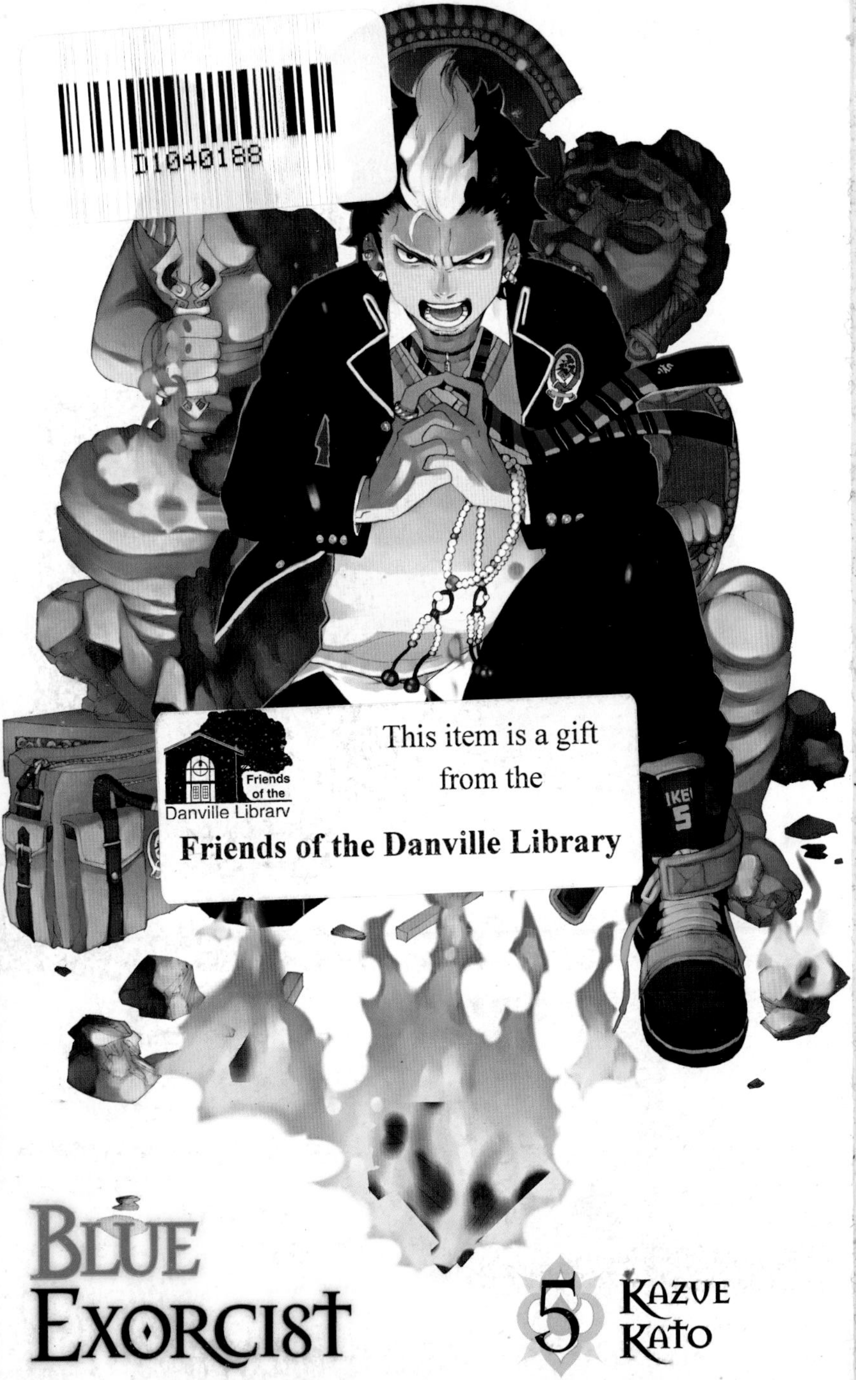

Blue Exorcist

5

Kazue Kato

BLUE EXORCIST

Contents

5

CAST OF CHARACTERS

RIN OKUMURA

Born of a human mother and Satan, the God of Demons, Rin Okumura has powers he can barely control. After Satan kills Father Fujimoto, Rin's foster father, Rin decides to become an Exorcist so he can someday defeat Satan. Now a first-year student at True Cross Academy and an Exwire at the Exorcism Cram School, he hopes to someday become a Knight. When he draws the Koma Sword, he manifests his internal power in the form of blue flames. He is currently training for the Exorcist Certification Exam, which he must pass in six months.

YUKIO OKUMURA

Rin's brother. Hoping to become a doctor, he's a genius who is the youngest student ever to become an instructor at the Exorcism Cram School. An instructor in Demon Pharmaceuticals, he possesses the titles of Doctor and Dragoon.

SHIEMI MORIYAMA

Daughter of the owner of Futsumaya, an exorcist supply shop. Inspired by Rin and Yukio, she became an Exwire and hopes to someday become an Exorcist. She has the ability to become a Tamer and can summon a baby Greenman.

RYUJI SUGURO

Heir to a venerable temple in Kyoto. After the Blue Night, he became an Exwire and hopes to become an Exorcist someday. He wants to achieve the titles of Dragoon and Aria.

RENZO SHIMA

Once a pupil of Suguro's father and now Suguro's friend. He's an Exwire who wants to become an Aria. He has an easygoing personality and is totally girl-crazy.

KONEKOMARU MIWA

Like Shima, he was once a pupil of Suguro's father and is now Suguro's friend. He's an Exwire who hopes to become an Exorcist someday. He is small in size and has a quiet and composed personality.

IZUMO KAMIKI

An Exwire with the blood of shrine maidens. She has the ability to become a Tamer and can summon two white foxes. Her friend Paku quit school, but she has continued attending.

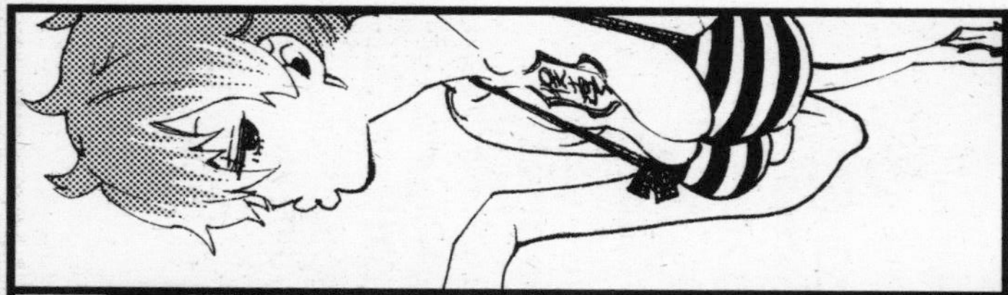

Shura Kirigakure

An upper-rank special investigator dispatched by Vatican Headquarters to True Cross Academy. A Senior Exorcist First Class who holds the titles of Knight, Tamer, Doctor and Aria. She was once Father Fujimoto's pupil and he asked her to teach swordsmanship to Rin.

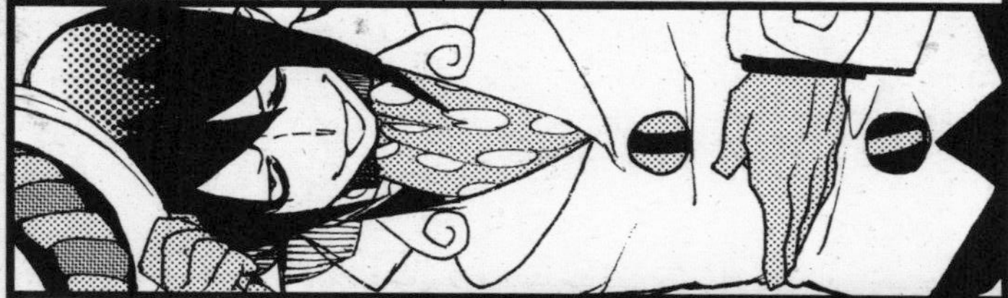

Mephisto Pheles

President of True Cross Academy and head of the Exorcism Cram School. He was Father Fujimoto's friend, and now he is Rin and Yukio's guardian. He plans to turn Rin into a weapon to use in the fight against Satan.

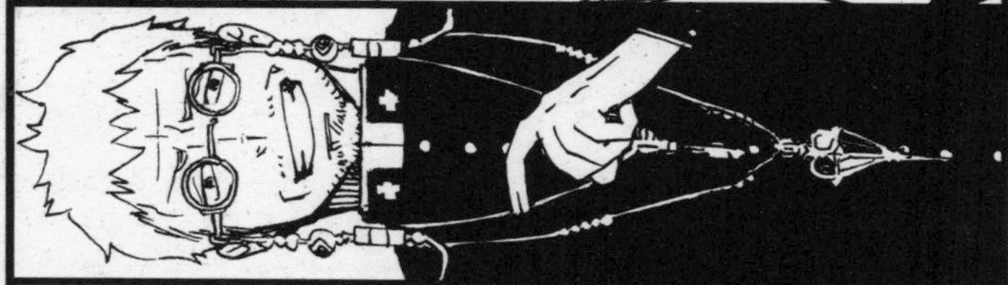

Shiro Fujimoto

The man who raised Rin and Yukio. He was a priest at True Cross Church. He held the rank of Paladin and once taught Demon Pharmaceuticals. Satan possessed him and he gave his life defending Rin.

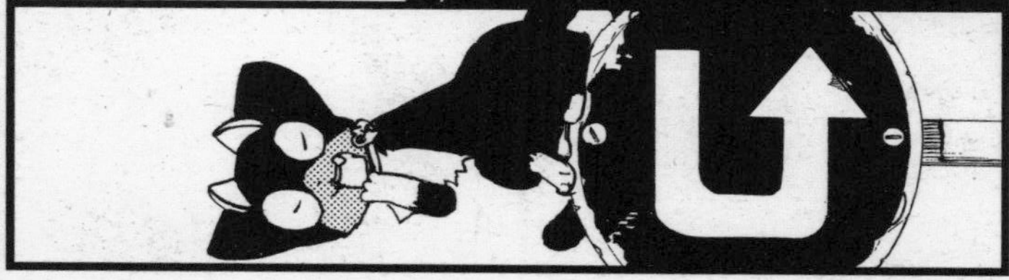

Kuro

A Cat Sídhe who was once Shiro's familiar. After Shiro's death, he began turning back into a demon. Rin saved him, and now the two are practically inseparable. His favorite drink is the catnip wine Shiro used to make.

◉ THE STORY SO FAR ◉

UNKNOWN TO RIN OKUMURA, BOTH HUMAN
AND DEMON BLOOD RUNS IN HIS VEINS. IN AN
ARGUMENT WITH HIS FOSTER FATHER, FATHER
FUJIMOTO, RIN LEARNS THAT SATAN IS HIS
TRUE FATHER. SATAN SUDDENLY APPEARS AND
TRIES TO DRAG RIN DOWN TO GEHENNA
BECAUSE RIN HAS INHERITED HIS POWER.
FATHER FUJIMOTO FIGHTS TO DEFEND RIN,
BUT DIES IN THE PROCESS. RIN DECIDES TO
BECOME AN EXORCIST SO HE CAN SOMEDAY
DEFEAT SATAN AND BEGINS STUDYING AT THE
EXORCISM CRAM SCHOOL UNDER THE
INSTRUCTION OF HIS TWIN BROTHER YUKIO,
WHO IS ALREADY AN EXORCIST.

AS SUMMER BREAK KICKS OFF, RIN AND THE
OTHER EXWIRES GO TO THE ACADEMY'S
FOREST DISTRICT FOR A THREE-DAY FOREST
CAMP. PART OF THE CAMP IS A TEST TO SELECT
WHO WILL GAIN THE RIGHT TO GO ON A REAL
MISSION. THE STUDENTS MUST WORK
TOGETHER OR THEY WILL FAIL THE TEST.

RIN HAS ALWAYS HANDLED EVERYTHING BY
HIMSELF, BUT HE LEARNS THE IMPORTANCE OF
HAVING FRIENDS LIKE SUGURO AND SHIEMI
AND DECIDES TO USE HIS POWER TO
HELP OTHERS.

⚜ THE STORY SO FAR ⚜

THE EXWIRES COMPLETE THE ASSIGNED TASK AND RETURN TO CAMP, BUT THEN AMAIMON ATTACKS. FACED WITH DANGER TO HIS FRIENDS, RIN REVEALS HIS FLAME IN A FIGHT AGAINST THE POWERFUL DEMON. MEPHISTO INTERVENES AND EVERYONE IS ALL RIGHT, BUT...

NOW THAT EVERYONE KNOWS RIN IS THE SON OF SATAN, HE MUST APPEAR AS EVIDENCE AT THE QUESTIONING OF MEPHISTO BY THE KNIGHTS OF THE TRUE CROSS.

MEPHISTO REVEALS THE SHOCKING FACT THAT SHIRO SECRETLY RAISED RIN IN ORDER TO USE HIM AS A WEAPON AGAINST SATAN. THE COURT LETS RIN GO ON CONDITION THAT HE PASS THE EXORCIST CERTIFICATION EXAM IN SIX MONTHS. UNDER THE SUPERVISION OF SHURA AND YUKIO, HE BEGINS LEARNING TO CONTROL HIS FLAME. THEN YUKIO GETS A PHONE CALL INFORMING HIM OF AN EMERGENCY!!

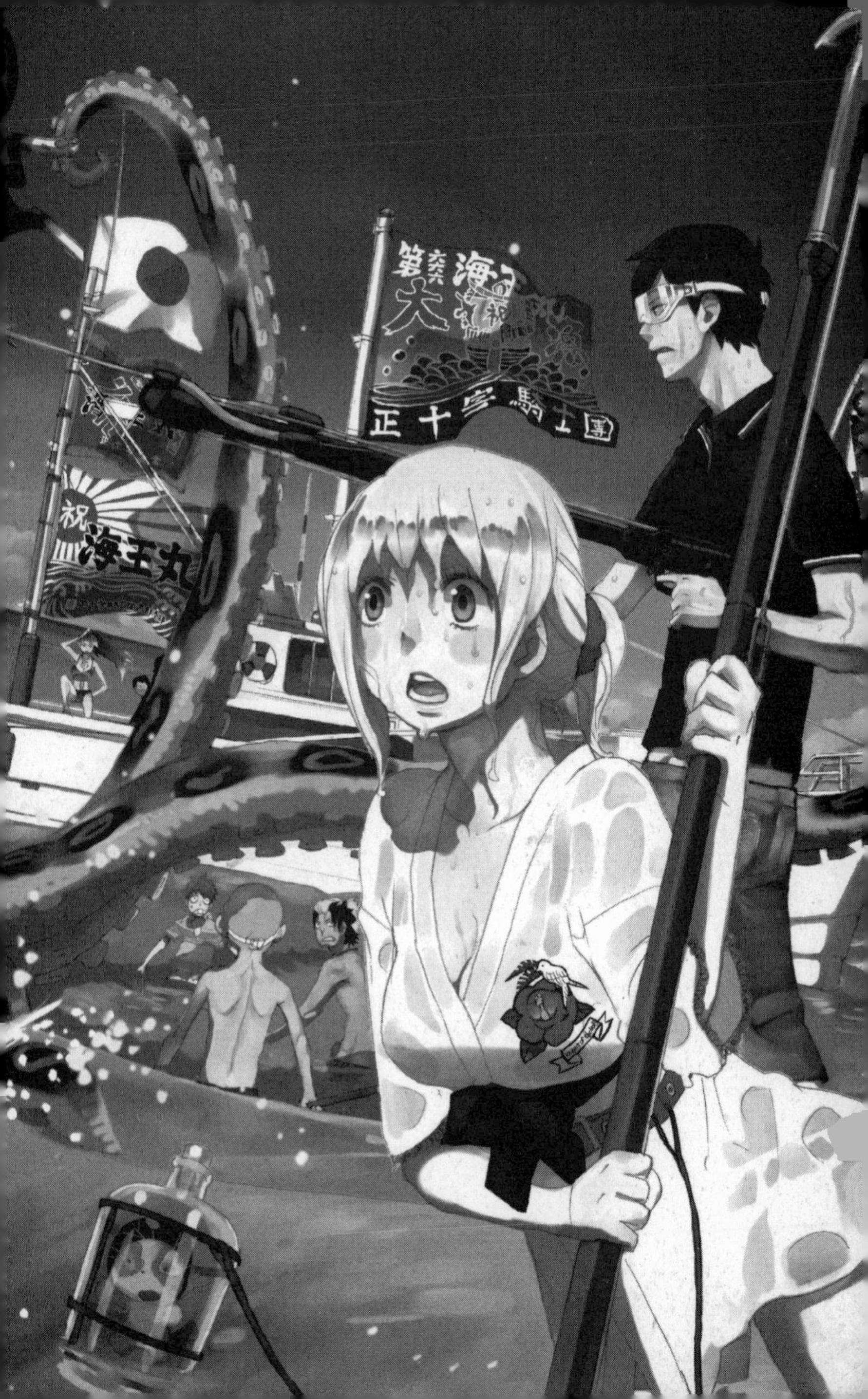
正十字騎士團
祝
海王丸

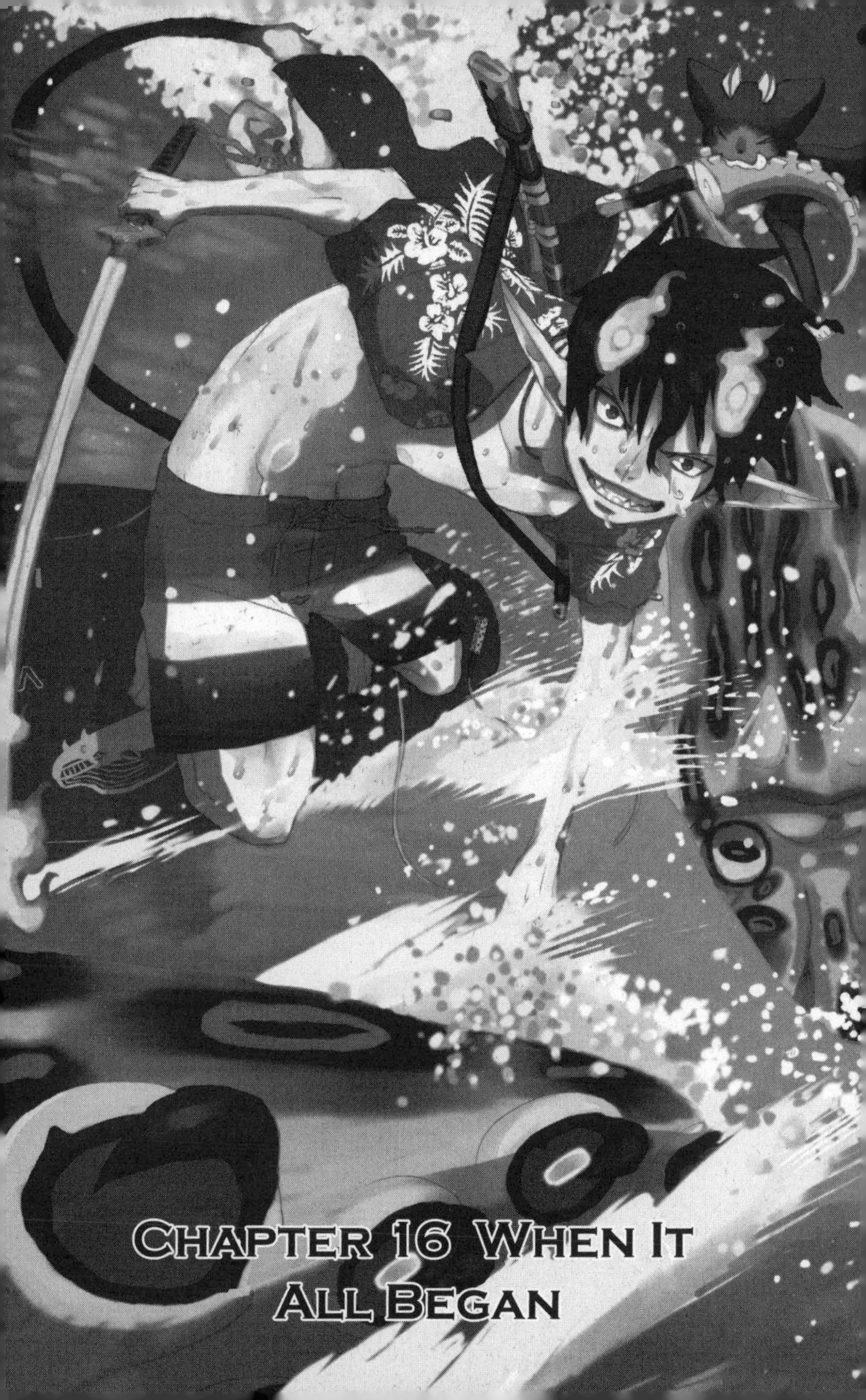
Chapter 16 When It
All Began

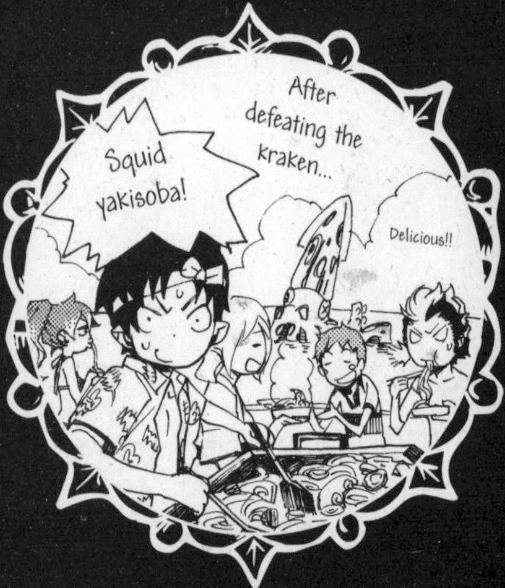
After defeating the kraken...
Squid yakisoba!
Delicious!!

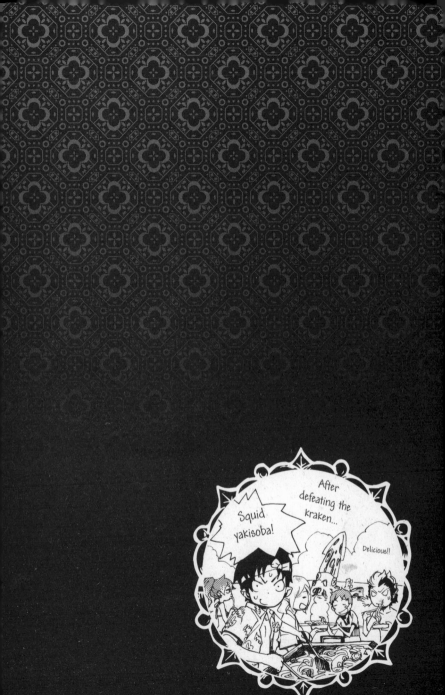

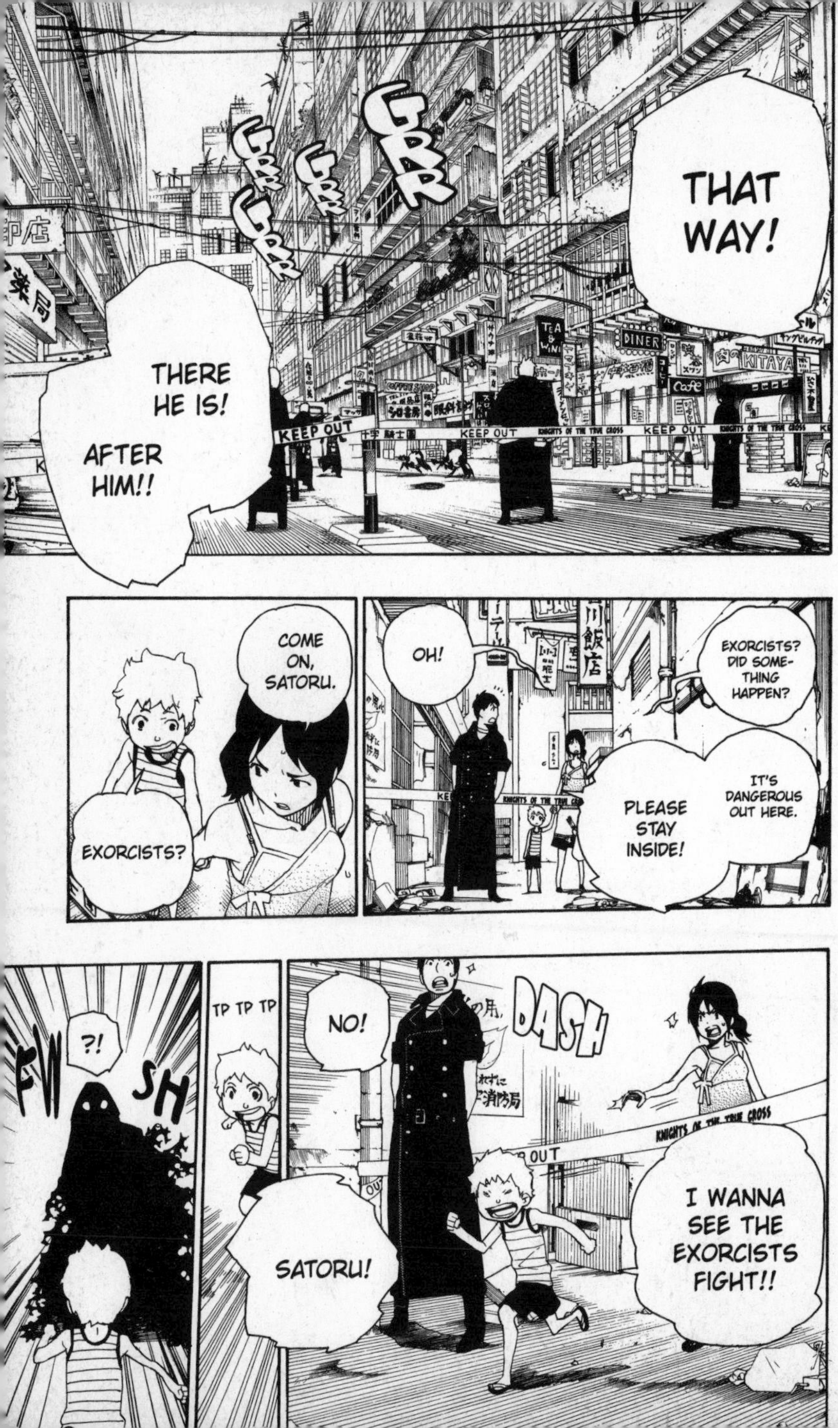
THAT WAY!
GRR
GRR
GRR
GRR
THERE HE IS!
AFTER HIM!!
KEEP OUT
KNIGHTS OF THE TRUE CROSS
DINER
KITAYA
EXORCISTS? DID SOME-THING HAPPEN?
OH!
IT'S DANGEROUS OUT HERE.
PLEASE STAY INSIDE!
COME ON, SATORU.
EXORCISTS?
DASH
NO!
I WANNA SEE THE EXORCISTS FIGHT!!
SATORU!
TP TP TP
?!
FWSH

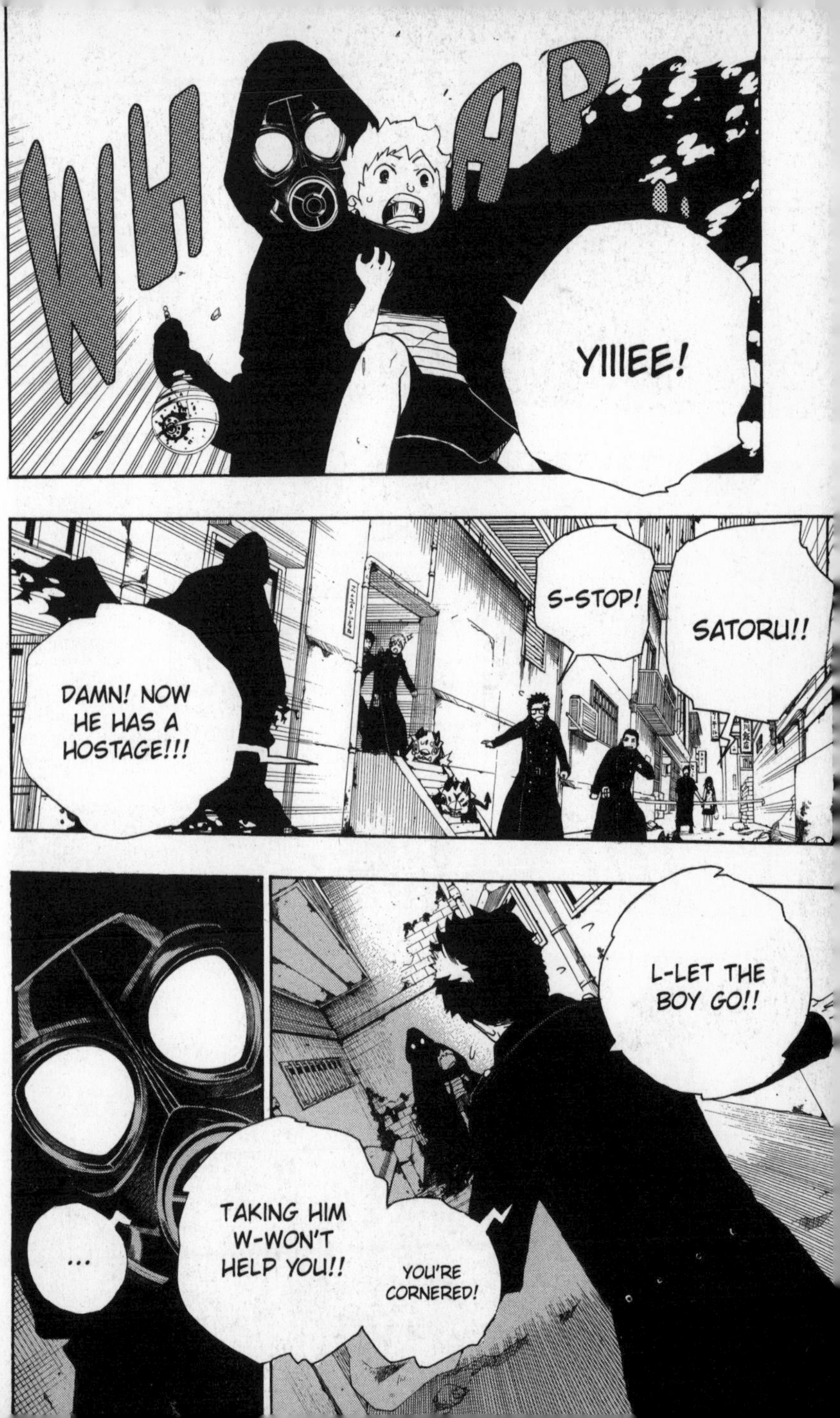
WHAP
YIIIEE!
SATORU!!
S-STOP!
DAMN! NOW HE HAS A HOSTAGE!!!
L-LET THE BOY GO!!
TAKING HIM W-WON'T HELP YOU!!
YOU'RE CORNERED!
...

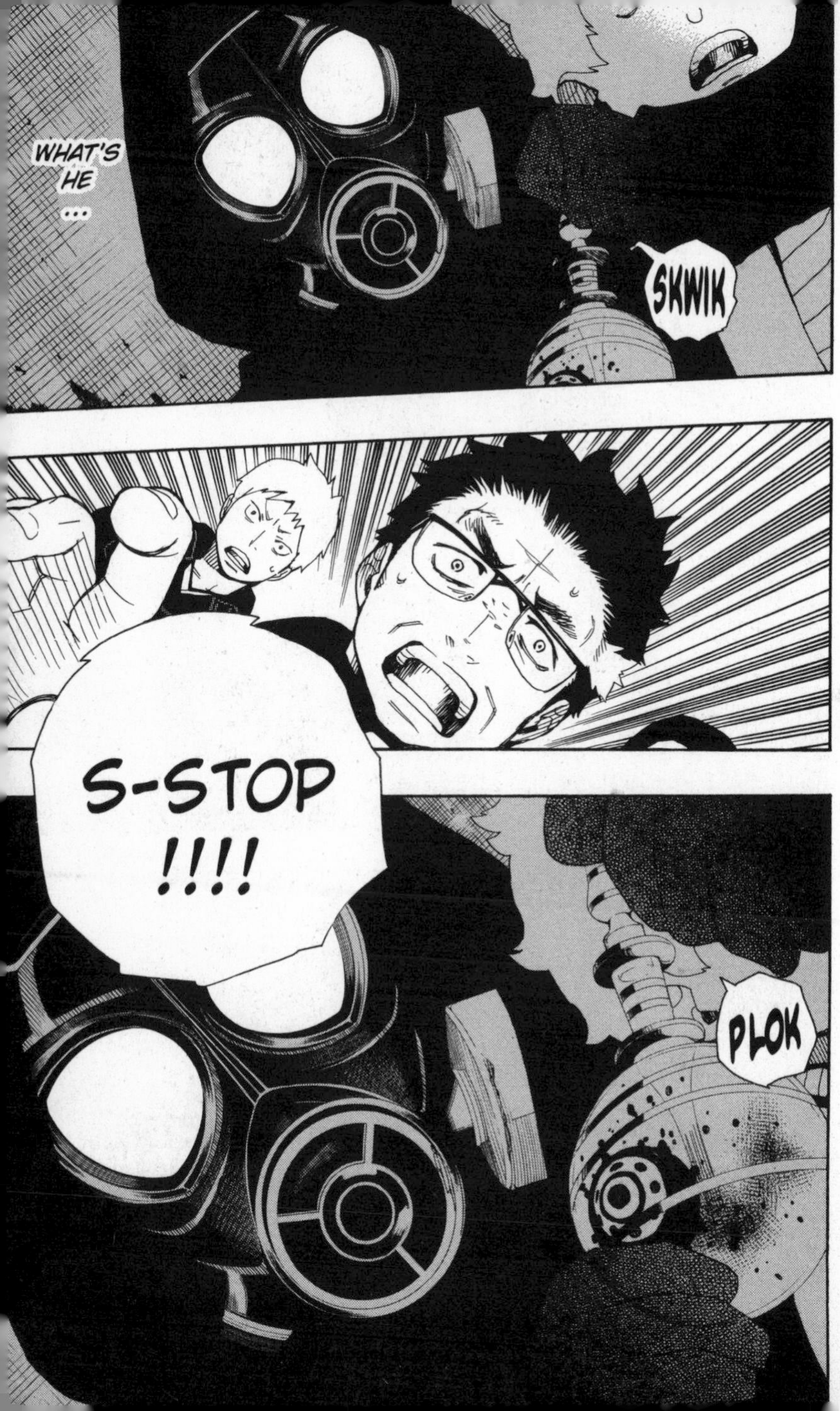
SKWIK
WHAT'S HE ...
S-STOP !!!!
PLOK

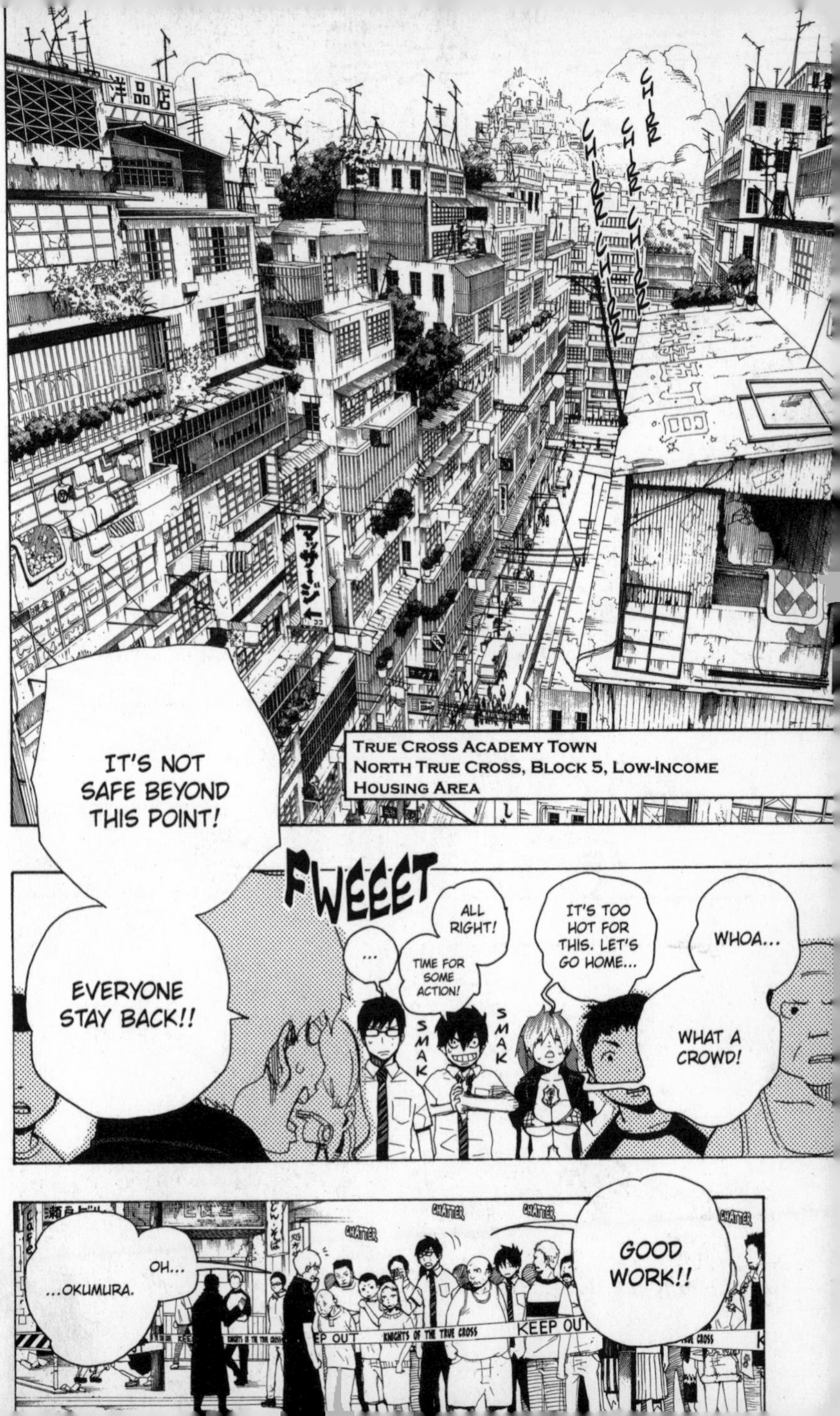
CHIRP CHIRP
CHIRP CHIRP
洋品店
マッサージ
True Cross Academy Town
North True Cross, Block 5, Low-Income Housing Area
IT'S NOT SAFE BEYOND THIS POINT!
WHOA...
WHAT A CROWD!
IT'S TOO HOT FOR THIS. LET'S GO HOME...
ALL RIGHT!
TIME FOR SOME ACTION!
SMAK SMAK
...
FWEEET
EVERYONE STAY BACK!!
GOOD WORK!!
CHATTER CHATTER CHATTER CHATTER
KEEP OUT
KNIGHTS OF THE TRUE CROSS
OH...
...OKUMURA.

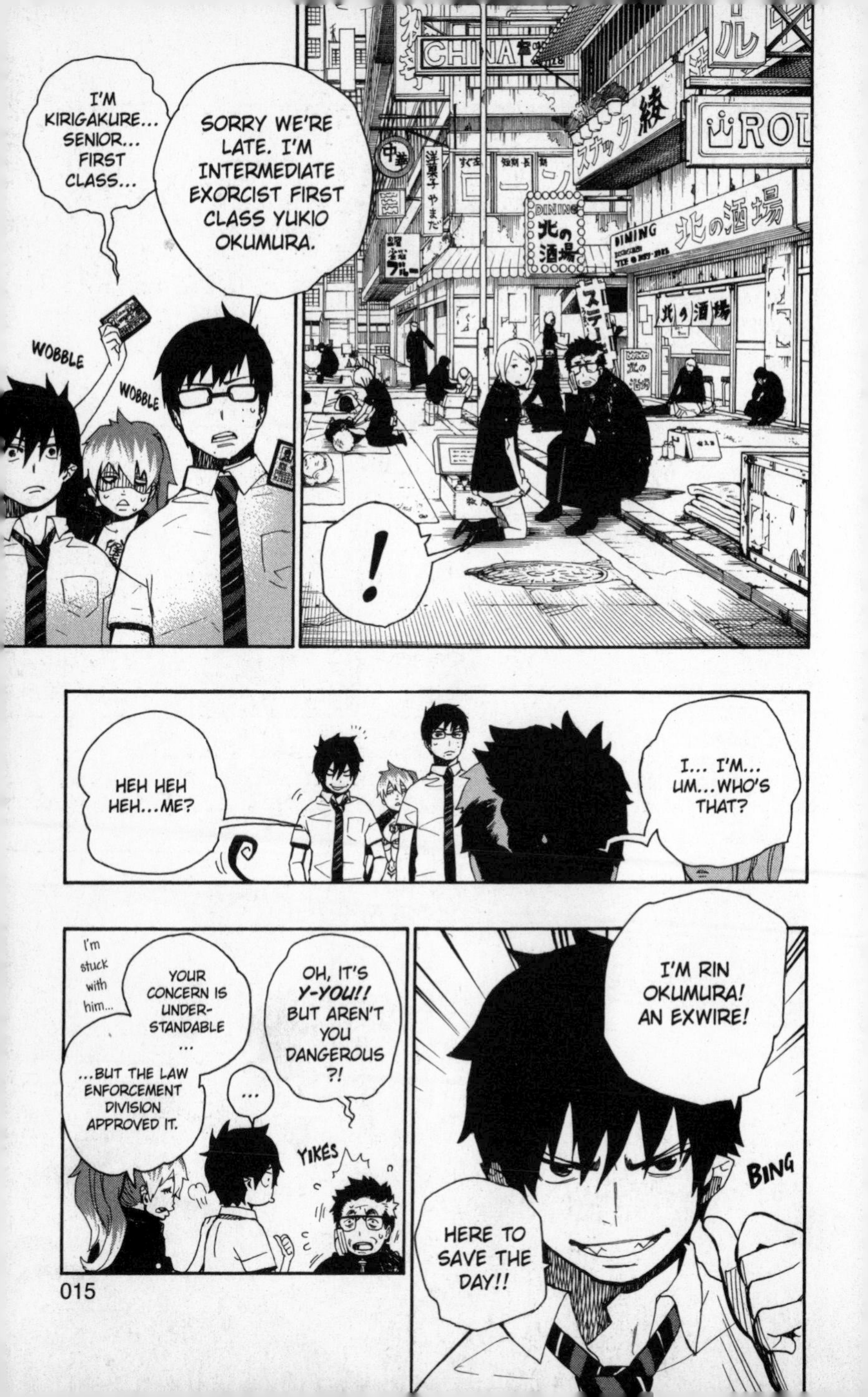
CHINA
DINING
北の酒場
!
SORRY WE'RE LATE. I'M INTERMEDIATE EXORCIST FIRST CLASS YUKIO OKUMURA.
I'M KIRIGAKURE... SENIOR... FIRST CLASS...
WOBBLE
WOBBLE
I... I'M... UM...WHO'S THAT?
HEH HEH HEH...ME?
I'M RIN OKUMURA! AN EXWIRE!
BING
HERE TO SAVE THE DAY!!
OH, IT'S *Y-YOU!!* BUT AREN'T YOU DANGEROUS ?!
YIKES
YOUR CONCERN IS UNDER-STANDABLE ...
...BUT THE LAW ENFORCEMENT DIVISION APPROVED IT.
I'm stuck with him...
...

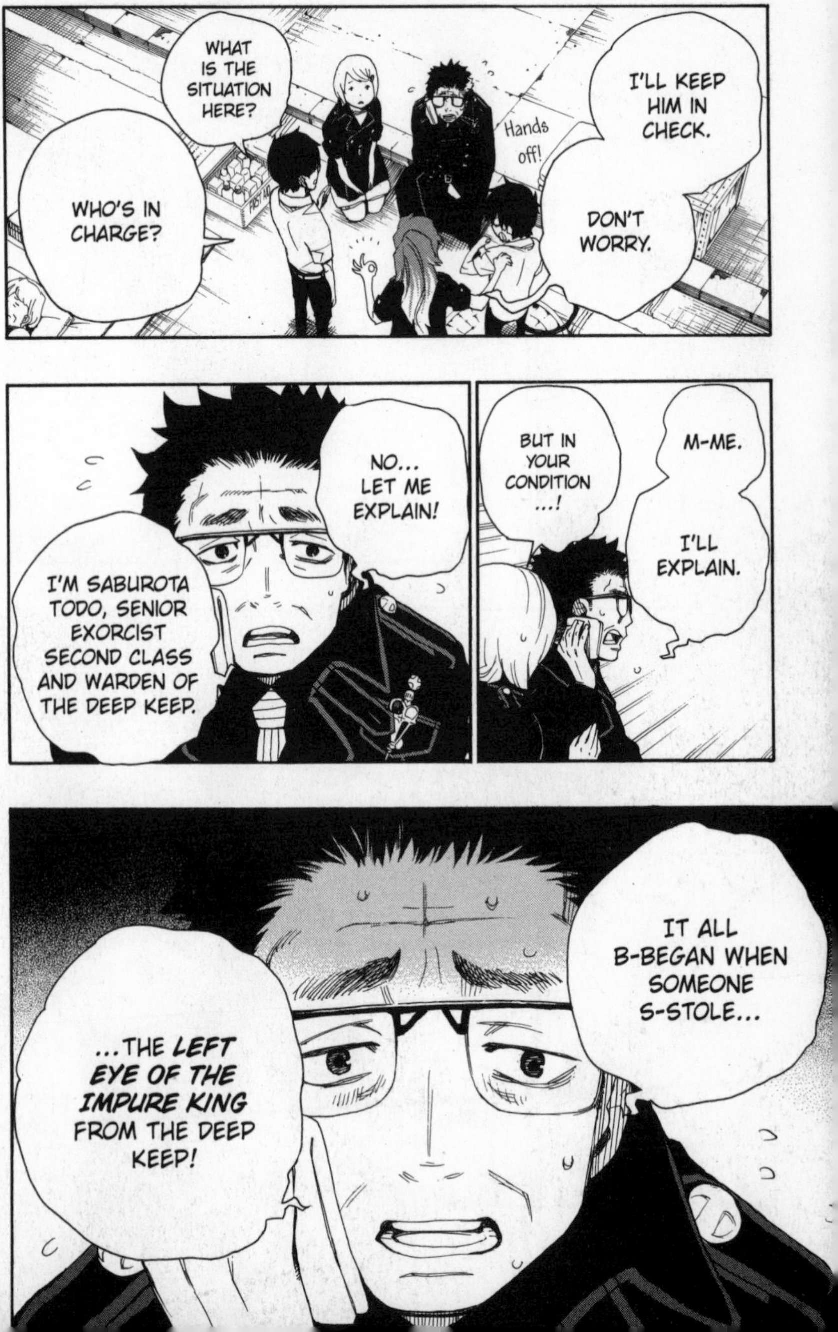
I'LL KEEP HIM IN CHECK.
DON'T WORRY.
Hands off!
WHAT IS THE SITUATION HERE?
WHO'S IN CHARGE?
M-ME.
I'LL EXPLAIN.
BUT IN YOUR CONDITION...!
NO... LET ME EXPLAIN!
I'M SABUROTA TODO, SENIOR EXORCIST SECOND CLASS AND WARDEN OF THE DEEP KEEP.
IT ALL B-BEGAN WHEN SOMEONE S-STOLE...
...THE *LEFT EYE OF THE IMPURE KING* FROM THE DEEP KEEP!

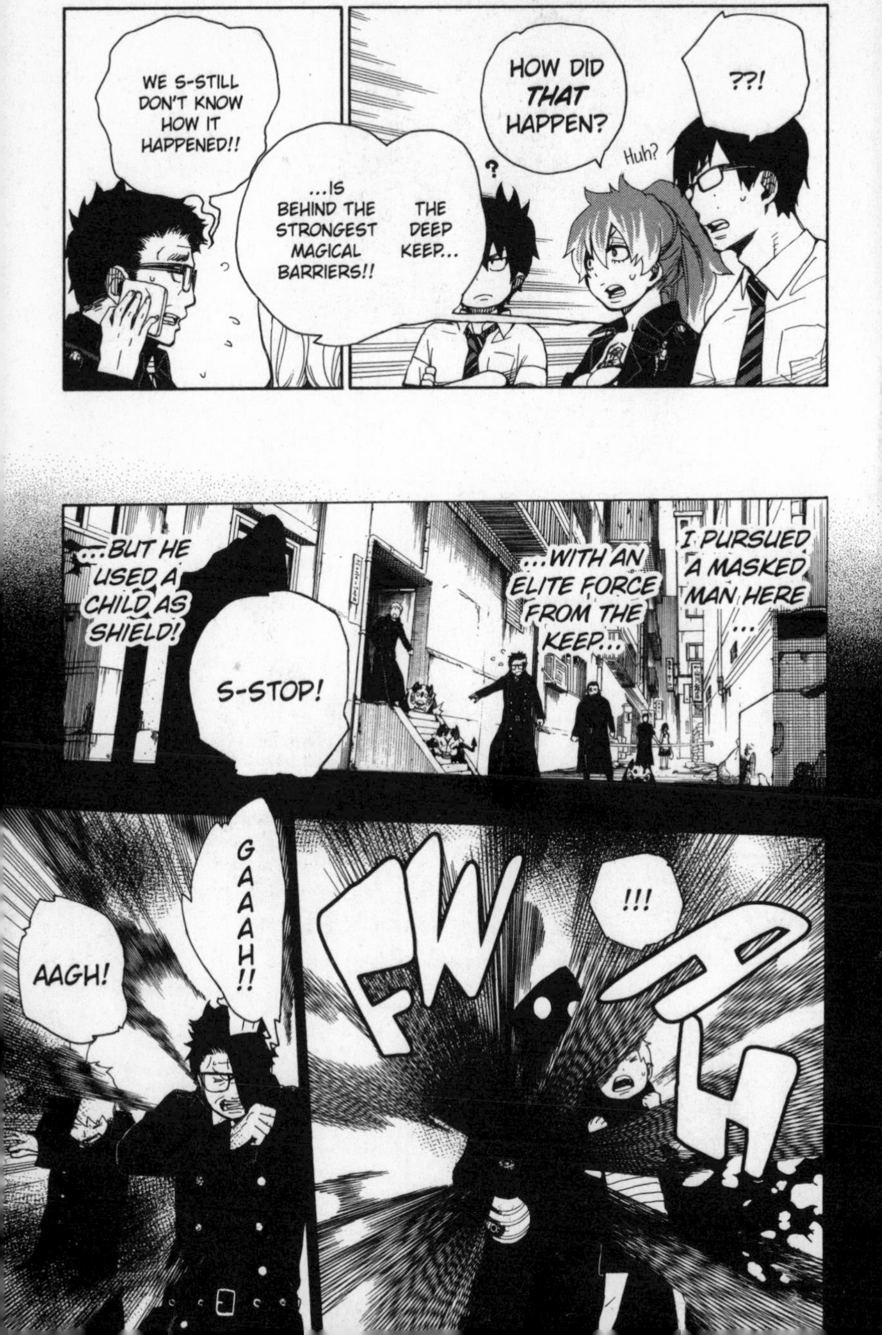
??!
Huh?
HOW DID THAT HAPPEN?
WE S-STILL DON'T KNOW HOW IT HAPPENED!!
THE DEEP KEEP... ...IS BEHIND THE STRONGEST MAGICAL BARRIERS!!
I PURSUED A MASKED MAN HERE...
...WITH AN ELITE FORCE FROM THE KEEP...
...BUT HE USED A CHILD AS SHIELD!
S-STOP!
!!!
FWAH
GAAAAH!!
AAGH!

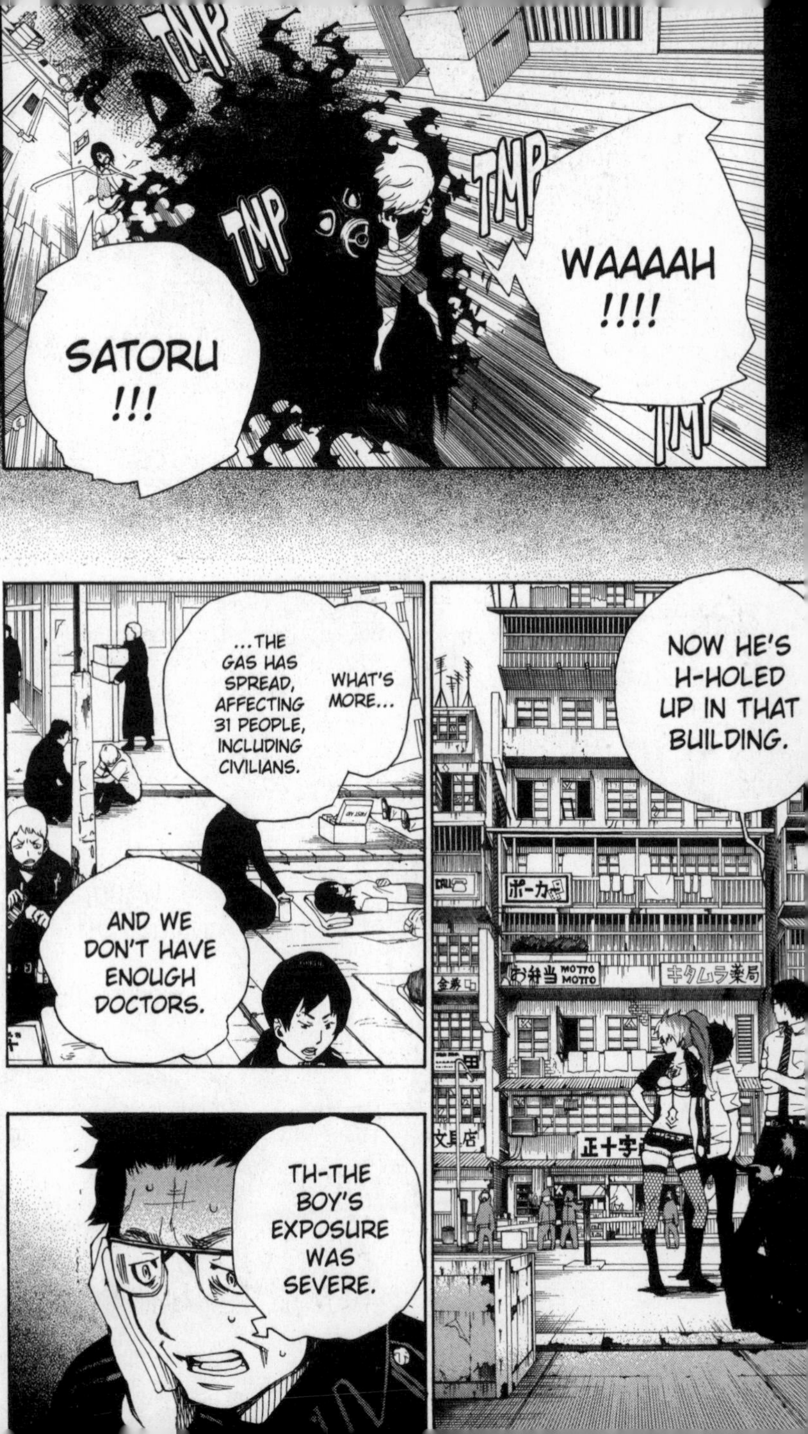
TMP
TMP
WAAAAH !!!!
TMP
TMP
SATORU !!!
NOW HE'S H-HOLED UP IN THAT BUILDING.
ポーカー
キタムラ薬局
お弁当
MOTTO MOTTO
文具店
WHAT'S MORE...
...THE GAS HAS SPREAD, AFFECTING 31 PEOPLE, INCLUDING CIVILIANS.
AND WE DON'T HAVE ENOUGH DOCTORS.
TH-THE BOY'S EXPOSURE WAS SEVERE.

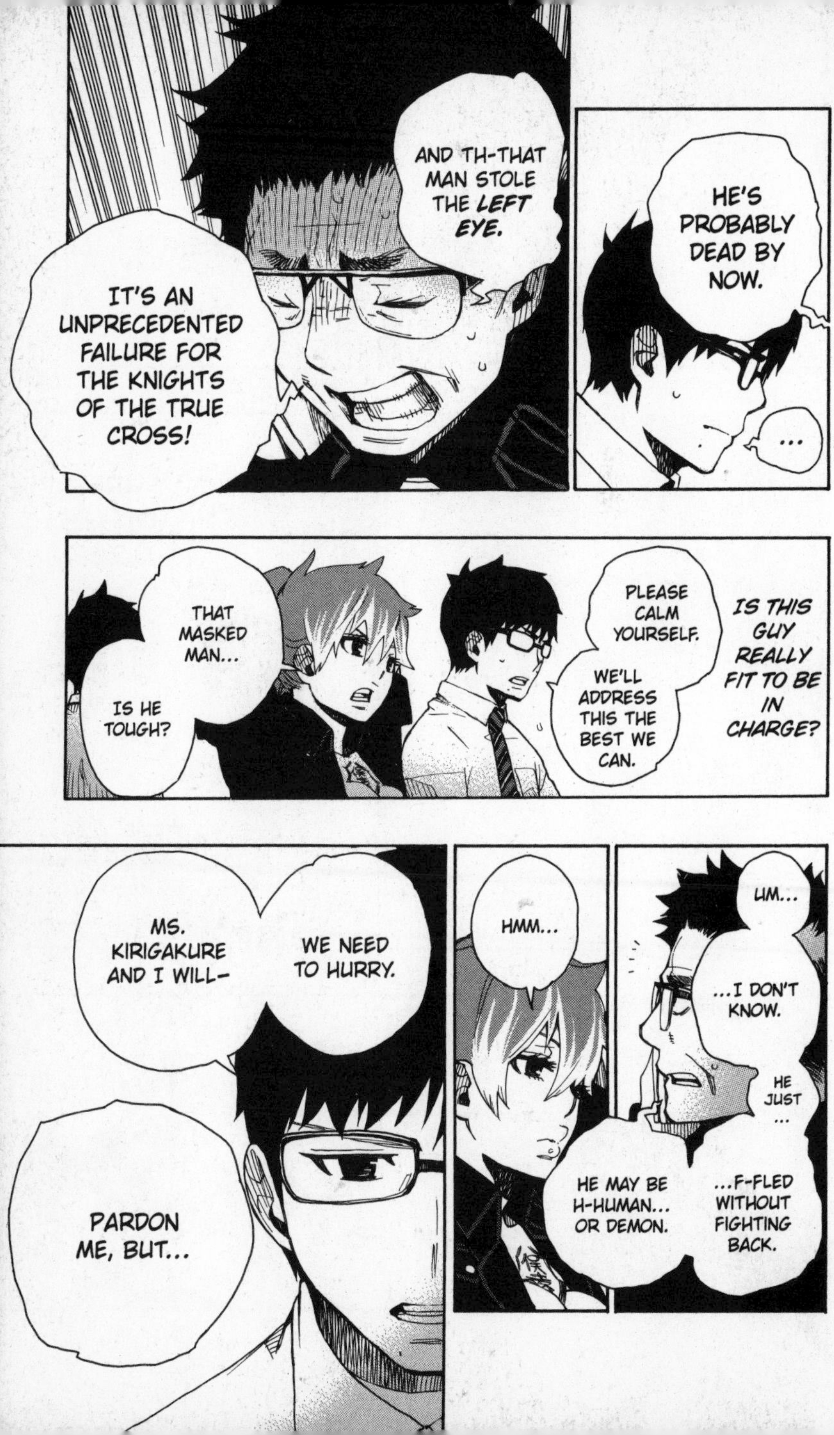
HE'S PROBABLY DEAD BY NOW.
...
AND TH-THAT MAN STOLE THE *LEFT EYE.*
IT'S AN UNPRECEDENTED FAILURE FOR THE KNIGHTS OF THE TRUE CROSS!
IS THIS GUY REALLY FIT TO BE IN CHARGE?
PLEASE CALM YOURSELF.
WE'LL ADDRESS THIS THE BEST WE CAN.
THAT MASKED MAN...
IS HE TOUGH?
UM...
...I DON'T KNOW.
HE JUST...
...F-FLED WITHOUT FIGHTING BACK.
HE MAY BE H-HUMAN... OR DEMON.
HMM...
WE NEED TO HURRY.
MS. KIRIGAKURE AND I WILL-
PARDON ME, BUT...

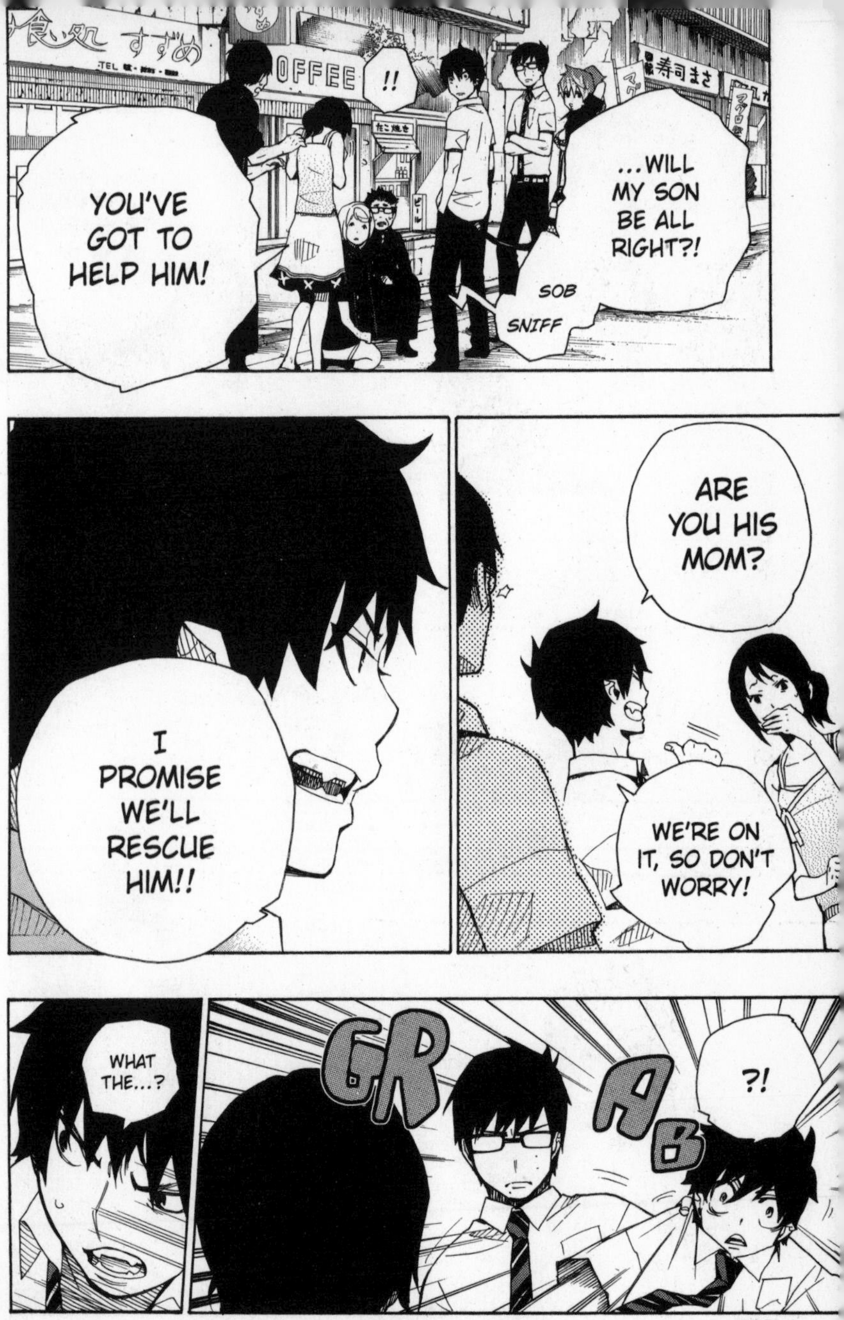
...WILL MY SON BE ALL RIGHT?!
SOB
SNIFF
!!
YOU'VE GOT TO HELP HIM!
ARE YOU HIS MOM?
WE'RE ON IT, SO DON'T WORRY!
I PROMISE WE'LL RESCUE HIM!!
?!
GRAB
WHAT THE...?

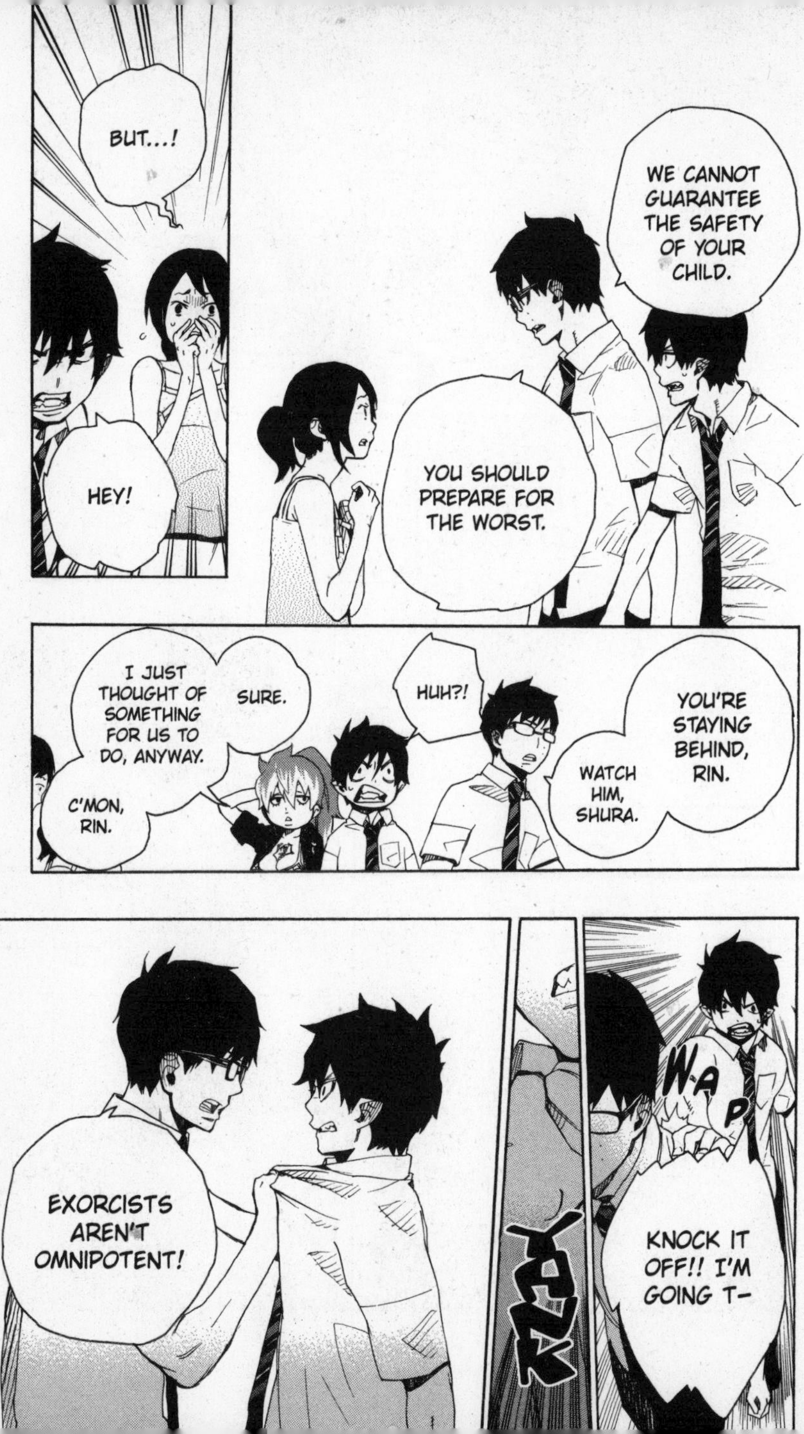
WE CANNOT GUARANTEE THE SAFETY OF YOUR CHILD.
YOU SHOULD PREPARE FOR THE WORST.
BUT...!
HEY!
YOU'RE STAYING BEHIND, RIN.
WATCH HIM, SHURA.
HUH?!
SURE.
I JUST THOUGHT OF SOMETHING FOR US TO DO, ANYWAY.
C'MON, RIN.
WAP
KNOCK IT OFF!! I'M GOING T-
YANK
EXORCISTS AREN'T OMNIPOTENT!

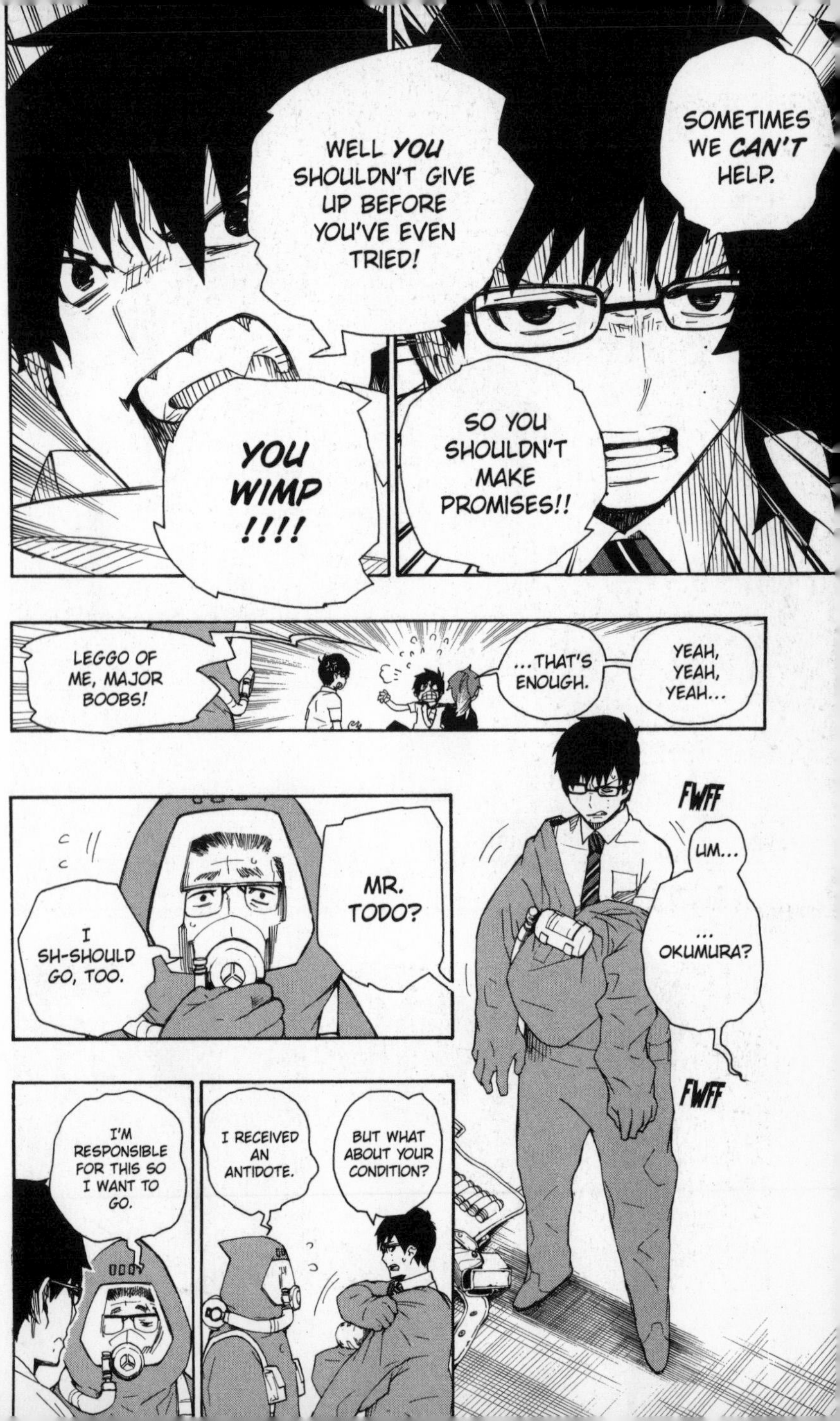
SOMETIMES WE CAN'T HELP.
SO YOU SHOULDN'T MAKE PROMISES!!
WELL YOU SHOULDN'T GIVE UP BEFORE YOU'VE EVEN TRIED!
YOU WIMP!!!!
YEAH, YEAH, YEAH...
...THAT'S ENOUGH.
LEGGO OF ME, MAJOR BOOBS!
FWFF
UM...
...OKUMURA?
FWFF
MR. TODO?
I SH-SHOULD GO, TOO.
BUT WHAT ABOUT YOUR CONDITION?
I RECEIVED AN ANTIDOTE.
I'M RESPONSIBLE FOR THIS SO I WANT TO GO.

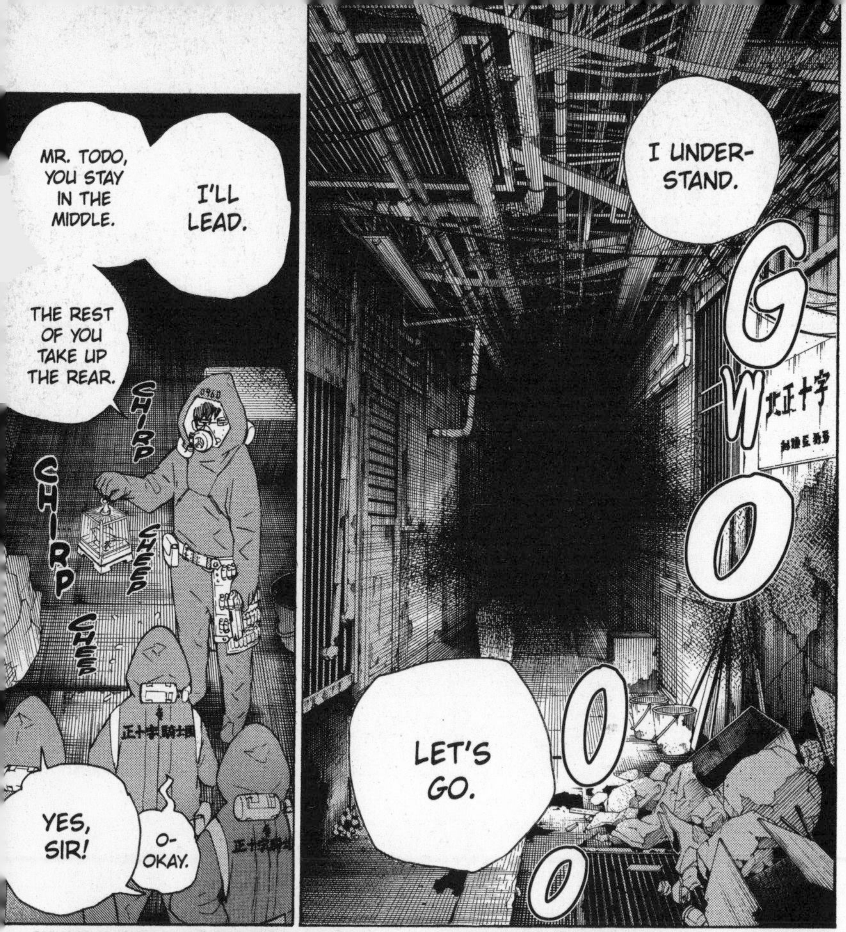
I UNDERSTAND.
GWOOOO
LET'S GO.
I'LL LEAD.
MR. TODO, YOU STAY IN THE MIDDLE.
THE REST OF YOU TAKE UP THE REAR.
CHIRP
CHIRP
CHEEP
CHEEP
O-OKAY.
YES, SIR!

JACKETS: KNIGHTS OF THE TRUE CROSS

SIGN: NORTH TRUE CROSS

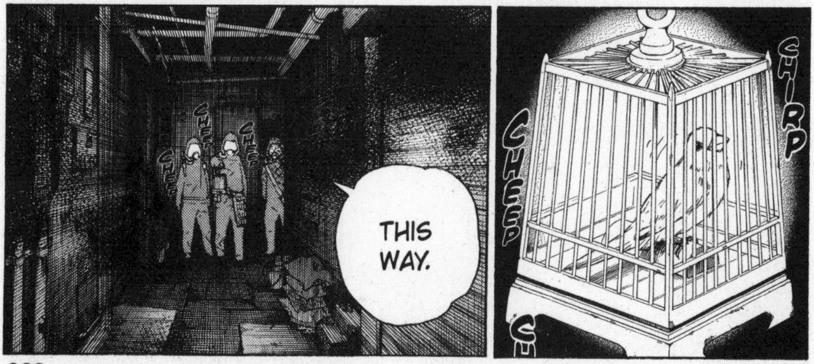
CHIRP
CHEEP
THIS WAY.

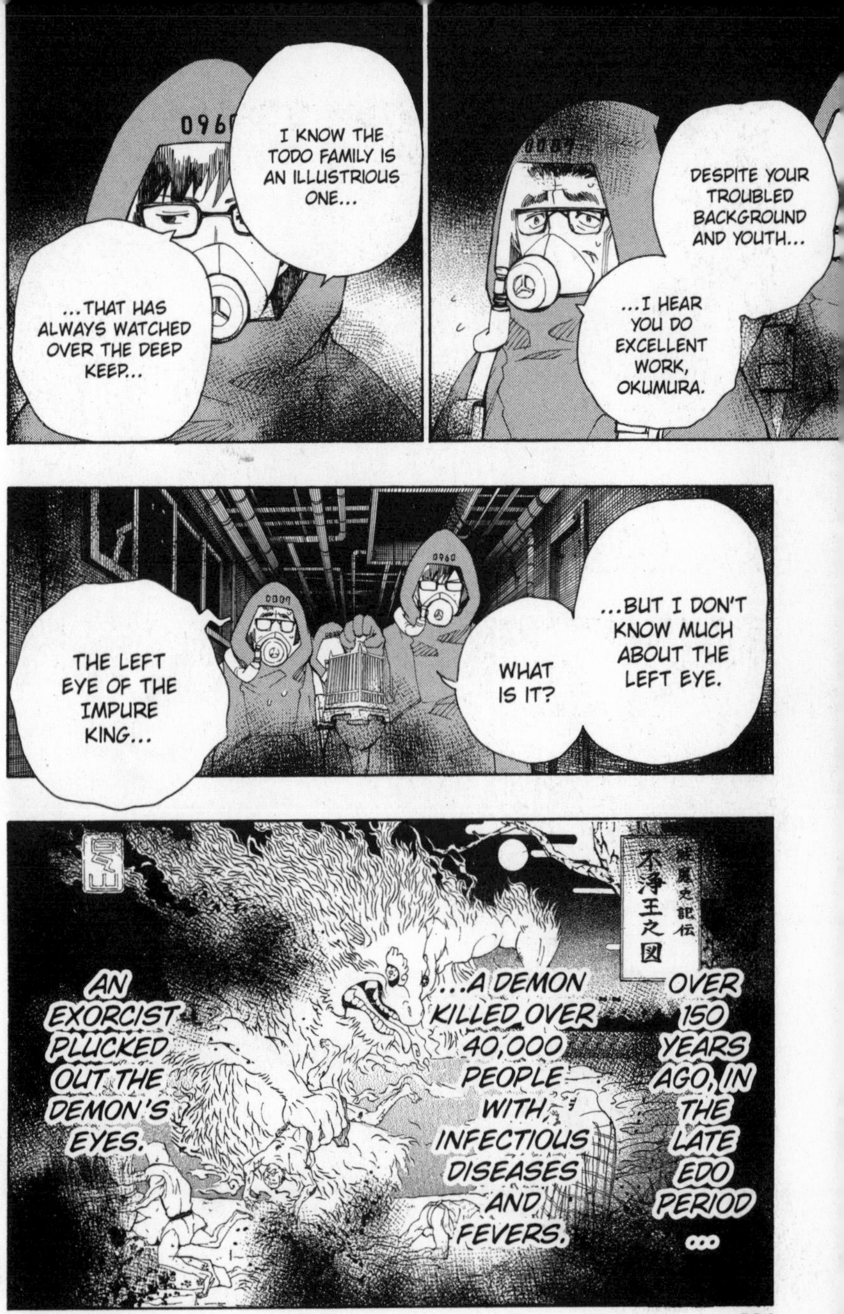
DESPITE YOUR TROUBLED BACKGROUND AND YOUTH...
...I HEAR YOU DO EXCELLENT WORK, OKUMURA.
I KNOW THE TODO FAMILY IS AN ILLUSTRIOUS ONE...
...THAT HAS ALWAYS WATCHED OVER THE DEEP KEEP...
...BUT I DON'T KNOW MUCH ABOUT THE LEFT EYE.
WHAT IS IT?
THE LEFT EYE OF THE IMPURE KING...
不浄王之図
OVER 150 YEARS AGO, IN THE LATE EDO PERIOD...
...A DEMON KILLED OVER 40,000 PEOPLE WITH INFECTIOUS DISEASES AND FEVERS.
AN EXORCIST PLUCKED OUT THE DEMON'S EYES.

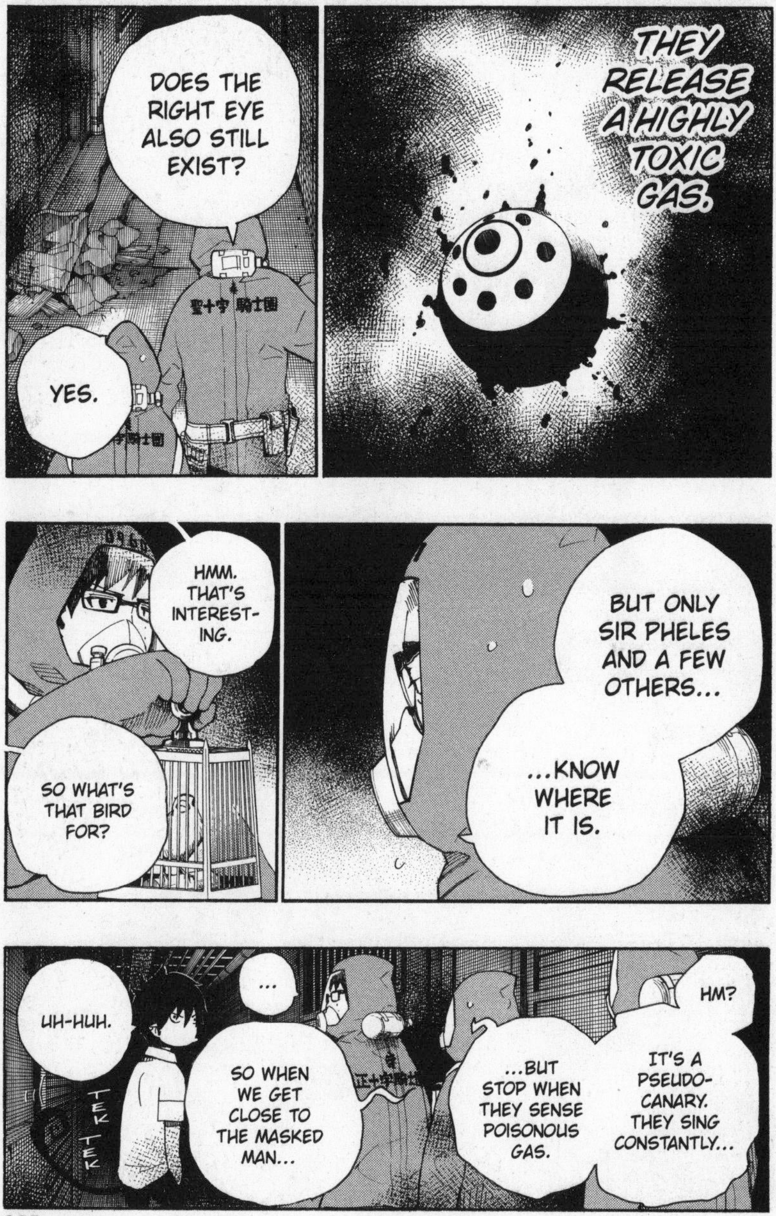
THEY RELEASE A HIGHLY TOXIC GAS.
DOES THE RIGHT EYE ALSO STILL EXIST?
YES.
BUT ONLY SIR PHELES AND A FEW OTHERS...
...KNOW WHERE IT IS.
HMM. THAT'S INTEREST-ING.
SO WHAT'S THAT BIRD FOR?
HM?
IT'S A PSEUDO-CANARY. THEY SING CONSTANTLY...
...BUT STOP WHEN THEY SENSE POISONOUS GAS.
SO WHEN WE GET CLOSE TO THE MASKED MAN...
...
UH-HUH.
TEK TEK

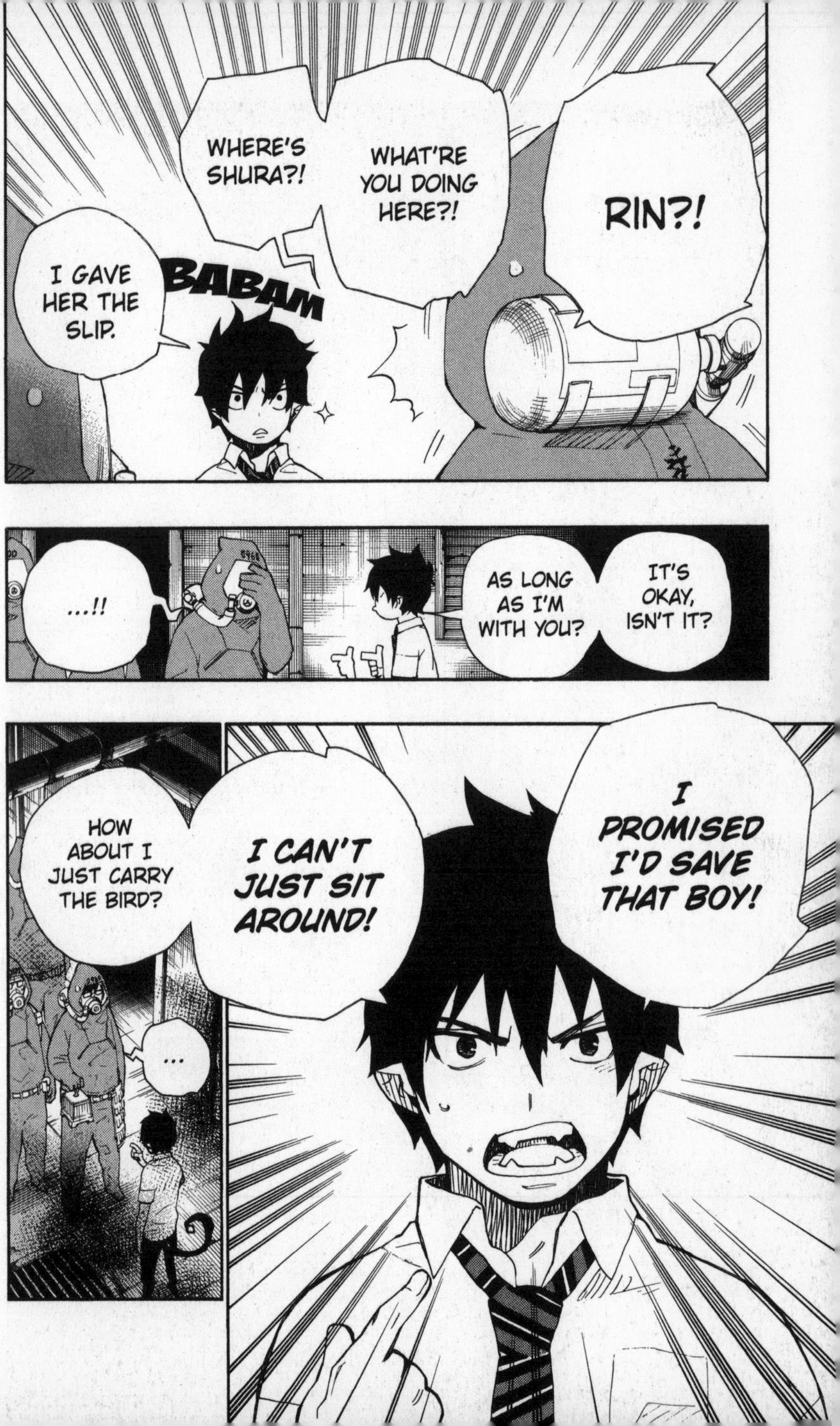
RIN?!
WHAT'RE YOU DOING HERE?!
WHERE'S SHURA?!
BABAM
I GAVE HER THE SLIP.
IT'S OKAY, ISN'T IT?
AS LONG AS I'M WITH YOU?
...!!
I PROMISED I'D SAVE THAT BOY!
I CAN'T JUST SIT AROUND!
HOW ABOUT I JUST CARRY THE BIRD?
...

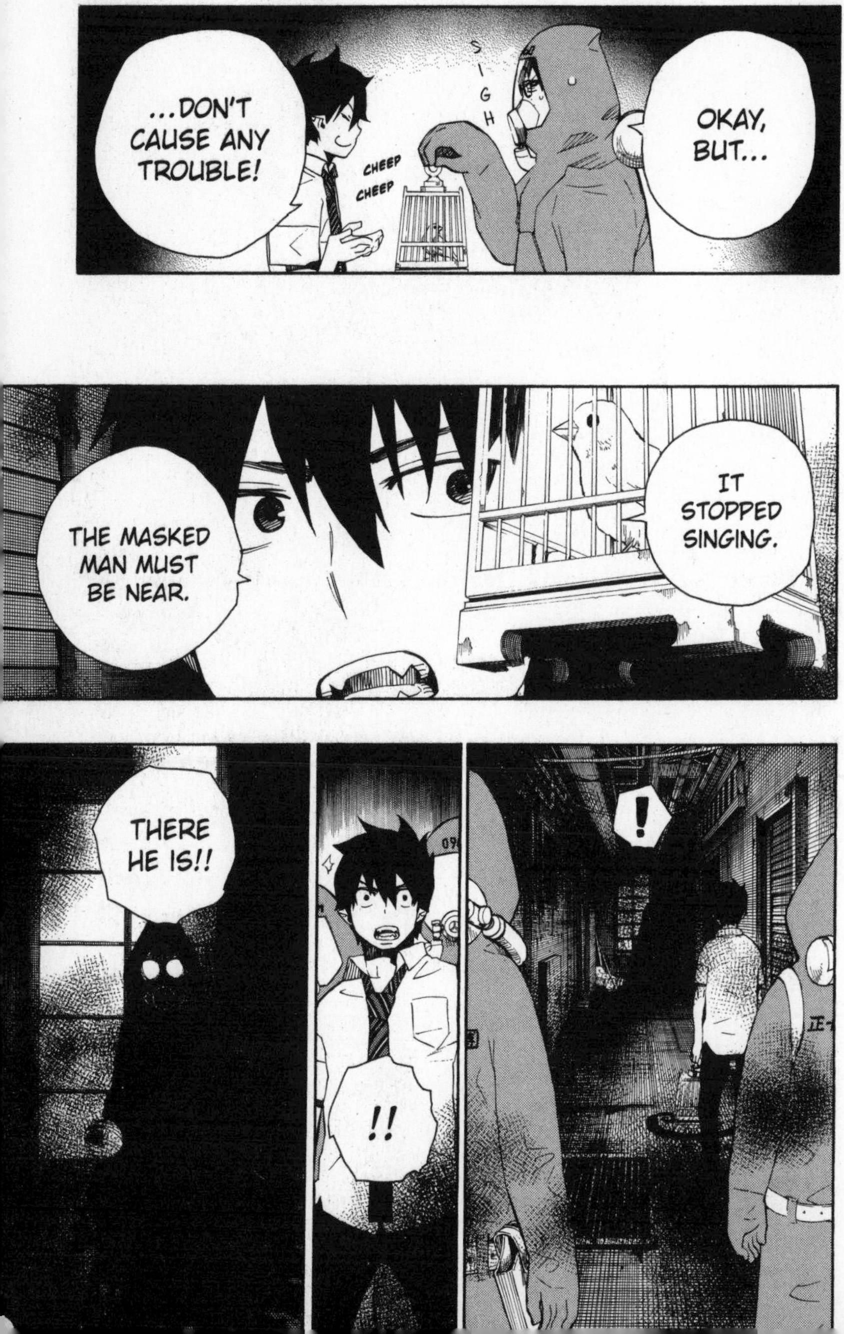
OKAY, BUT...
SIGH
CHEEP CHEEP
...DON'T CAUSE ANY TROUBLE!
IT STOPPED SINGING.
THE MASKED MAN MUST BE NEAR.
!
!!
THERE HE IS!!

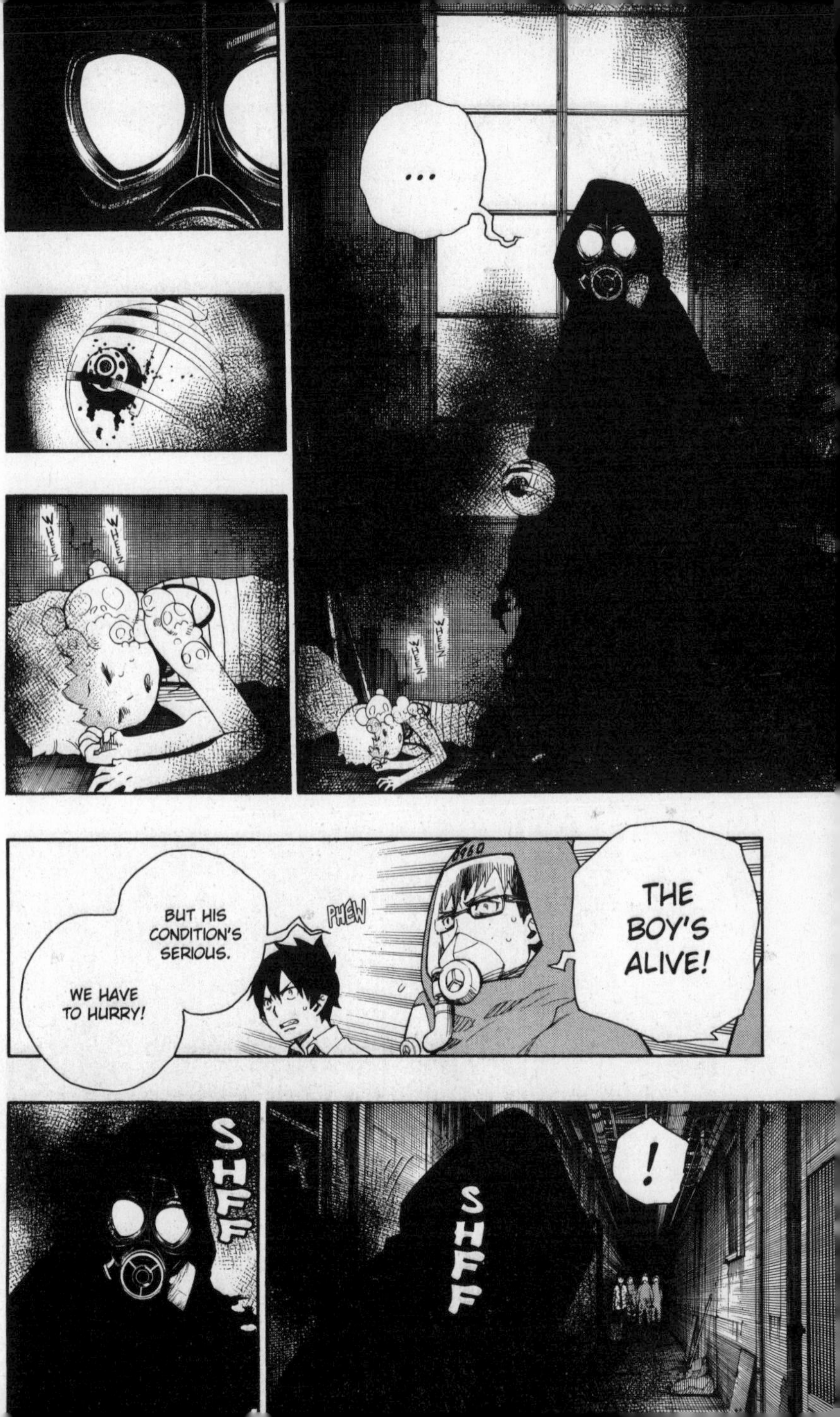
...
WHEEZ
WHEEZ
WHEEZ
WHEEZ
THE BOY'S ALIVE!
PHEW
BUT HIS CONDITION'S SERIOUS.
WE HAVE TO HURRY!
!
SHFF
SHFF

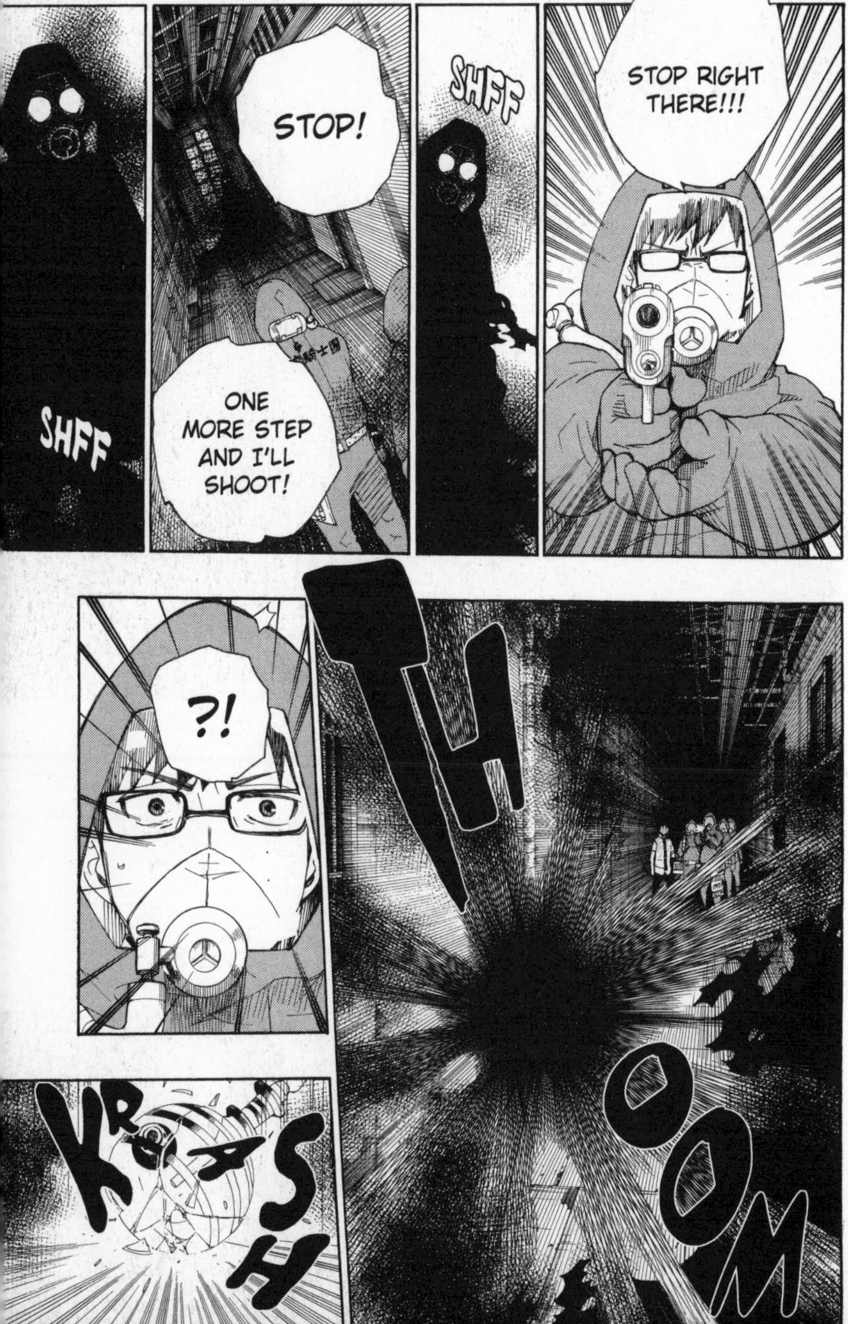

STOP RIGHT THERE!!!
SHFF
STOP!
ONE MORE STEP AND I'LL SHOOT!
SHFF
THOOOM
?!
KRASH

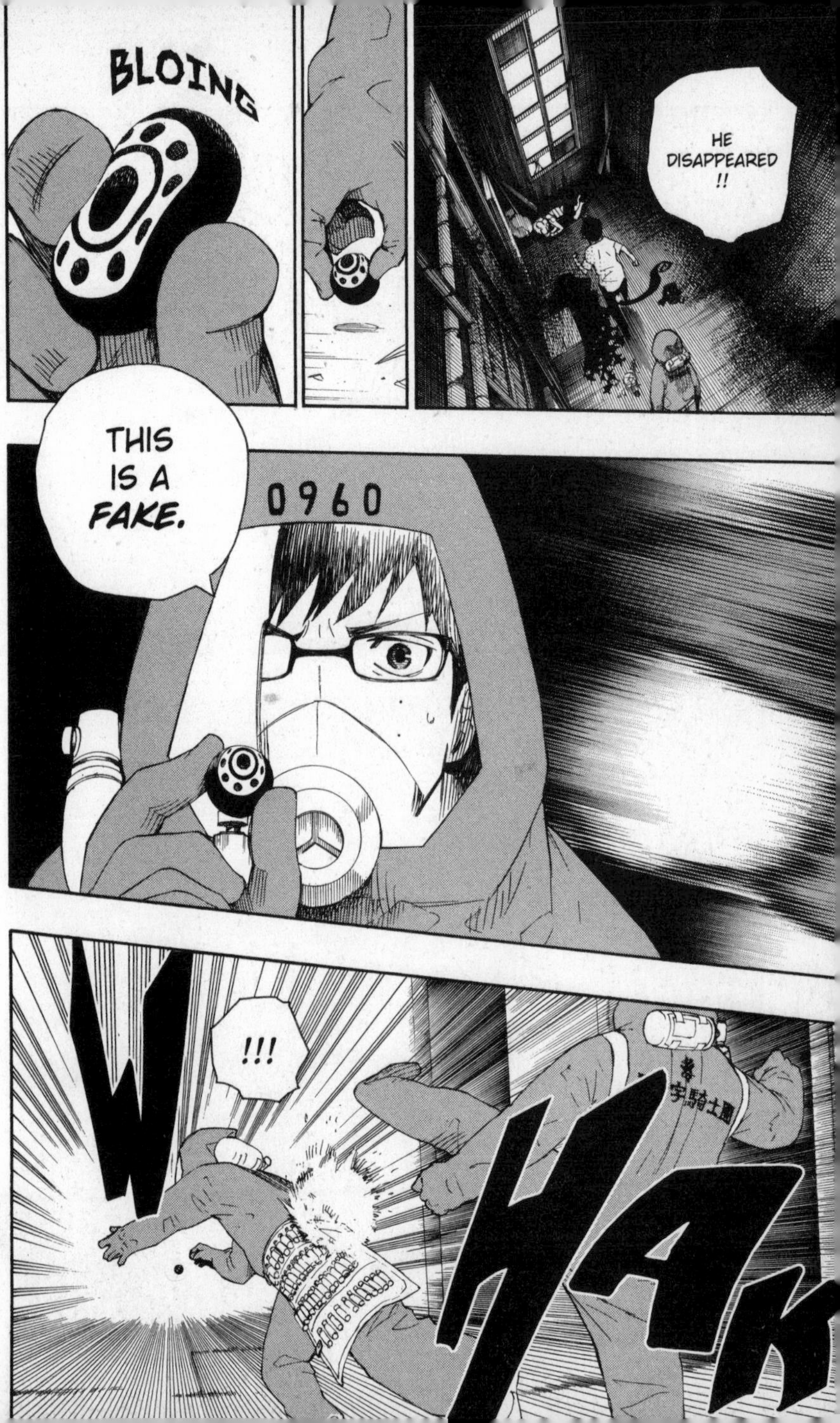

HE DISAPPEARED !!
BLOING
THIS IS A FAKE.
0960
!!!
WHAK

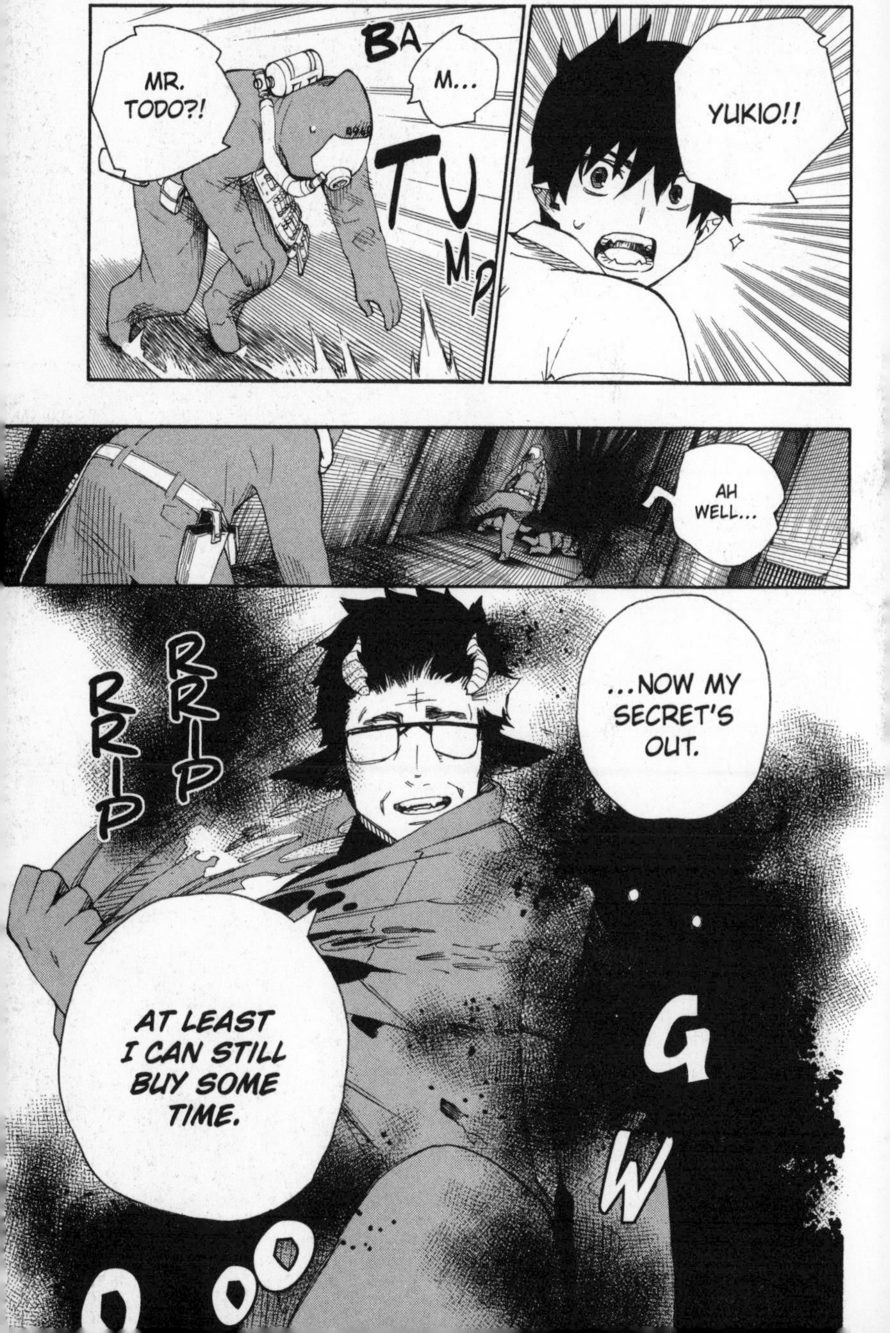
YUKIO!!
M...
BA
TUMP
MR. TODO?!
AH WELL...
...NOW MY SECRET'S OUT.
RRIP
RRIP
AT LEAST I CAN STILL BUY SOME TIME.
GWOOO

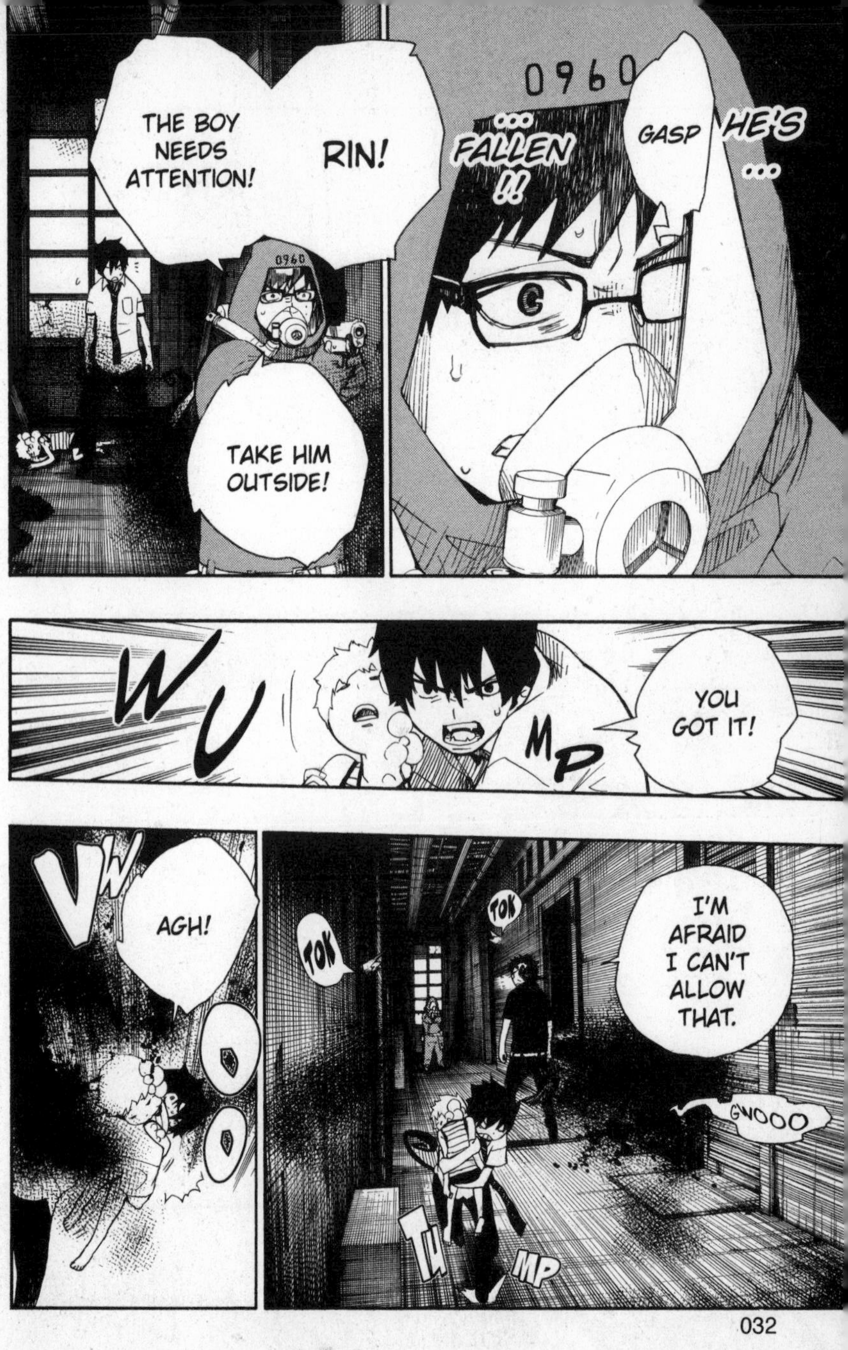
0960
HE'S ...
GASP
... FALLEN !!
RIN!
THE BOY NEEDS ATTENTION!
0960
TAKE HIM OUTSIDE!
YOU GOT IT!
WUMP
I'M AFRAID I CAN'T ALLOW THAT.
TOK
TOK
GWOOO
THUMP
AGH!
VWOOO

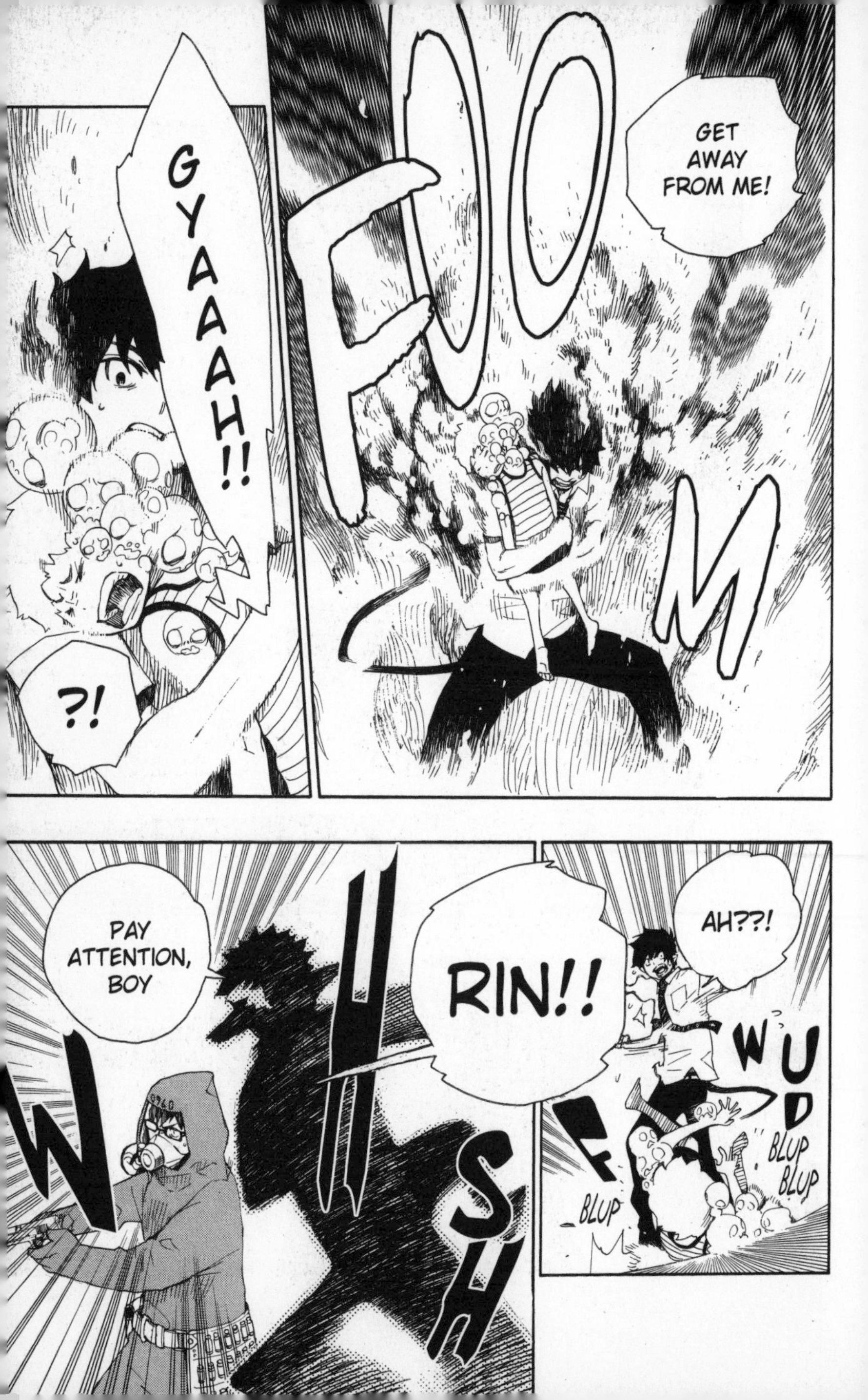
GET AWAY FROM ME!
FOOM
GYAAAH!!
?!
AH??!
WUD
F
BLUP
BLUP
BLUP
RIN!!
PAY ATTENTION, BOY
WHSH

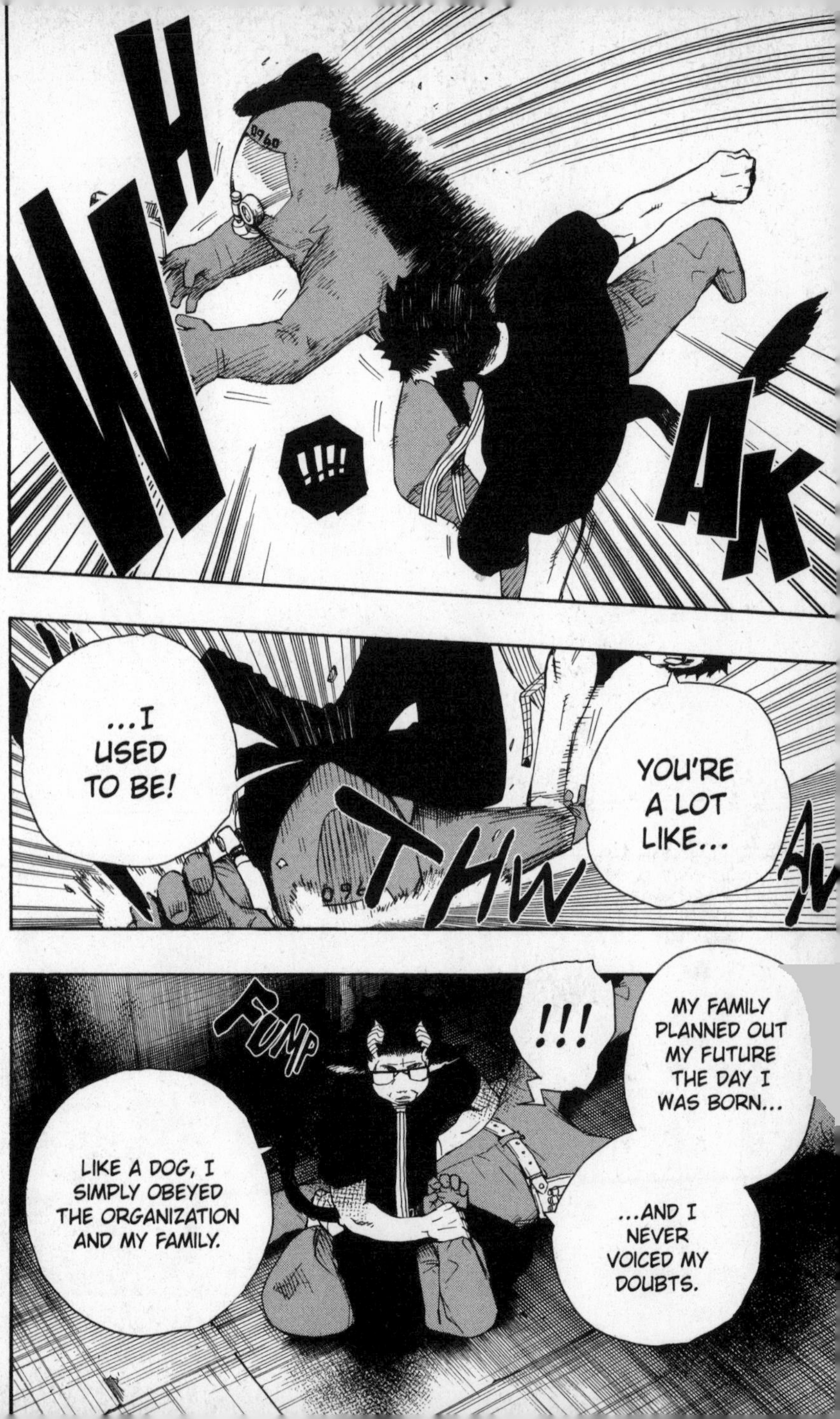
WHAK
!!!!
YOU'RE A LOT LIKE...
THWA
...I USED TO BE!
MY FAMILY PLANNED OUT MY FUTURE THE DAY I WAS BORN...
!!!
FUMP
...AND I NEVER VOICED MY DOUBTS.
LIKE A DOG, I SIMPLY OBEYED THE ORGANIZATION AND MY FAMILY.

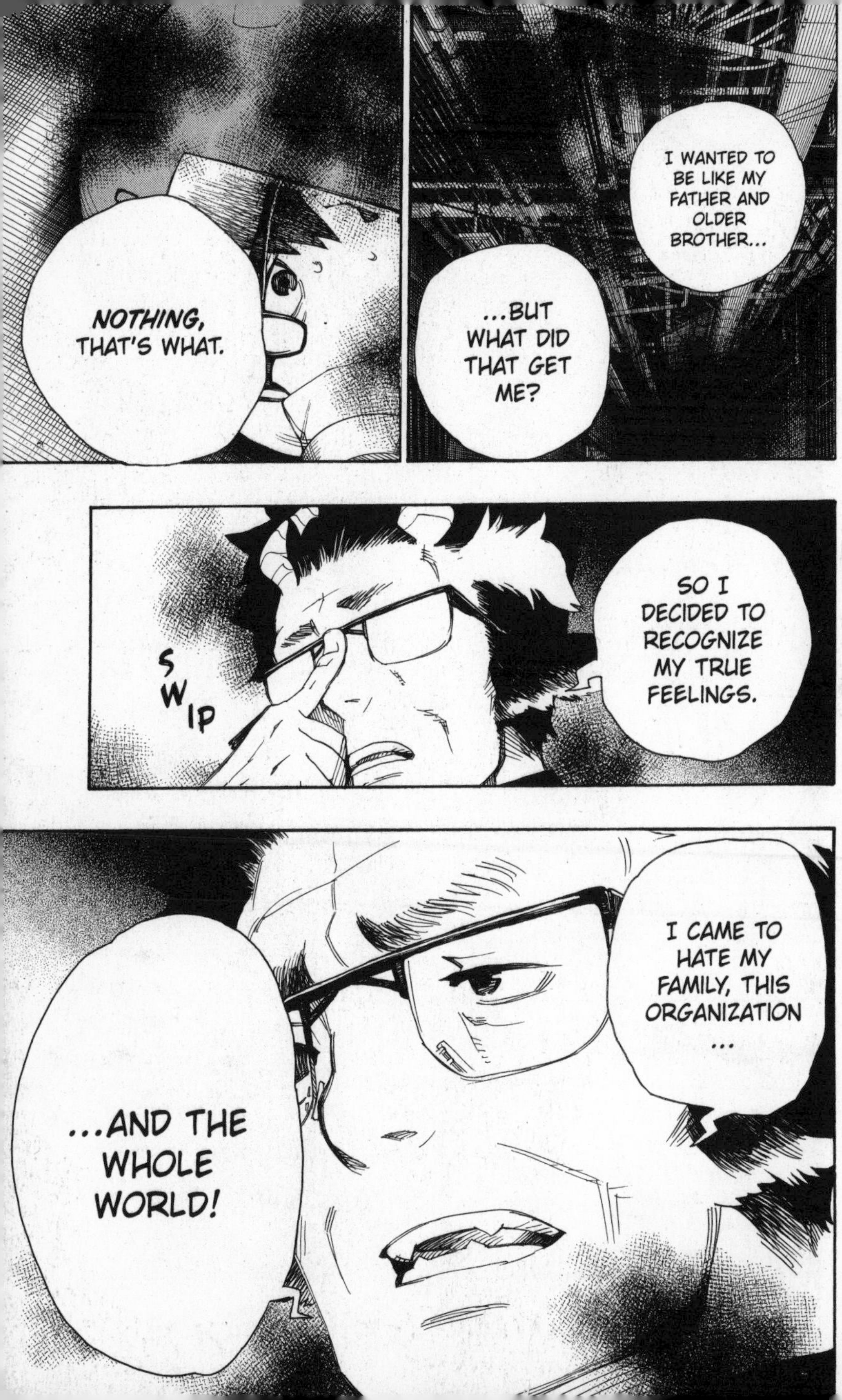
I WANTED TO BE LIKE MY FATHER AND OLDER BROTHER...
...BUT WHAT DID THAT GET ME?
NOTHING, THAT'S WHAT.
SO I DECIDED TO RECOGNIZE MY TRUE FEELINGS.
SWIP
I CAME TO HATE MY FAMILY, THIS ORGANIZATION ...
...AND THE WHOLE WORLD!

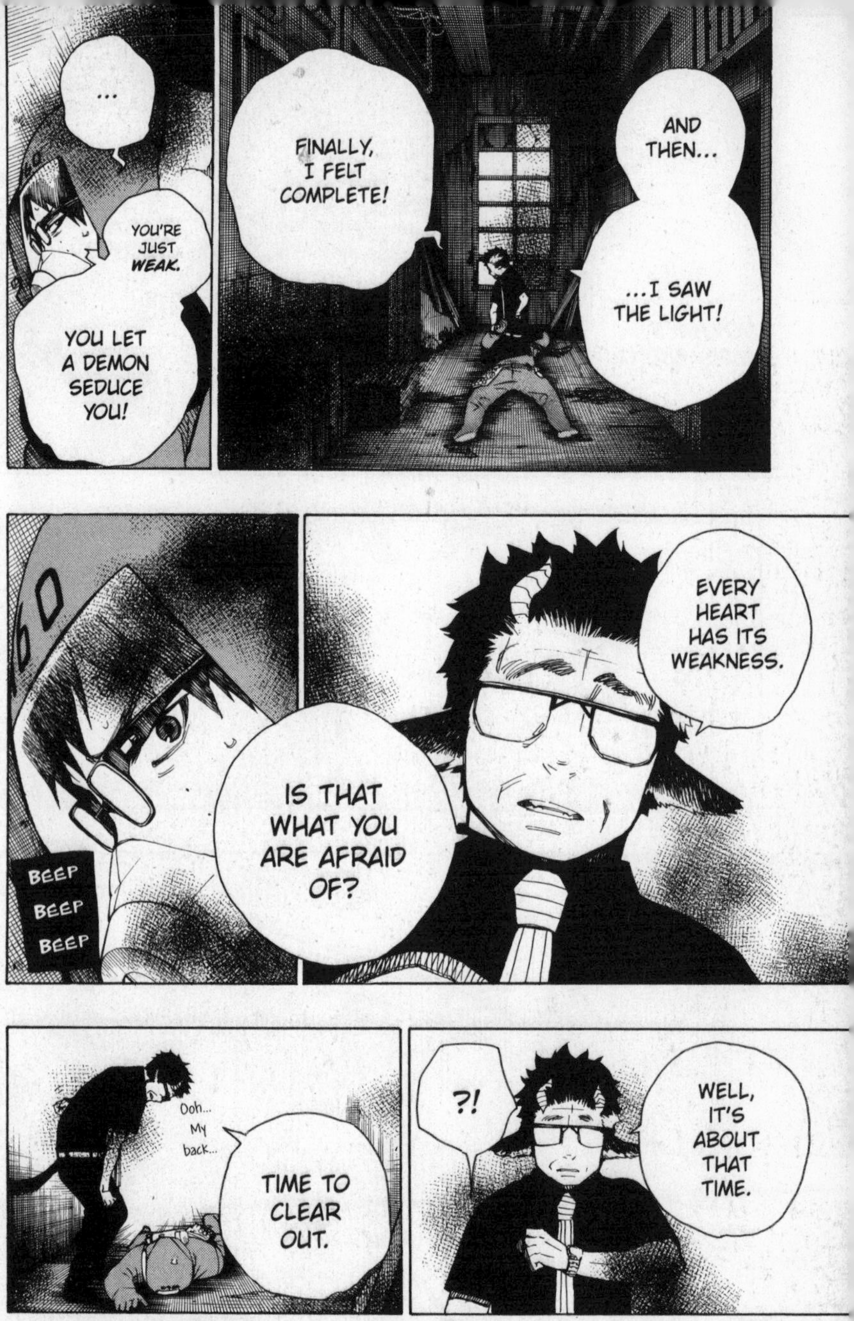
AND THEN...
...I SAW THE LIGHT!
FINALLY, I FELT COMPLETE!
...
YOU'RE JUST WEAK.
YOU LET A DEMON SEDUCE YOU!
EVERY HEART HAS ITS WEAKNESS.
IS THAT WHAT YOU ARE AFRAID OF?
BEEP BEEP BEEP
WELL, IT'S ABOUT THAT TIME.
?!
Ooh... My back...
TIME TO CLEAR OUT.

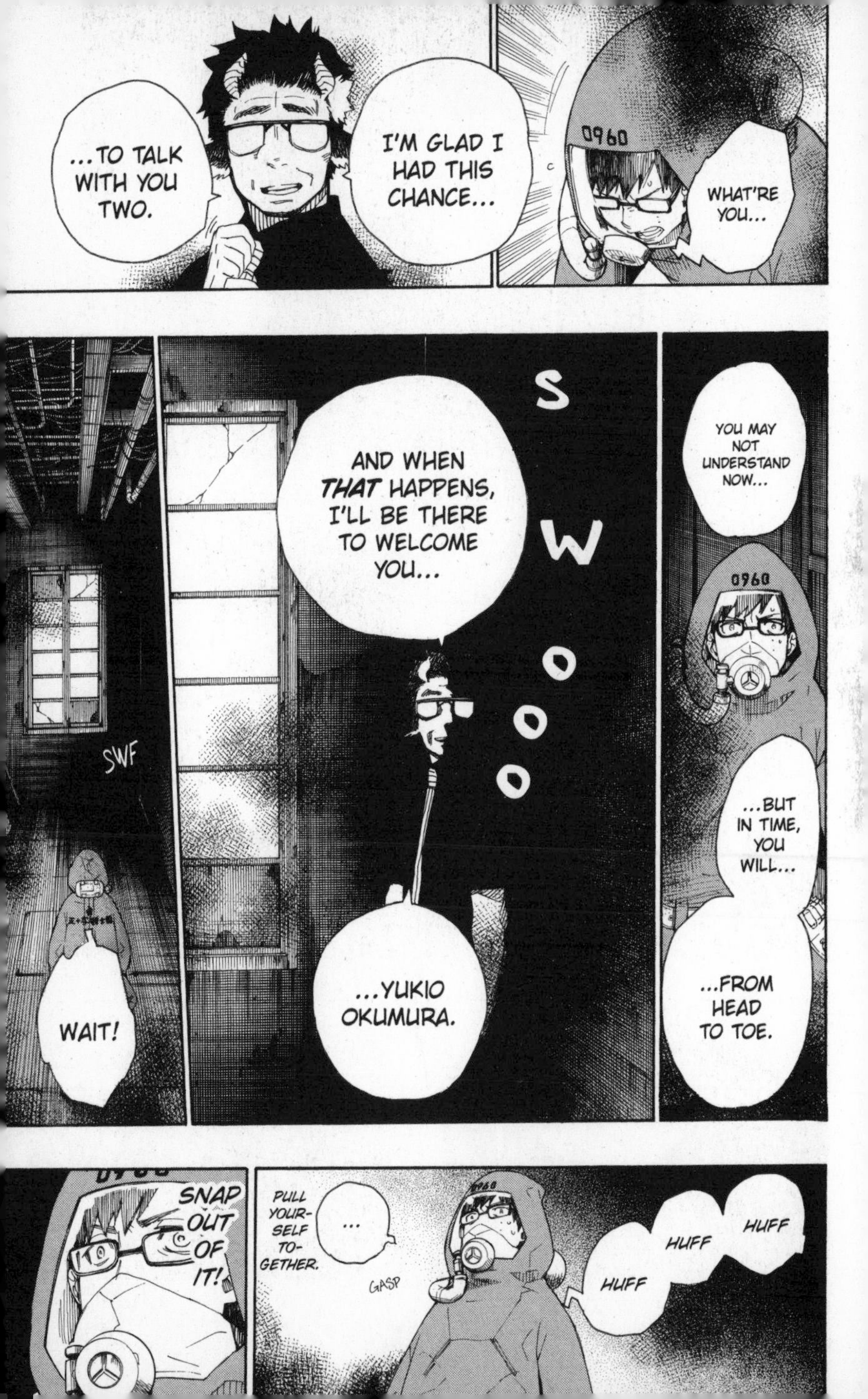
WHAT'RE YOU...
I'M GLAD I HAD THIS CHANCE...
...TO TALK WITH YOU TWO.
YOU MAY NOT UNDERSTAND NOW...
...BUT IN TIME, YOU WILL...
...FROM HEAD TO TOE.
SWOOOO
AND WHEN *THAT* HAPPENS, I'LL BE THERE TO WELCOME YOU...
...YUKIO OKUMURA.
SWF
WAIT!
HUFF
HUFF
HUFF
...
GASP
PULL YOUR-SELF TO-GETHER.
SNAP OUT OF IT!

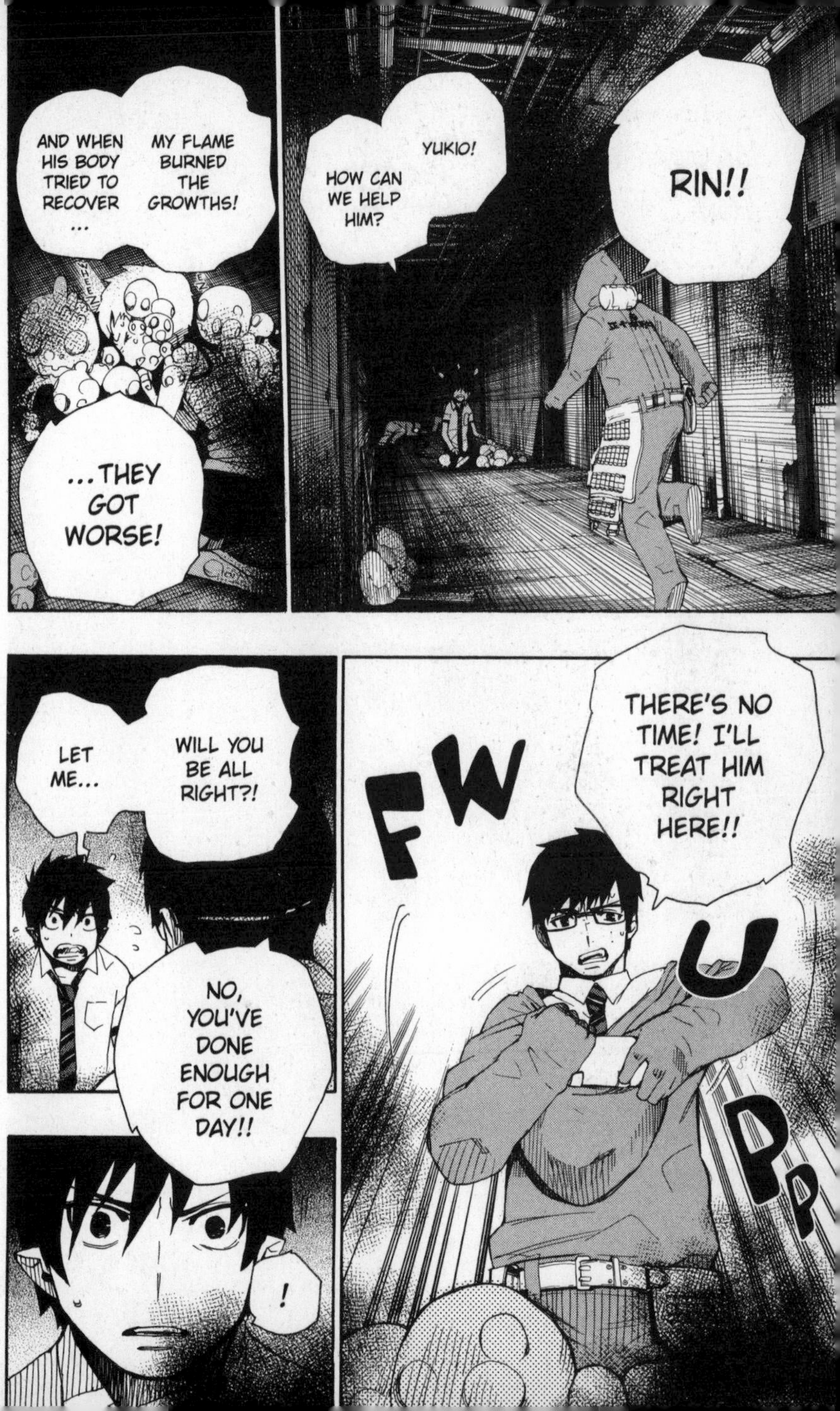
RIN!!
YUKIO!
HOW CAN WE HELP HIM?
MY FLAME BURNED THE GROWTHS!
AND WHEN HIS BODY TRIED TO RECOVER...
...THEY GOT WORSE!
THERE'S NO TIME! I'LL TREAT HIM RIGHT HERE!!
FWUPP
WILL YOU BE ALL RIGHT?!
LET ME...
NO, YOU'VE DONE ENOUGH FOR ONE DAY!!
!

CONCEN-
TRATE!

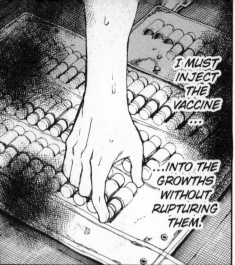

I MUST
INJECT
THE
VACCINE
...

...INTO THE
GROWTHS
WITHOUT
RUPTURING
THEM!

HUFF

HUFF

HUFF

...!

HUFF

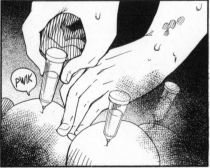

PWIK

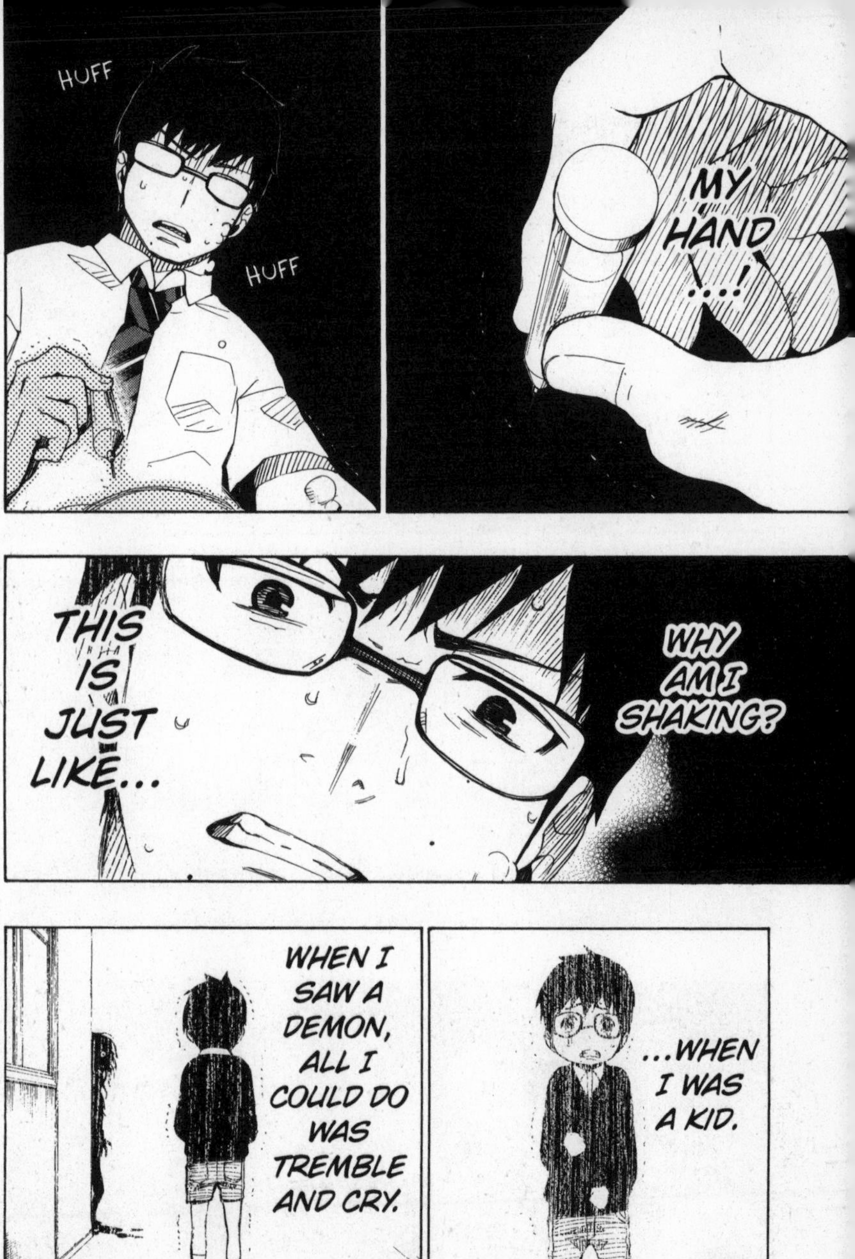
MY HAND...!
HUFF
HUFF
WHY AM I SHAKING?
THIS IS JUST LIKE...
...WHEN I WAS A KID.
WHEN I SAW A DEMON, ALL I COULD DO WAS TREMBLE AND CRY.

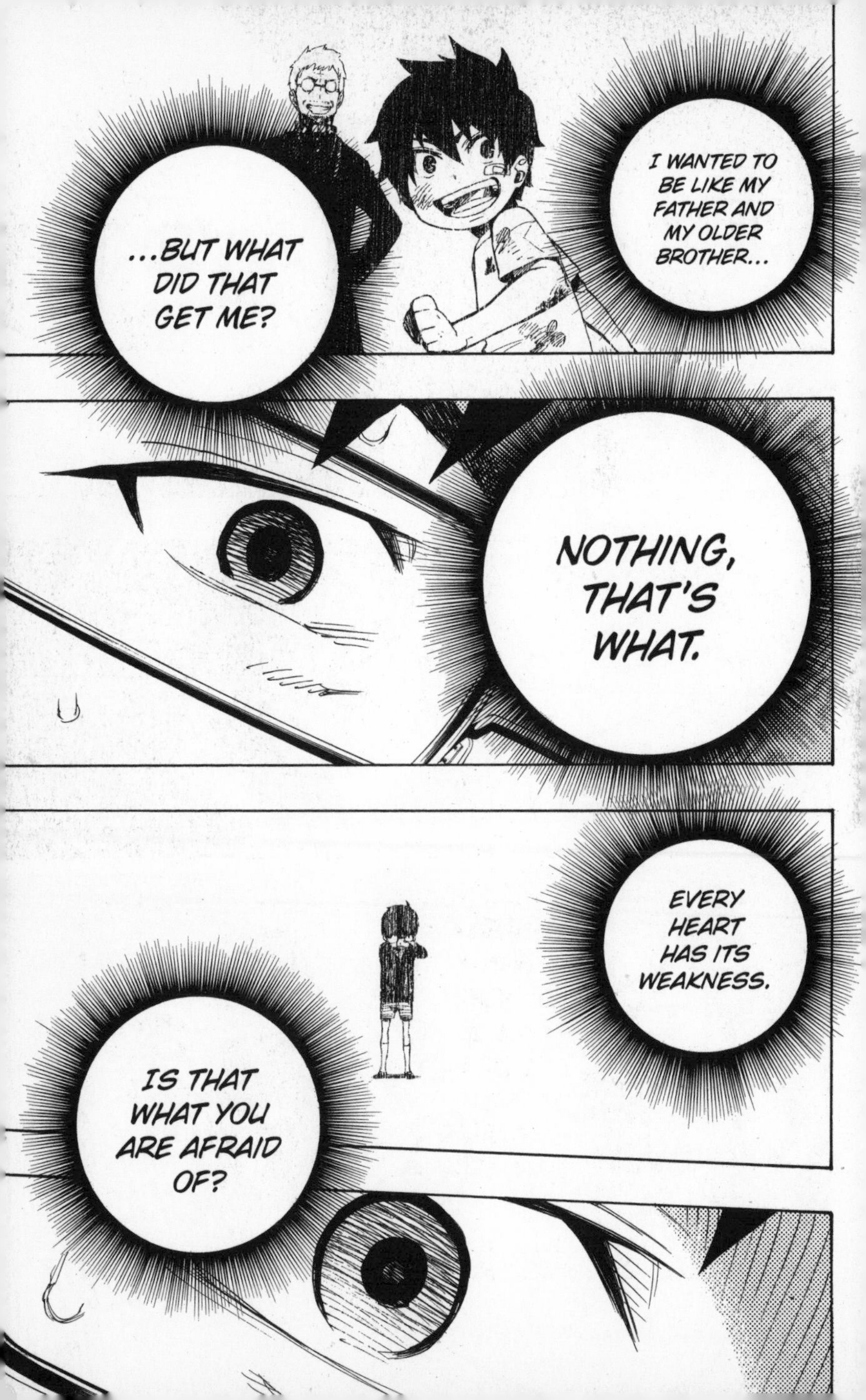
I WANTED TO BE LIKE MY FATHER AND MY OLDER BROTHER...
...BUT WHAT DID THAT GET ME?
NOTHING, THAT'S WHAT.
EVERY HEART HAS ITS WEAKNESS.
IS THAT WHAT YOU ARE AFRAID OF?

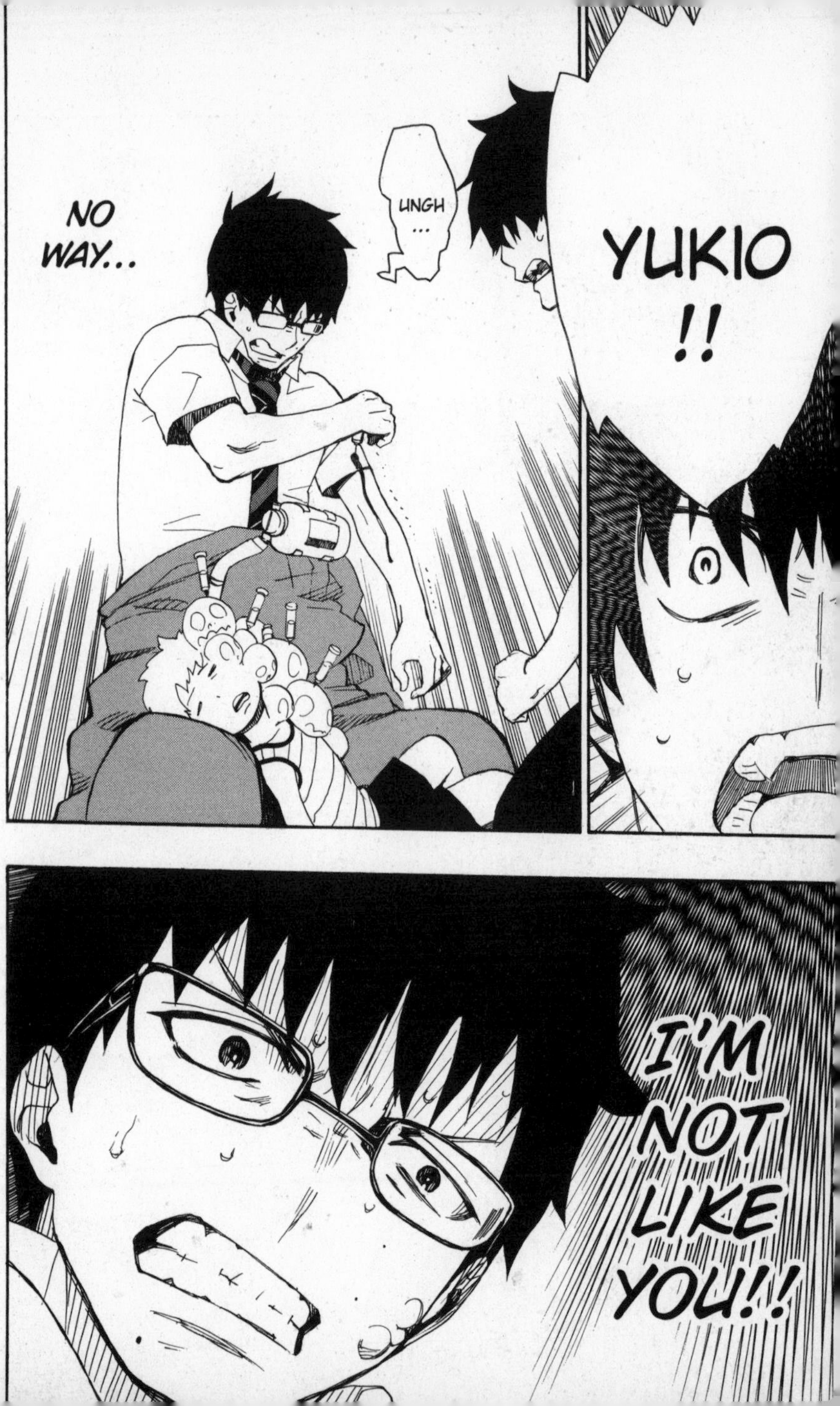
YUKIO !!
UNGH ...
NO WAY...
I'M NOT LIKE YOU!!

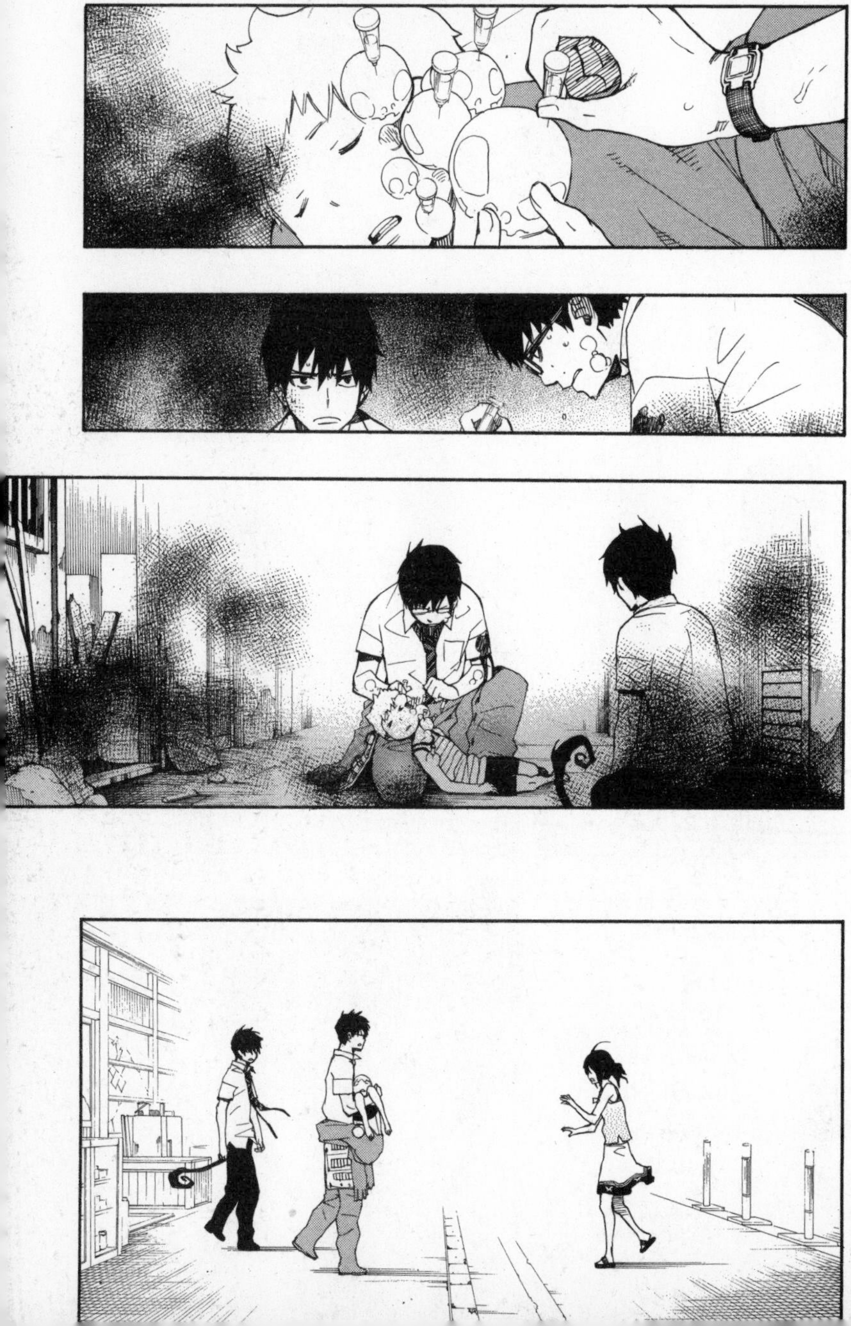

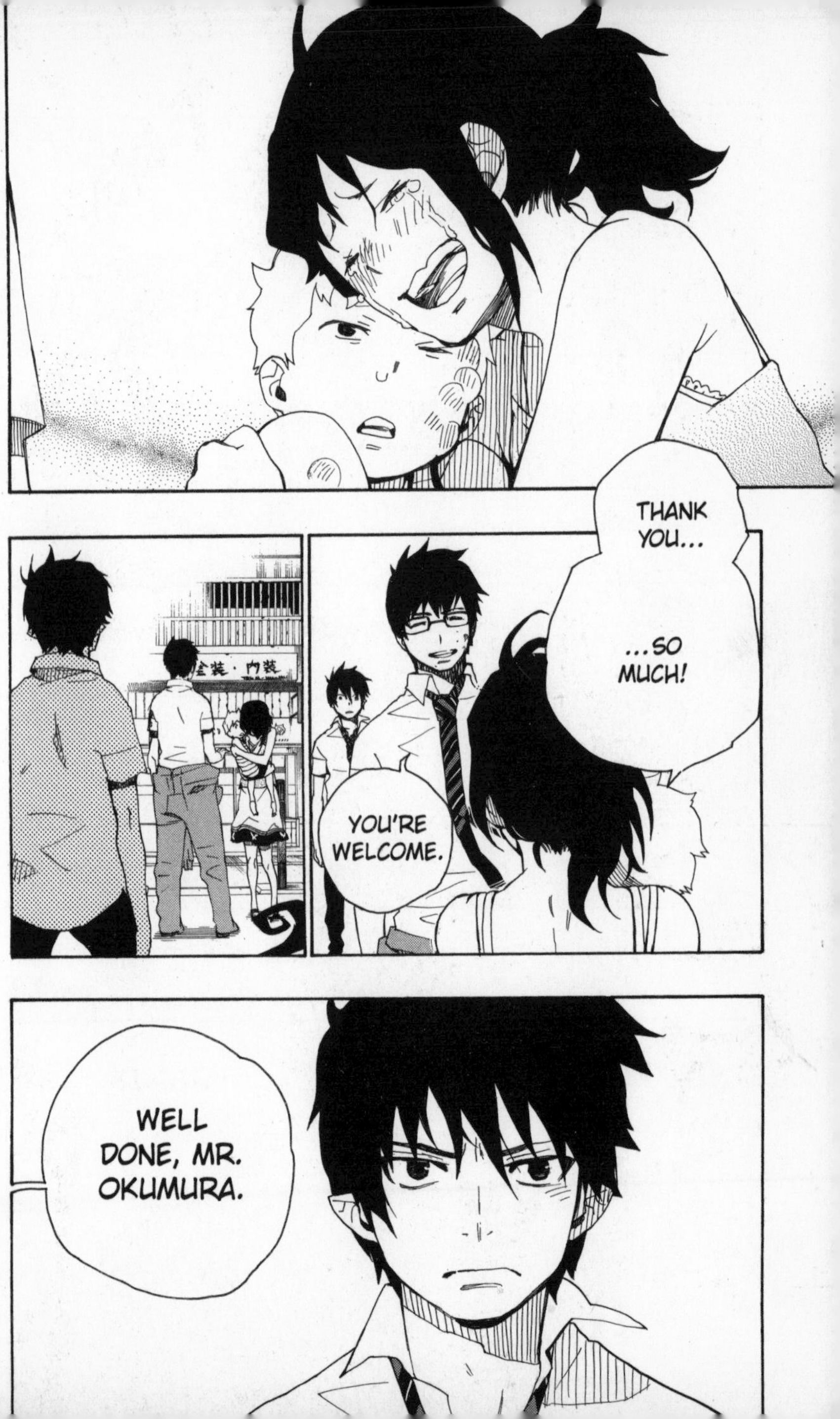
THANK YOU...
...SO MUCH!
YOU'RE WELCOME.
WELL DONE, MR. OKUMURA.

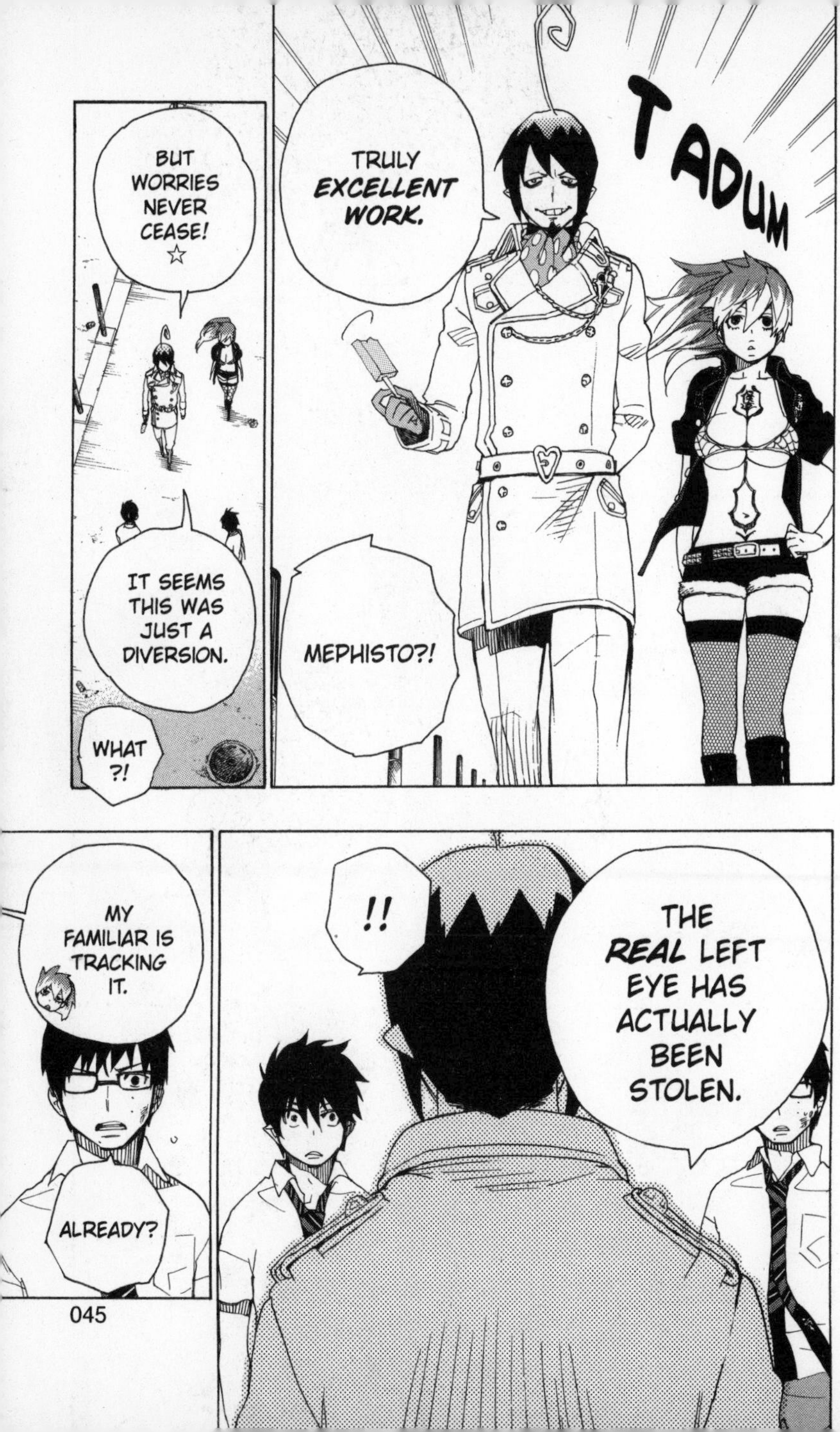
TADUM
TRULY EXCELLENT WORK.
MEPHISTO?!
BUT WORRIES NEVER CEASE! ☆
IT SEEMS THIS WAS JUST A DIVERSION.
WHAT?!
THE REAL LEFT EYE HAS ACTUALLY BEEN STOLEN.
!!
MY FAMILIAR IS TRACKING IT.
ALREADY?

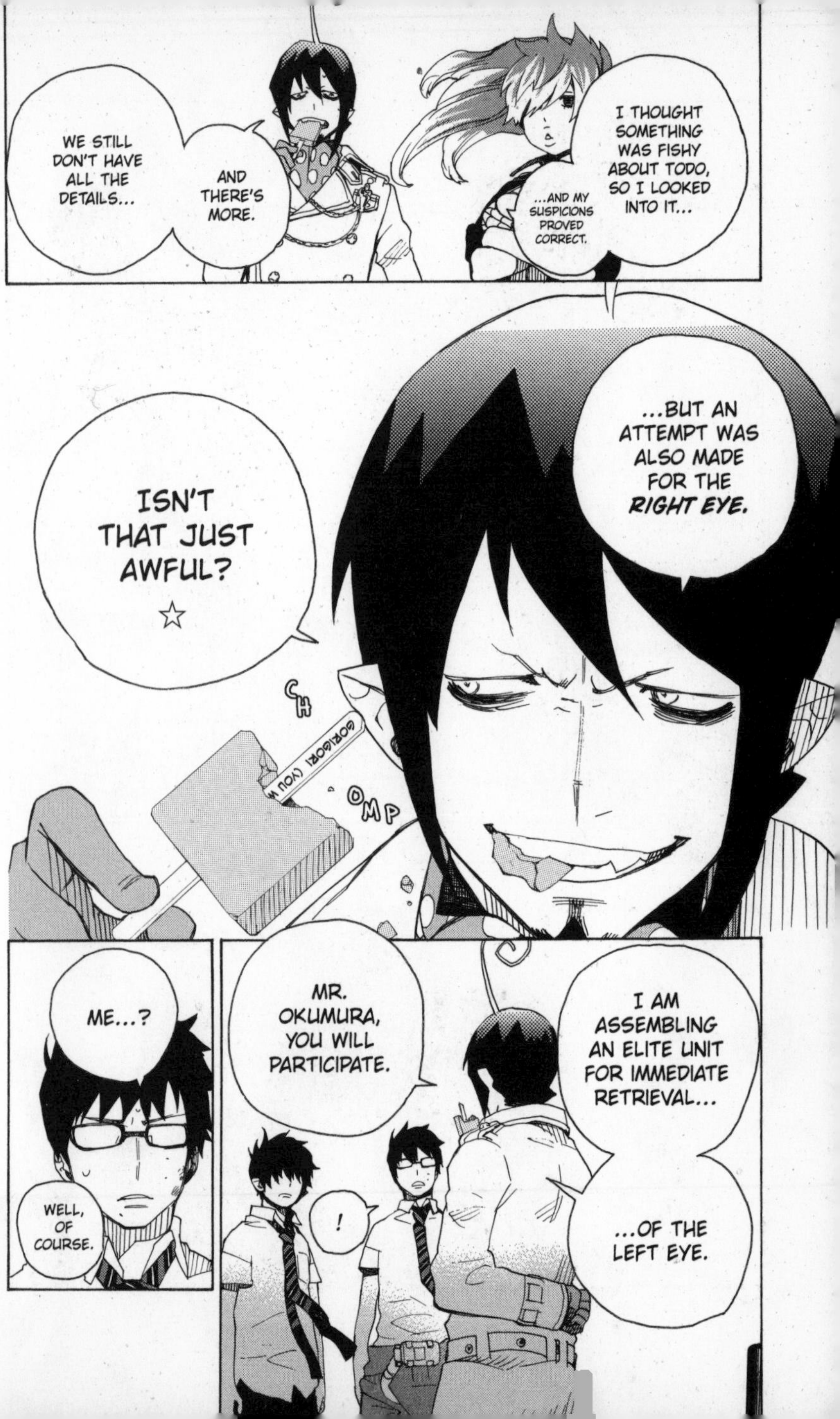
I THOUGHT SOMETHING WAS FISHY ABOUT TODO, SO I LOOKED INTO IT...
...AND MY SUSPICIONS PROVED CORRECT.
AND THERE'S MORE.
WE STILL DON'T HAVE ALL THE DETAILS...
...BUT AN ATTEMPT WAS ALSO MADE FOR THE *RIGHT EYE.*
ISN'T THAT JUST AWFUL? ☆
CH
OMP
GORIGORI (YOU W
I AM ASSEMBLING AN ELITE UNIT FOR IMMEDIATE RETRIEVAL...
...OF THE LEFT EYE.
!
MR. OKUMURA, YOU WILL PARTICIPATE.
ME...?
WELL, OF COURSE.

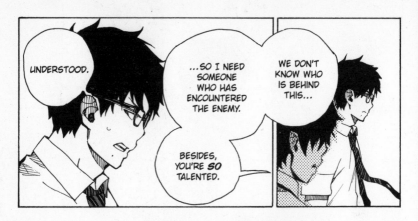

WE DON'T KNOW WHO IS BEHIND THIS...
...SO I NEED SOMEONE WHO HAS ENCOUNTERED THE ENEMY.
BESIDES, YOU'RE **SO** TALENTED.
UNDERSTOOD.
MEET AT THE BASE...
...IN ONE HOUR.
KEEP OUT
KNIGHTS OF THE TRUE CROSS
KEEP OUT
KEEP OUT
COFFEE SHOP
Cafe
SHURA ...
...I'M LEAVING RIN WITH YOU.
OKAY.
HMPH.
THAT'S ONE RAPIDLY AGING 15-YEAR-OLD!
He'll go bald young.
...

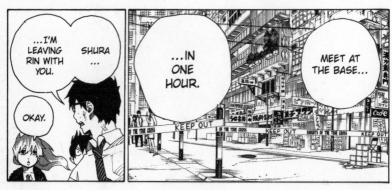

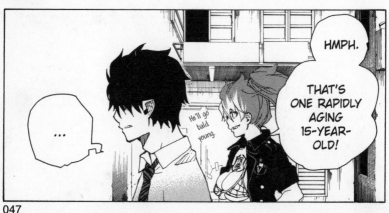

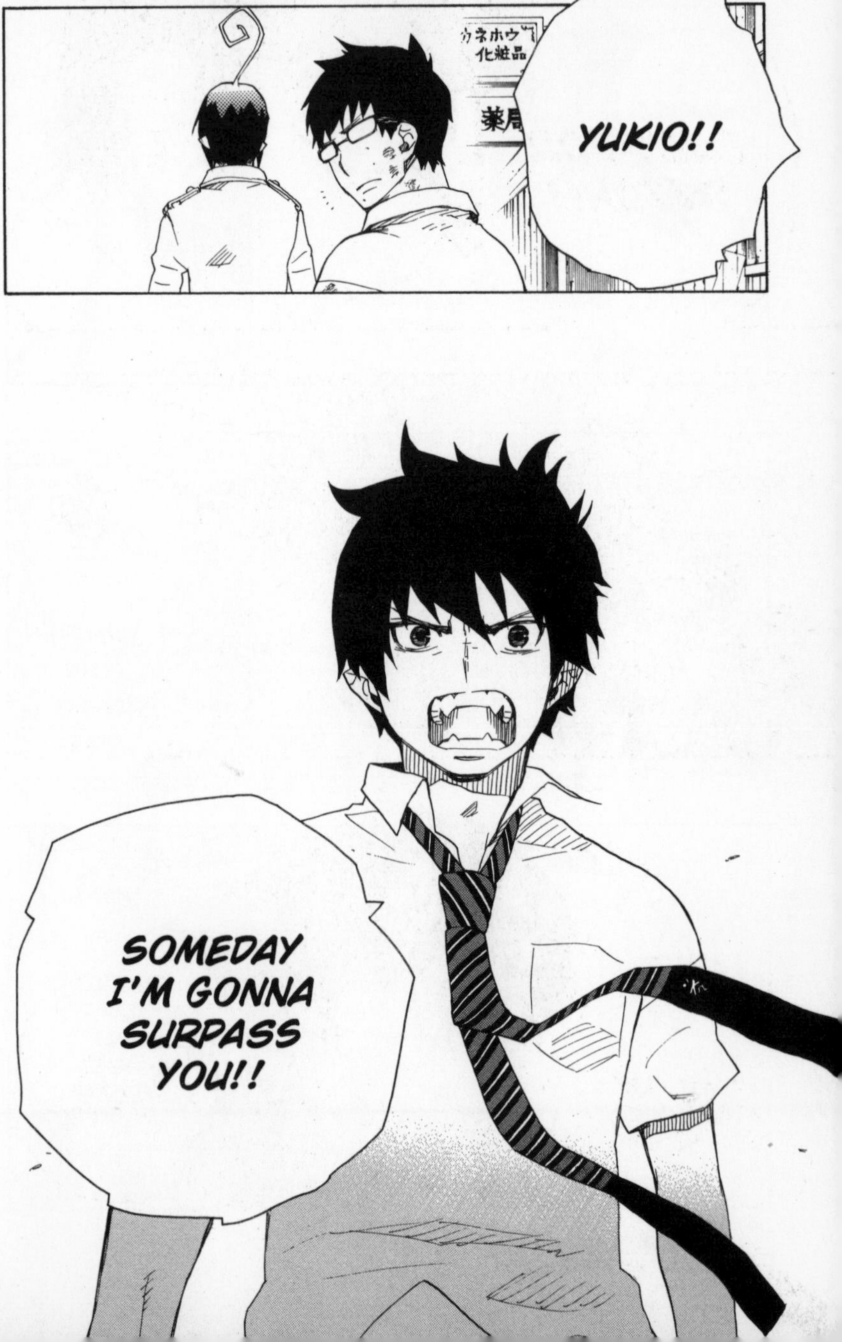
YUKIO!!
カネホウ
化粧品
SOMEDAY I'M GONNA SURPASS YOU!!

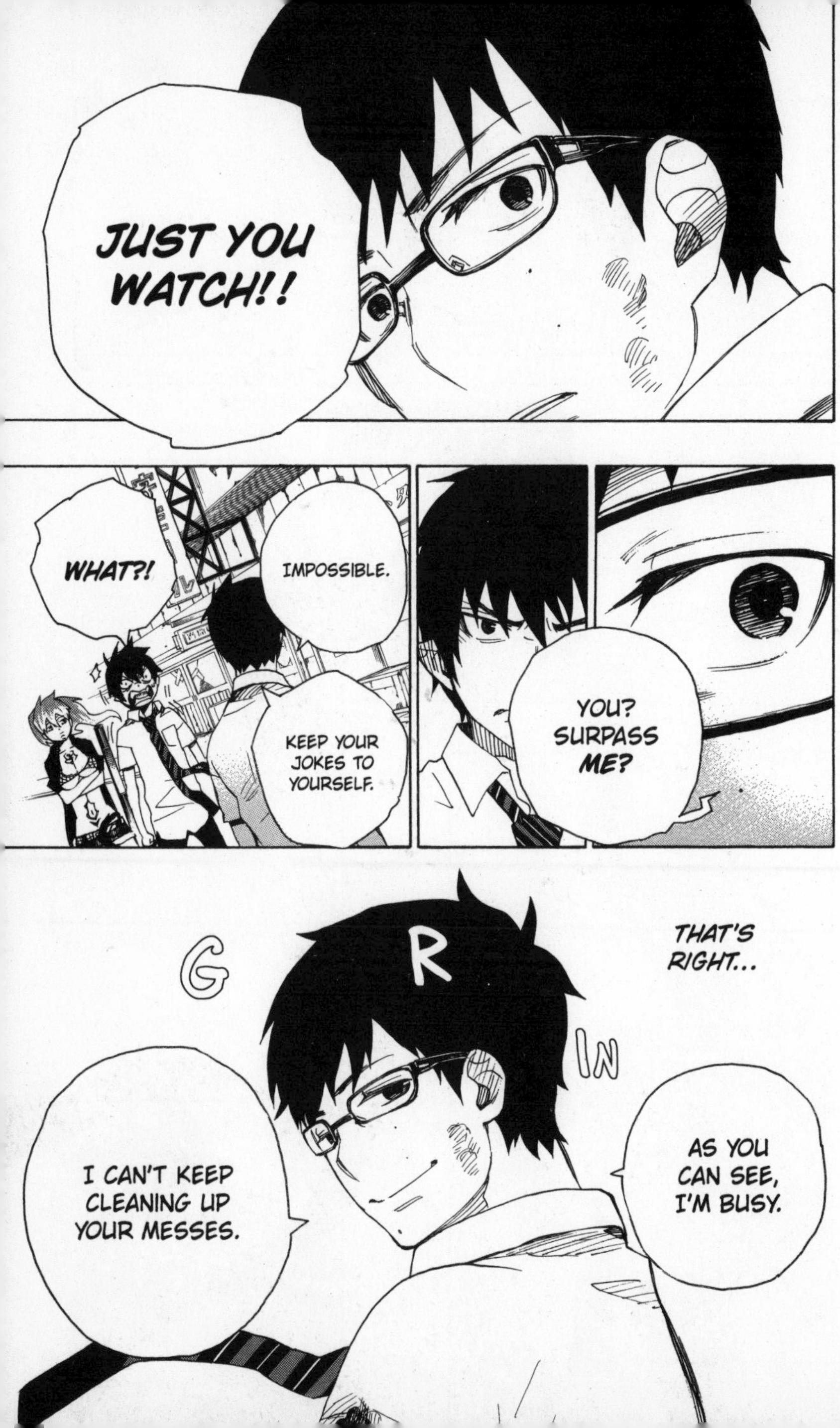
JUST YOU WATCH!!
YOU? SURPASS ME?
IMPOSSIBLE.
KEEP YOUR JOKES TO YOURSELF.
WHAT?!
THAT'S RIGHT...
GRIN
AS YOU CAN SEE, I'M BUSY.
I CAN'T KEEP CLEANING UP YOUR MESSES.

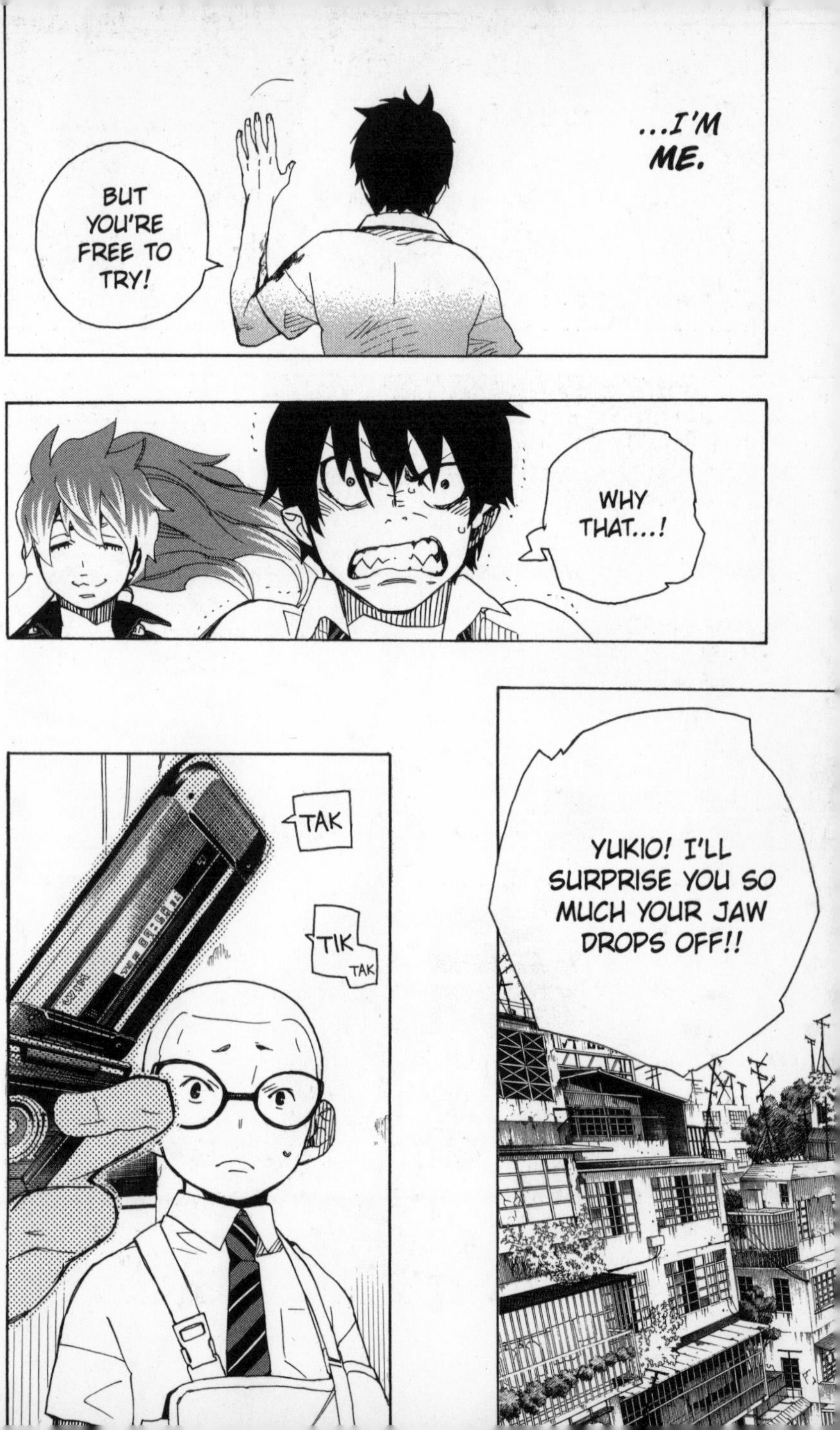
...I'M ME.
BUT YOU'RE FREE TO TRY!
WHY THAT...!
YUKIO! I'LL SURPRISE YOU SO MUCH YOUR JAW DROPS OFF!!
TAK
TIK
TAK

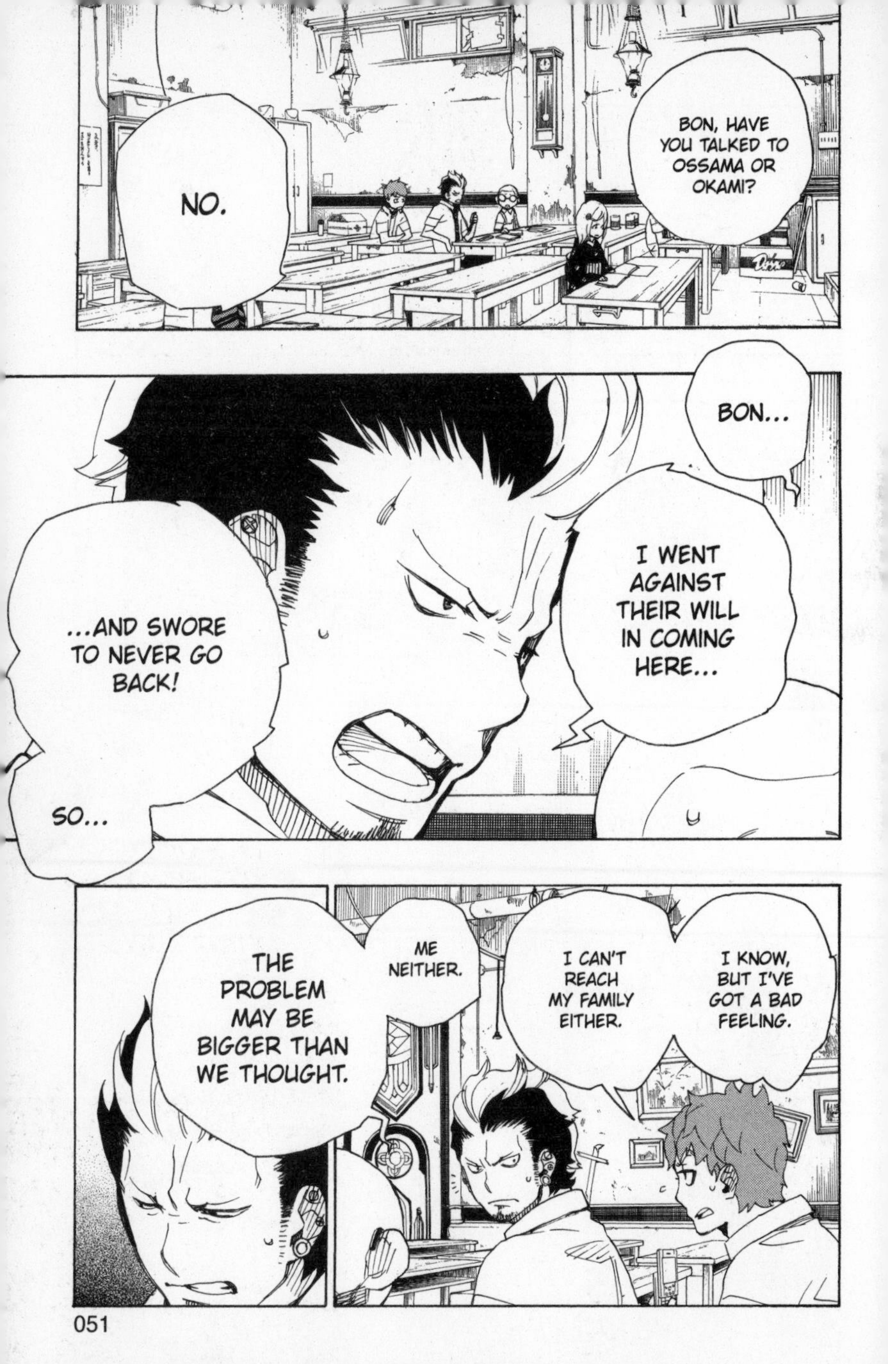
BON, HAVE YOU TALKED TO OSSAMA OR OKAMI?
NO.
BON...
I WENT AGAINST THEIR WILL IN COMING HERE...
...AND SWORE TO NEVER GO BACK!
SO...
I KNOW, BUT I'VE GOT A BAD FEELING.
I CAN'T REACH MY FAMILY EITHER.
ME NEITHER.
THE PROBLEM MAY BE BIGGER THAN WE THOUGHT.

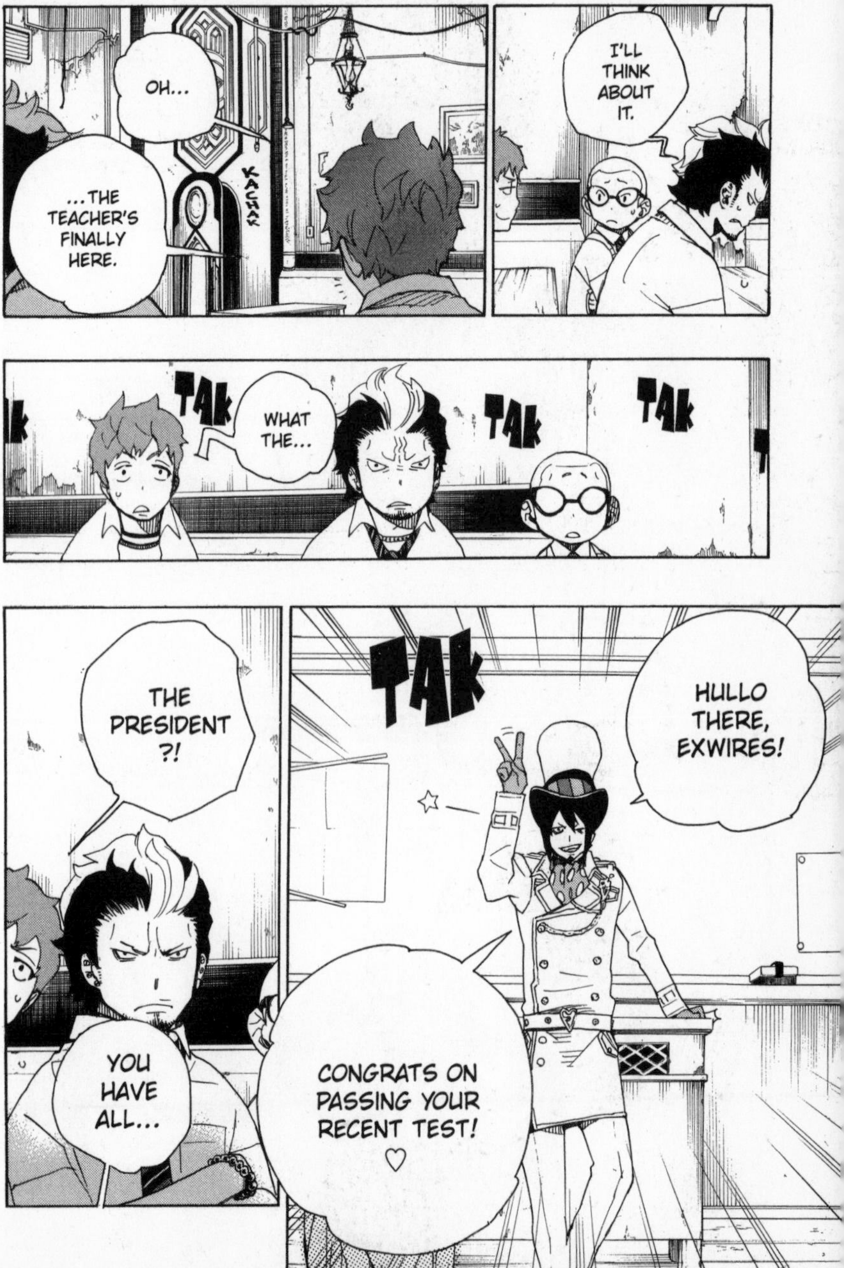
I'LL THINK ABOUT IT.
OH...
...THE TEACHER'S FINALLY HERE.
KACHAK
TAK
TAK
WHAT THE...
TAK
HULLO THERE, EXWIRES!
TAK
CONGRATS ON PASSING YOUR RECENT TEST! ♡
THE PRESIDENT ?!
YOU HAVE ALL...

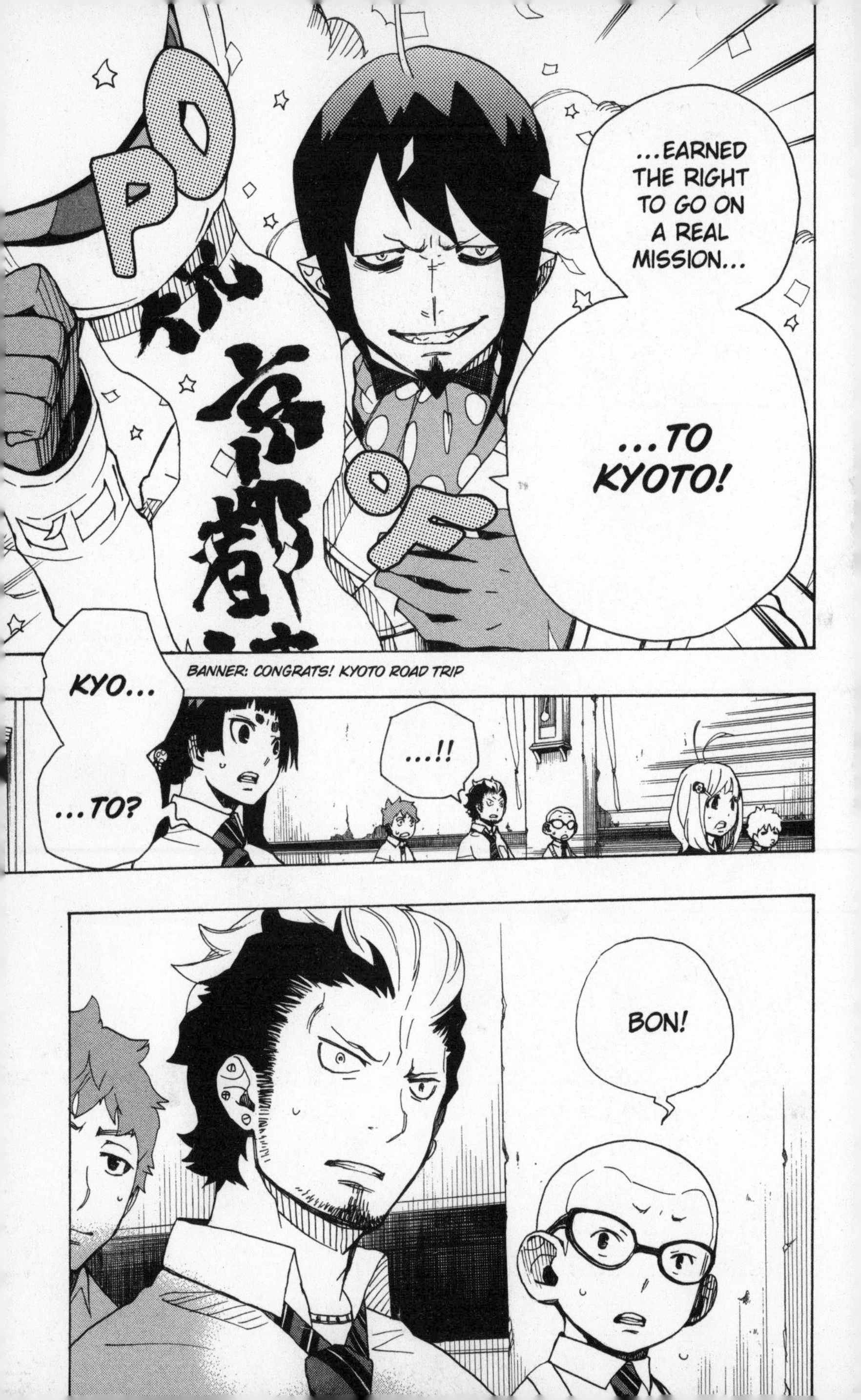
PO
OF
...EARNED THE RIGHT TO GO ON A REAL MISSION...
...TO KYOTO!
BANNER: CONGRATS! KYOTO ROAD TRIP
KYO... ...TO?
...!!
BON!

Blue Exorcist Chapter 16 When it All Began

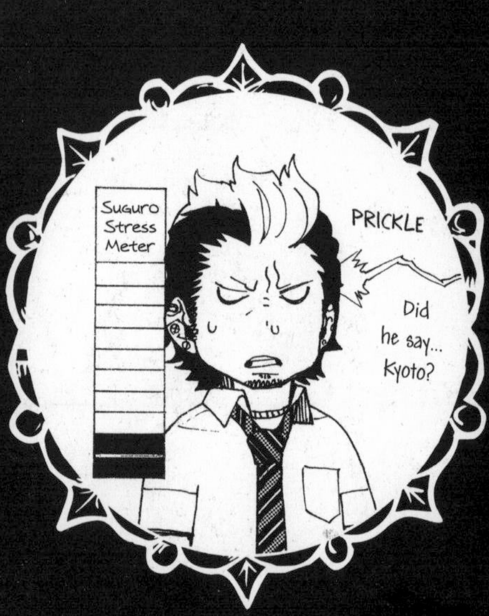
Suguro Stress Meter
PRICKLE
Did he say... Kyoto?

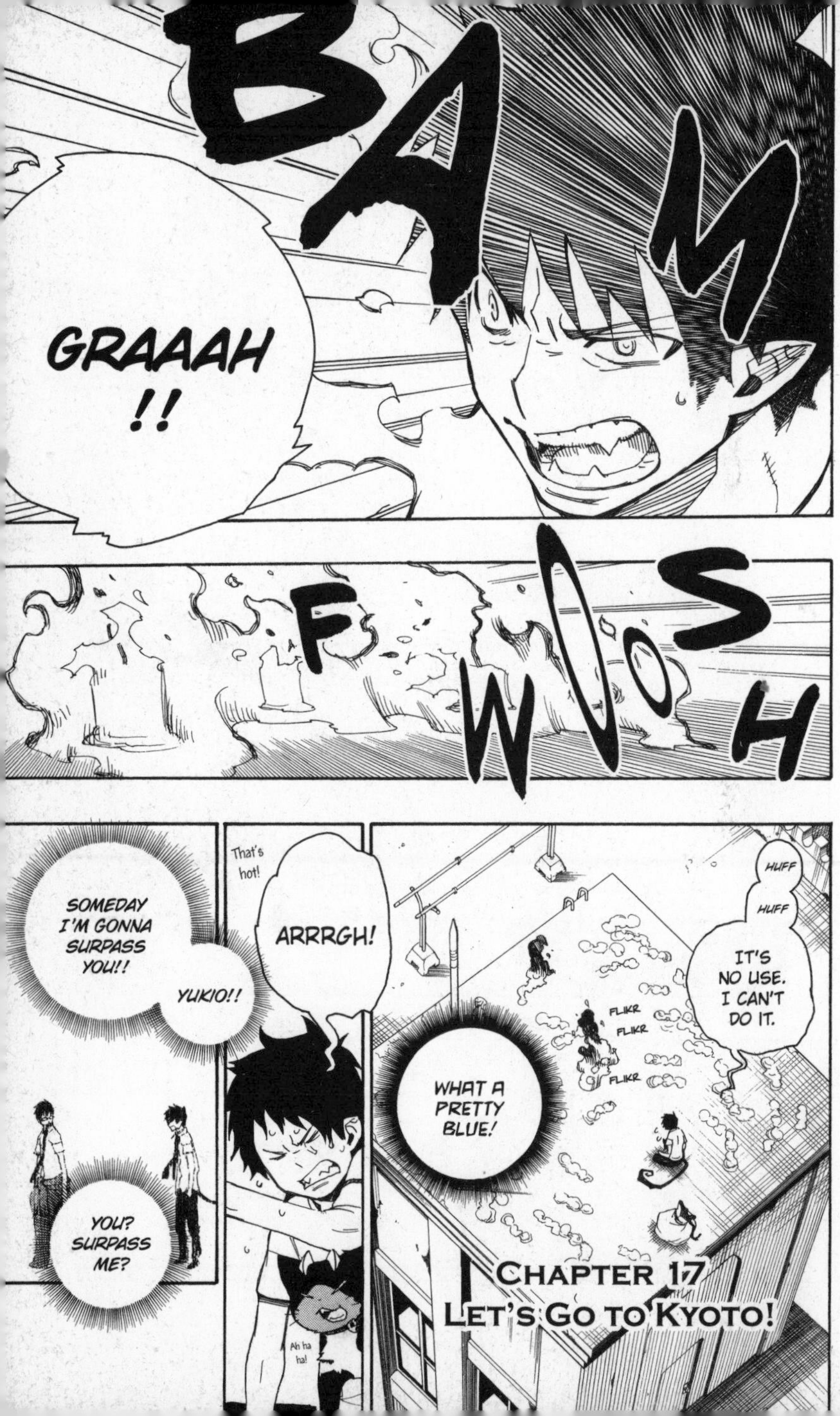
BAM
GRAAAH !!
FWOOSH
HUFF
HUFF
IT'S NO USE. I CAN'T DO IT.
FLIKR
FLIKR
FLIKR
WHAT A PRETTY BLUE!
Chapter 17
Let's Go to Kyoto!
That's hot!
ARRRGH!
Ah ha ha!
SOMEDAY I'M GONNA SURPASS YOU!!
YUKIO!!
YOU? SURPASS ME?

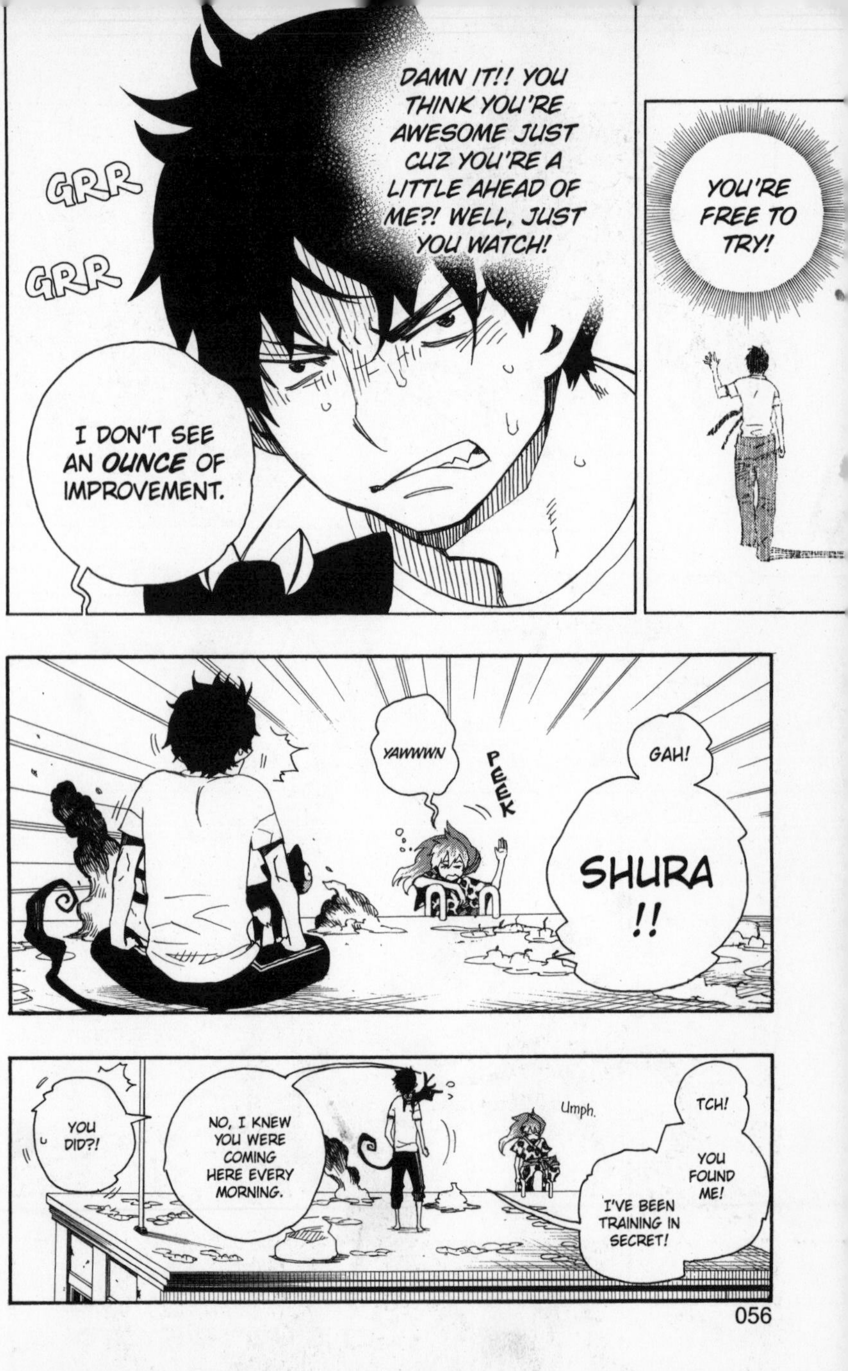
YOU'RE FREE TO TRY!
DAMN IT!! YOU THINK YOU'RE AWESOME JUST CUZ YOU'RE A LITTLE AHEAD OF ME?! WELL, JUST YOU WATCH!
GRR
GRR
I DON'T SEE AN OUNCE OF IMPROVEMENT.
GAH!
SHURA !!
PEEK
YAWWWN
TCH!
YOU FOUND ME!
I'VE BEEN TRAINING IN SECRET!
Umph.
NO, I KNEW YOU WERE COMING HERE EVERY MORNING.
YOU DID?!

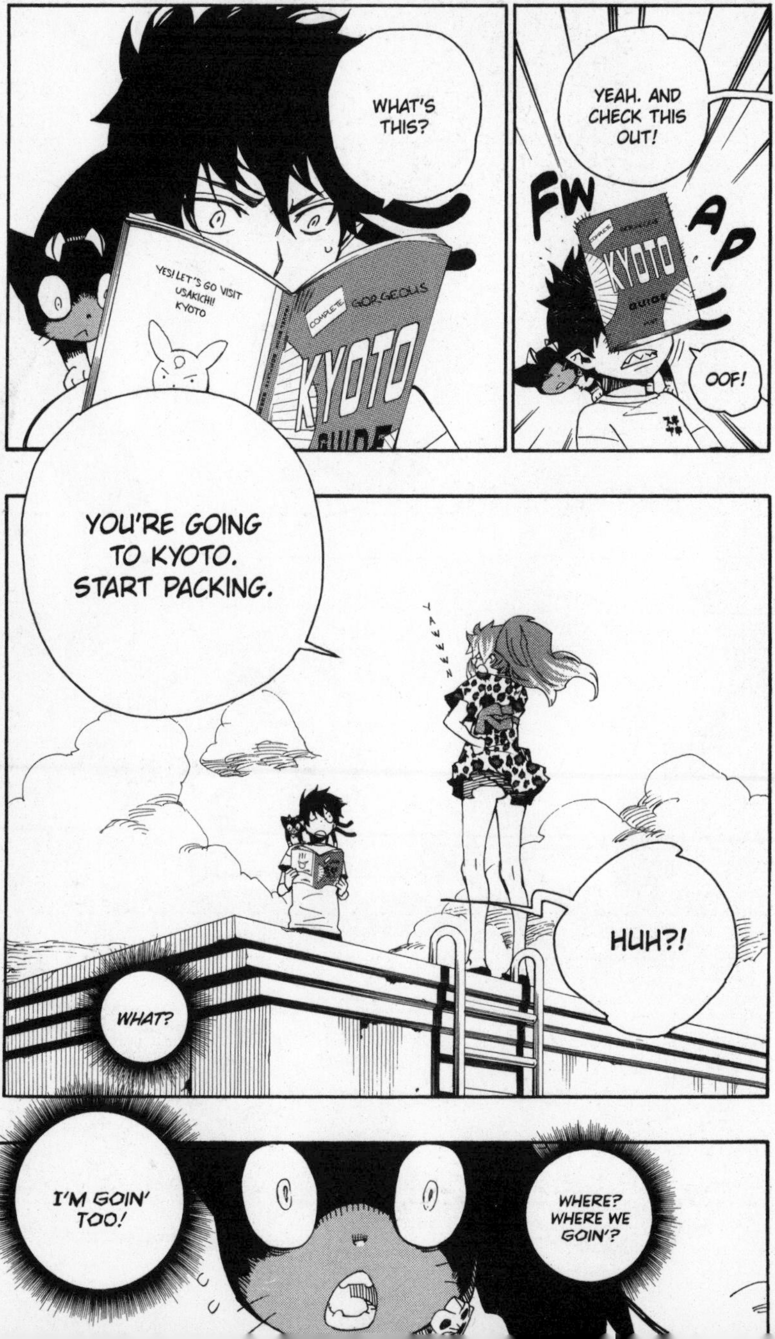
YEAH. AND CHECK THIS OUT!
FW AP
COMPLETE KYOTO GUIDE
OOF!
WHAT'S THIS?
YES! LET'S GO VISIT USAKICHI! KYOTO
COMPLETE GORGEOUS KYOTO GUIDE
YOU'RE GOING TO KYOTO. START PACKING.
HUH?!
WHAT?
WHERE? WHERE WE GOIN'?
I'M GOIN' TOO!

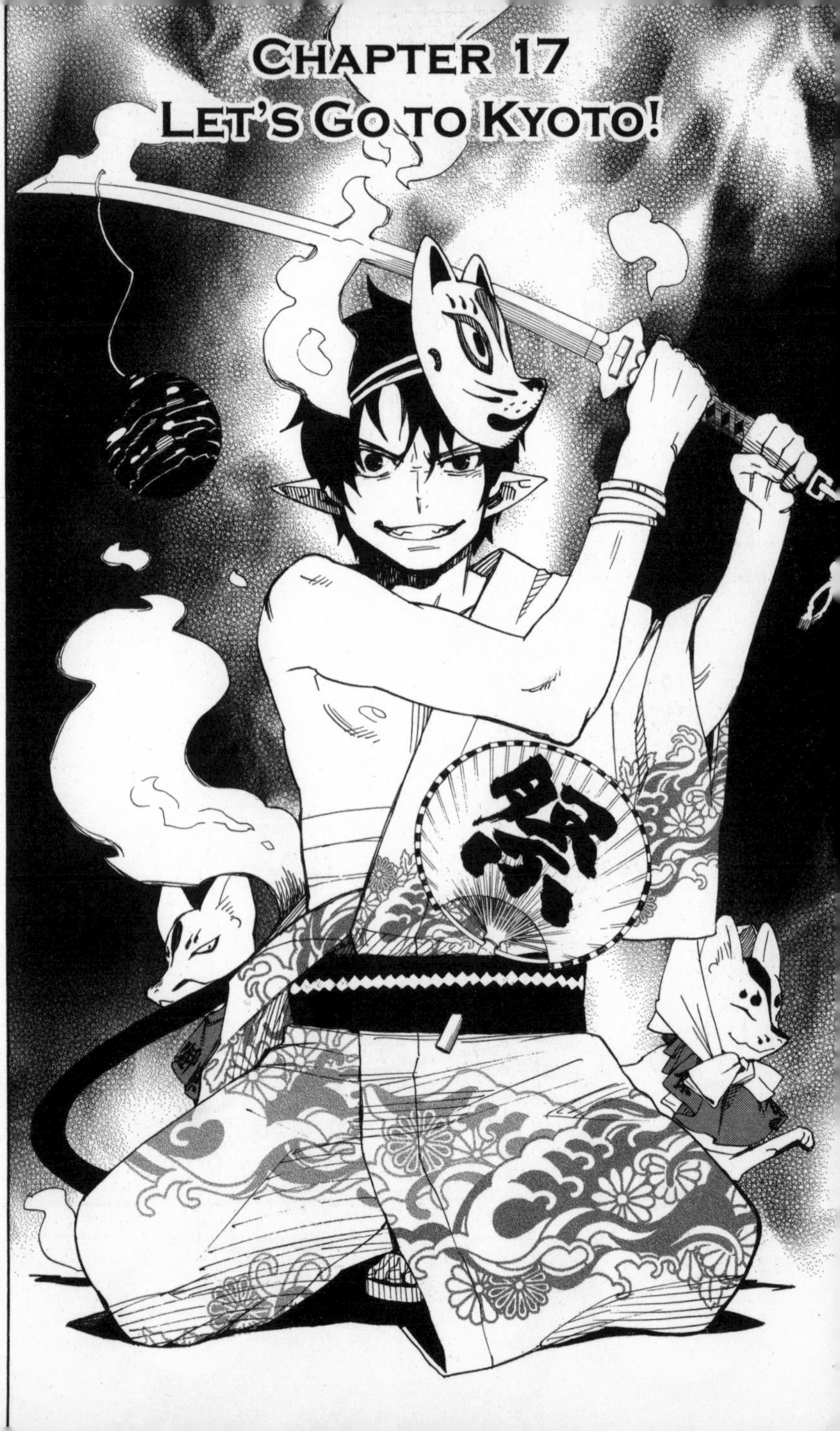
CHAPTER 17
LET'S GO TO KYOTO!
祭

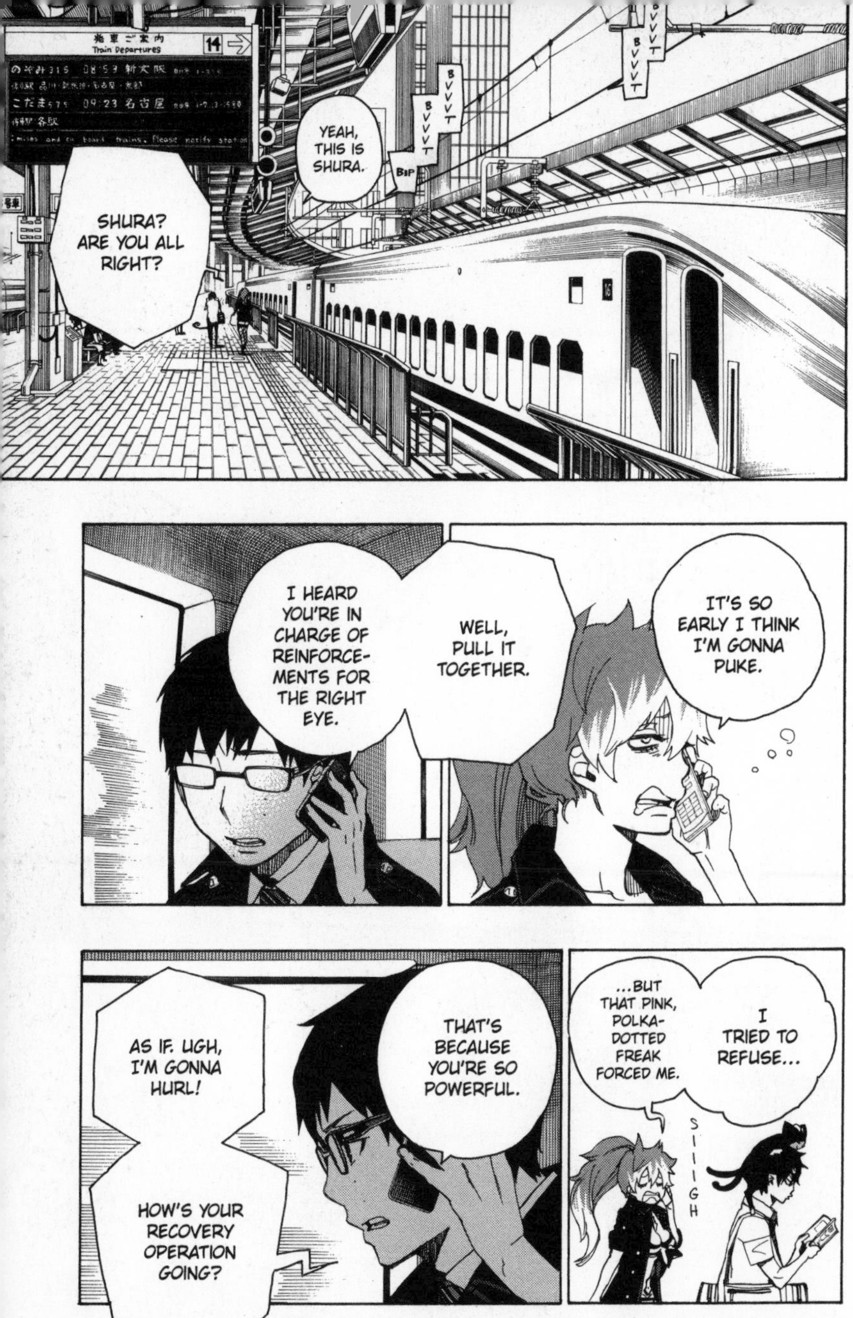
BVVVT
BVVVT
BVVVT
BIP
YEAH, THIS IS SHURA.
Train Departures
14
SHURA? ARE YOU ALL RIGHT?
IT'S SO EARLY I THINK I'M GONNA PUKE.
WELL, PULL IT TOGETHER.
I HEARD YOU'RE IN CHARGE OF REINFORCE-MENTS FOR THE RIGHT EYE.
I TRIED TO REFUSE...
...BUT THAT PINK, POLKA-DOTTED FREAK FORCED ME.
SIIIGH
THAT'S BECAUSE YOU'RE SO POWERFUL.
AS IF. UGH, I'M GONNA HURL!
HOW'S YOUR RECOVERY OPERATION GOING?

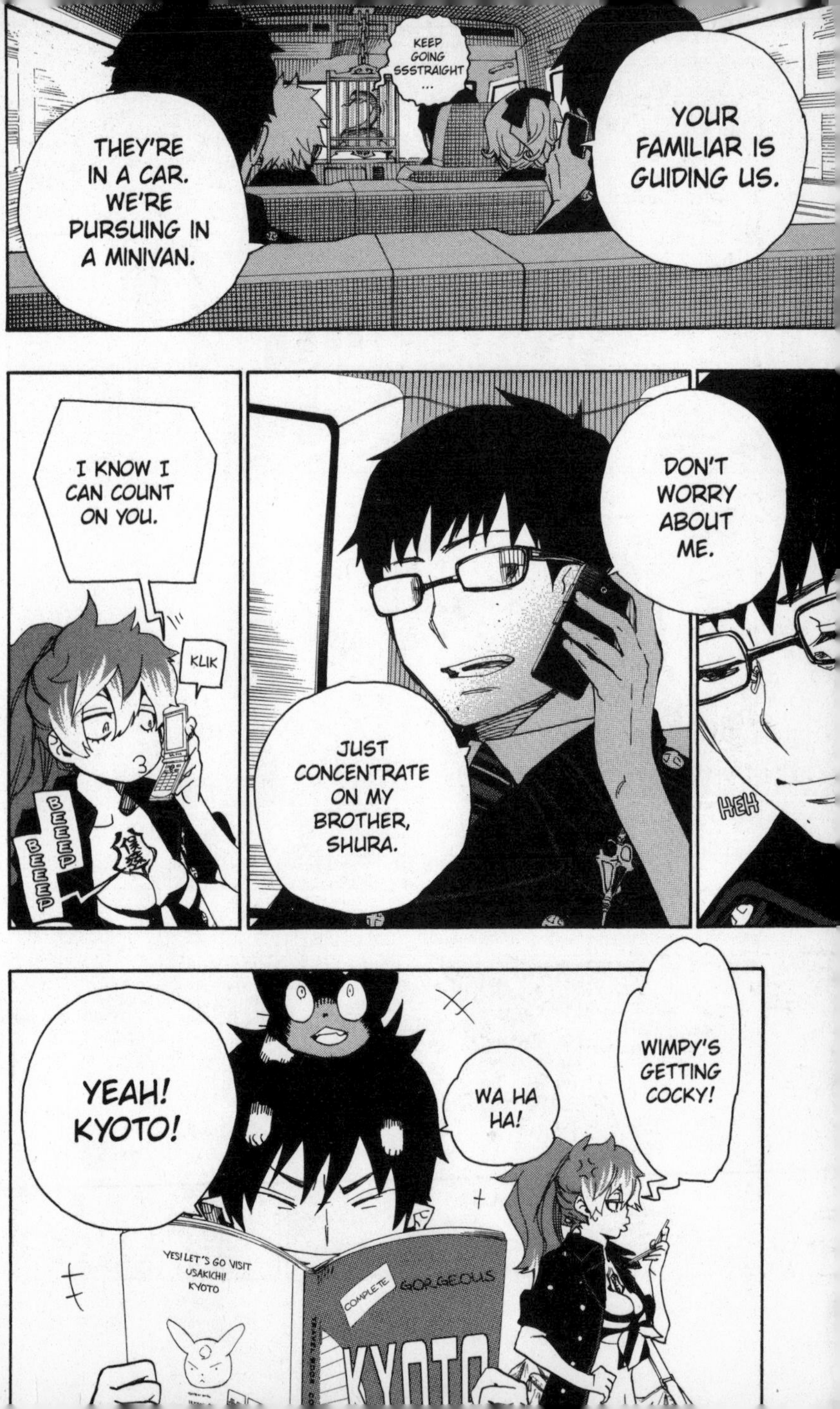
KEEP GOING SSSTRAIGHT ...
YOUR FAMILIAR IS GUIDING US.
THEY'RE IN A CAR. WE'RE PURSUING IN A MINIVAN.
DON'T WORRY ABOUT ME.
HEH
JUST CONCENTRATE ON MY BROTHER, SHURA.
I KNOW I CAN COUNT ON YOU.
KLIK
BEEEEP BEEEEP
WIMPY'S GETTING COCKY!
WA HA HA!
YEAH! KYOTO!
YES! LET'S GO VISIT USAKICHI! KYOTO
COMPLETE
GORGEOUS
KYOTO

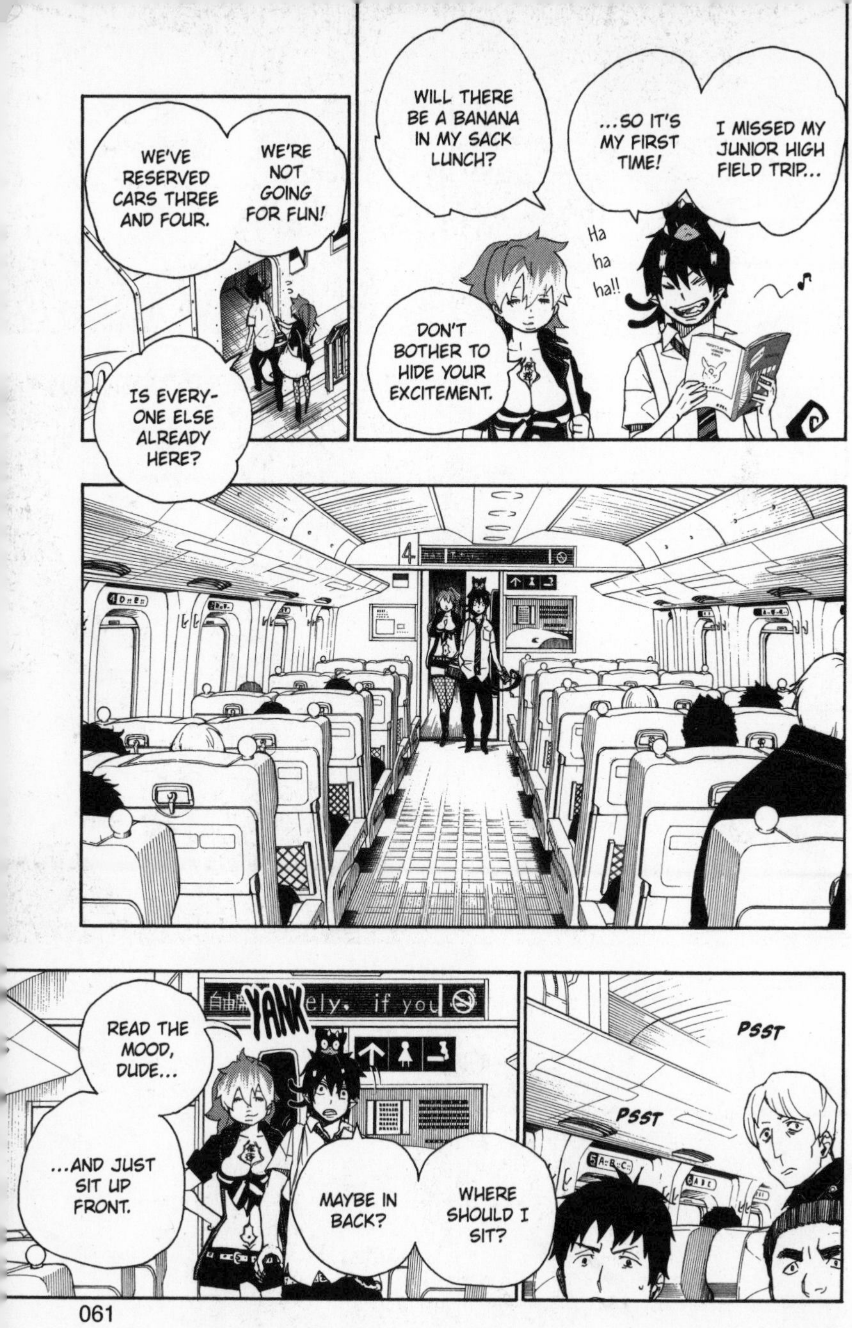
I MISSED MY JUNIOR HIGH FIELD TRIP...
...SO IT'S MY FIRST TIME!
Ha ha ha!!
WILL THERE BE A BANANA IN MY SACK LUNCH?
DON'T BOTHER TO HIDE YOUR EXCITEMENT.
WE'RE NOT GOING FOR FUN!
WE'VE RESERVED CARS THREE AND FOUR.
IS EVERY-ONE ELSE ALREADY HERE?
4
PSST
PSST
WHERE SHOULD I SIT?
MAYBE IN BACK?
YANK
READ THE MOOD, DUDE...
...AND JUST SIT UP FRONT.

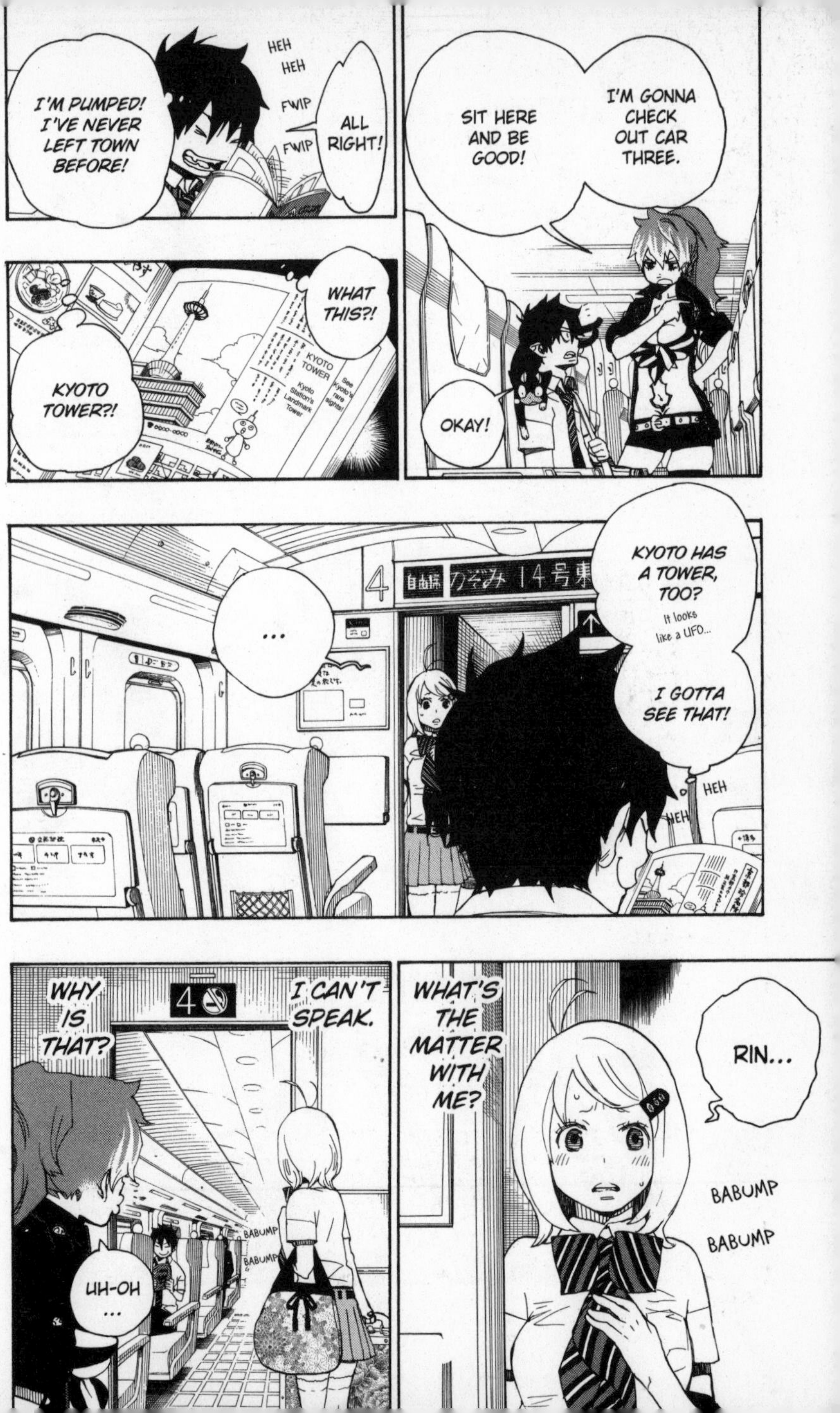

I'M GONNA CHECK OUT CAR THREE.
SIT HERE AND BE GOOD!
OKAY!
HEH HEH
ALL RIGHT!
FWIP FWIP
I'M PUMPED! I'VE NEVER LEFT TOWN BEFORE!
WHAT THIS?!
KYOTO TOWER
See Kyoto's rare sights!
Kyoto Station's Landmark Tower
KYOTO TOWER?!
KYOTO HAS A TOWER, TOO?
It looks like a UFO...
I GOTTA SEE THAT!
HEH HEH
...
RIN...
BABUMP BABUMP
WHAT'S THE MATTER WITH ME?
I CAN'T SPEAK.
WHY IS THAT?
BABUMP BABUMP
UH-OH ...

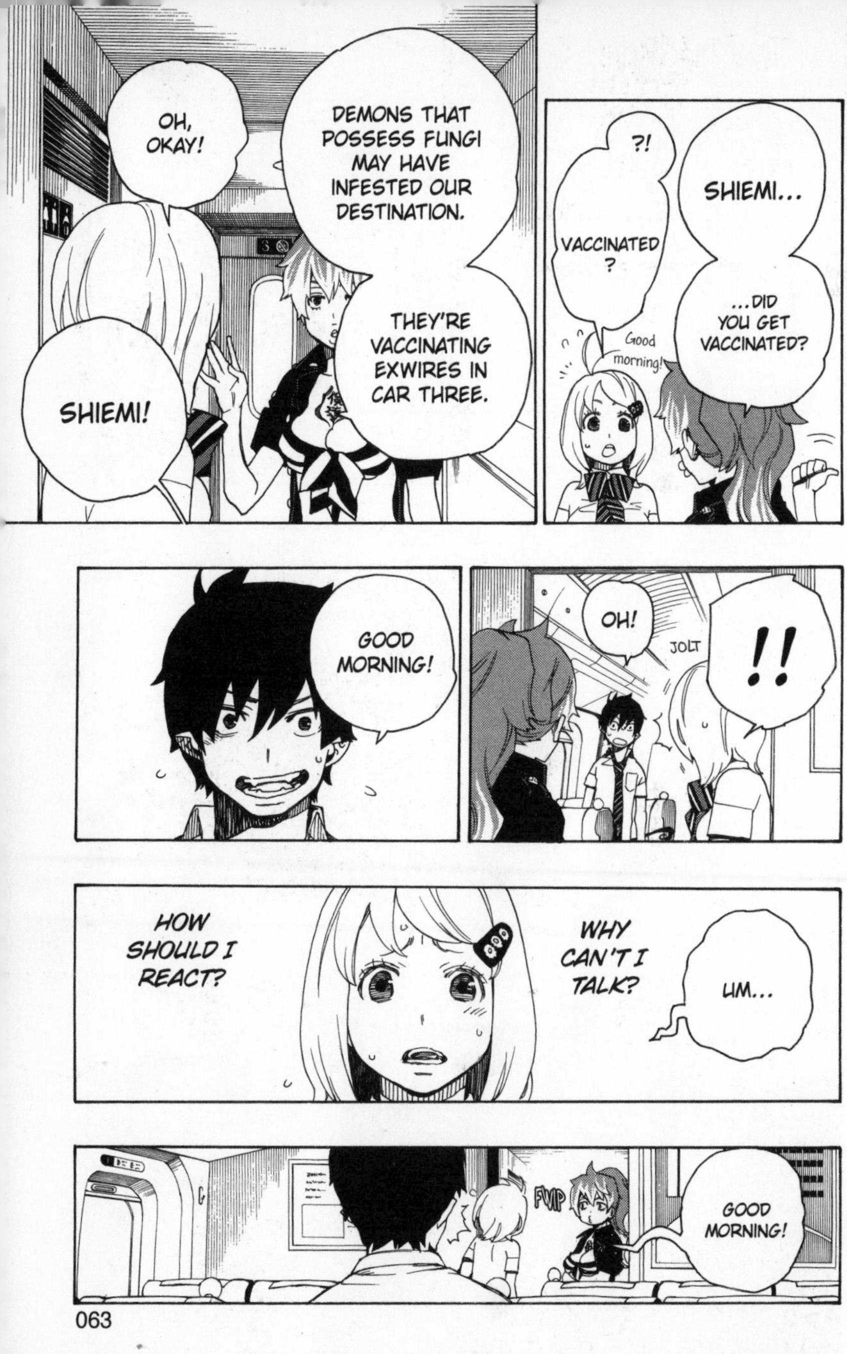
SHIEMI...
...DID YOU GET VACCINATED?
?!
VACCINATED?
Good morning!
DEMONS THAT POSSESS FUNGI MAY HAVE INFESTED OUR DESTINATION.
OH, OKAY!
THEY'RE VACCINATING EXWIRES IN CAR THREE.
SHIEMI!
!!
JOLT
OH!
GOOD MORNING!
UM...
WHY CAN'T I TALK?
HOW SHOULD I REACT?
GOOD MORNING!
FWIP

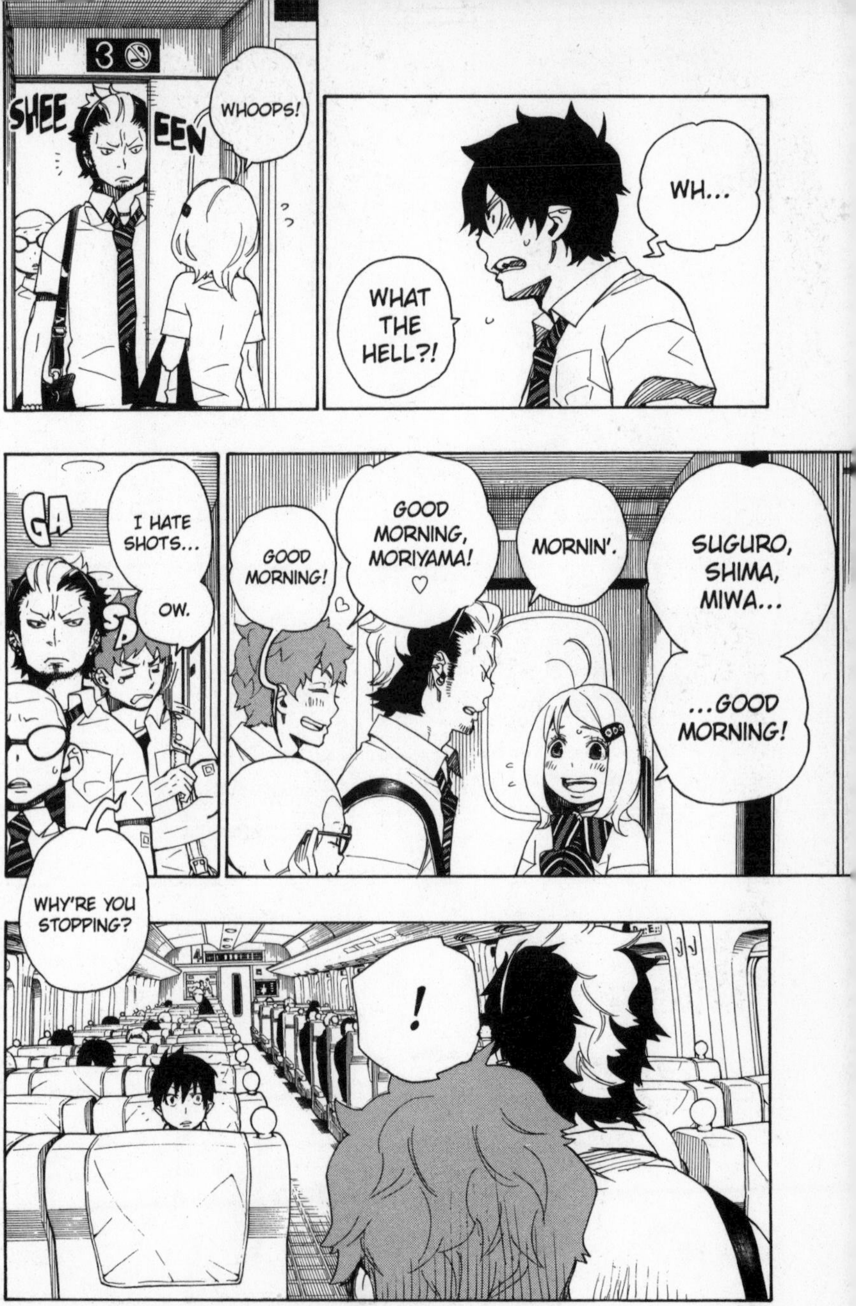
WH...
WHAT THE HELL?!
WHOOPS!
SHEE
EEN
SUGURO, SHIMA, MIWA...
...GOOD MORNING!
MORNIN'.
GOOD MORNING, MORIYAMA! ♡
GOOD MORNING!
I HATE SHOTS...
OW.
GA
SP
WHY'RE YOU STOPPING?
!

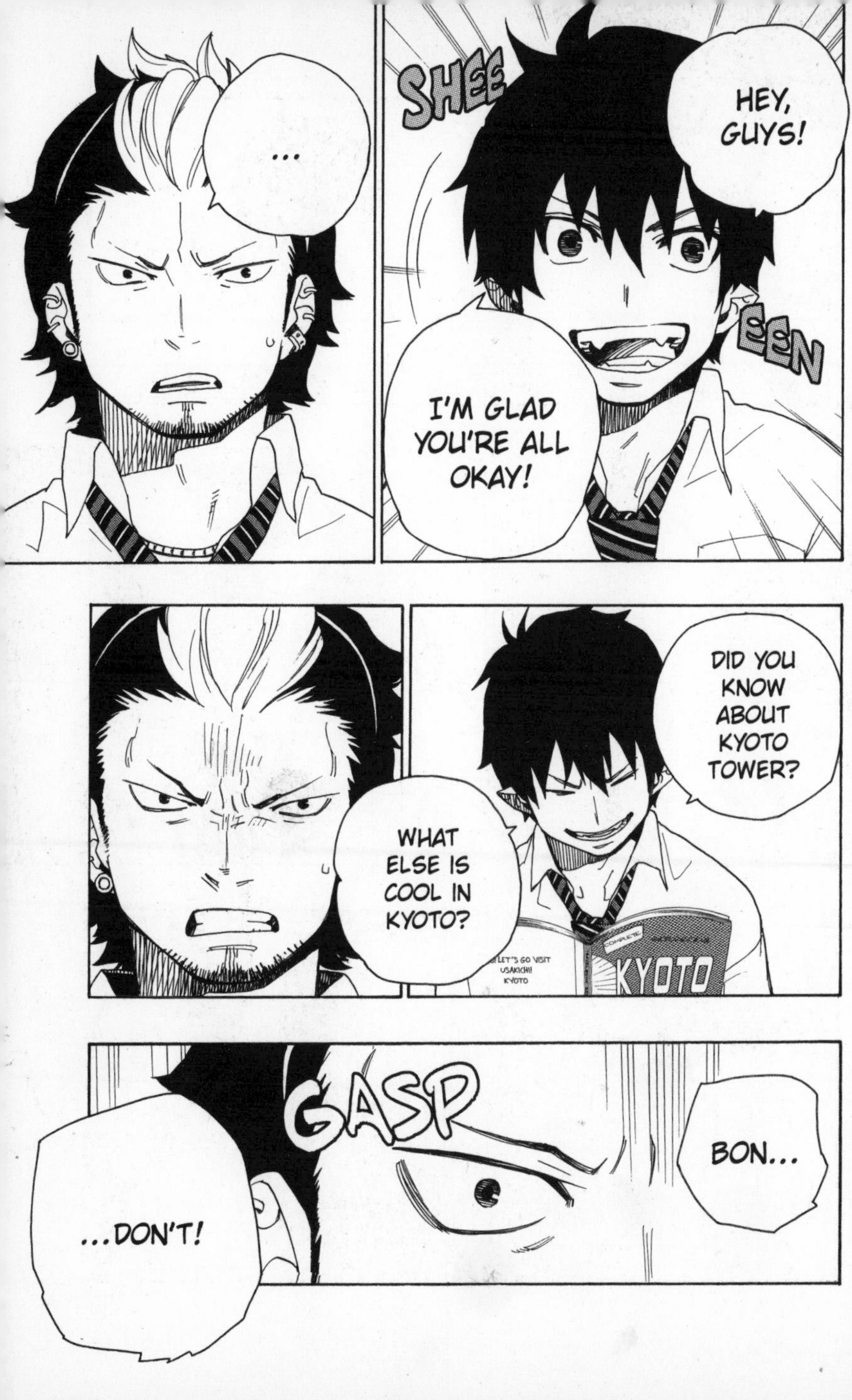
SHEE
EEN
HEY, GUYS!
I'M GLAD YOU'RE ALL OKAY!
...
DID YOU KNOW ABOUT KYOTO TOWER?
WHAT ELSE IS COOL IN KYOTO?
COMPLETE
KYOTO
LET'S GO VISIT USAKICHI! KYOTO
GASP
BON...
...DON'T!

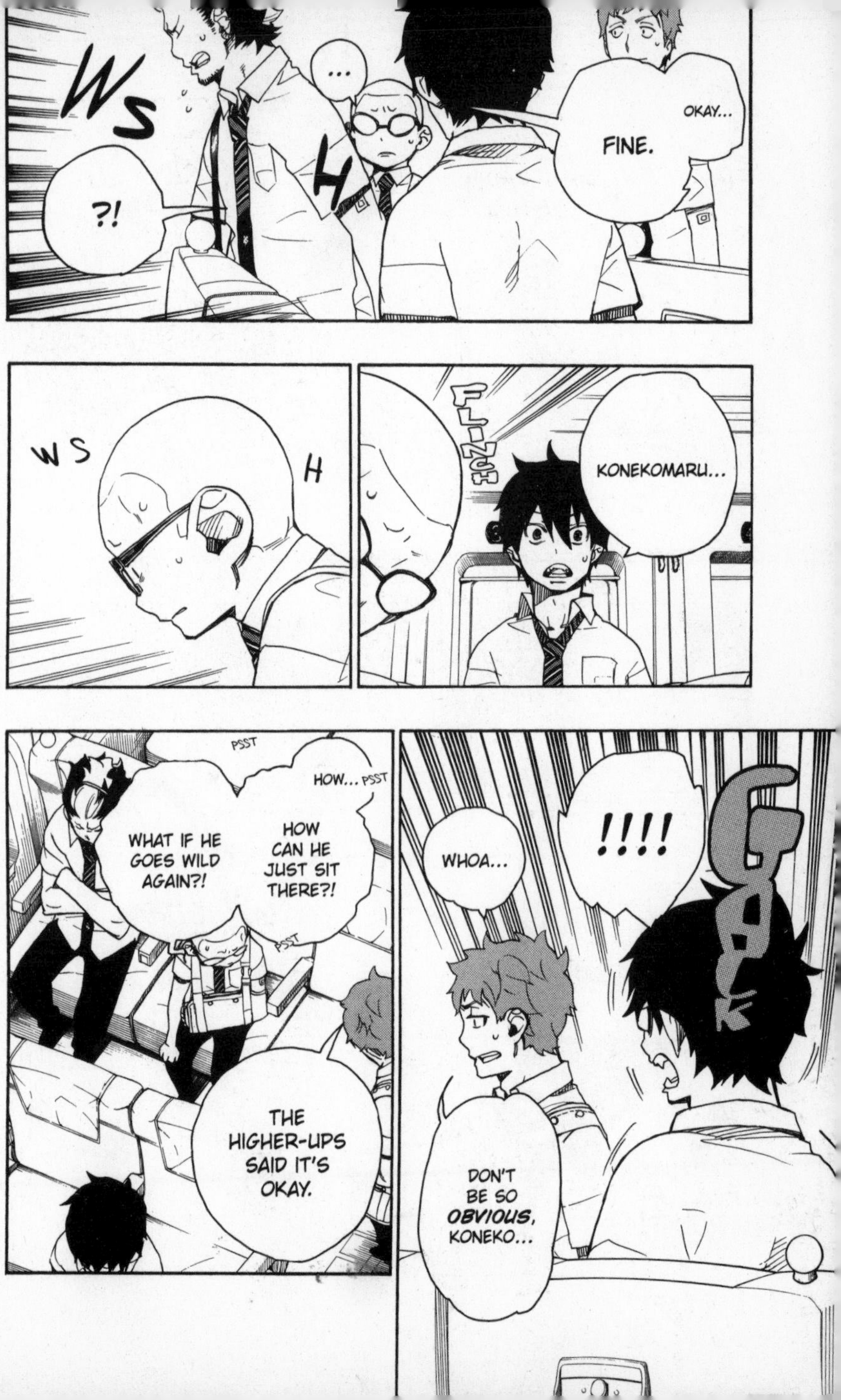
OKAY... FINE.
...
WSH
?!
FLINCH
KONEKOMARU...
WS H
!!!!
WHOA...
DON'T BE SO *OBVIOUS*, KONEKO...
PSST
HOW... PSST
HOW CAN HE JUST SIT THERE?!
WHAT IF HE GOES WILD AGAIN?!
PSST
THE HIGHER-UPS SAID IT'S OKAY.

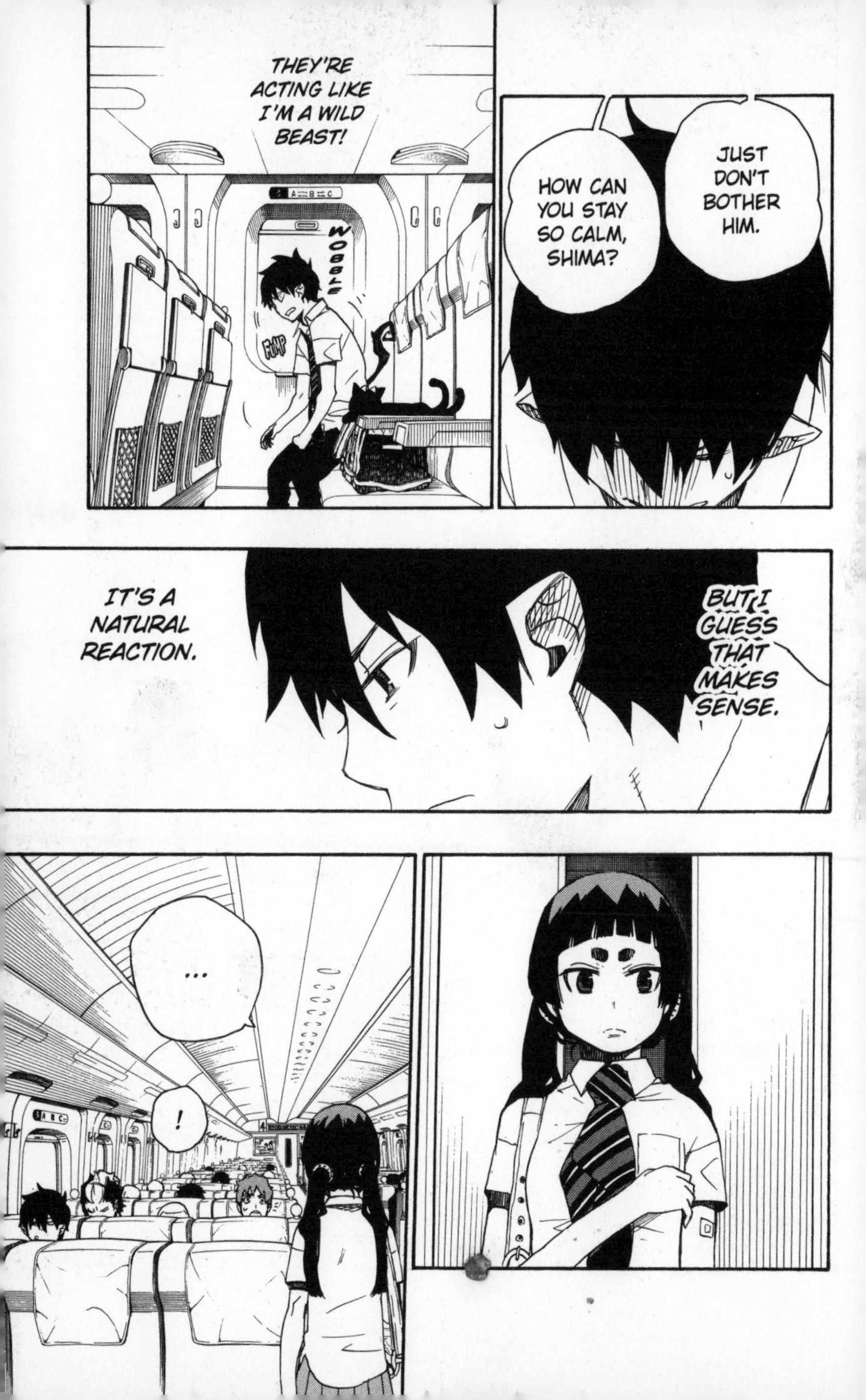
JUST DON'T BOTHER HIM.
HOW CAN YOU STAY SO CALM, SHIMA?
THEY'RE ACTING LIKE I'M A WILD BEAST!
WOBBLE
FUMP
BUT I GUESS THAT MAKES SENSE.
IT'S A NATURAL REACTION.
...
!

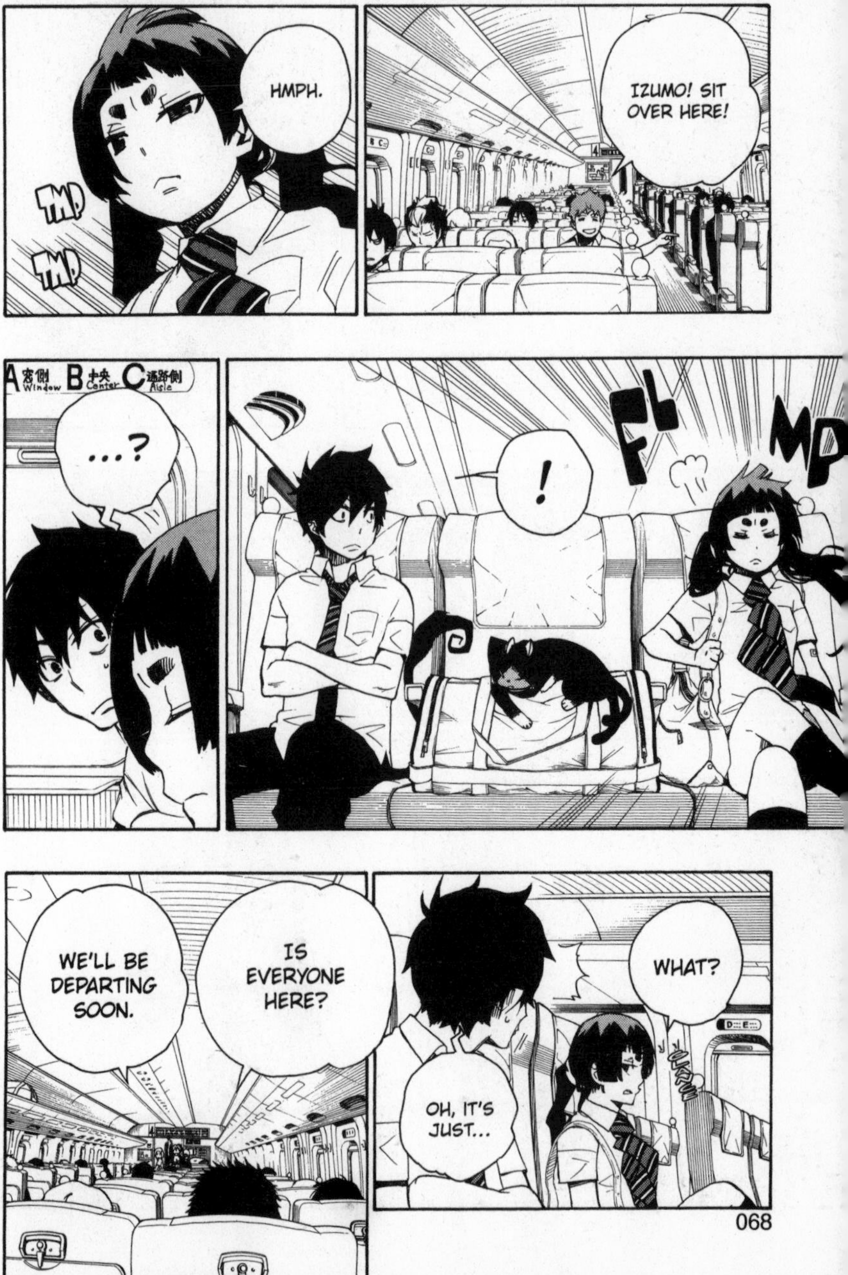
IZUMO! SIT OVER HERE!
HMPH.
TMP
TMP
FL
MP
!
A 窓側 Window B 中央 Center C 通路側 Aisle
...?
WHAT?
OH, IT'S JUST...
IS EVERYONE HERE?
WE'LL BE DEPARTING SOON.

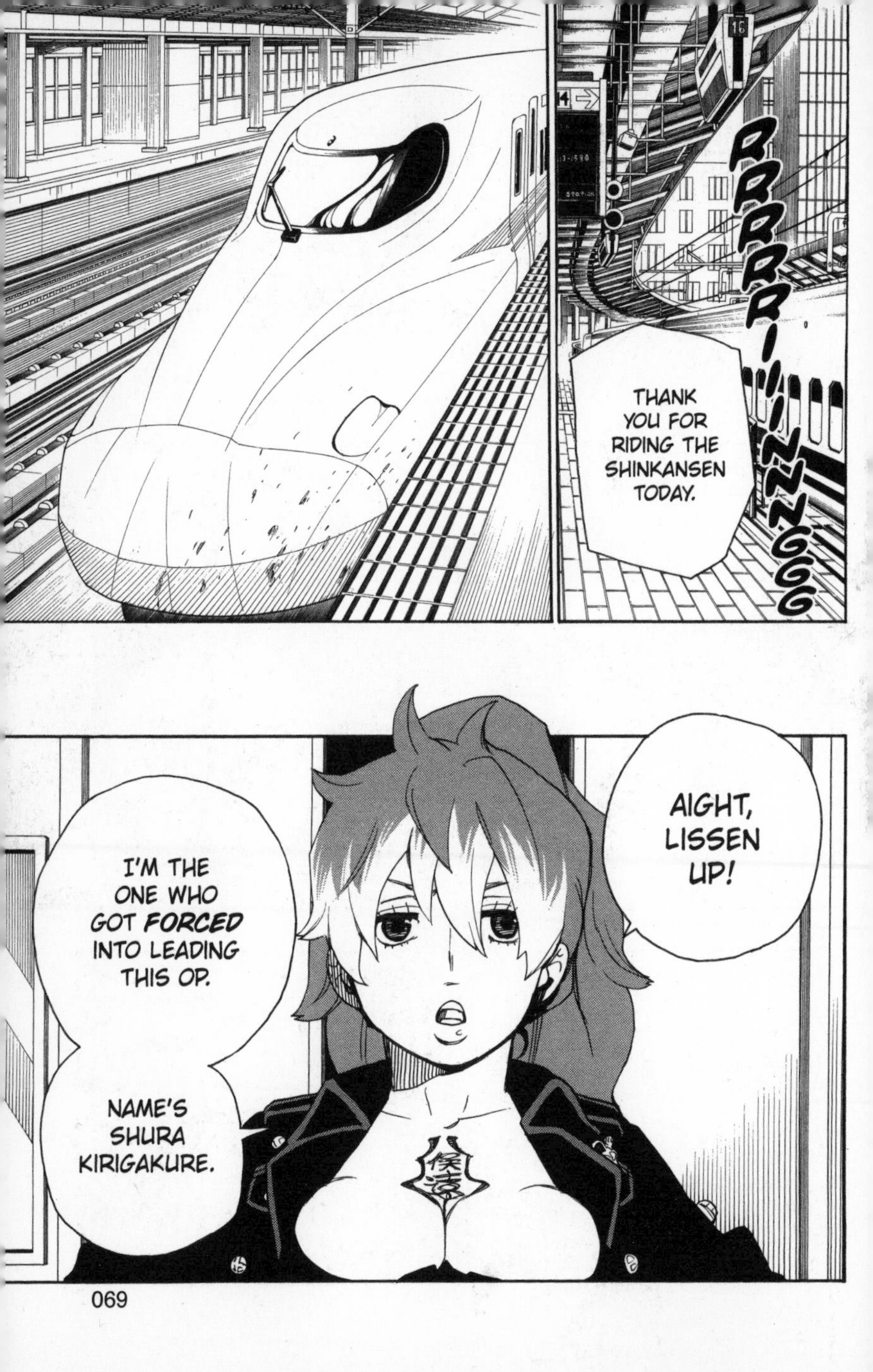
THANK YOU FOR RIDING THE SHINKANSEN TODAY.
RRRRRRI-I-I-INNNGGG
AIGHT, LISSEN UP!
I'M THE ONE WHO GOT *FORCED* INTO LEADING THIS OP.
NAME'S SHURA KIRIGAKURE.

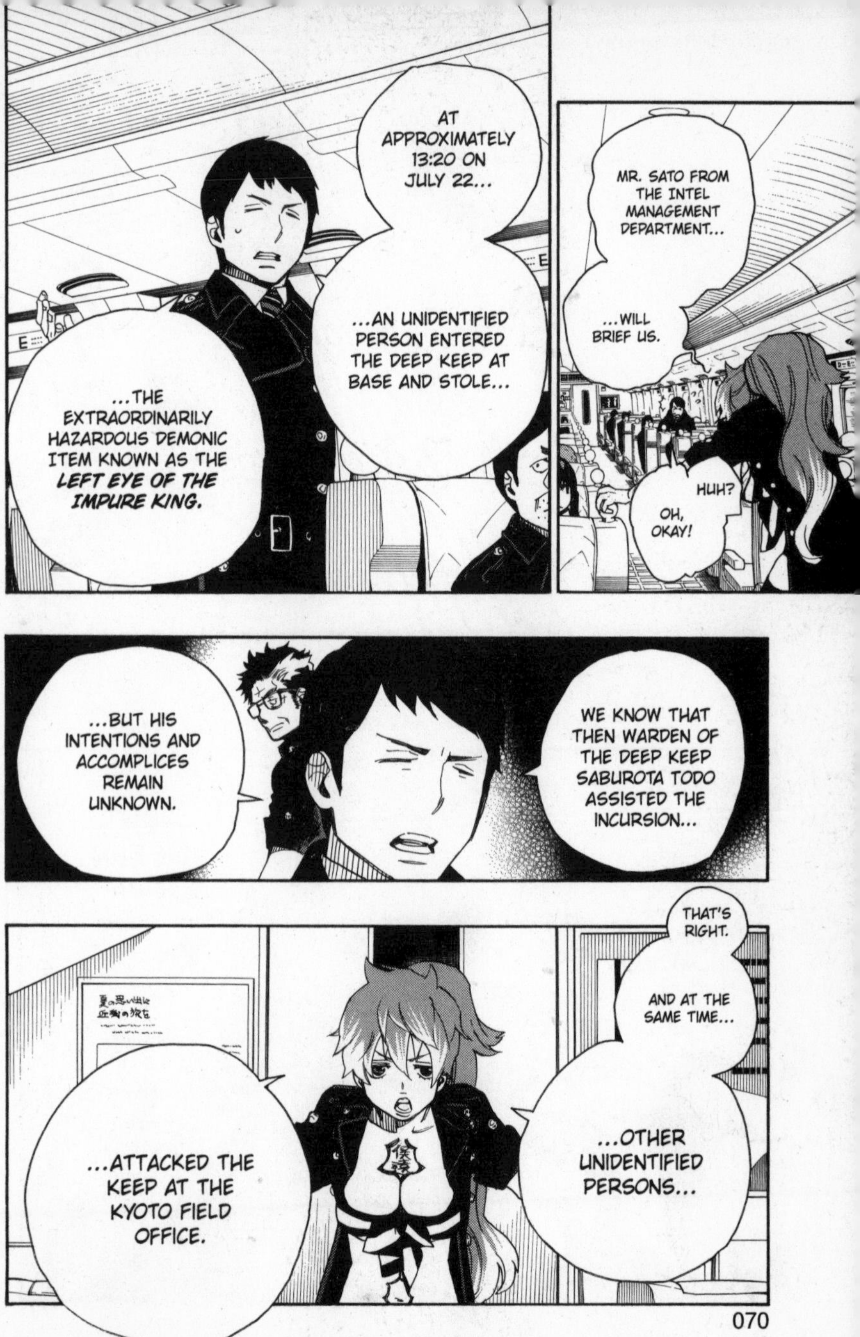
MR. SATO FROM THE INTEL MANAGEMENT DEPARTMENT...
...WILL BRIEF US.
HUH?
OH, OKAY!
AT APPROXIMATELY 13:20 ON JULY 22...
...AN UNIDENTIFIED PERSON ENTERED THE DEEP KEEP AT BASE AND STOLE...
...THE EXTRAORDINARILY HAZARDOUS DEMONIC ITEM KNOWN AS THE *LEFT EYE OF THE IMPURE KING.*
WE KNOW THAT THEN WARDEN OF THE DEEP KEEP SABUROTA TODO ASSISTED THE INCURSION...
...BUT HIS INTENTIONS AND ACCOMPLICES REMAIN UNKNOWN.
THAT'S RIGHT.
AND AT THE SAME TIME...
...OTHER UNIDENTIFIED PERSONS...
...ATTACKED THE KEEP AT THE KYOTO FIELD OFFICE.

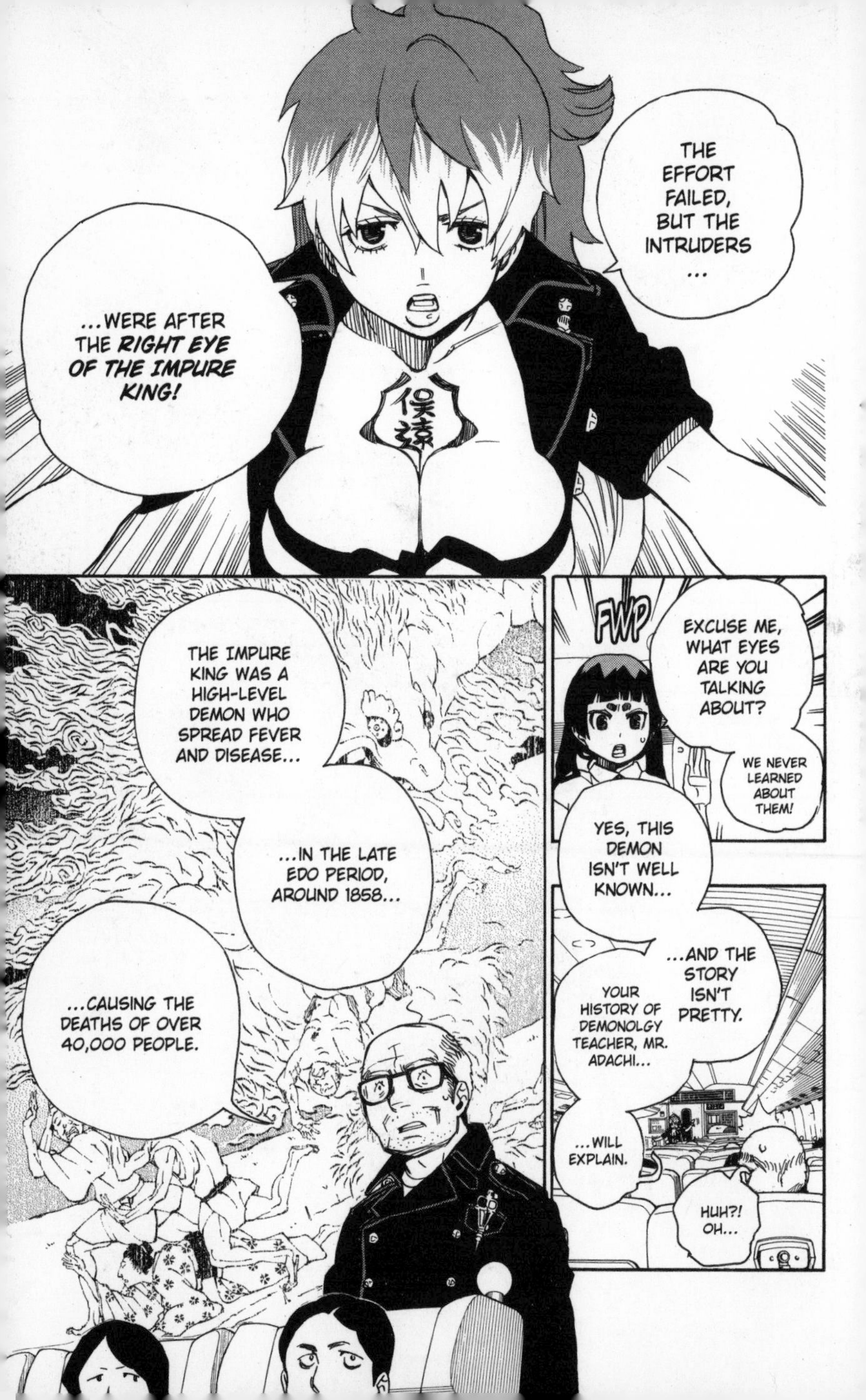
THE EFFORT FAILED, BUT THE INTRUDERS...
...WERE AFTER THE *RIGHT EYE OF THE IMPURE KING!*
FWP
EXCUSE ME, WHAT EYES ARE YOU TALKING ABOUT?
WE NEVER LEARNED ABOUT THEM!
YES, THIS DEMON ISN'T WELL KNOWN...
...AND THE STORY ISN'T PRETTY.
YOUR HISTORY OF DEMONOLGY TEACHER, MR. ADACHI...
...WILL EXPLAIN.
HUH?! OH...
THE IMPURE KING WAS A HIGH-LEVEL DEMON WHO SPREAD FEVER AND DISEASE...
...IN THE LATE EDO PERIOD, AROUND 1858...
...CAUSING THE DEATHS OF OVER 40,000 PEOPLE.

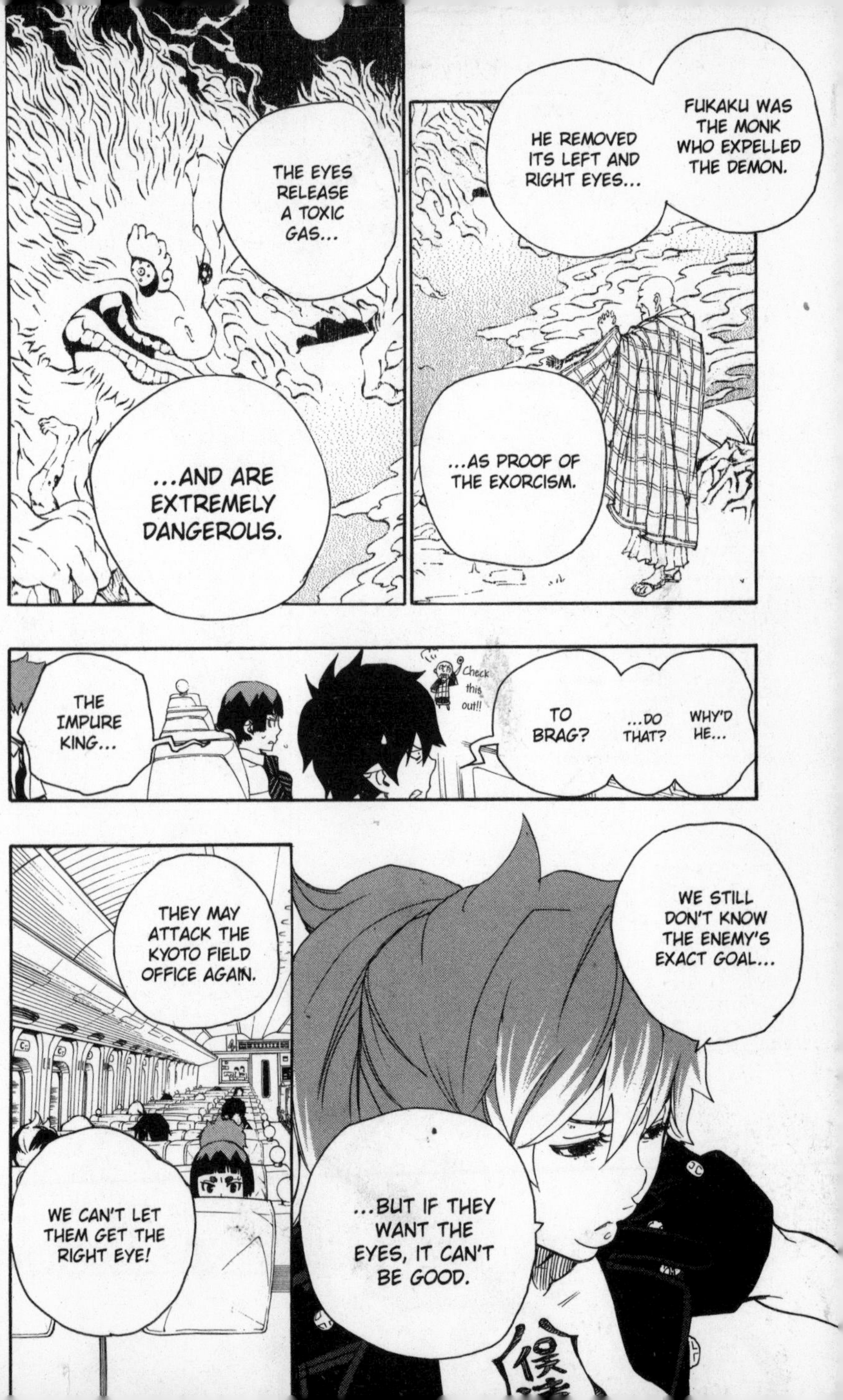
FUKAKU WAS THE MONK WHO EXPELLED THE DEMON.
HE REMOVED ITS LEFT AND RIGHT EYES...
...AS PROOF OF THE EXORCISM.
THE EYES RELEASE A TOXIC GAS...
...AND ARE EXTREMELY DANGEROUS.
WHY'D HE...
...DO THAT?
TO BRAG?
Check this out!!
THE IMPURE KING...
WE STILL DON'T KNOW THE ENEMY'S EXACT GOAL...
...BUT IF THEY WANT THE EYES, IT CAN'T BE GOOD.
THEY MAY ATTACK THE KYOTO FIELD OFFICE AGAIN.
WE CAN'T LET THEM GET THE RIGHT EYE!

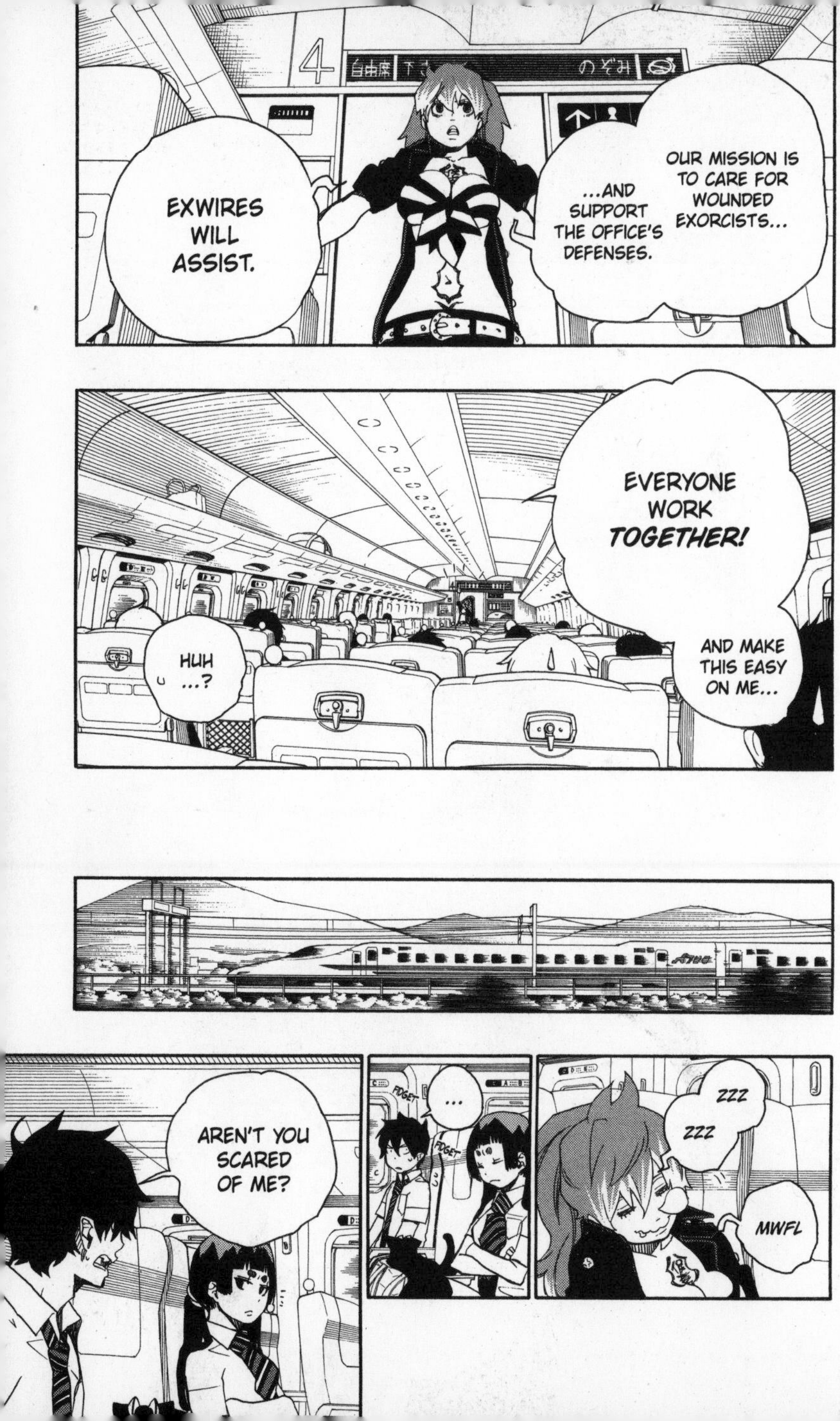
OUR MISSION IS TO CARE FOR WOUNDED EXORCISTS...
...AND SUPPORT THE OFFICE'S DEFENSES.
EXWIRES WILL ASSIST.
EVERYONE WORK *TOGETHER!*
AND MAKE THIS EASY ON ME...
HUH ...?
ZZZ
ZZZ
MWFL
FIDGET
...
FIDGET
AREN'T YOU SCARED OF ME?

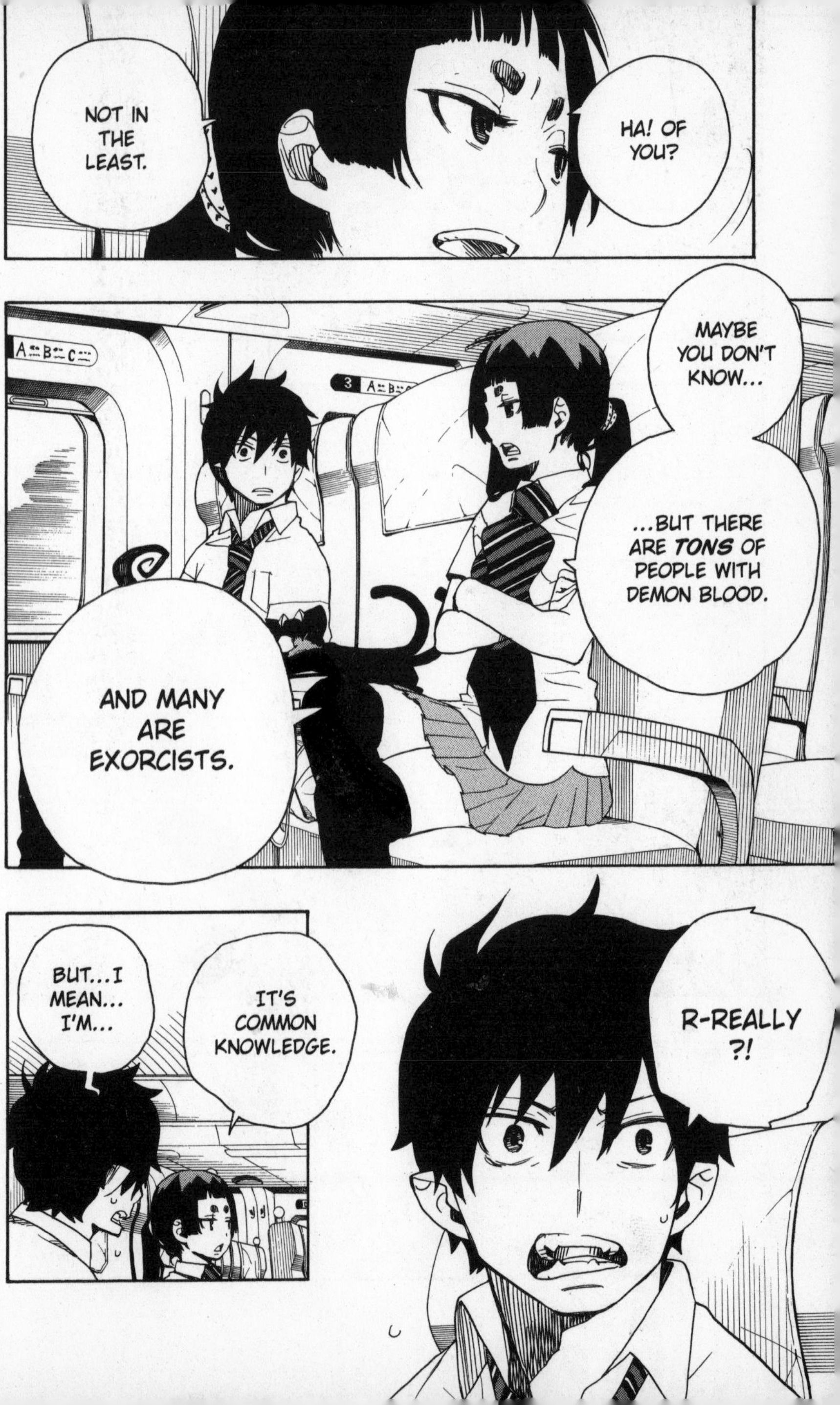
HA! OF YOU?
NOT IN THE LEAST.
MAYBE YOU DON'T KNOW...
...BUT THERE ARE **TONS** OF PEOPLE WITH DEMON BLOOD.
AND MANY ARE EXORCISTS.
R-REALLY ?!
IT'S COMMON KNOWLEDGE.
BUT...I MEAN... I'M...

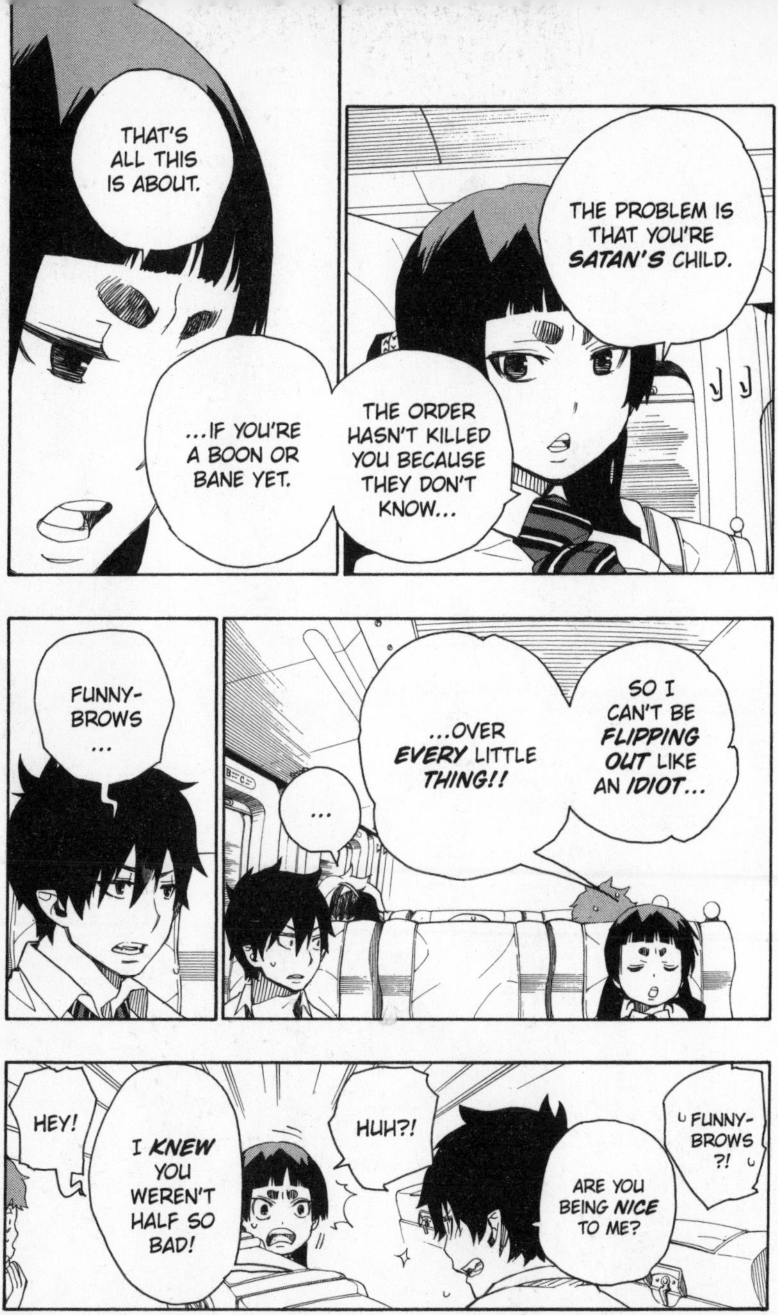
THE PROBLEM IS THAT YOU'RE SATAN'S CHILD.
THE ORDER HASN'T KILLED YOU BECAUSE THEY DON'T KNOW...
...IF YOU'RE A BOON OR BANE YET.
THAT'S ALL THIS IS ABOUT.
SO I CAN'T BE FLIPPING OUT LIKE AN IDIOT...
...OVER EVERY LITTLE THING!!
...
FUNNY-BROWS ...
FUNNY-BROWS ?!
ARE YOU BEING NICE TO ME?
HUH?!
I KNEW YOU WEREN'T HALF SO BAD!
HEY!

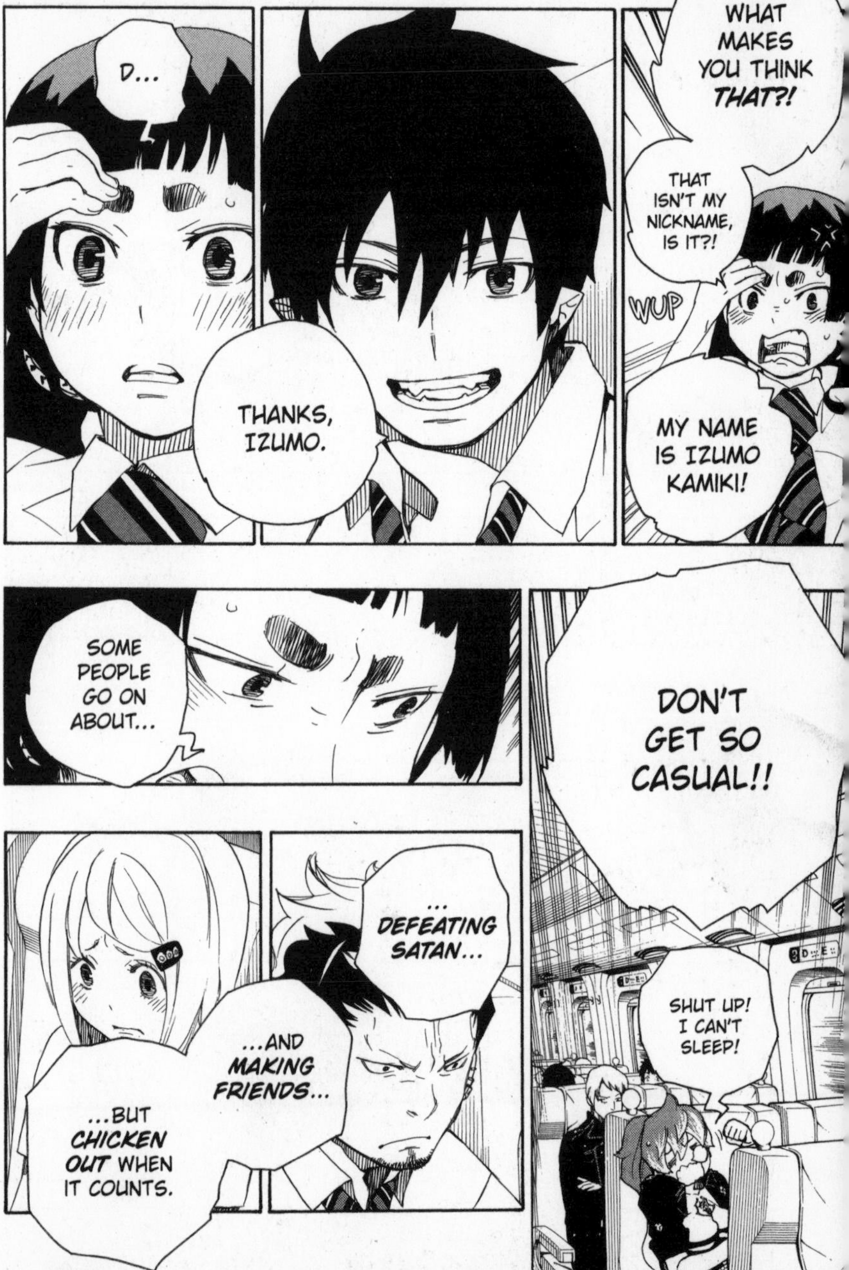
WHAT MAKES YOU THINK THAT?!
THAT ISN'T MY NICKNAME, IS IT?!
WUP
MY NAME IS IZUMO KAMIKI!
THANKS, IZUMO.
D...
DON'T GET SO CASUAL!!
SHUT UP! I CAN'T SLEEP!
SOME PEOPLE GO ON ABOUT...
... DEFEATING SATAN...
...AND MAKING FRIENDS...
...BUT CHICKEN OUT WHEN IT COUNTS.

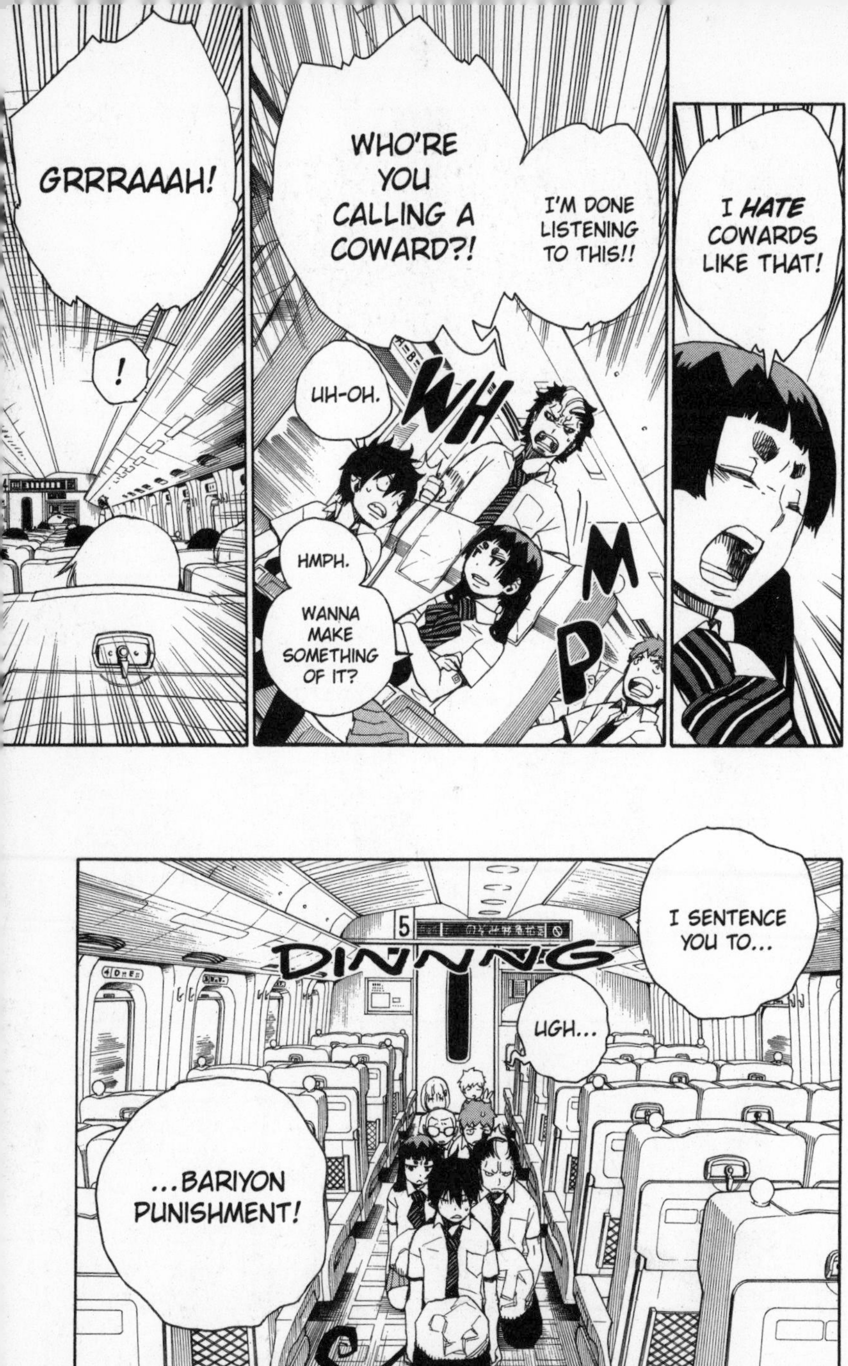
I HATE COWARDS LIKE THAT!
WHO'RE YOU CALLING A COWARD?!
I'M DONE LISTENING TO THIS!!
WHMP
UH-OH.
HMPH.
WANNA MAKE SOMETHING OF IT?
GRRRAAAH!
!
I SENTENCE YOU TO...
DINNNG
UGH...
...BARIYON PUNISHMENT!

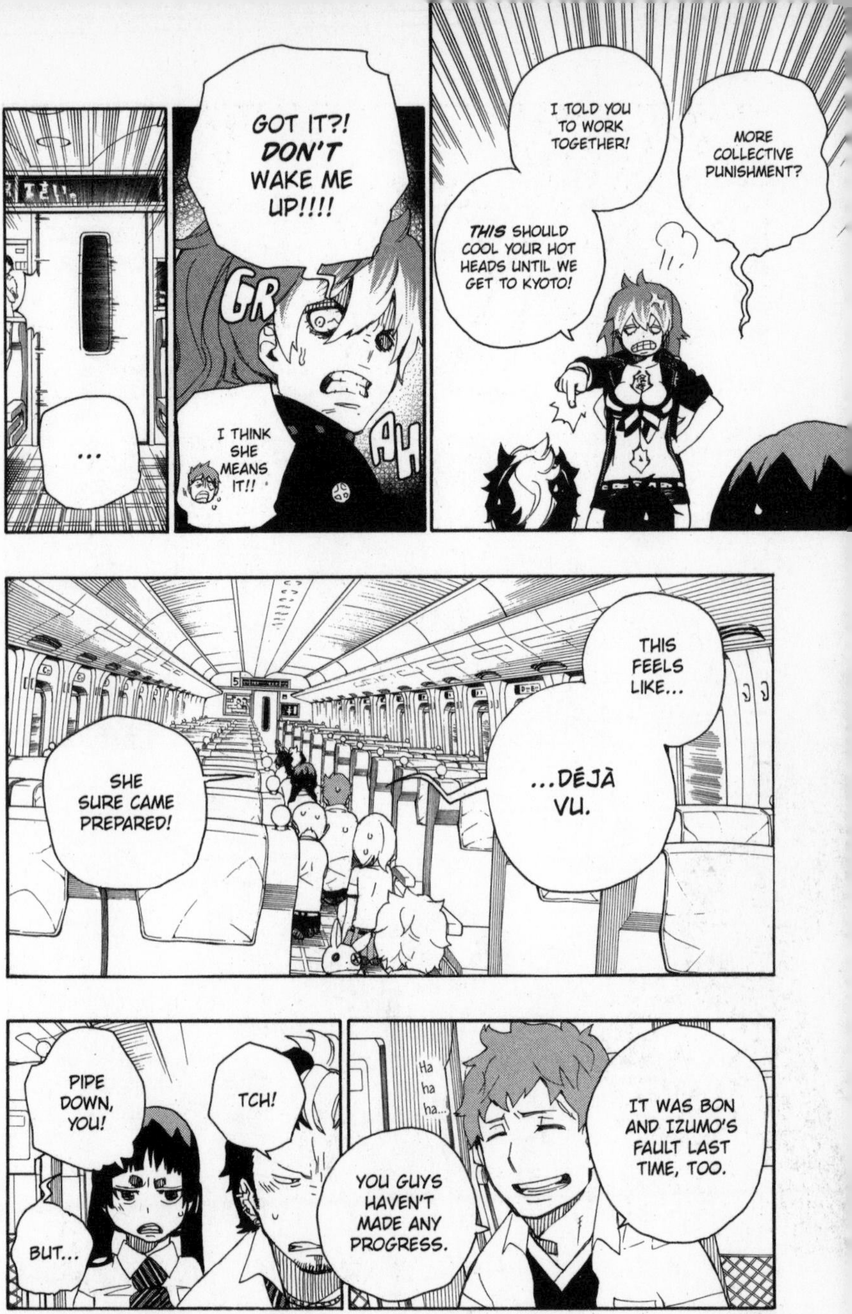
I TOLD YOU TO WORK TOGETHER!
THIS SHOULD COOL YOUR HOT HEADS UNTIL WE GET TO KYOTO!
MORE COLLECTIVE PUNISHMENT?
GOT IT?! DON'T WAKE ME UP!!!!
GR
AH
I THINK SHE MEANS IT!!
...
THIS FEELS LIKE...
...DÉJÀ VU.
SHE SURE CAME PREPARED!
IT WAS BON AND IZUMO'S FAULT LAST TIME, TOO.
Ha ha ha...
YOU GUYS HAVEN'T MADE ANY PROGRESS.
TCH!
PIPE DOWN, YOU!
BUT...

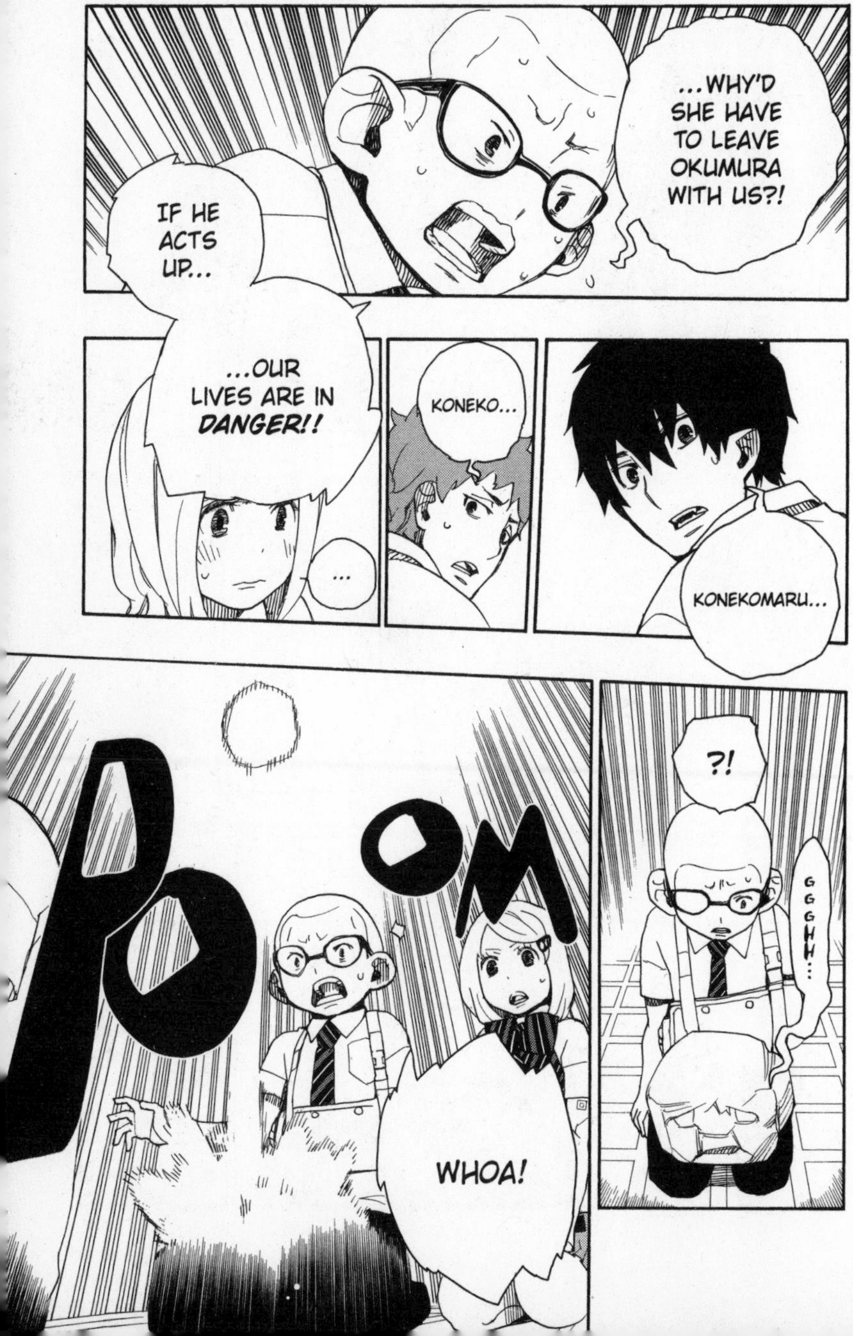
...WHY'D SHE HAVE TO LEAVE OKUMURA WITH US?!
IF HE ACTS UP...
...OUR LIVES ARE IN DANGER!!
KONEKOMARU...
KONEKO...
...
?!
GGGHH...
BOOM
WHOA!

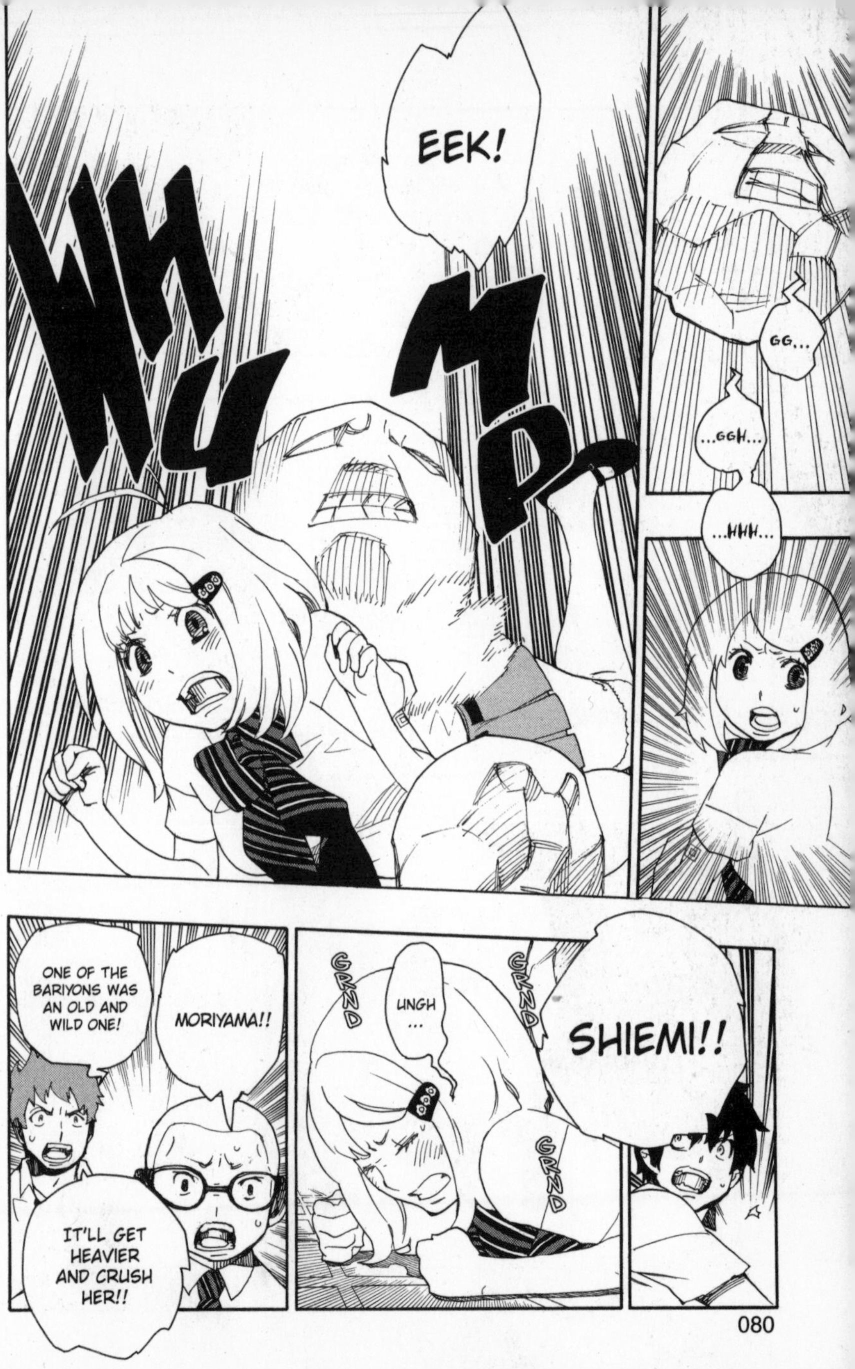
GG...
...GGH...
...HHH...
EEK!
WHUMP
SHIEMI!!
GRND
UNGH ...
GRND
GRND
MORIYAMA!!
ONE OF THE BARIYONS WAS AN OLD AND WILD ONE!
IT'LL GET HEAVIER AND CRUSH HER!!

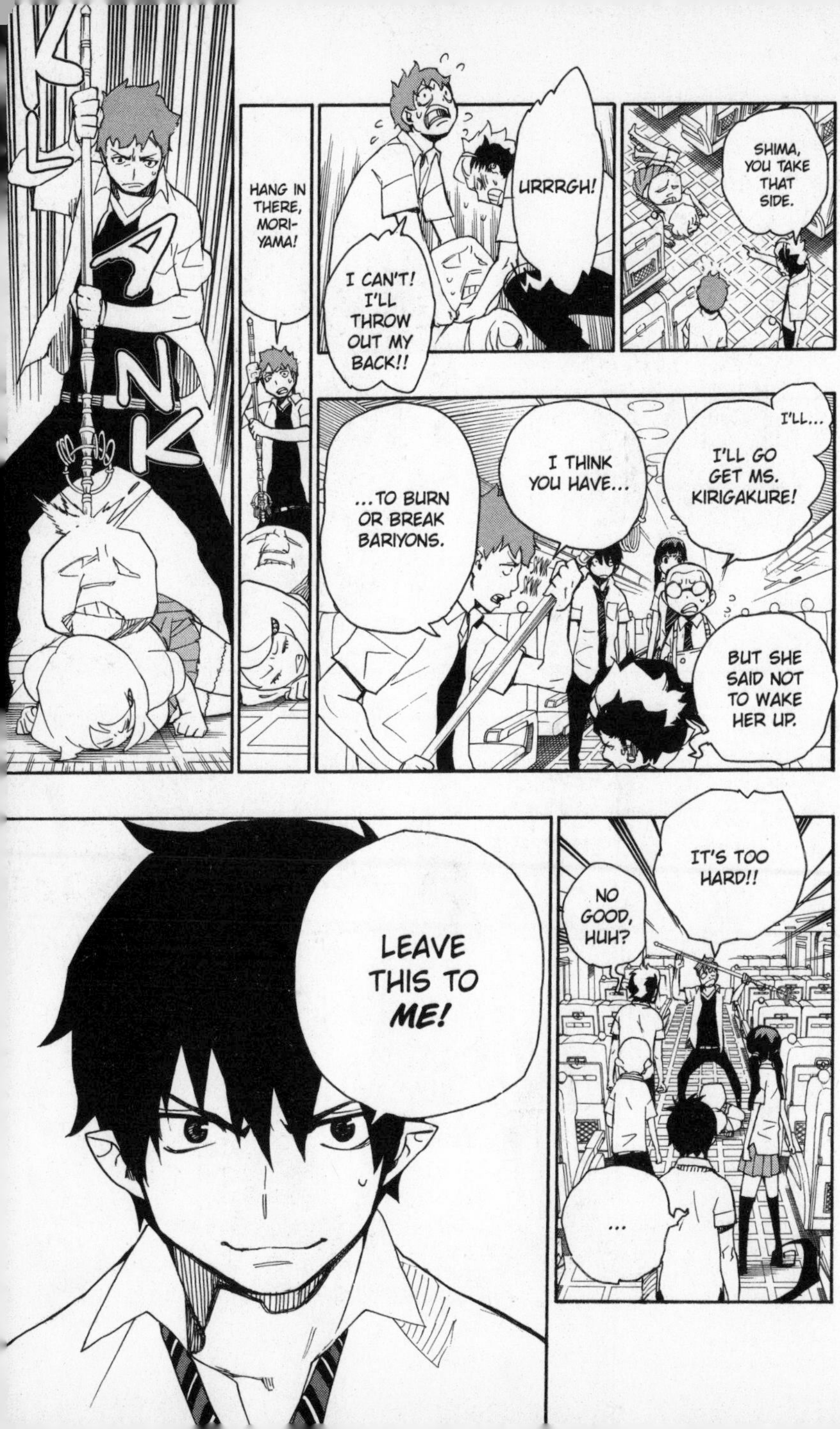
SHIMA, YOU TAKE THAT SIDE.
URRRGH!
I CAN'T! I'LL THROW OUT MY BACK!!
I'LL...
I'LL GO GET MS. KIRIGAKURE!
BUT SHE SAID NOT TO WAKE HER UP.
I THINK YOU HAVE...
...TO BURN OR BREAK BARIYONS.
HANG IN THERE, MORI-YAMA!
KLANK
IT'S TOO HARD!!
NO GOOD, HUH?
...
LEAVE THIS TO ME!

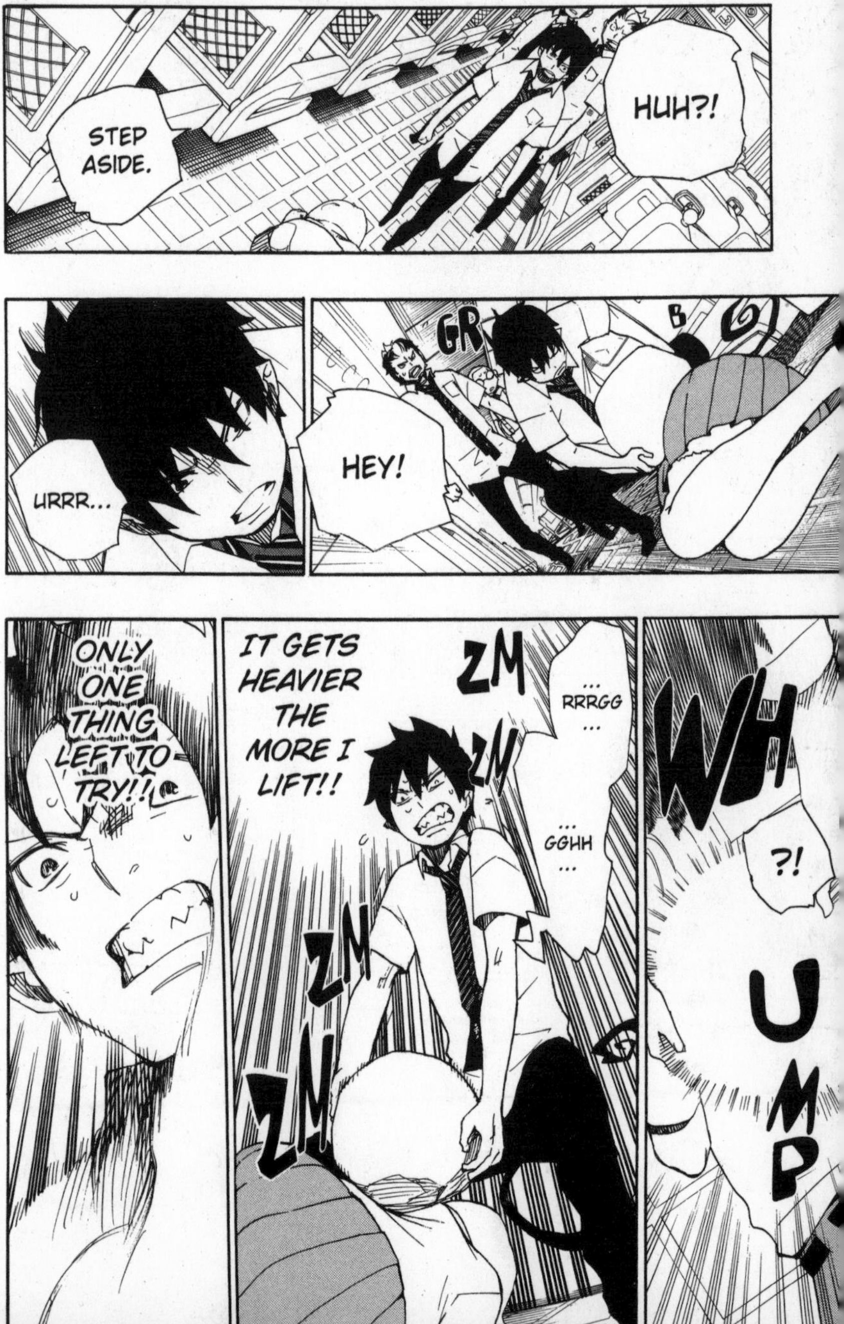
HUH?!
STEP ASIDE.
B
GR
HEY!
URRR...
WH
?!
UMP
ZM
...RRRGG...
IT GETS HEAVIER THE MORE I LIFT!!
ZM
...GGHH...
ZM
ZM
ONLY ONE THING LEFT TO TRY!!

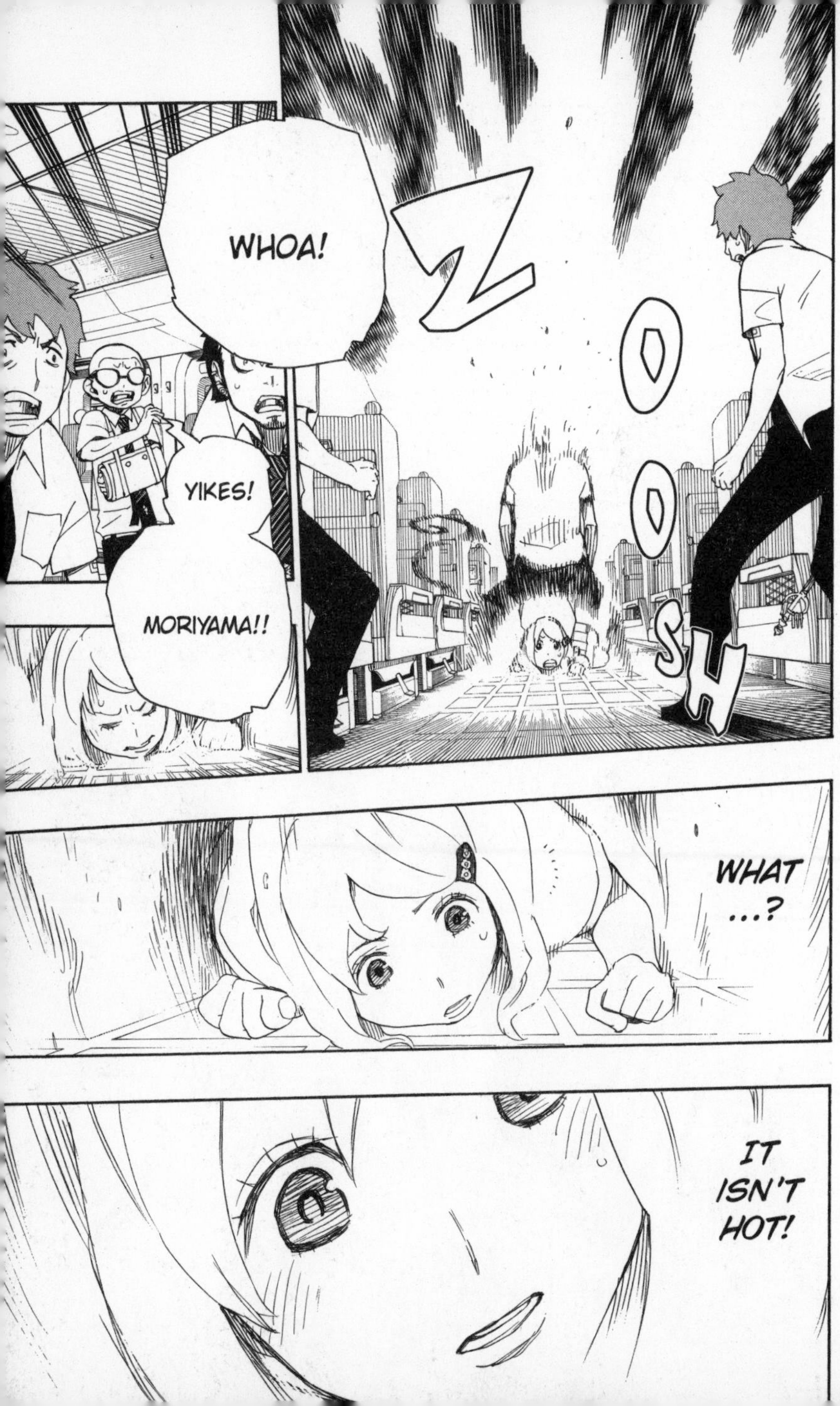
ZOOSH
WHOA!
YIKES!
MORIYAMA!!
WHAT ...?
IT ISN'T HOT!

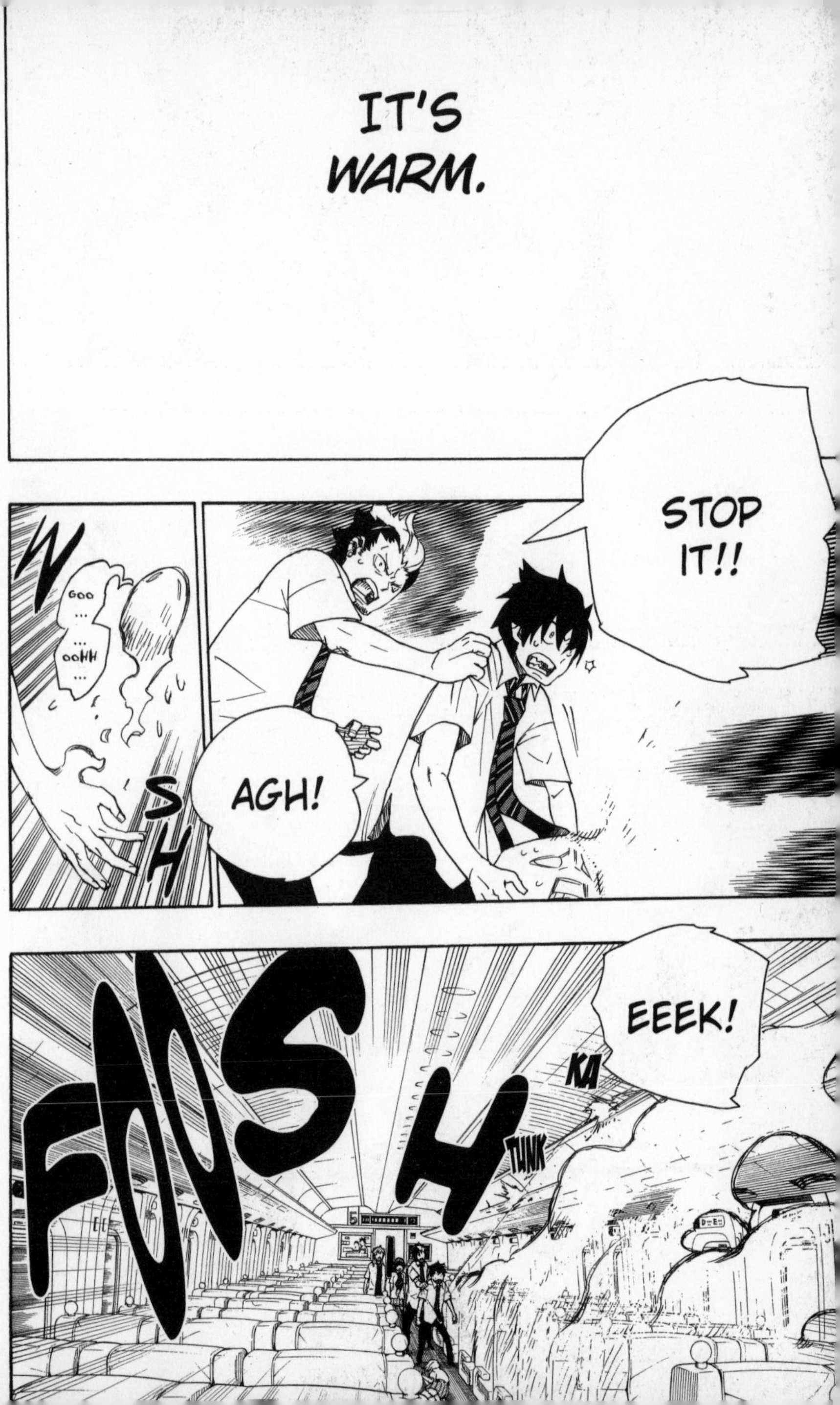
IT'S WARM.
STOP IT!!
AGH!
W
GOO... ...OOHH...
SH
EEEK!
KA
TUNK
FOOSH

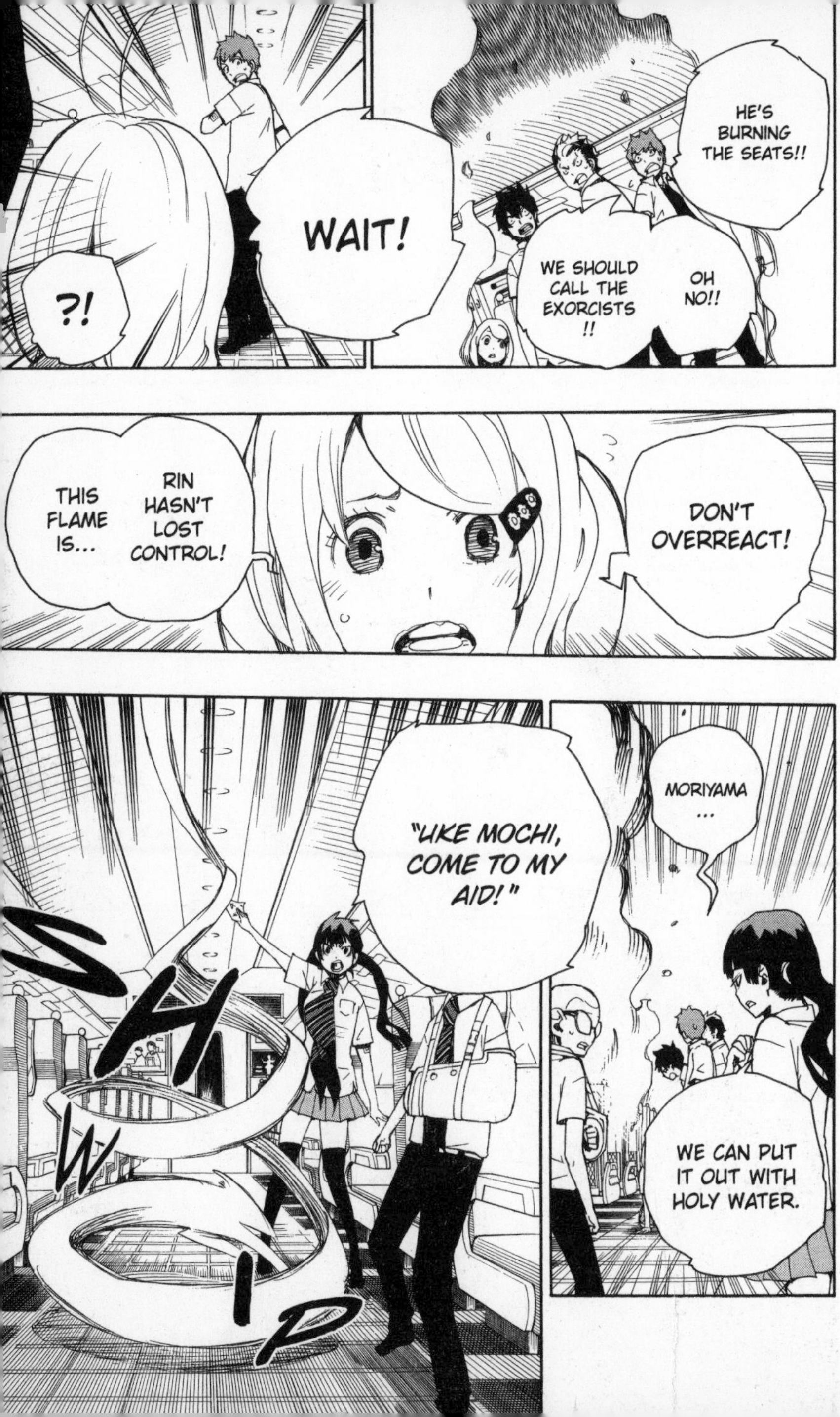
HE'S BURNING THE SEATS!!
OH NO!!
WE SHOULD CALL THE EXORCISTS !!
WAIT!
?!
DON'T OVERREACT!
RIN HASN'T LOST CONTROL!
THIS FLAME IS...
MORIYAMA ...
WE CAN PUT IT OUT WITH HOLY WATER.
"UKE MOCHI, COME TO MY AID!"
SHWIP

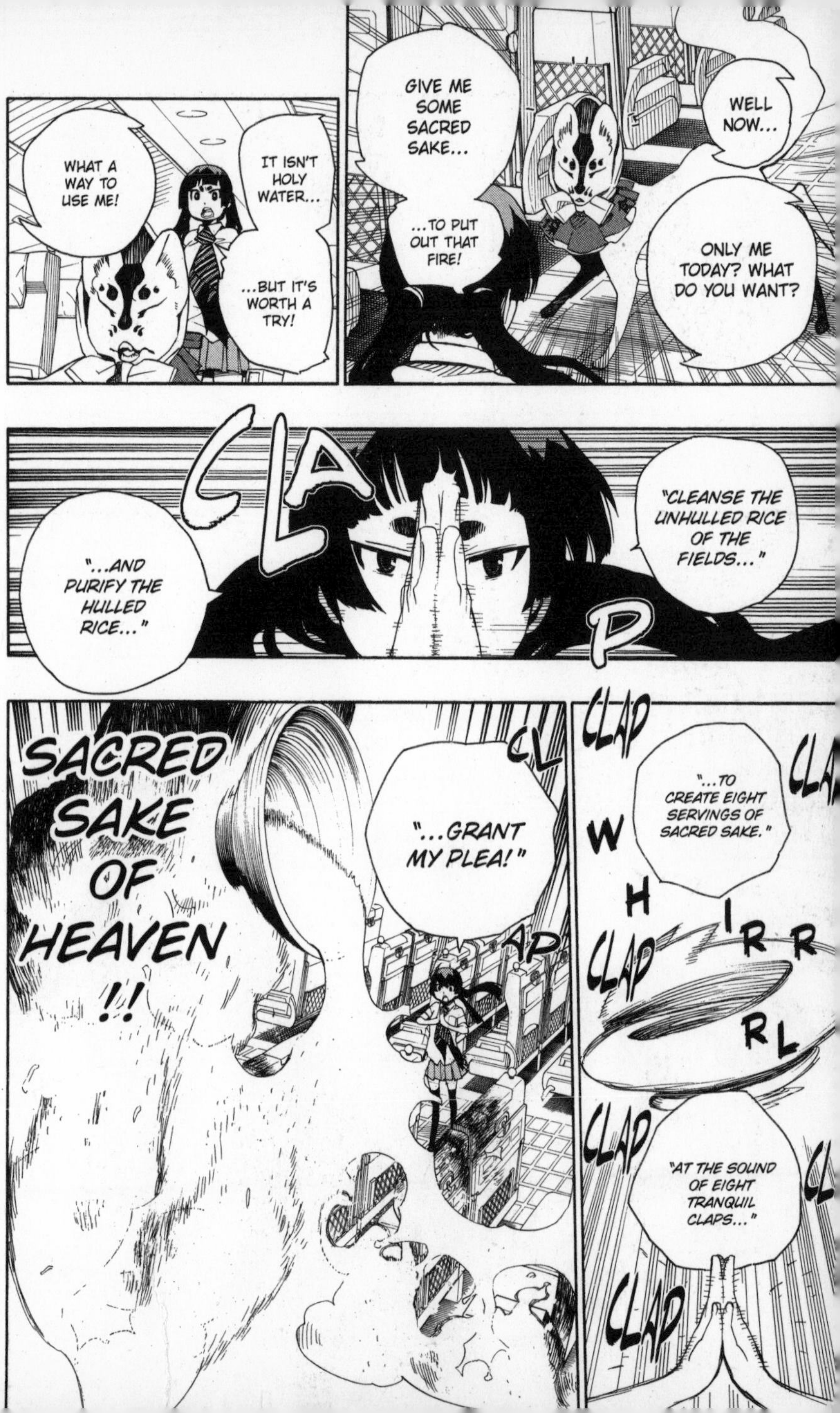
WELL NOW...
ONLY ME TODAY? WHAT DO YOU WANT?
GIVE ME SOME SACRED SAKE...
...TO PUT OUT THAT FIRE!
IT ISN'T HOLY WATER...
...BUT IT'S WORTH A TRY!
WHAT A WAY TO USE ME!
CLAP
"CLEANSE THE UNHULLED RICE OF THE FIELDS..."
"...AND PURIFY THE HULLED RICE..."
CLAP
CLA
"...TO CREATE EIGHT SERVINGS OF SACRED SAKE."
WHIRRRL
CLAP
CLAP
CL
"AT THE SOUND OF EIGHT TRANQUIL CLAPS..."
CLAP
CLAP
"...GRANT MY PLEA!"
SACRED SAKE OF HEAVEN!!

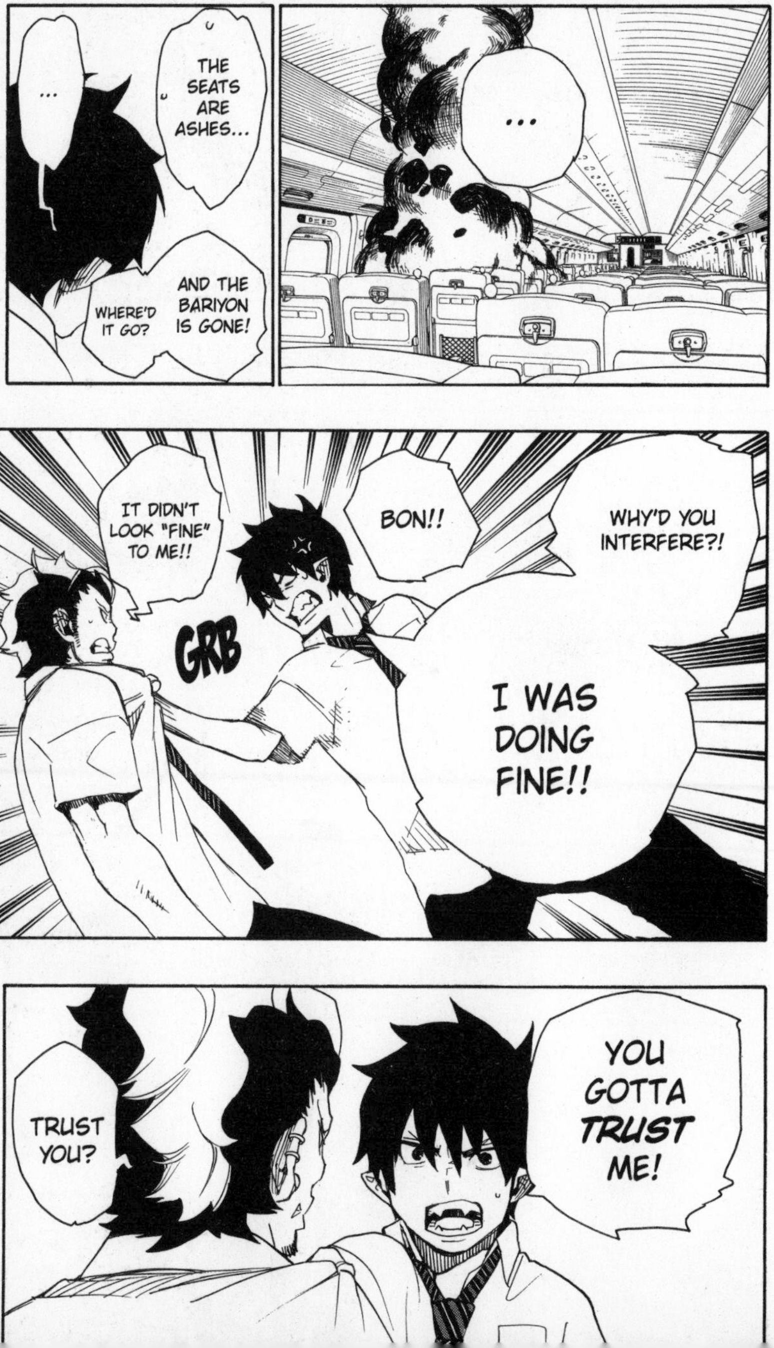
...
THE SEATS ARE ASHES...
...
AND THE BARIYON IS GONE!
WHERE'D IT GO?
WHY'D YOU INTERFERE?!
BON!!
I WAS DOING FINE!!
IT DIDN'T LOOK "FINE" TO ME!!
GRB
YOU GOTTA TRUST ME!
TRUST YOU?

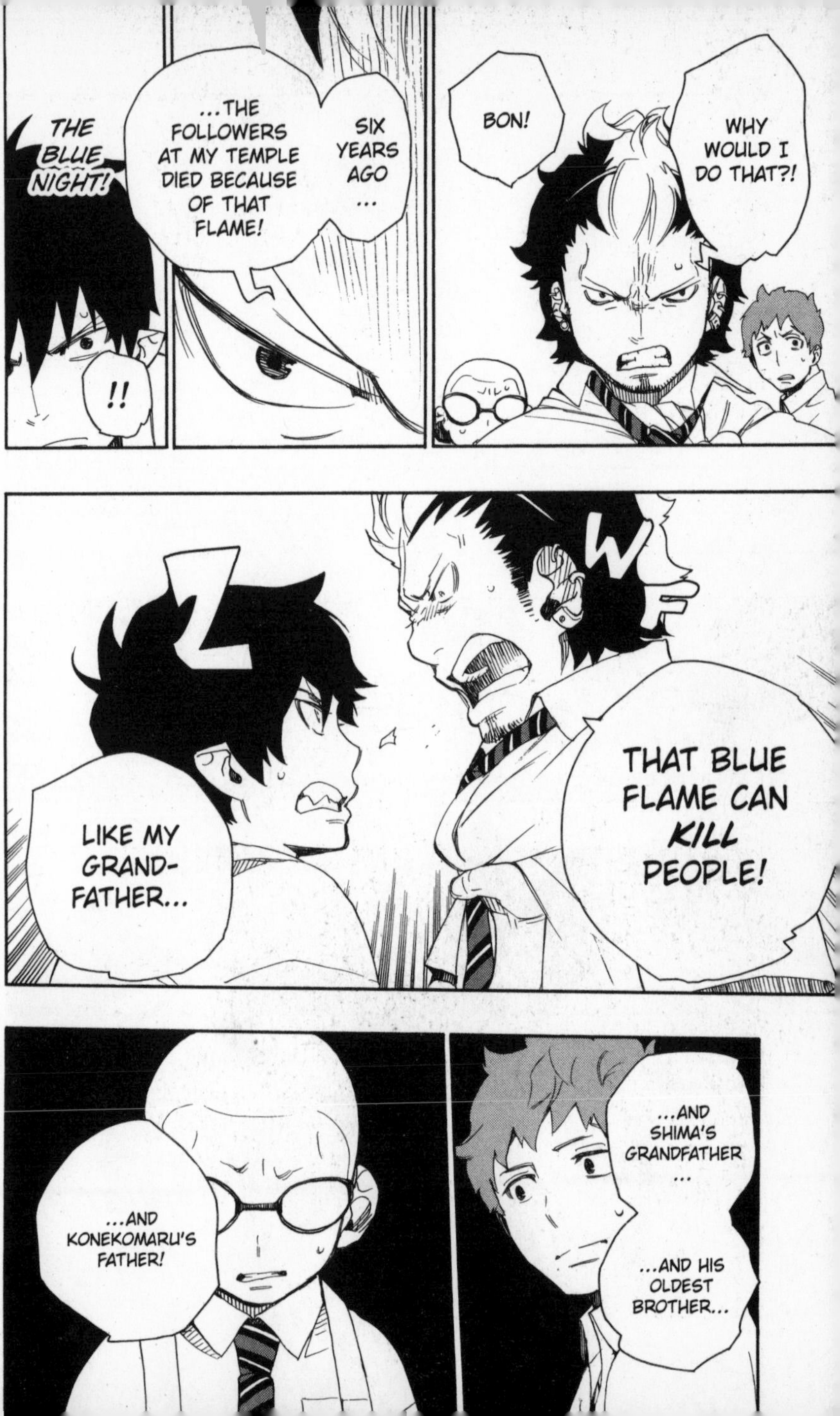
WHY WOULD I DO THAT?!
BON!
SIX YEARS AGO...
...THE FOLLOWERS AT MY TEMPLE DIED BECAUSE OF THAT FLAME!
THE BLUE NIGHT!
!!
THAT BLUE FLAME CAN KILL PEOPLE!
LIKE MY GRAND-FATHER...
...AND SHIMA'S GRANDFATHER...
...AND HIS OLDEST BROTHER...
...AND KONEKOMARU'S FATHER!

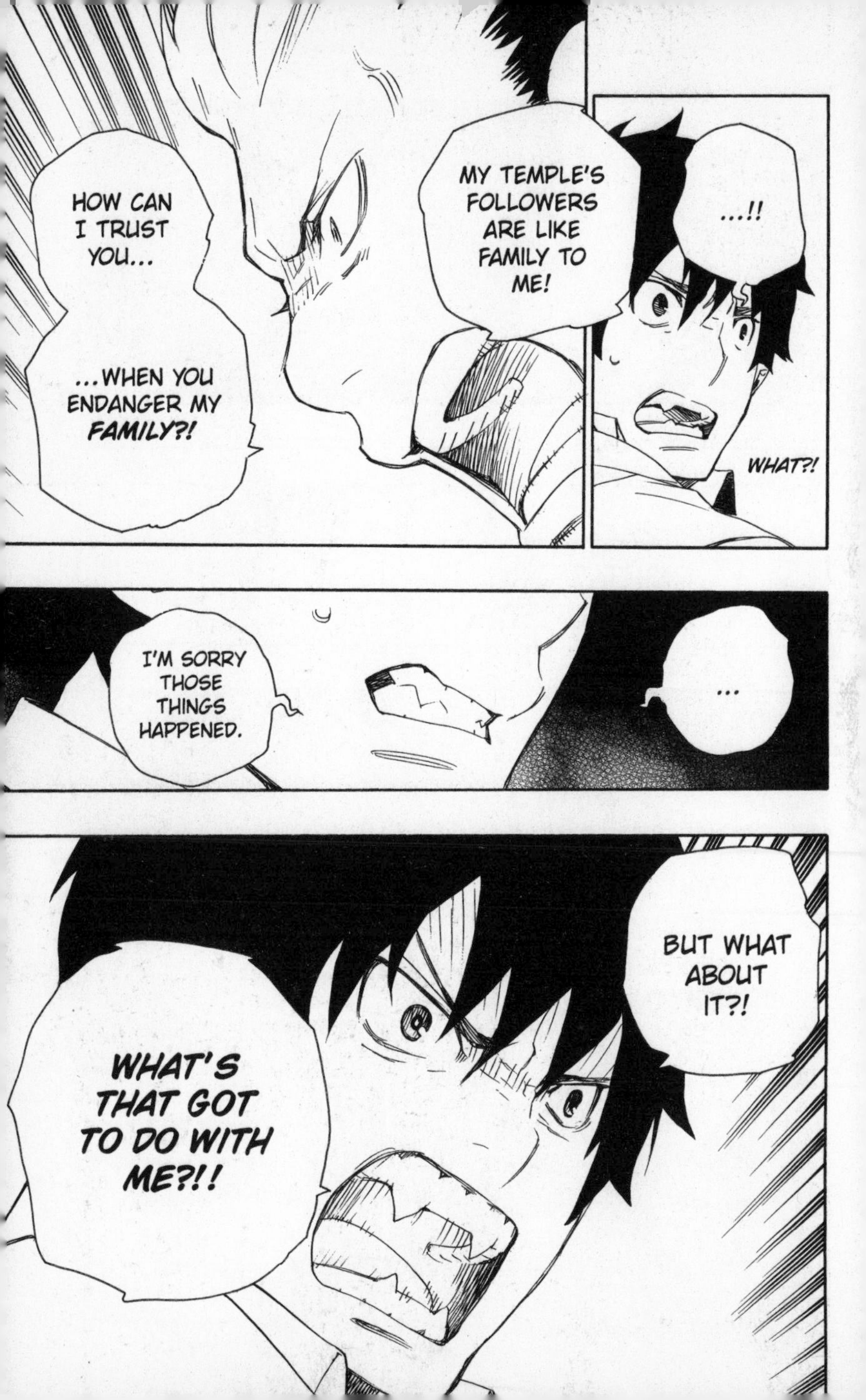
...!!
WHAT?!
MY TEMPLE'S FOLLOWERS ARE LIKE FAMILY TO ME!
HOW CAN I TRUST YOU...
...WHEN YOU ENDANGER MY *FAMILY?!*
...
I'M SORRY THOSE THINGS HAPPENED.
BUT WHAT ABOUT IT?!
WHAT'S THAT GOT TO DO WITH ME?!!

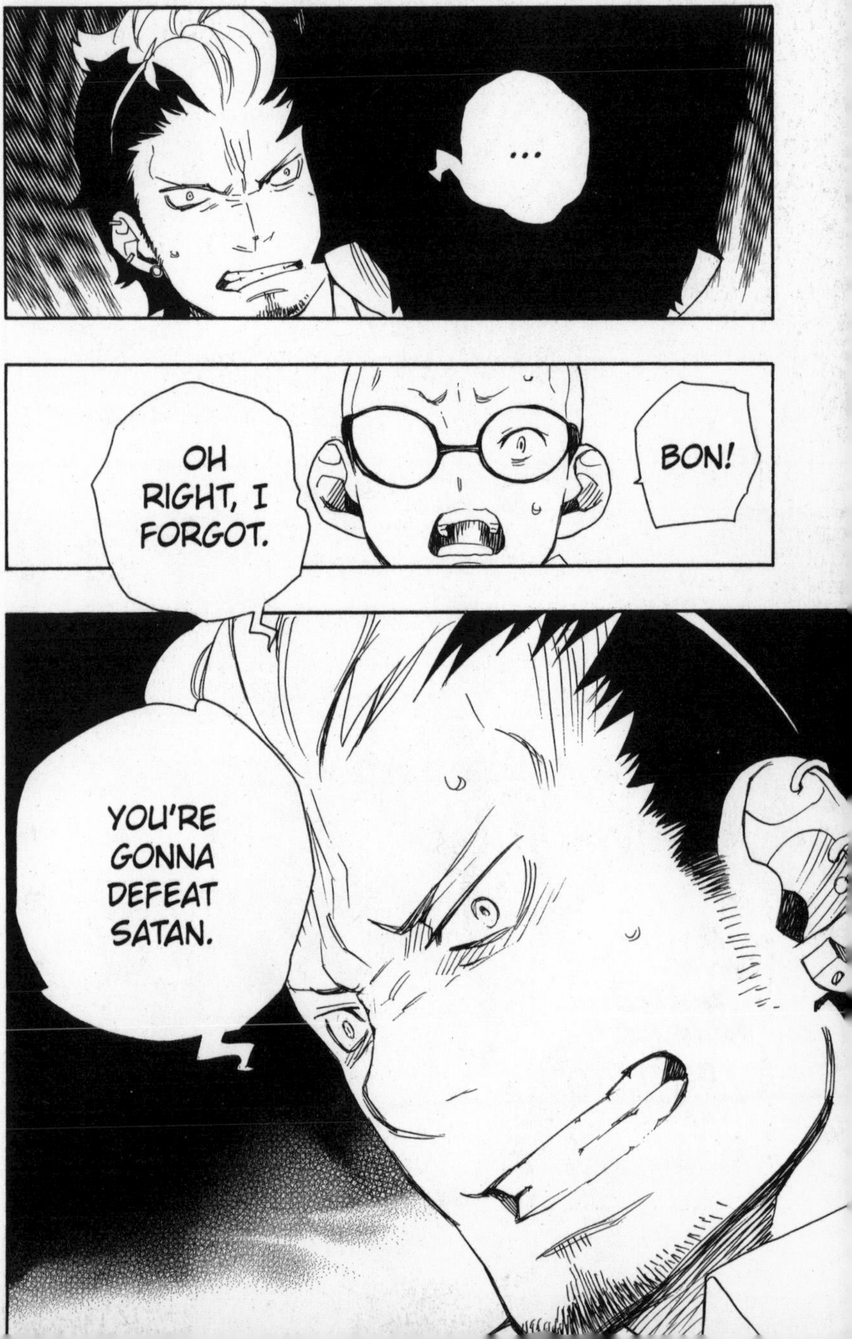
...
BON!
OH RIGHT, I FORGOT.
YOU'RE GONNA DEFEAT SATAN.

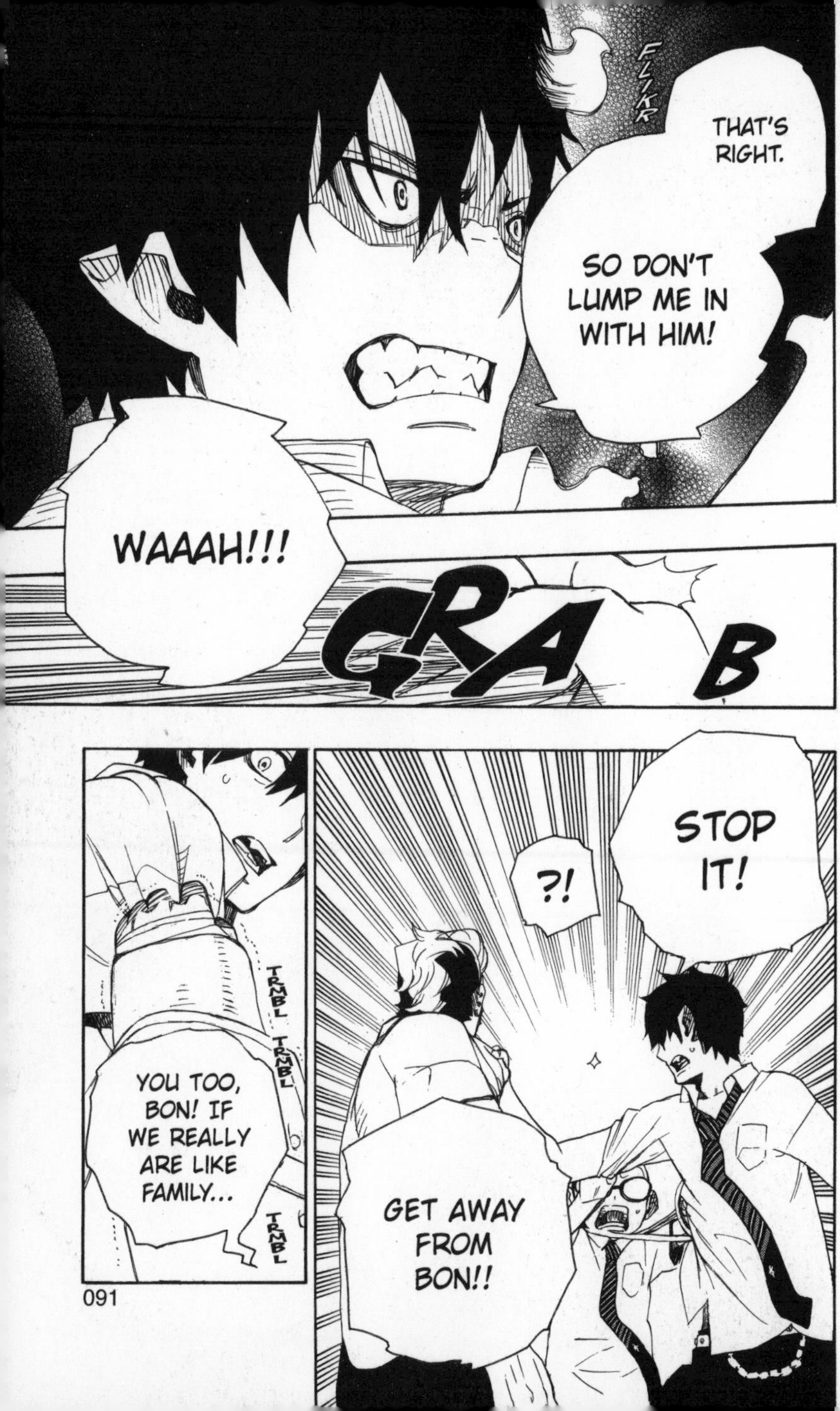
FLIKR
THAT'S RIGHT.
SO DON'T LUMP ME IN WITH HIM!
WAAAH!!!
GRAB
STOP IT!
?!
GET AWAY FROM BON!!
TRMBL TRMBL
YOU TOO, BON! IF WE REALLY ARE LIKE FAMILY...
TRMBL

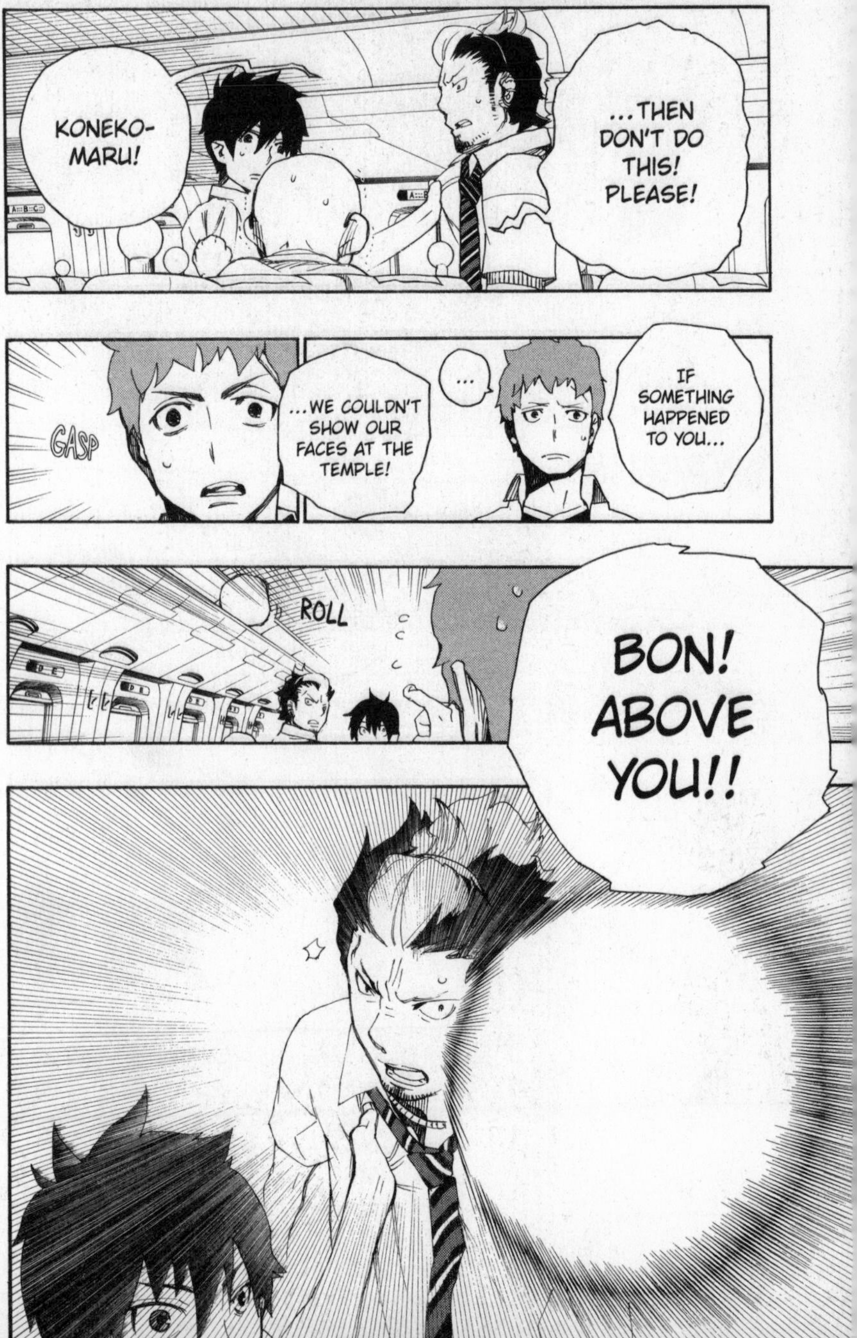
...THEN DON'T DO THIS! PLEASE!
KONEKO-MARU!
IF SOMETHING HAPPENED TO YOU...
...
...WE COULDN'T SHOW OUR FACES AT THE TEMPLE!
GASP
BON! ABOVE YOU!!
ROLL

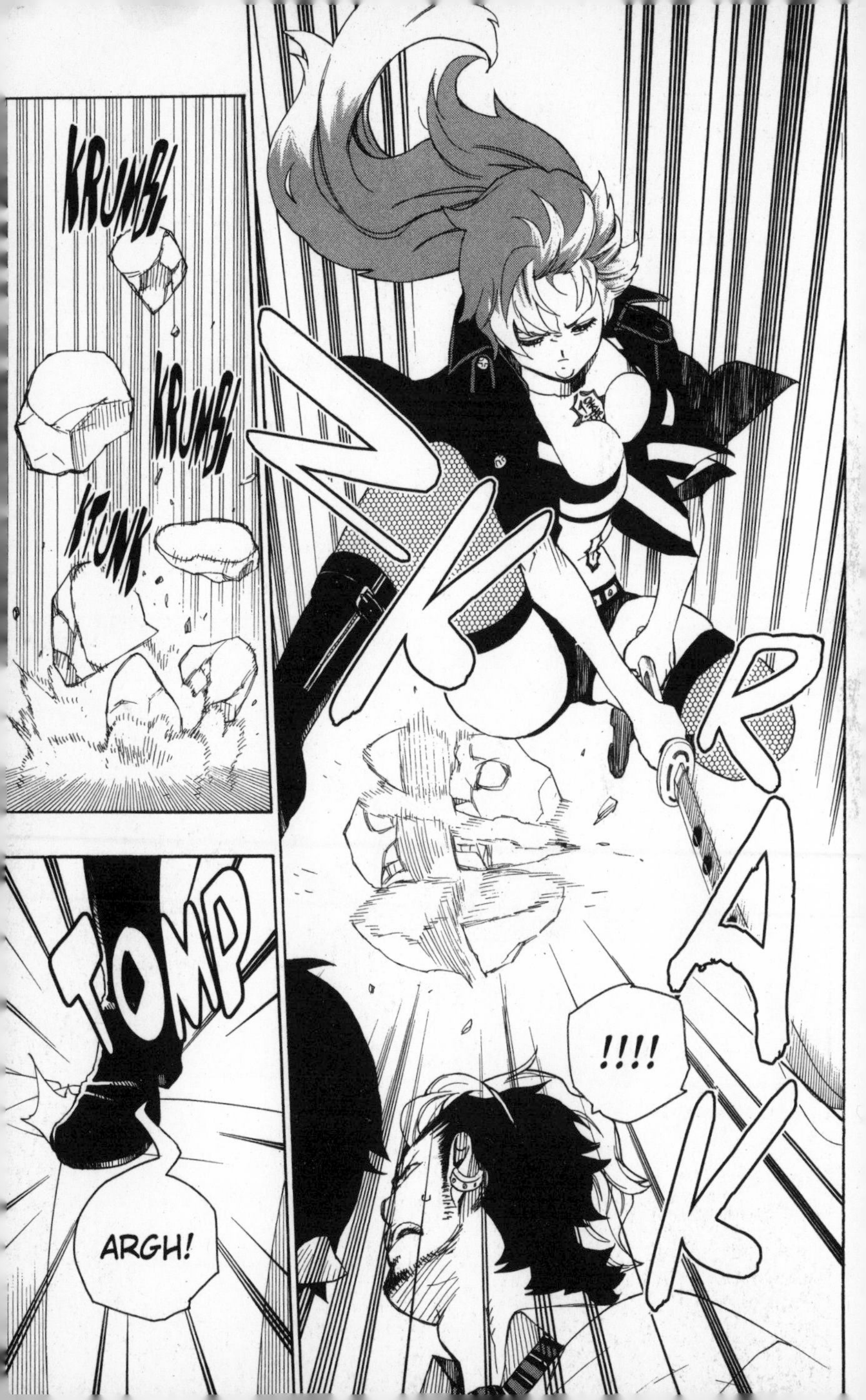
ZKRAK
!!!!
KRUMBL
KRUMBL
KTUNK
TOMP
ARGH!

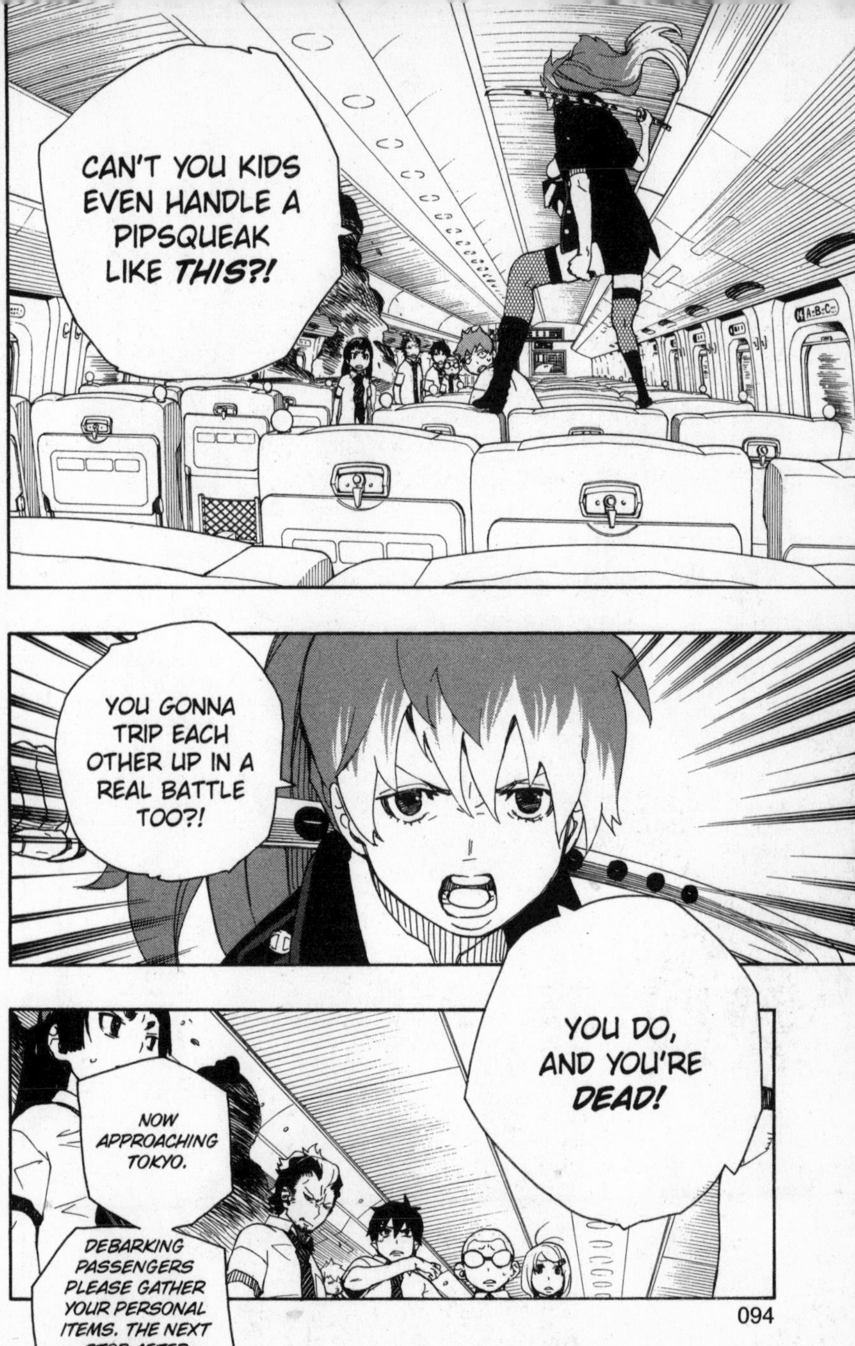
CAN'T YOU KIDS EVEN HANDLE A PIPSQUEAK LIKE *THIS?!*
YOU GONNA TRIP EACH OTHER UP IN A REAL BATTLE TOO?!
YOU DO, AND YOU'RE *DEAD!*
NOW APPROACHING TOKYO.
DEBARKING PASSENGERS PLEASE GATHER YOUR PERSONAL ITEMS. THE NEXT STOP AFTER KYOTO IS...

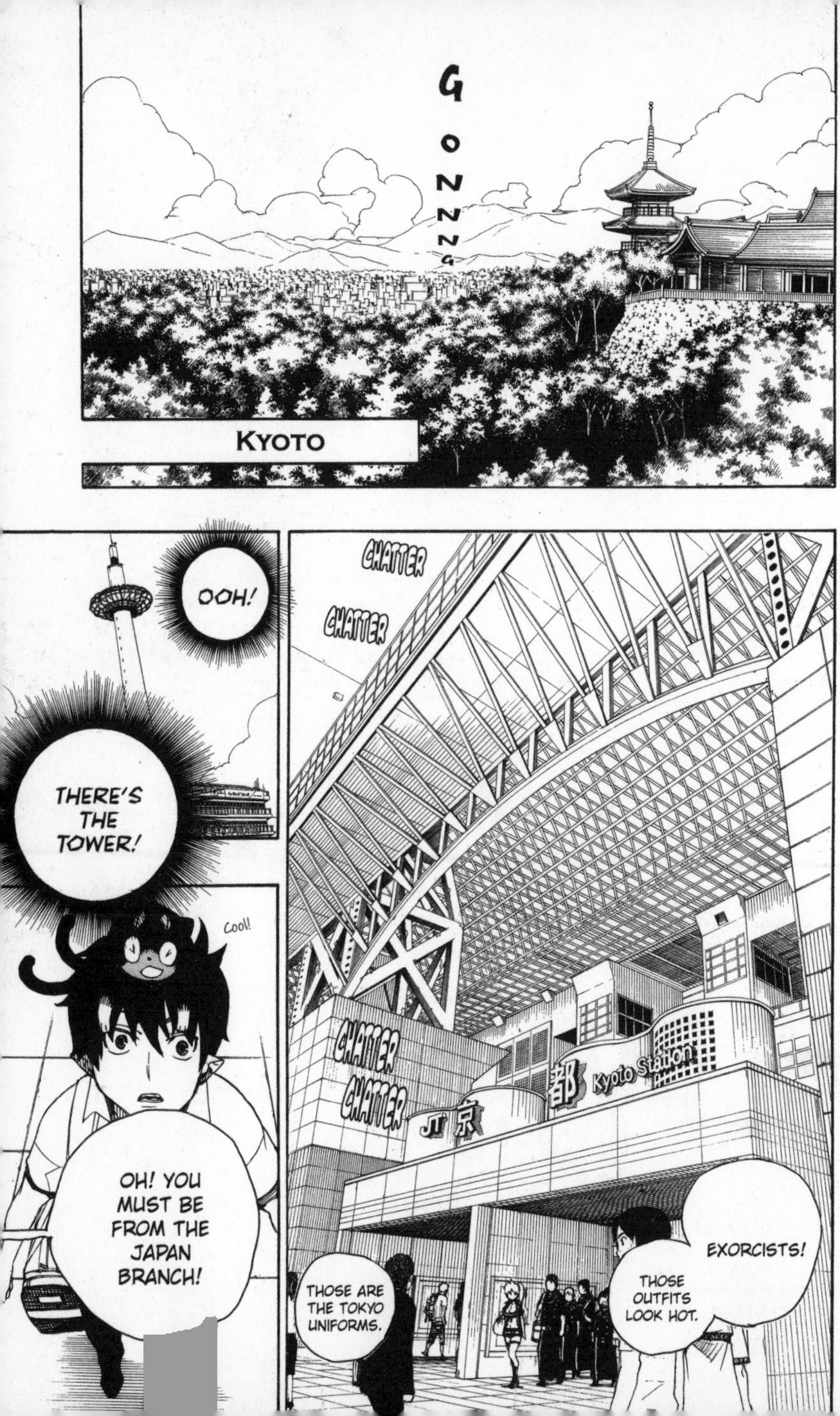
GONNNG
KYOTO
CHATTER
CHATTER
CHATTER
CHATTER
京都 Kyoto Station
EXORCISTS!
THOSE OUTFITS LOOK HOT.
THOSE ARE THE TOKYO UNIFORMS.
OOH!
THERE'S THE TOWER!
Cool!
OH! YOU MUST BE FROM THE JAPAN BRANCH!

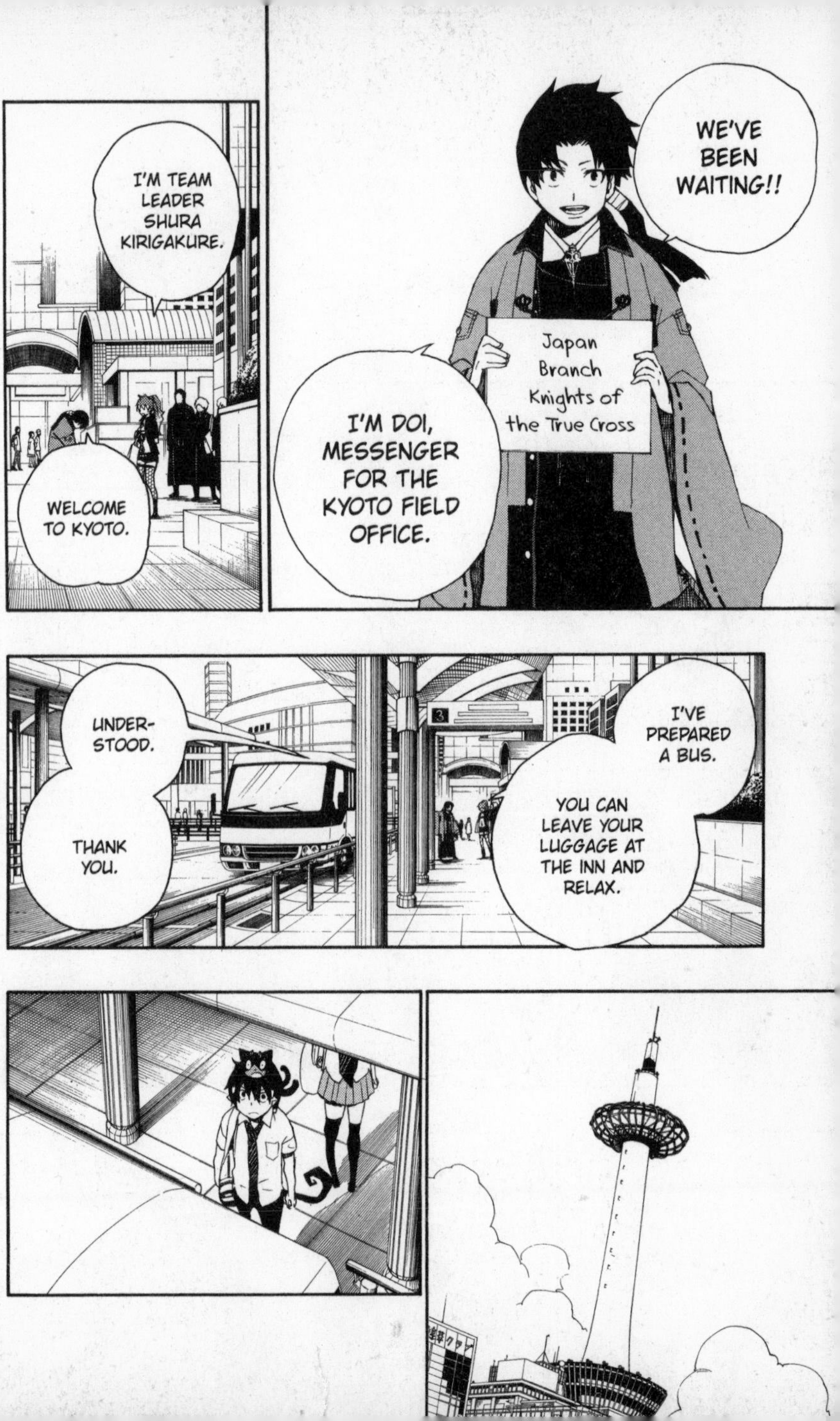
WE'VE BEEN WAITING!!
Japan Branch Knights of the True Cross
I'M DOI, MESSENGER FOR THE KYOTO FIELD OFFICE.
I'M TEAM LEADER SHURA KIRIGAKURE.
WELCOME TO KYOTO.
I'VE PREPARED A BUS.
YOU CAN LEAVE YOUR LUGGAGE AT THE INN AND RELAX.
UNDER-STOOD.
THANK YOU.

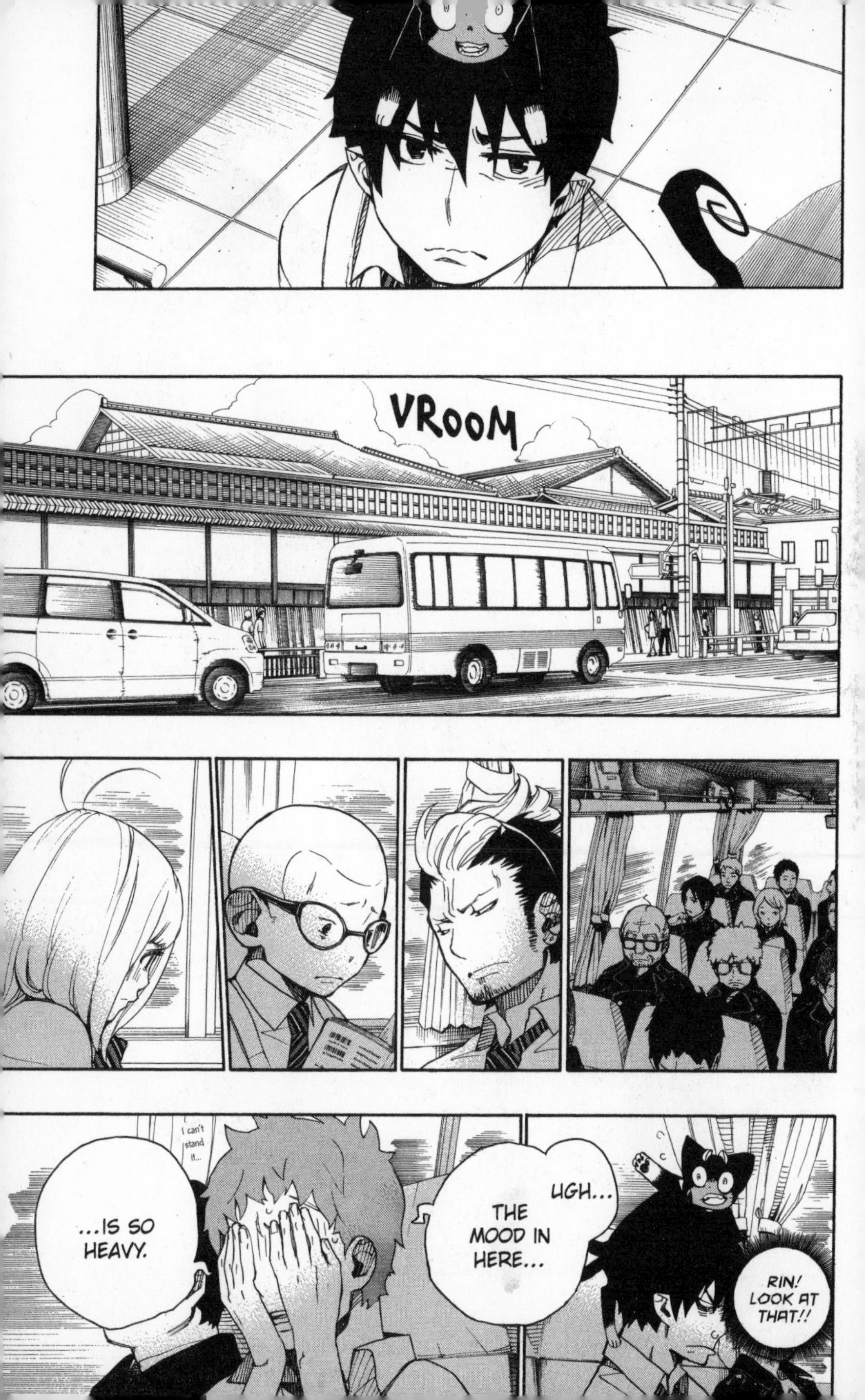
VROOM
RIN! LOOK AT THAT!!
UGH... THE MOOD IN HERE...
I can't stand it...
...IS SO HEAVY.

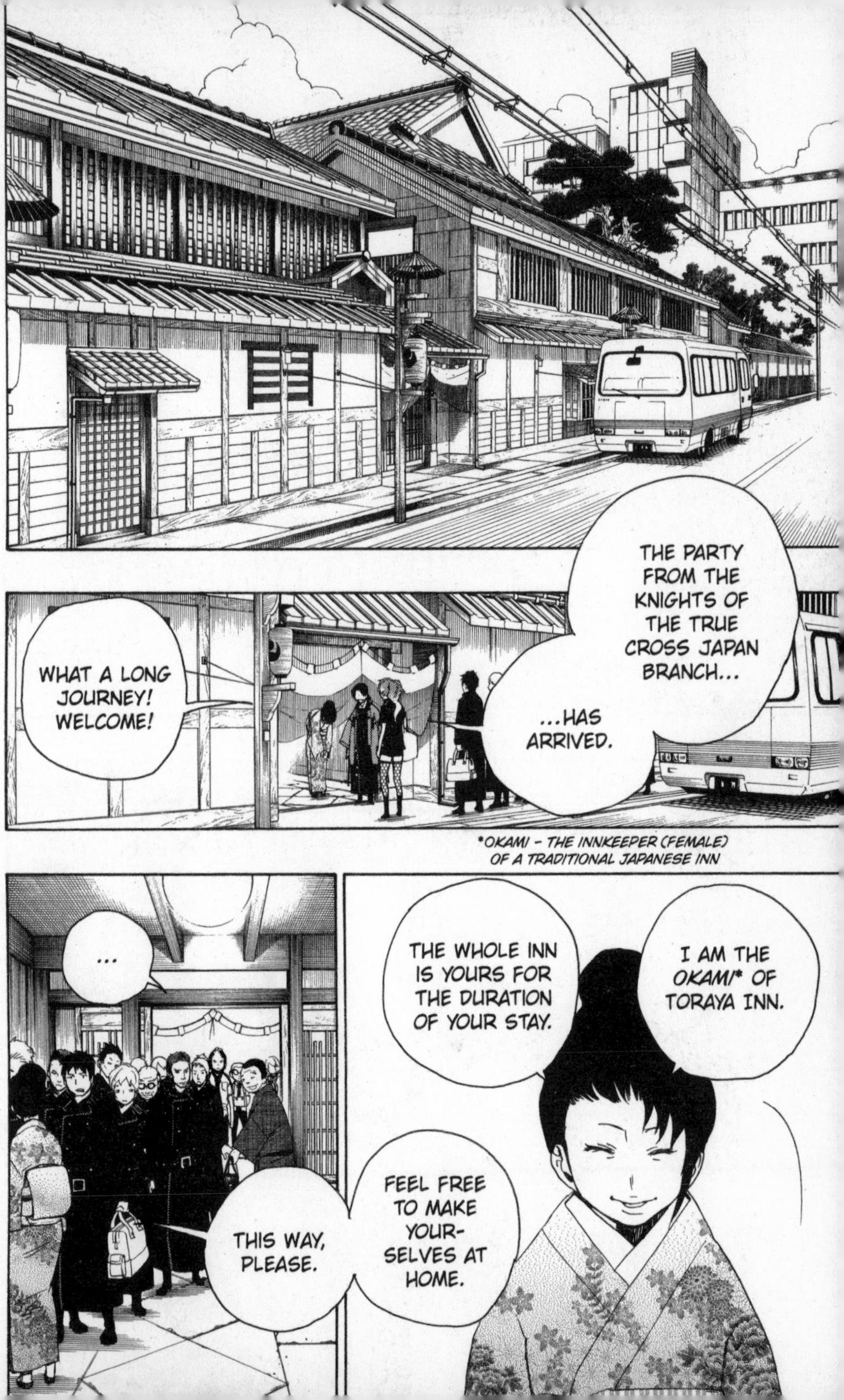
THE PARTY FROM THE KNIGHTS OF THE TRUE CROSS JAPAN BRANCH...
...HAS ARRIVED.
WHAT A LONG JOURNEY! WELCOME!
I AM THE *OKAMI** OF TORAYA INN.
THE WHOLE INN IS YOURS FOR THE DURATION OF YOUR STAY.
FEEL FREE TO MAKE YOUR-SELVES AT HOME.
...
THIS WAY, PLEASE.

**OKAMI* - THE INNKEEPER (FEMALE) OF A TRADITIONAL JAPANESE INN*

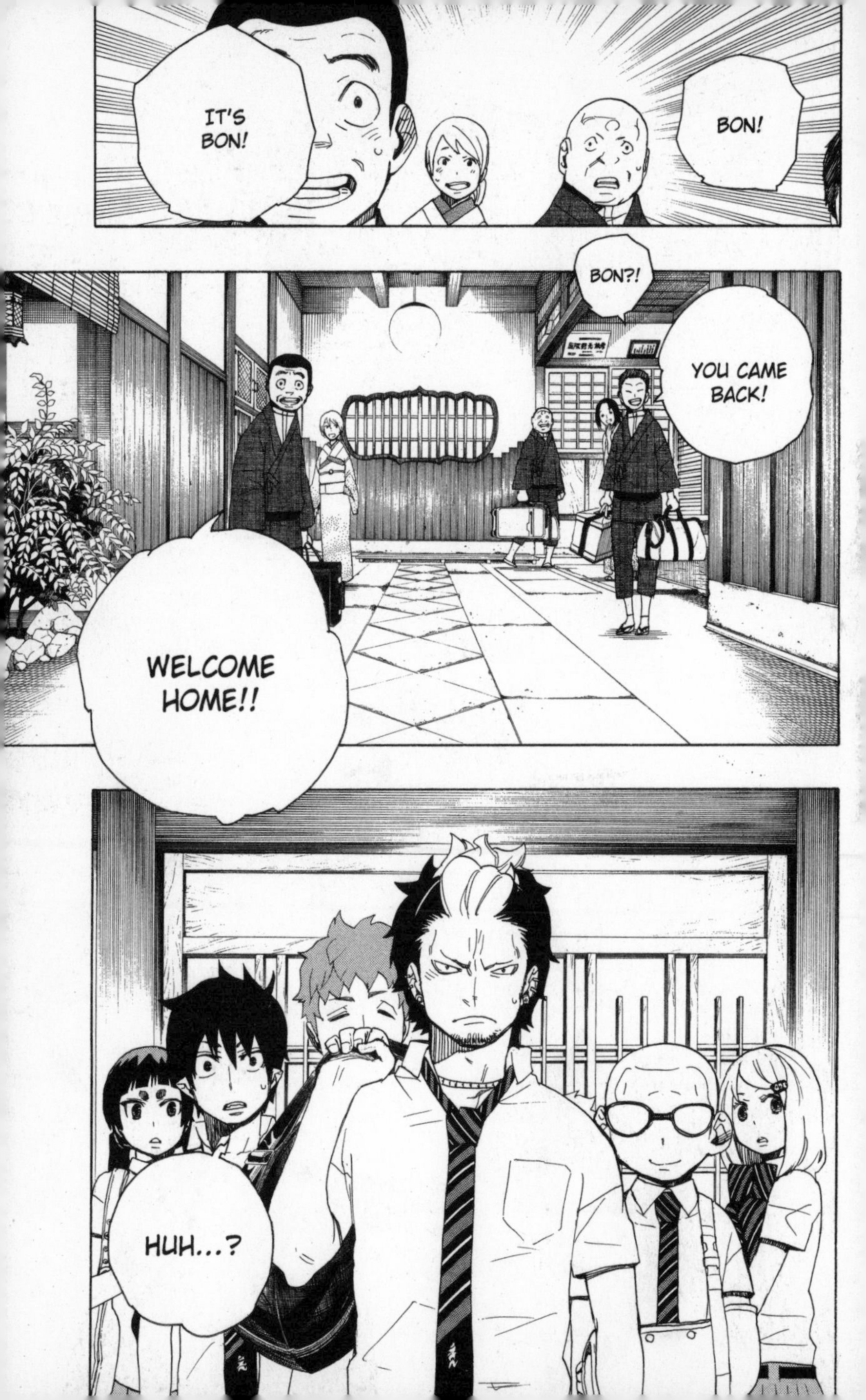
BON!
IT'S BON!
BON?!
YOU CAME BACK!
WELCOME HOME!!
HUH...?

Blue Exorcist Chapter 17 Let's Go to Kyoto!

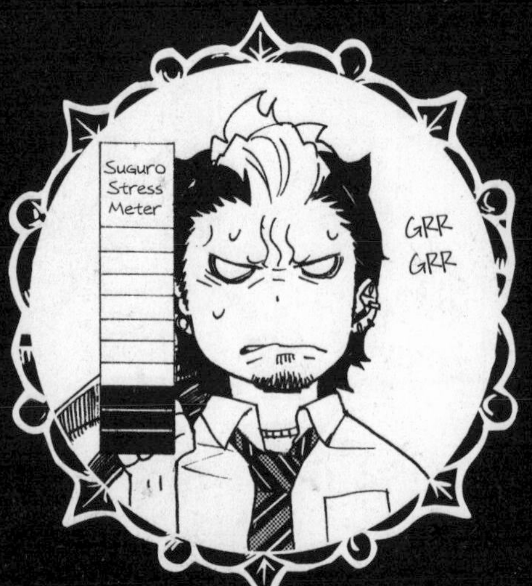

Suguro Stress Meter
GRR GRR

Chapter 18 Discord

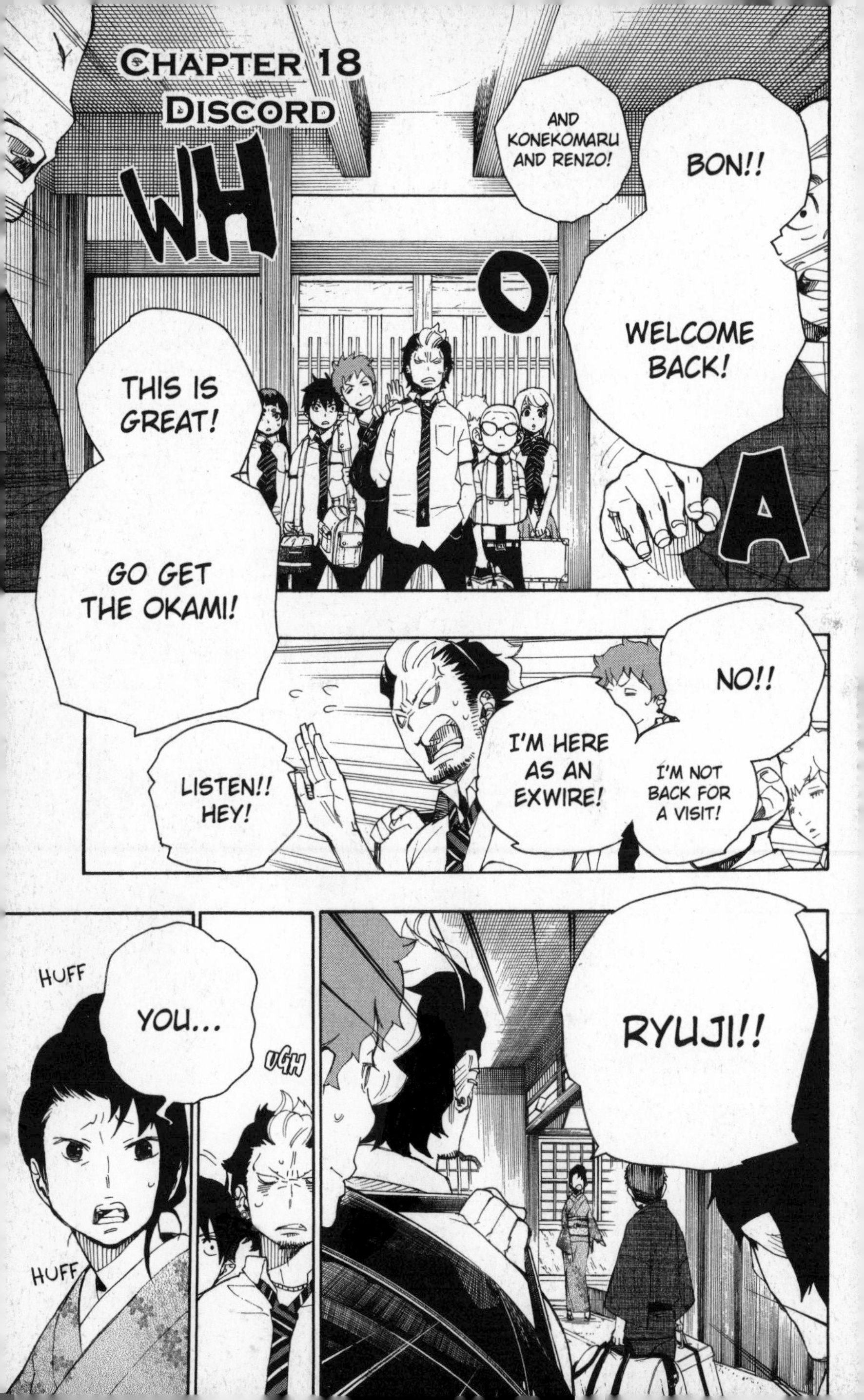
BON!!
AND KONEKOMARU AND RENZO!
WELCOME BACK!
WH O A
THIS IS GREAT!
GO GET THE OKAMI!
NO!!
I'M NOT BACK FOR A VISIT!
I'M HERE AS AN EXWIRE!
LISTEN!! HEY!
RYUJI!!
UGH
HUFF
YOU...
HUFF

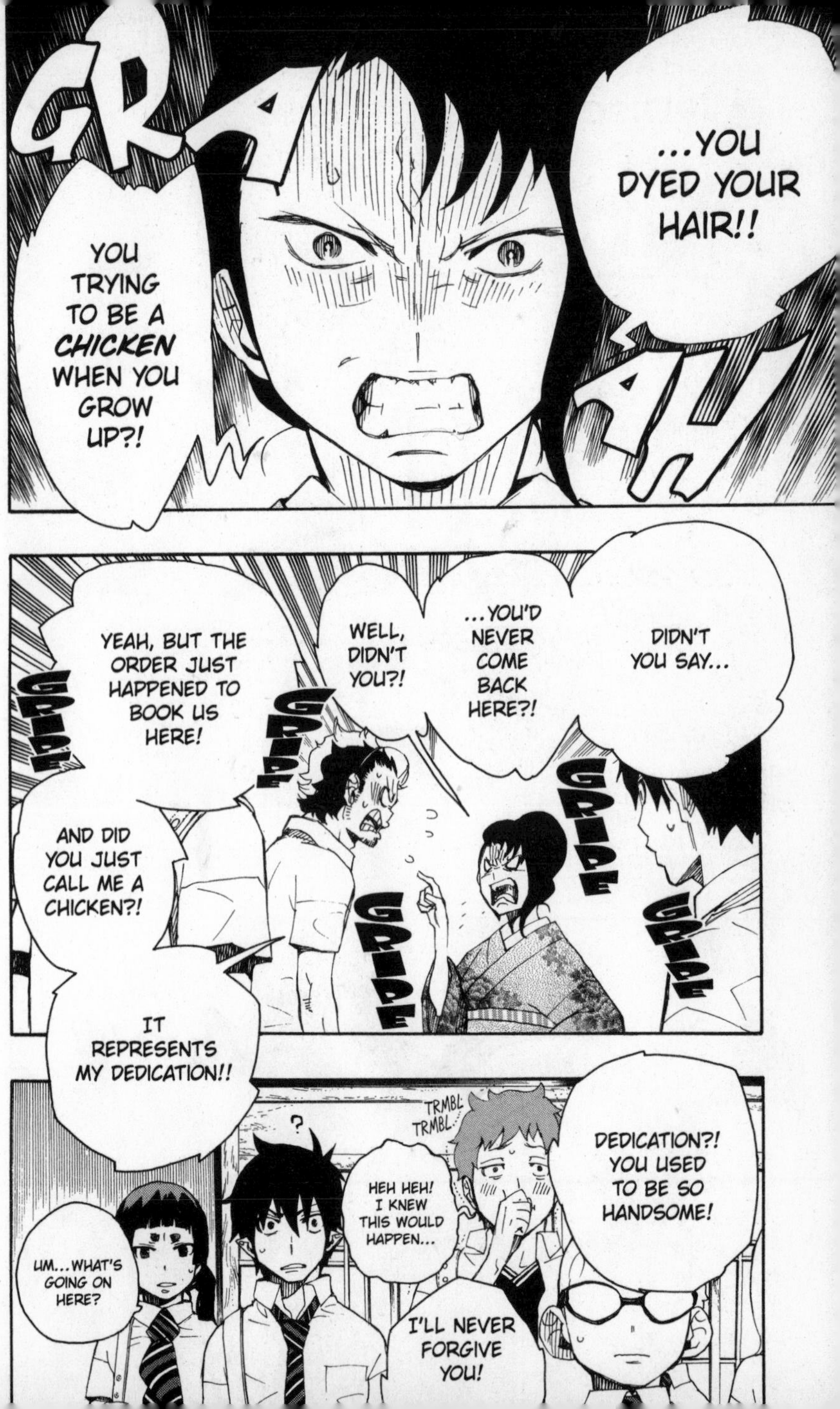
GRAAH
...YOU DYED YOUR HAIR!!
YOU TRYING TO BE A *CHICKEN* WHEN YOU GROW UP?!
DIDN'T YOU SAY...
...YOU'D NEVER COME BACK HERE?!
WELL, DIDN'T YOU?!
GRIDE GRIDE
GRIDE GRIDE
YEAH, BUT THE ORDER JUST HAPPENED TO BOOK US HERE!
AND DID YOU JUST CALL ME A CHICKEN?!
IT REPRESENTS MY DEDICATION!!
DEDICATION?! YOU USED TO BE SO HANDSOME!
I'LL NEVER FORGIVE YOU!
TRMBL TRMBL
HEH HEH! I KNEW THIS WOULD HAPPEN...
?
UM...WHAT'S GOING ON HERE?

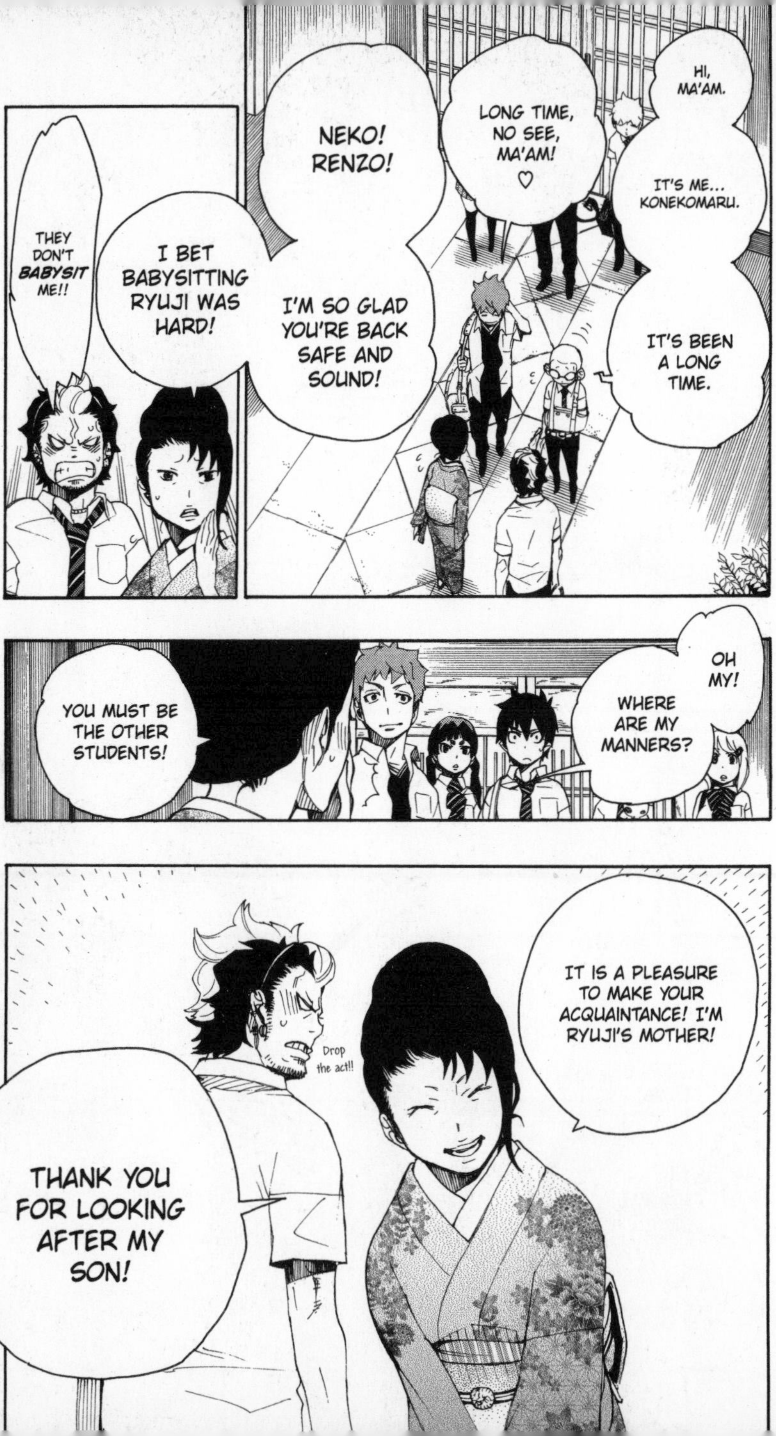
HI, MA'AM.
IT'S ME... KONEKOMARU.
IT'S BEEN A LONG TIME.
LONG TIME, NO SEE, MA'AM! ♡
NEKO! RENZO!
I'M SO GLAD YOU'RE BACK SAFE AND SOUND!
I BET BABYSITTING RYUJI WAS HARD!
THEY DON'T *BABYSIT* ME!!
OH MY!
WHERE ARE MY MANNERS?
YOU MUST BE THE OTHER STUDENTS!
IT IS A PLEASURE TO MAKE YOUR ACQUAINTANCE! I'M RYUJI'S MOTHER!
Drop the act!!
THANK YOU FOR LOOKING AFTER MY SON!

Chapter 18 Discord

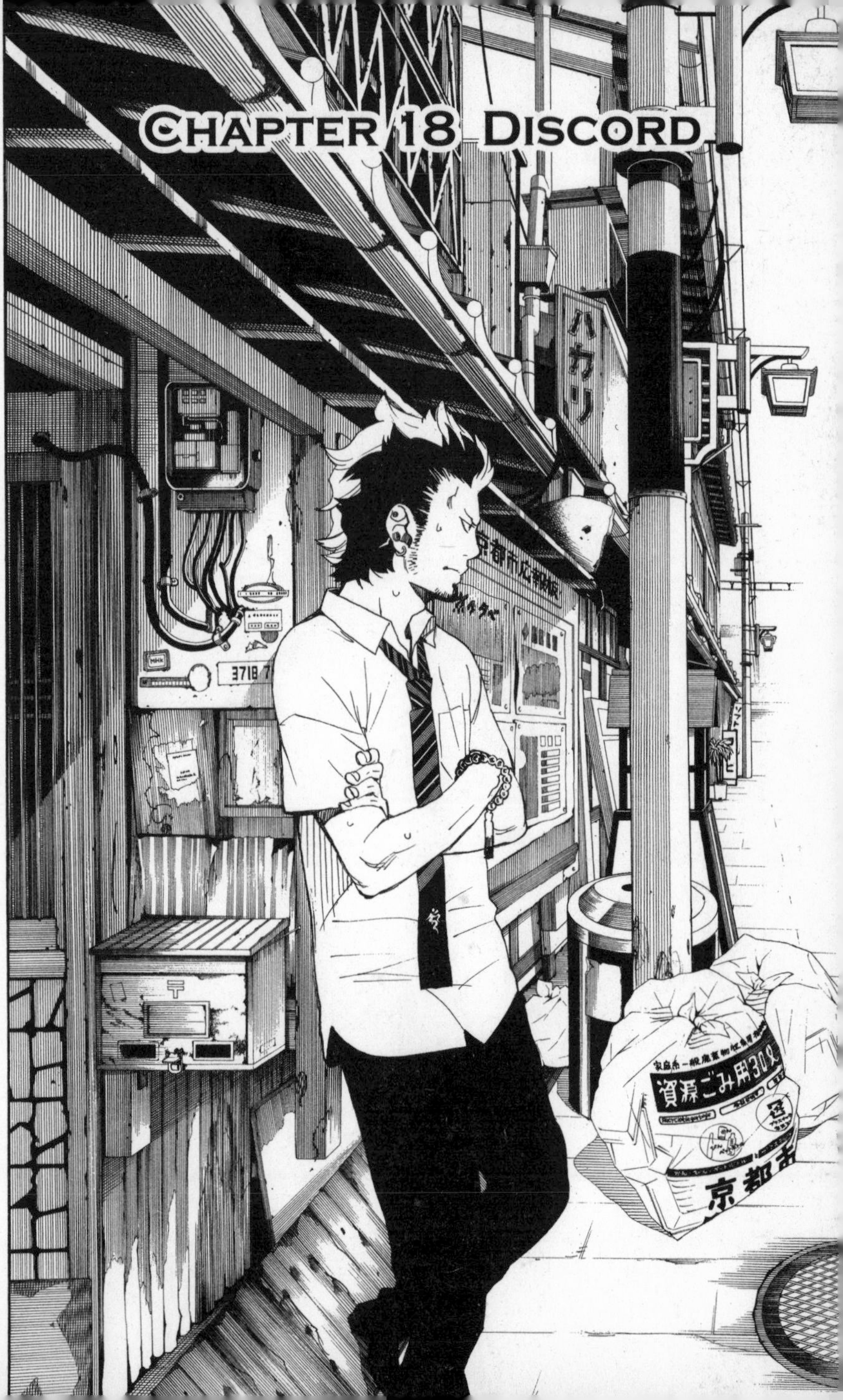
ハカリ
資源ごみ用
京都市

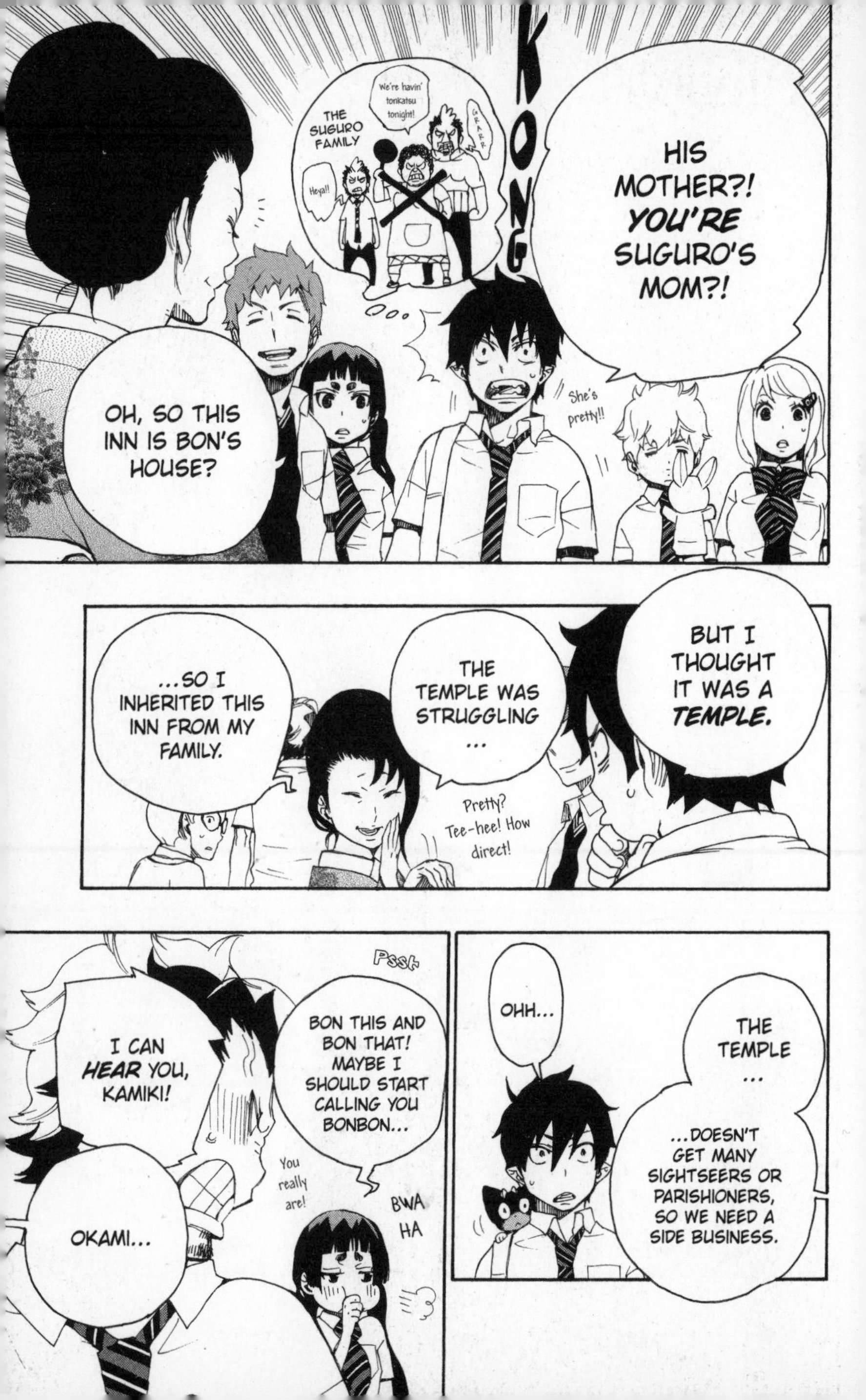
HIS MOTHER?! YOU'RE SUGURO'S MOM?!
KONG
THE SUGURO FAMILY
We're havin' tonkatsu tonight!
GRARR
Heya!!
She's pretty!!
OH, SO THIS INN IS BON'S HOUSE?
BUT I THOUGHT IT WAS A TEMPLE.
THE TEMPLE WAS STRUGGLING...
Pretty? Tee-hee! How direct!
...SO I INHERITED THIS INN FROM MY FAMILY.
THE TEMPLE...
...DOESN'T GET MANY SIGHTSEERS OR PARISHIONERS, SO WE NEED A SIDE BUSINESS.
OHH...
Pssh
BON THIS AND BON THAT! MAYBE I SHOULD START CALLING YOU BONBON...
I CAN HEAR YOU, KAMIKI!
You really are!
BWA HA
OKAMI...

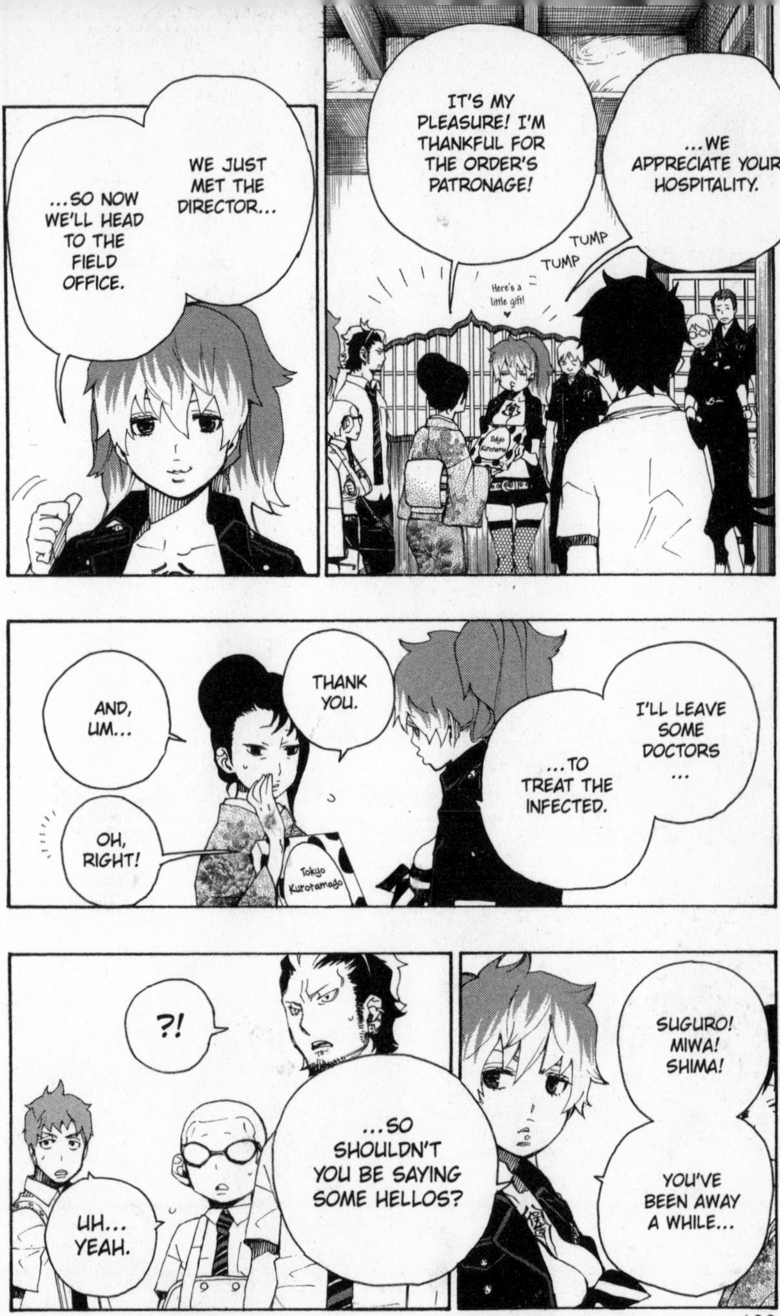
...WE APPRECIATE YOUR HOSPITALITY.
IT'S MY PLEASURE! I'M THANKFUL FOR THE ORDER'S PATRONAGE!
TUMP
TUMP
Here's a little gift!
WE JUST MET THE DIRECTOR...
...SO NOW WE'LL HEAD TO THE FIELD OFFICE.
I'LL LEAVE SOME DOCTORS...
...TO TREAT THE INFECTED.
THANK YOU.
AND, UM...
OH, RIGHT!
Tokyo Kurotamago
SUGURO! MIWA! SHIMA!
YOU'VE BEEN AWAY A WHILE...
...SO SHOULDN'T YOU BE SAYING SOME HELLOS?
?!
UH... YEAH.

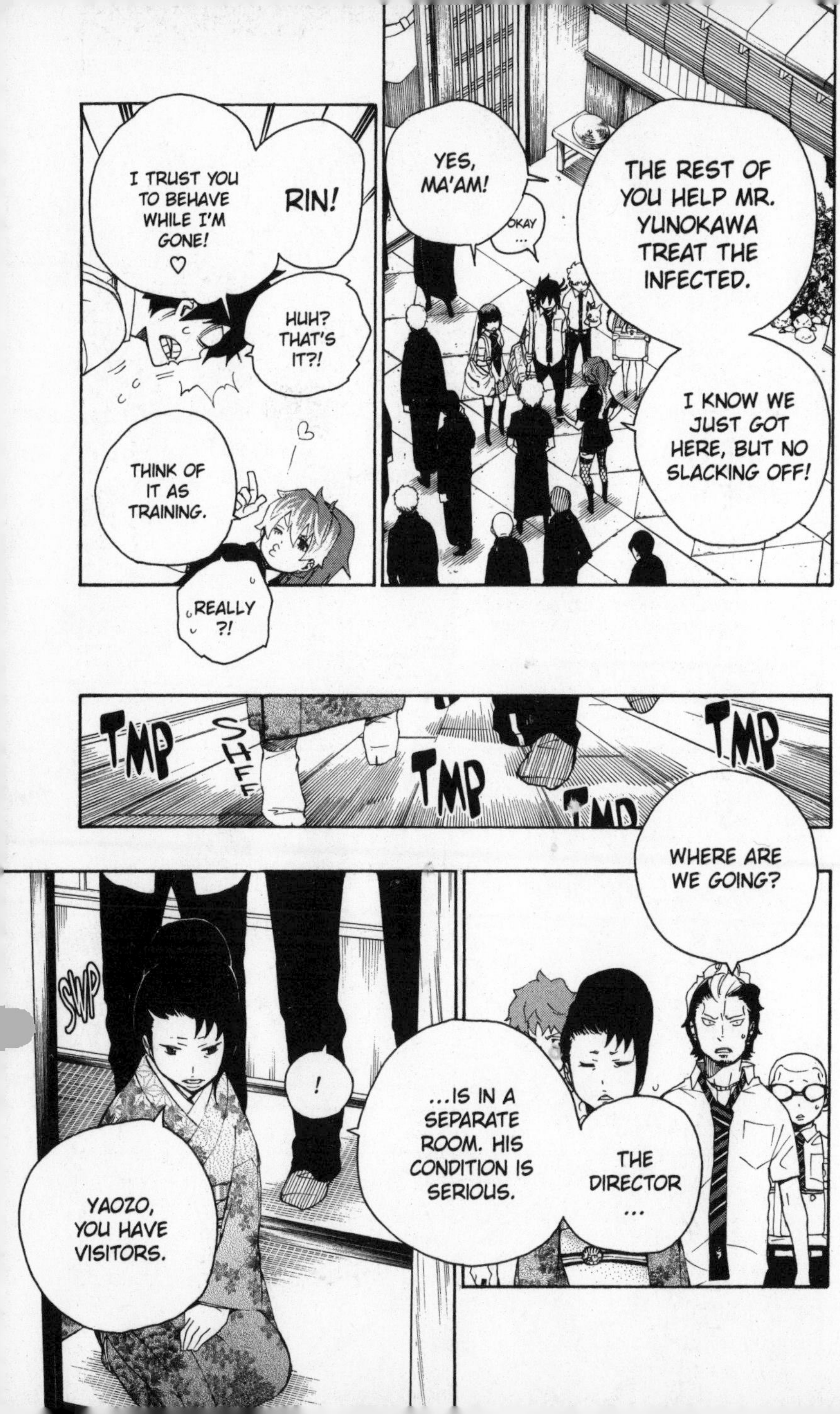
THE REST OF YOU HELP MR. YUNOKAWA TREAT THE INFECTED.
I KNOW WE JUST GOT HERE, BUT NO SLACKING OFF!
YES, MA'AM!
OKAY ...
RIN!
I TRUST YOU TO BEHAVE WHILE I'M GONE! ♡
HUH? THAT'S IT?!
THINK OF IT AS TRAINING.
REALLY ?!
TMP
TMP
TMP
SHFF
TMP
WHERE ARE WE GOING?
THE DIRECTOR ...
...IS IN A SEPARATE ROOM. HIS CONDITION IS SERIOUS.
SWP
!
YAOZO, YOU HAVE VISITORS.

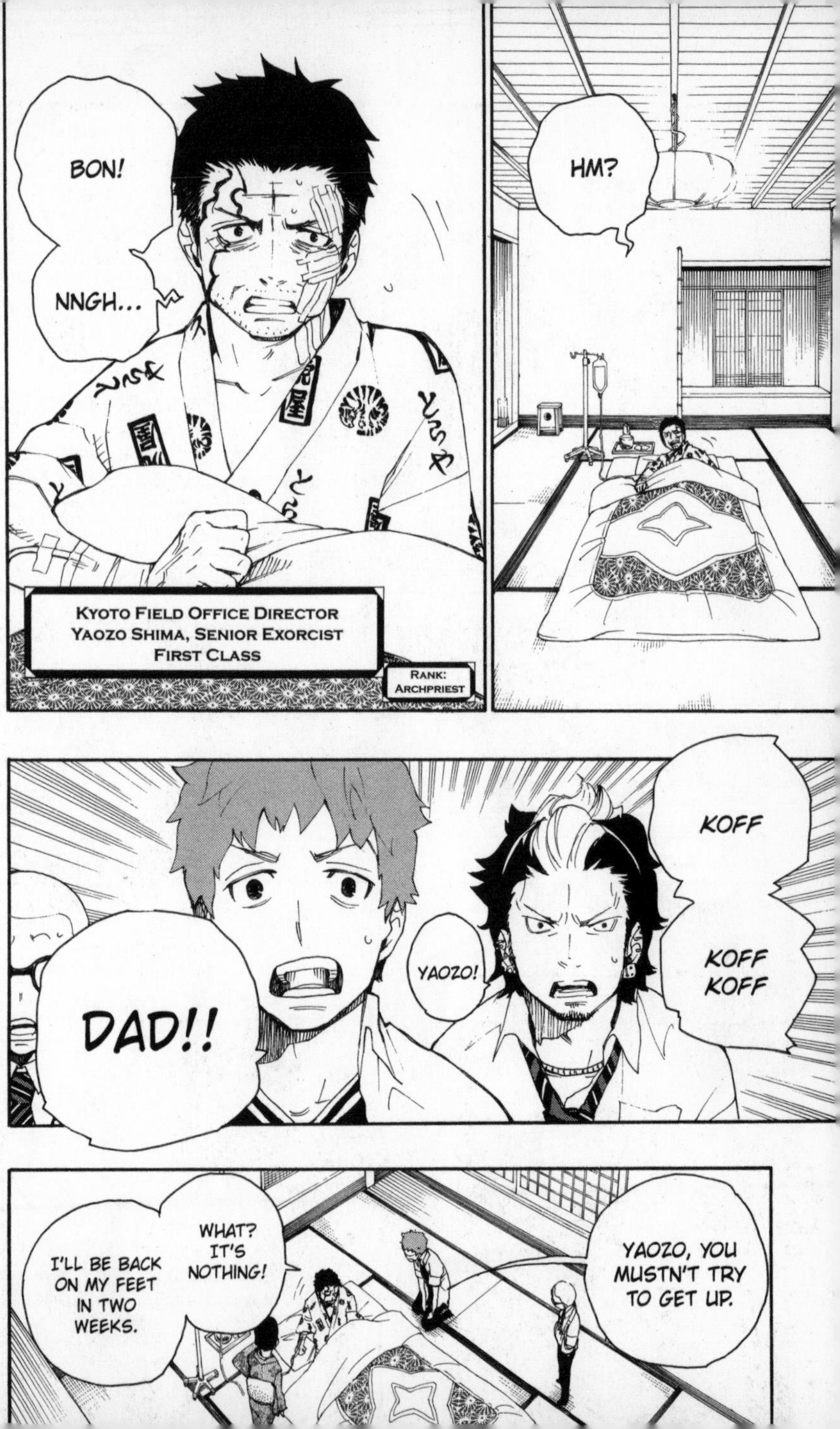
HM?
BON!
NNGH...
Kyoto Field Office Director
Yaozo Shima, Senior Exorcist
First Class
Rank:
Archpriest
KOFF
KOFF KOFF
YAOZO!
DAD!!
YAOZO, YOU MUSTN'T TRY TO GET UP.
WHAT? IT'S NOTHING!
I'LL BE BACK ON MY FEET IN TWO WEEKS.

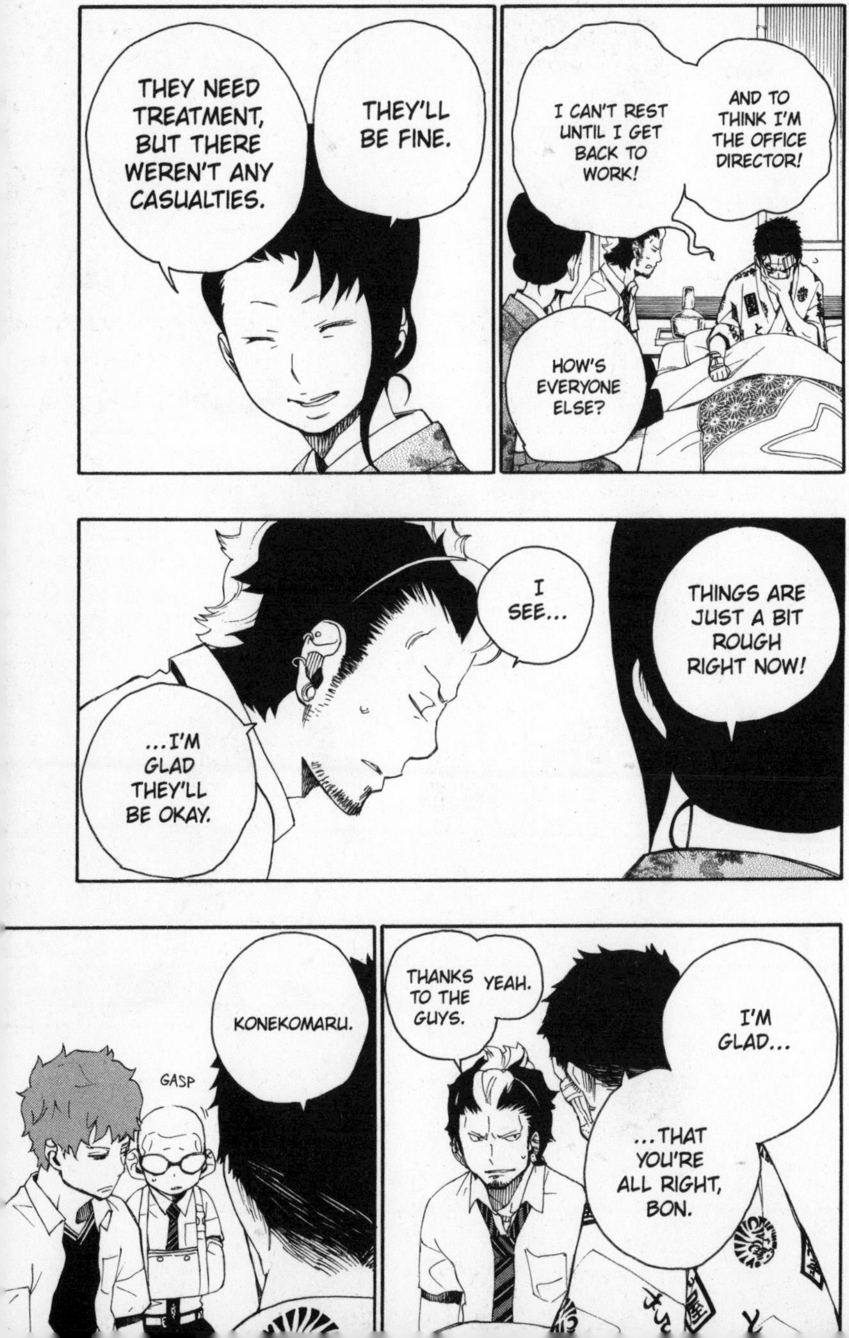
AND TO THINK I'M THE OFFICE DIRECTOR!
I CAN'T REST UNTIL I GET BACK TO WORK!
HOW'S EVERYONE ELSE?
THEY'LL BE FINE.
THEY NEED TREATMENT, BUT THERE WEREN'T ANY CASUALTIES.
THINGS ARE JUST A BIT ROUGH RIGHT NOW!
I SEE...
...I'M GLAD THEY'LL BE OKAY.
I'M GLAD...
...THAT YOU'RE ALL RIGHT, BON.
YEAH.
THANKS TO THE GUYS.
KONEKOMARU.
GASP

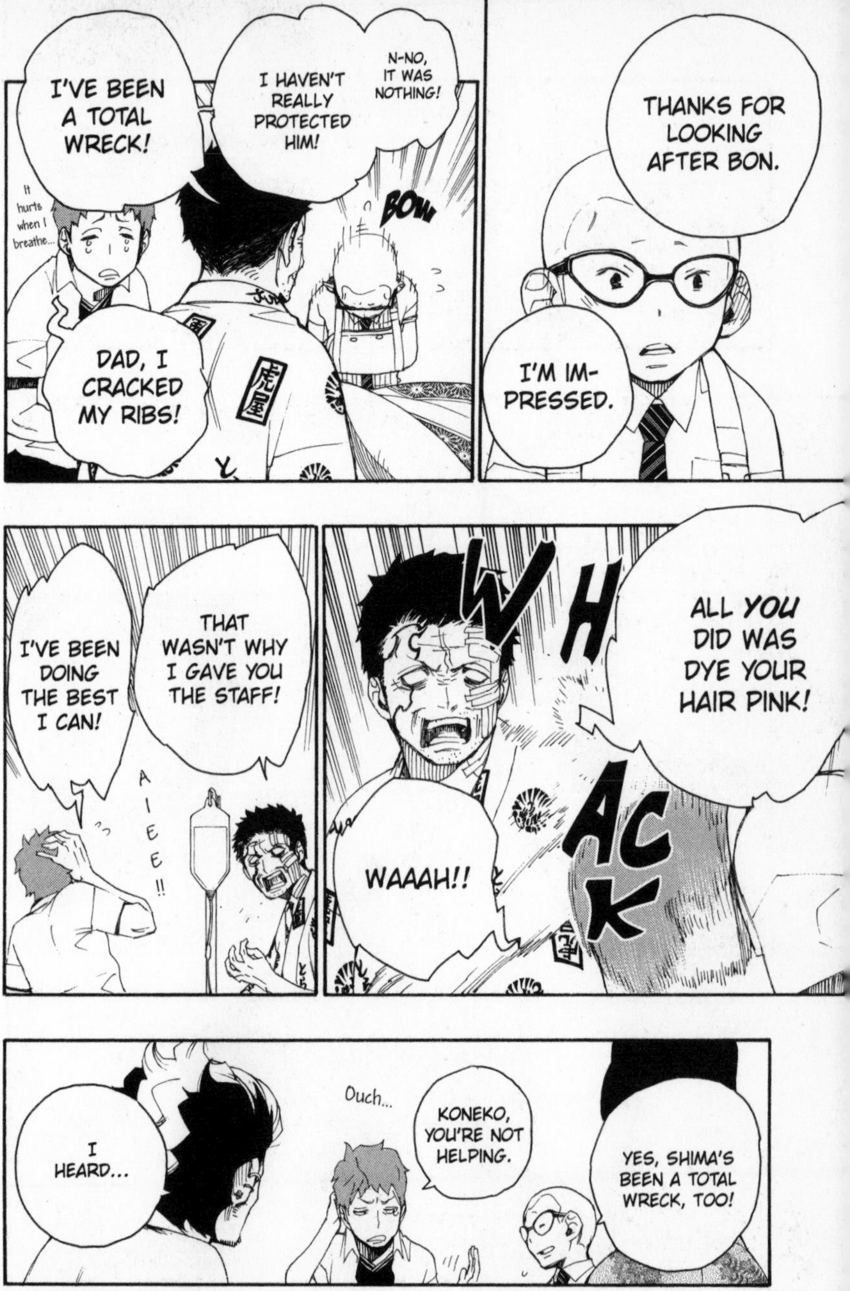
THANKS FOR LOOKING AFTER BON.
I'M IM-PRESSED.
N-NO, IT WAS NOTHING!
BOW
I HAVEN'T REALLY PROTECTED HIM!
I'VE BEEN A TOTAL WRECK!
It hurts when I breathe...
DAD, I CRACKED MY RIBS!
ALL *YOU* DID WAS DYE YOUR HAIR PINK!
WHACK
WAAAH!!
THAT WASN'T WHY I GAVE YOU THE STAFF!
I'VE BEEN DOING THE BEST I CAN!
AIEE!!
YES, SHIMA'S BEEN A TOTAL WRECK, TOO!
KONEKO, YOU'RE NOT HELPING.
Ouch...
I HEARD...

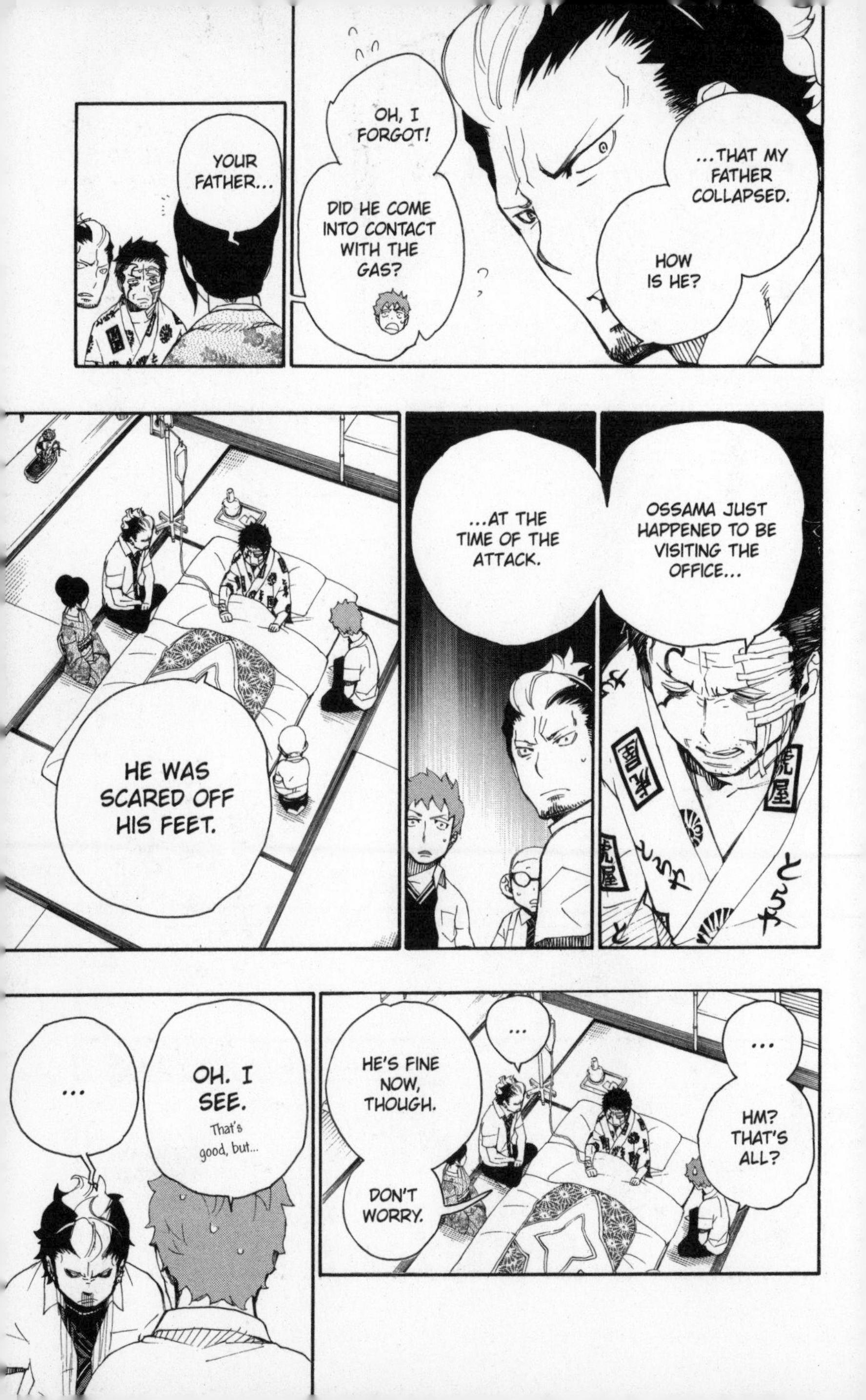
...THAT MY FATHER COLLAPSED.
HOW IS HE?
OH, I FORGOT!
DID HE COME INTO CONTACT WITH THE GAS?
YOUR FATHER...
OSSAMA JUST HAPPENED TO BE VISITING THE OFFICE...
...AT THE TIME OF THE ATTACK.
HE WAS SCARED OFF HIS FEET.
...
HM? THAT'S ALL?
...
HE'S FINE NOW, THOUGH.
DON'T WORRY.
OH. I SEE.
That's good, but...
...

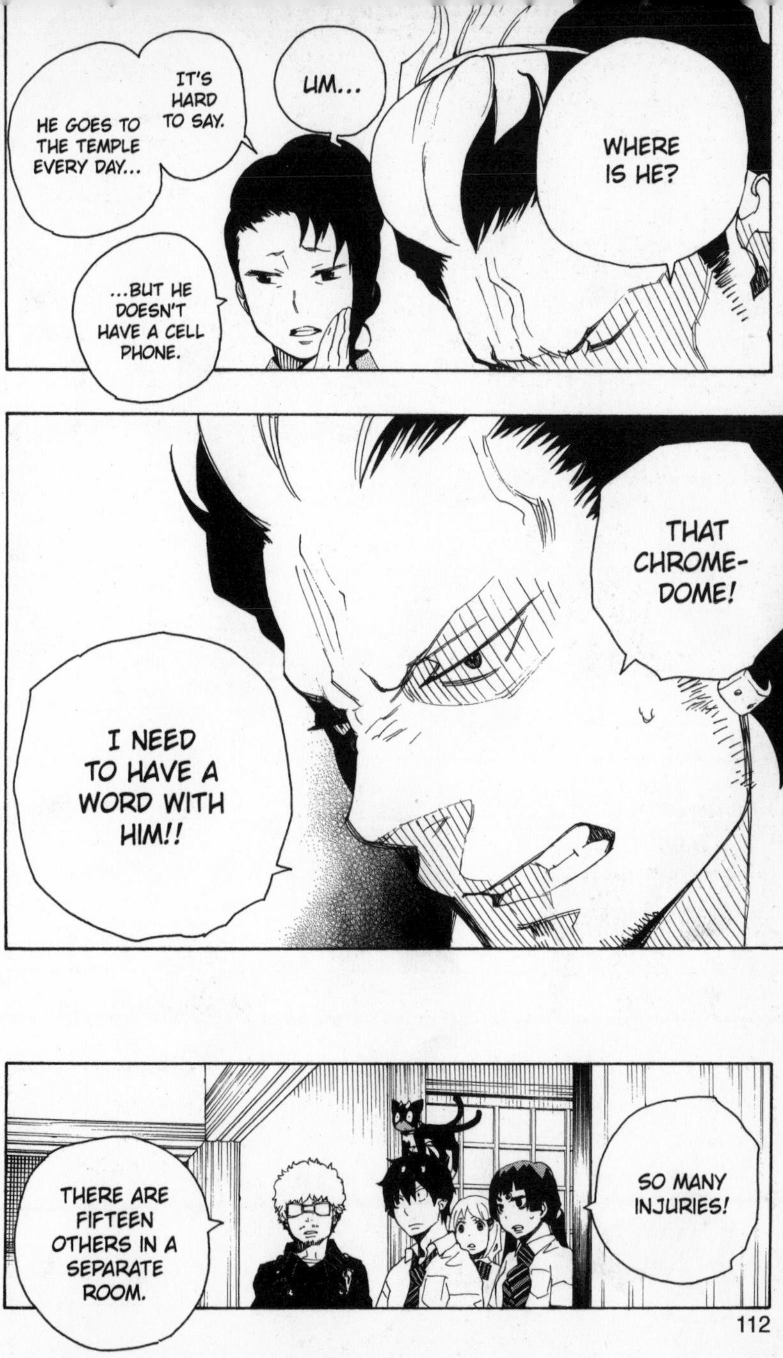
WHERE IS HE?
UM...
IT'S HARD TO SAY.
HE GOES TO THE TEMPLE EVERY DAY...
...BUT HE DOESN'T HAVE A CELL PHONE.
THAT CHROME-DOME!
I NEED TO HAVE A WORD WITH HIM!!
SO MANY INJURIES!
THERE ARE FIFTEEN OTHERS IN A SEPARATE ROOM.

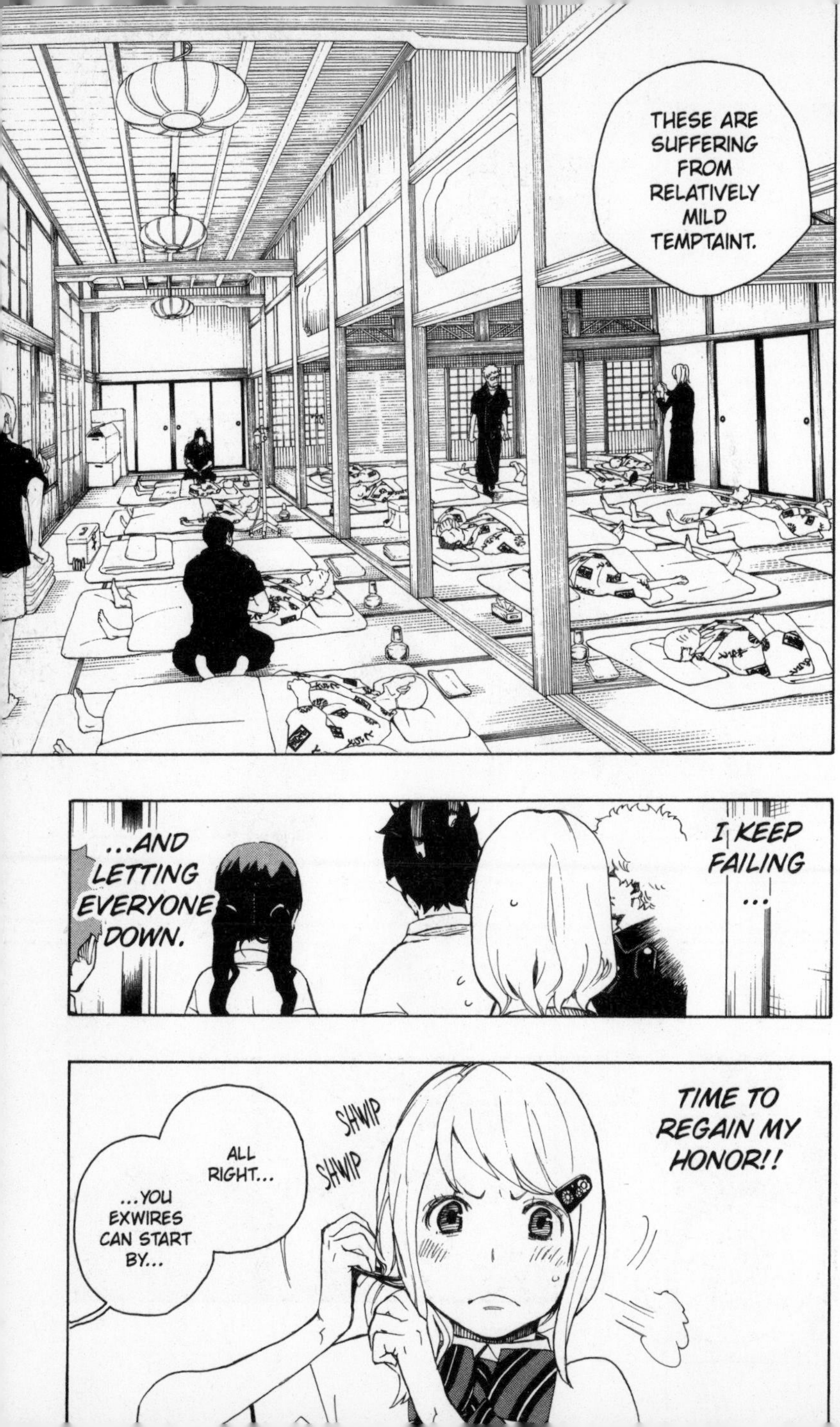
THESE ARE SUFFERING FROM RELATIVELY MILD TEMPTAINT.
I KEEP FAILING...
...AND LETTING EVERYONE DOWN.
TIME TO REGAIN MY HONOR!!
SHWIP
SHWIP
ALL RIGHT... ...YOU EXWIRES CAN START BY...

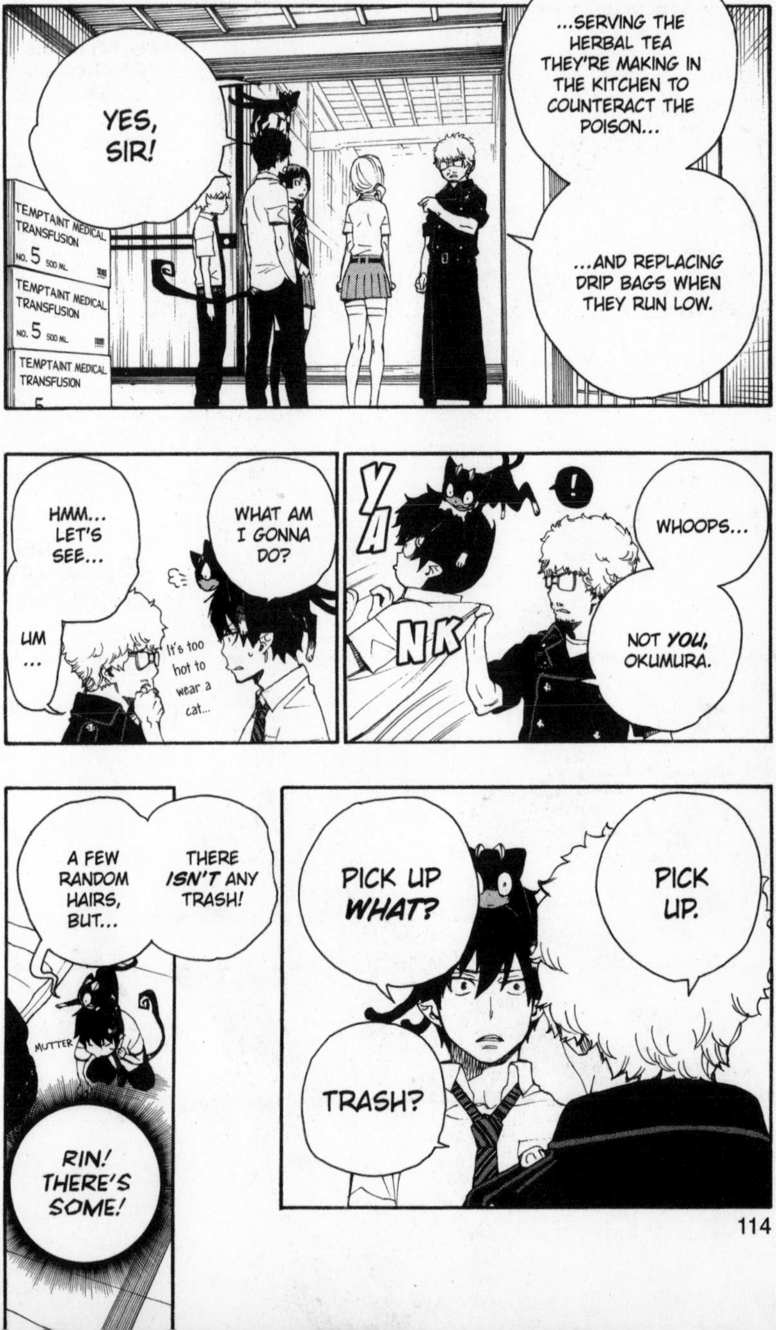
...SERVING THE HERBAL TEA THEY'RE MAKING IN THE KITCHEN TO COUNTERACT THE POISON...
...AND REPLACING DRIP BAGS WHEN THEY RUN LOW.
YES, SIR!
TEMPTAINT MEDICAL TRANSFUSION NO. 5 500 ML
TEMPTAINT MEDICAL TRANSFUSION NO. 5 500 ML
TEMPTAINT MEDICAL TRANSFUSION
YANK
!
WHOOPS...
NOT *YOU*, OKUMURA.
WHAT AM I GONNA DO?
HMM... LET'S SEE...
UM ...
It's too hot to wear a cat...
PICK UP.
PICK UP *WHAT?*
TRASH?
THERE *ISN'T* ANY TRASH!
A FEW RANDOM HAIRS, BUT...
MUTTER
RIN! THERE'S SOME!

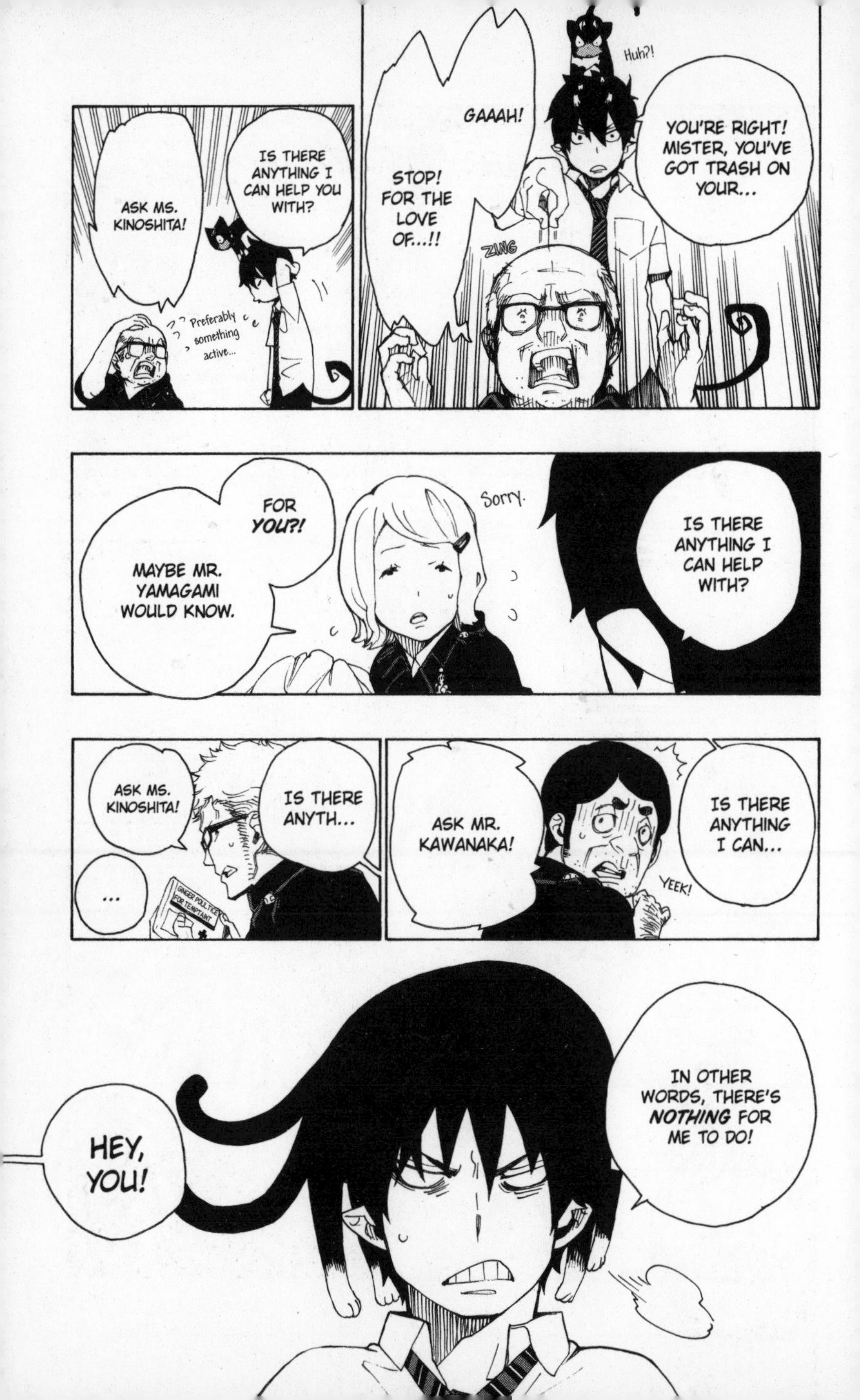

Huh?!
YOU'RE RIGHT! MISTER, YOU'VE GOT TRASH ON YOUR...
GAAAH!
ZING
STOP! FOR THE LOVE OF...!!
IS THERE ANYTHING I CAN HELP YOU WITH?
Preferably something active...
ASK MS. KINOSHITA!
IS THERE ANYTHING I CAN HELP WITH?
Sorry.
FOR *YOU?!*
MAYBE MR. YAMAGAMI WOULD KNOW.
IS THERE ANYTHING I CAN...
YEEK!
ASK MR. KAWANAKA!
IS THERE ANYTH...
ASK MS. KINOSHITA!
...
IN OTHER WORDS, THERE'S *NOTHING* FOR ME TO DO!
HEY, YOU!

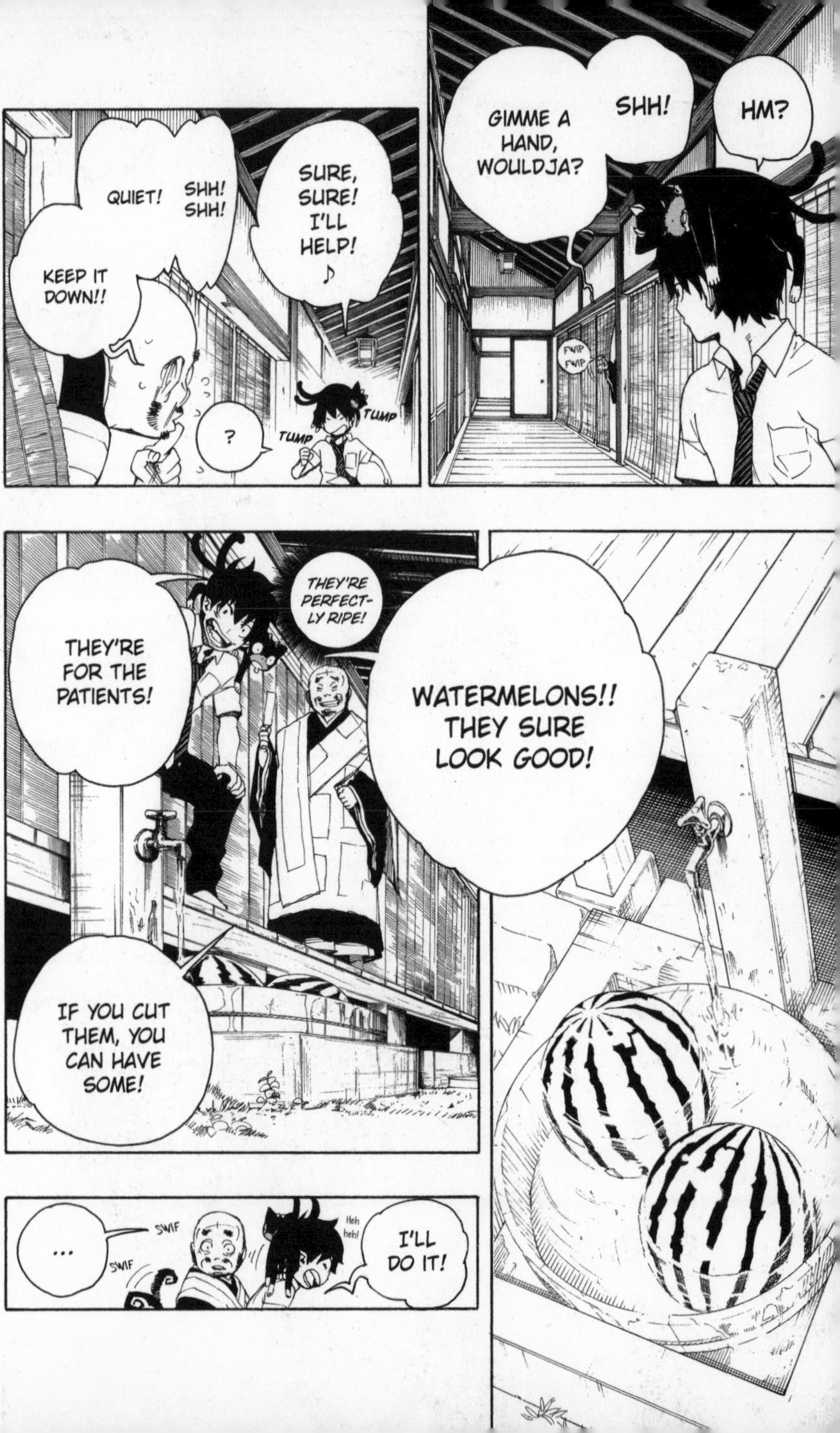
HM?
SHH!
GIMME A HAND, WOULDJA?
FWIP FWIP
SURE, SURE! I'LL HELP! ♪
SHH! SHH!
QUIET!
KEEP IT DOWN!!
TUMP
TUMP
?
WATERMELONS!! THEY SURE LOOK GOOD!
THEY'RE PERFECTLY RIPE!
THEY'RE FOR THE PATIENTS!
IF YOU CUT THEM, YOU CAN HAVE SOME!
I'LL DO IT!
Heh heh!
SWIF
SWIF
...

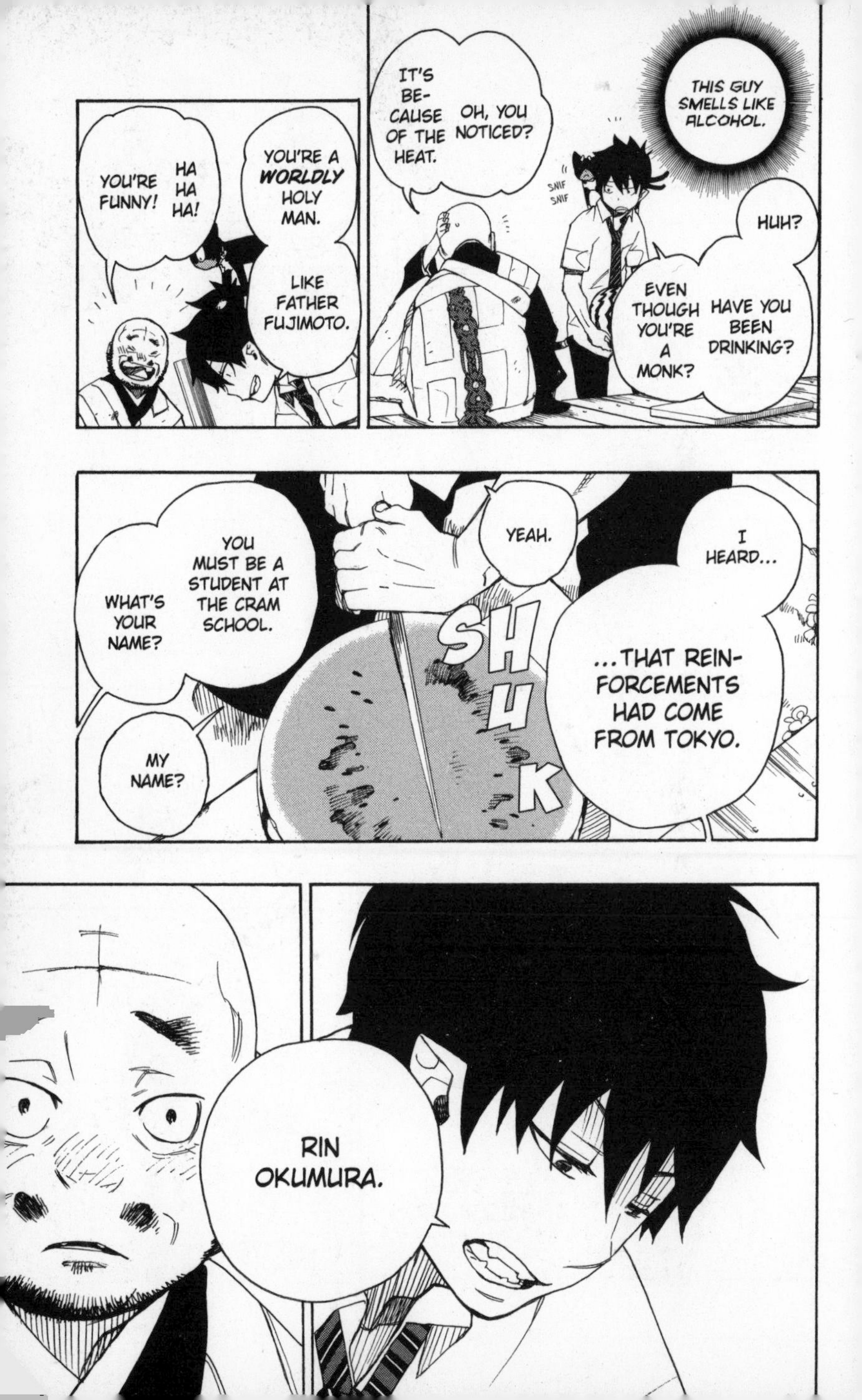
THIS GUY SMELLS LIKE ALCOHOL.
SNIF SNIF
HUH?
HAVE YOU BEEN DRINKING?
EVEN THOUGH YOU'RE A MONK?
OH, YOU NOTICED?
IT'S BE-CAUSE OF THE HEAT.
YOU'RE A *WORLDLY* HOLY MAN.
LIKE FATHER FUJIMOTO.
HA HA HA!
YOU'RE FUNNY!
I HEARD...
...THAT REIN-FORCEMENTS HAD COME FROM TOKYO.
YEAH.
SHUK
YOU MUST BE A STUDENT AT THE CRAM SCHOOL.
WHAT'S YOUR NAME?
MY NAME?
RIN OKUMURA.

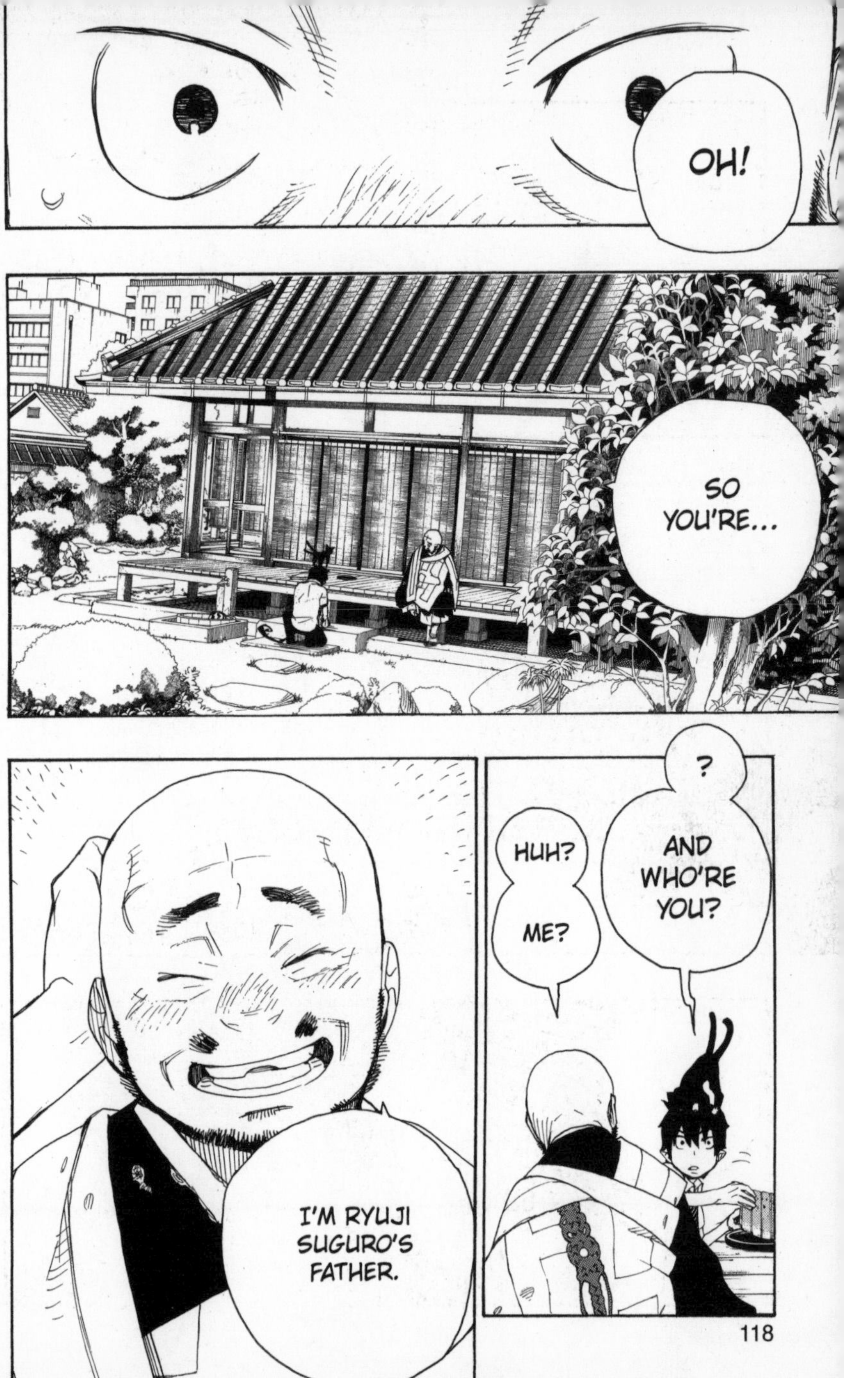
OH!
SO YOU'RE...
?
AND WHO'RE YOU?
HUH?
ME?
I'M RYUJI SUGURO'S FATHER.

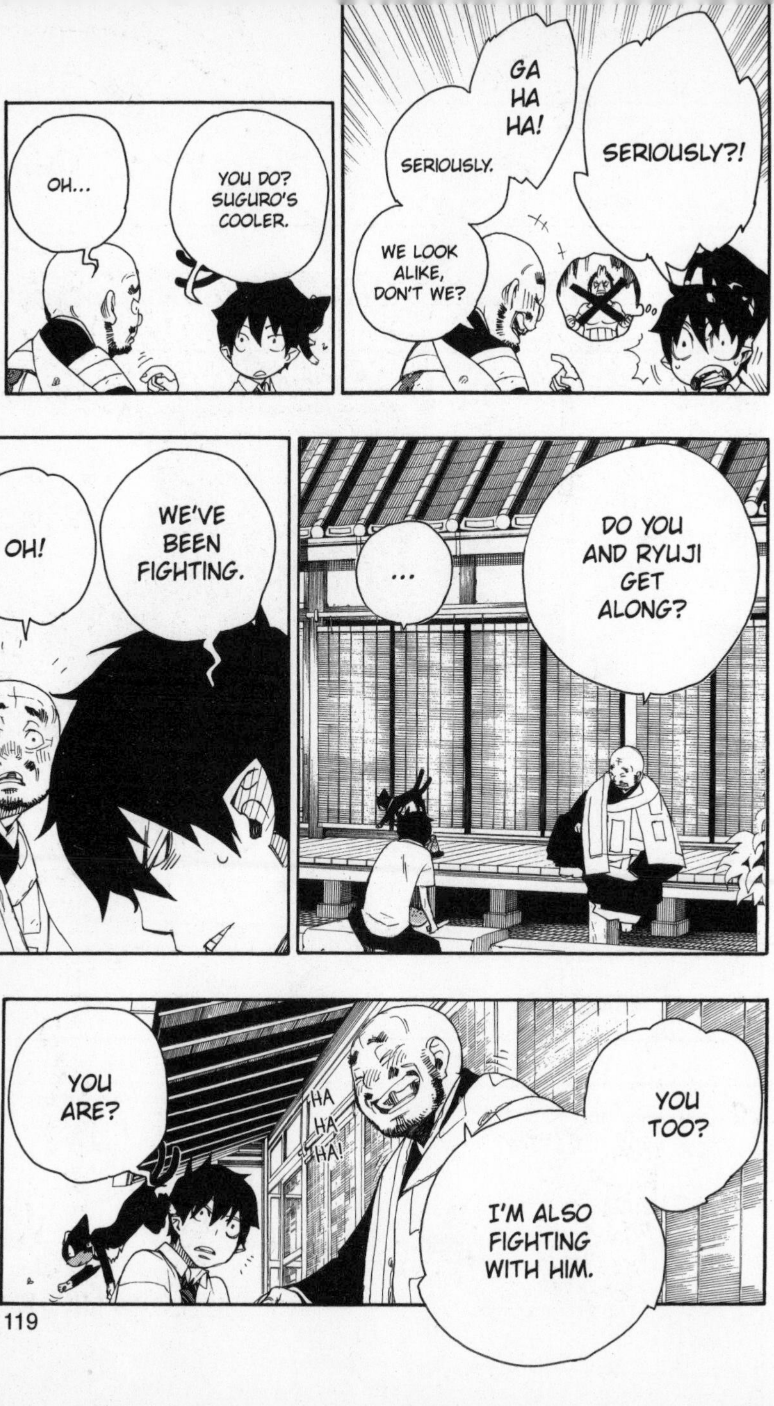
SERIOUSLY?!
GA HA HA!
SERIOUSLY.
WE LOOK ALIKE, DON'T WE?
YOU DO? SUGURO'S COOLER.
OH...
DO YOU AND RYUJI GET ALONG?
...
WE'VE BEEN FIGHTING.
OH!
YOU TOO?
I'M ALSO FIGHTING WITH HIM.
HA HA HA!
YOU ARE?

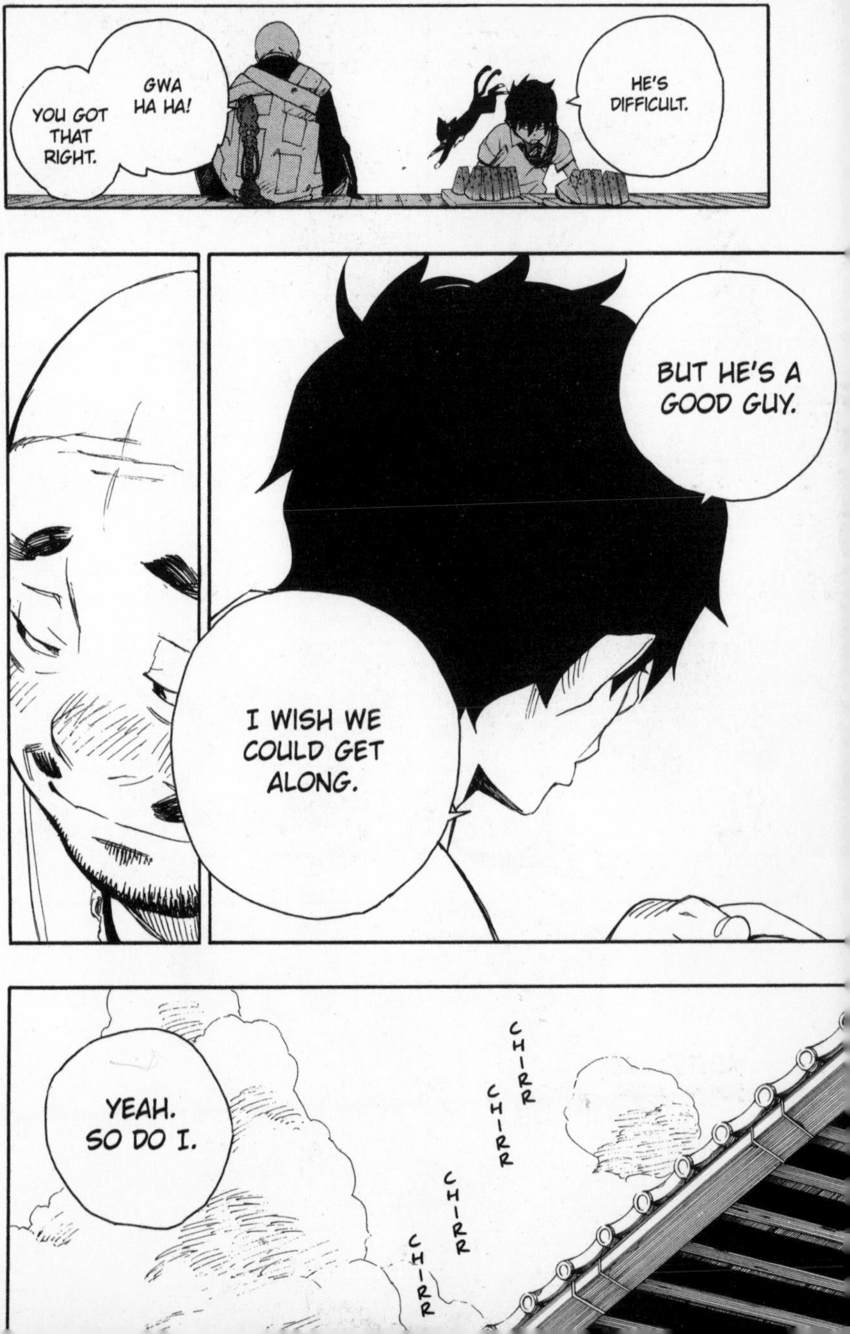
HE'S DIFFICULT.
GWA HA HA!
YOU GOT THAT RIGHT.
BUT HE'S A GOOD GUY.
I WISH WE COULD GET ALONG.
CHIRR
CHIRR
CHIRR
CHIRR
YEAH. SO DO I.

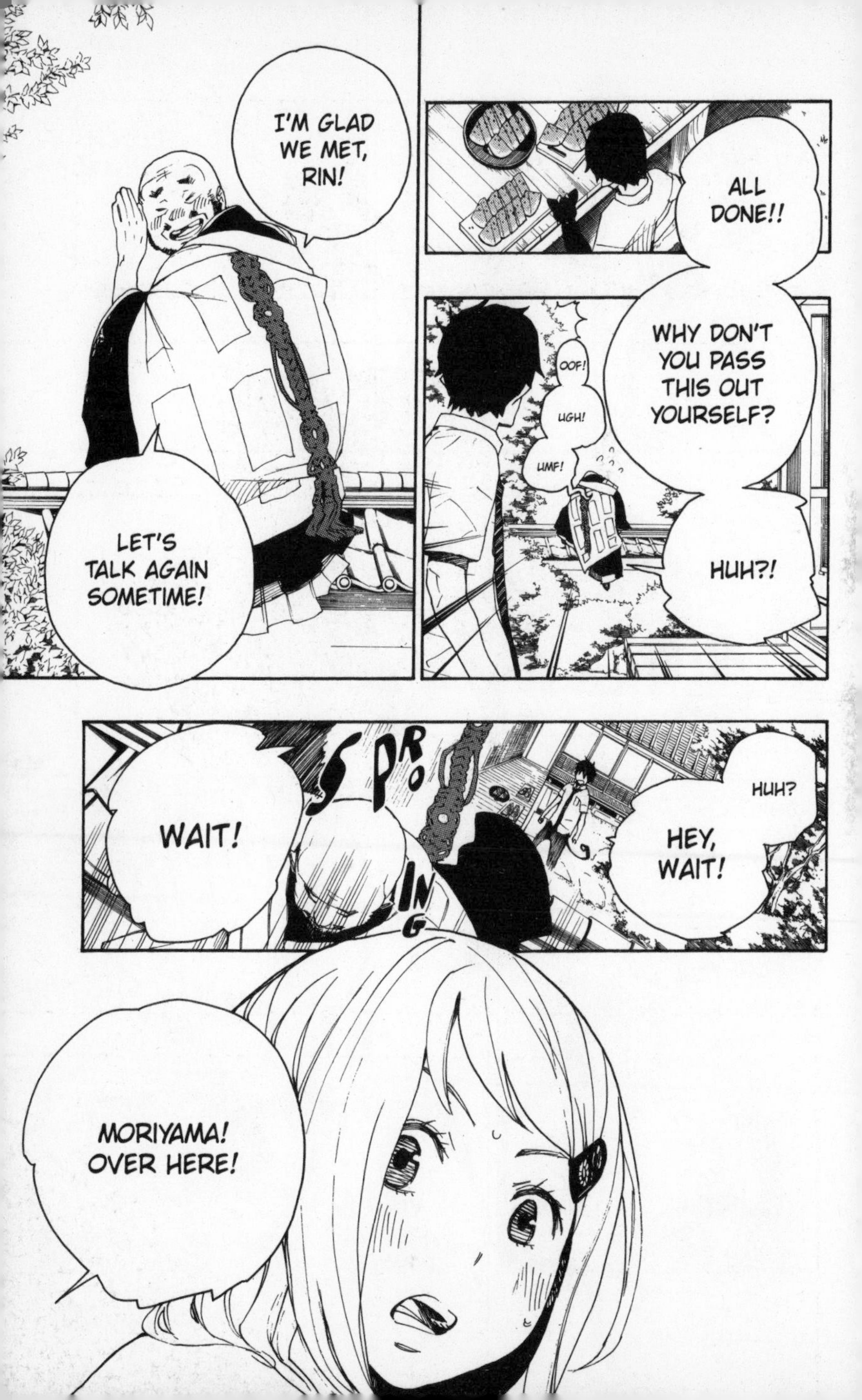

ALL DONE!!
WHY DON'T YOU PASS THIS OUT YOURSELF?
OOF!
UGH!
UMF!
HUH?!
I'M GLAD WE MET, RIN!
LET'S TALK AGAIN SOMETIME!
HUH?
HEY, WAIT!
SPROING
WAIT!
MORIYAMA! OVER HERE!

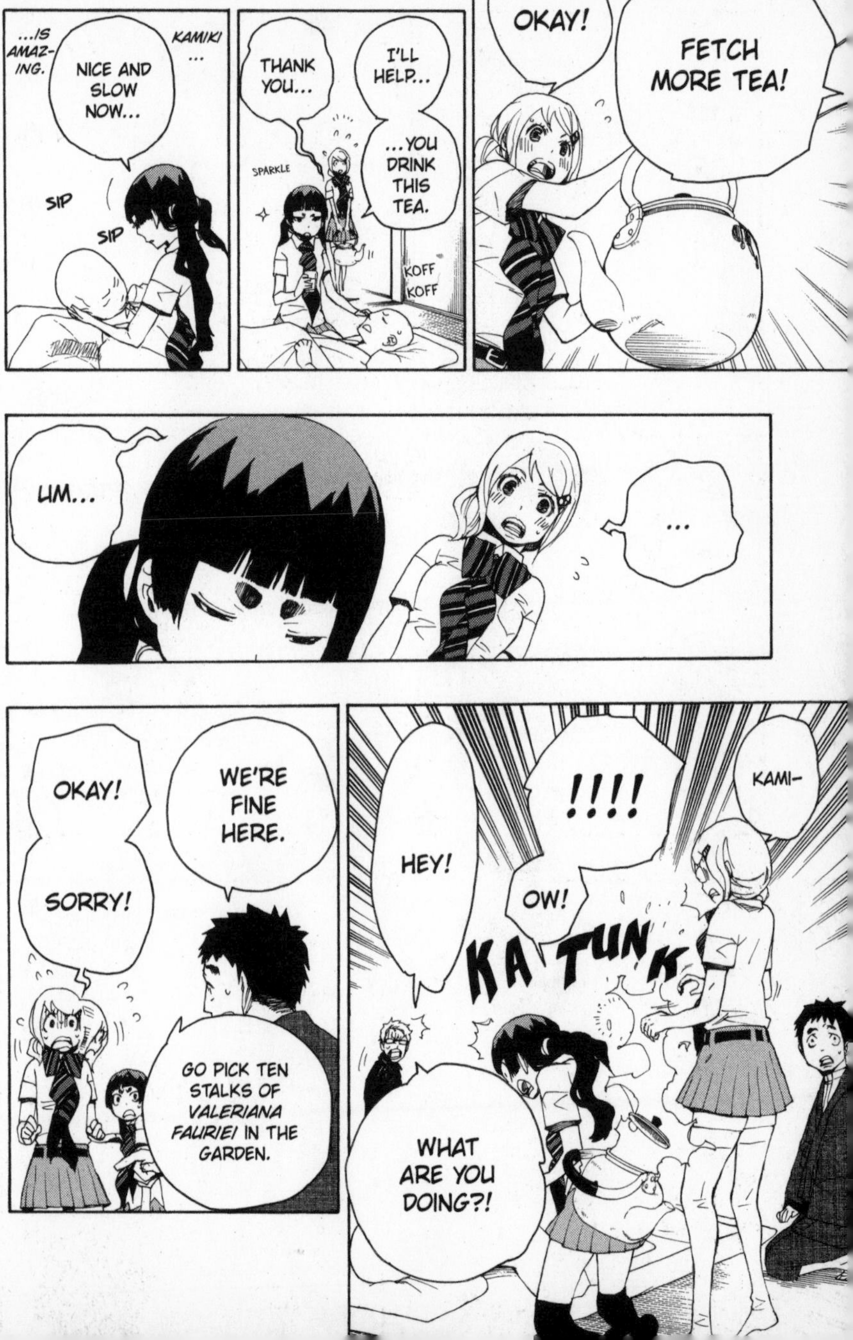
FETCH MORE TEA!
OKAY!
I'LL HELP...
...YOU DRINK THIS TEA.
THANK YOU...
SPARKLE
KOFF KOFF
KAMIKI...
NICE AND SLOW NOW...
...IS AMAZ-ING.
SIP
SIP
...
UM...
KAMI-
!!!!
OW!
HEY!
KA TUNK
WHAT ARE YOU DOING?!
WE'RE FINE HERE.
OKAY!
SORRY!
GO PICK TEN STALKS OF VALERIANA FAURIEI IN THE GARDEN.

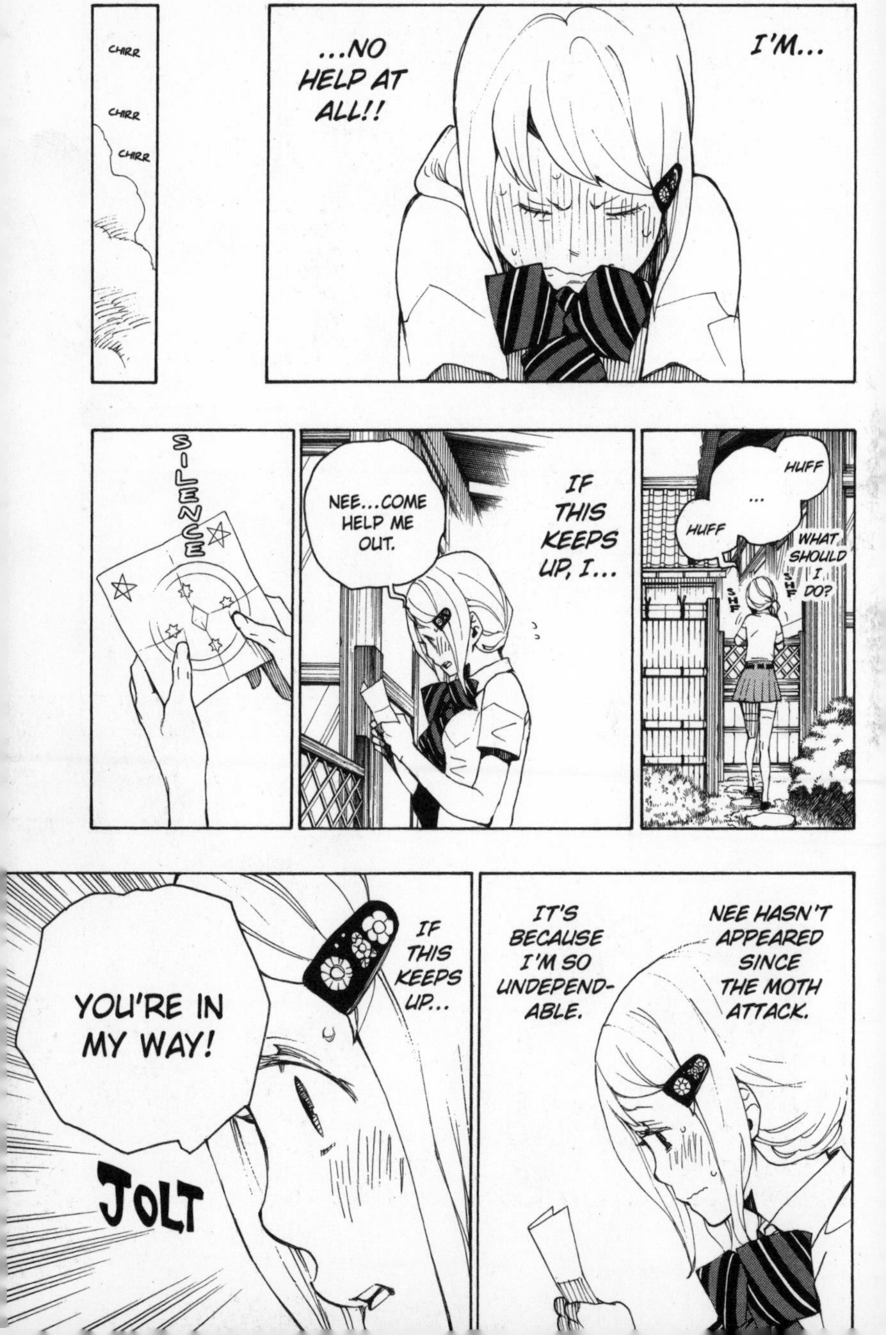
I'M...
...NO HELP AT ALL!!
CHIRR
CHIRR
CHIRR
HUFF
...
WHAT SHOULD I DO?
SHF
HUFF
SHF
IF THIS KEEPS UP, I...
NEE...COME HELP ME OUT.
SILENCE
NEE HASN'T APPEARED SINCE THE MOTH ATTACK.
IT'S BECAUSE I'M SO UNDEPEND-ABLE.
IF THIS KEEPS UP...
YOU'RE IN MY WAY!
JOLT

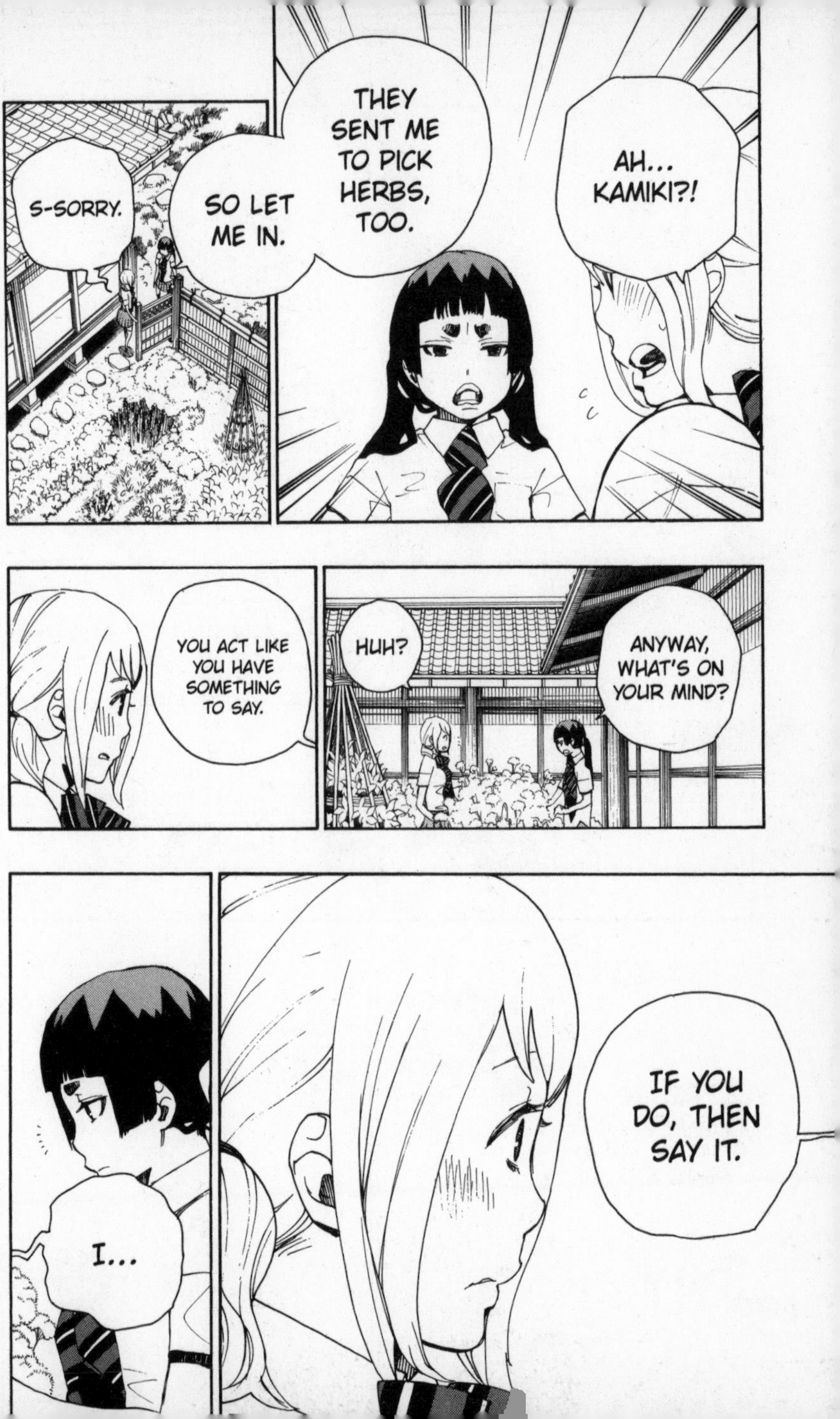
AH... KAMIKI?!
THEY SENT ME TO PICK HERBS, TOO.
SO LET ME IN.
S-SORRY.
ANYWAY, WHAT'S ON YOUR MIND?
HUH?
YOU ACT LIKE YOU HAVE SOMETHING TO SAY.
IF YOU DO, THEN SAY IT.
I...

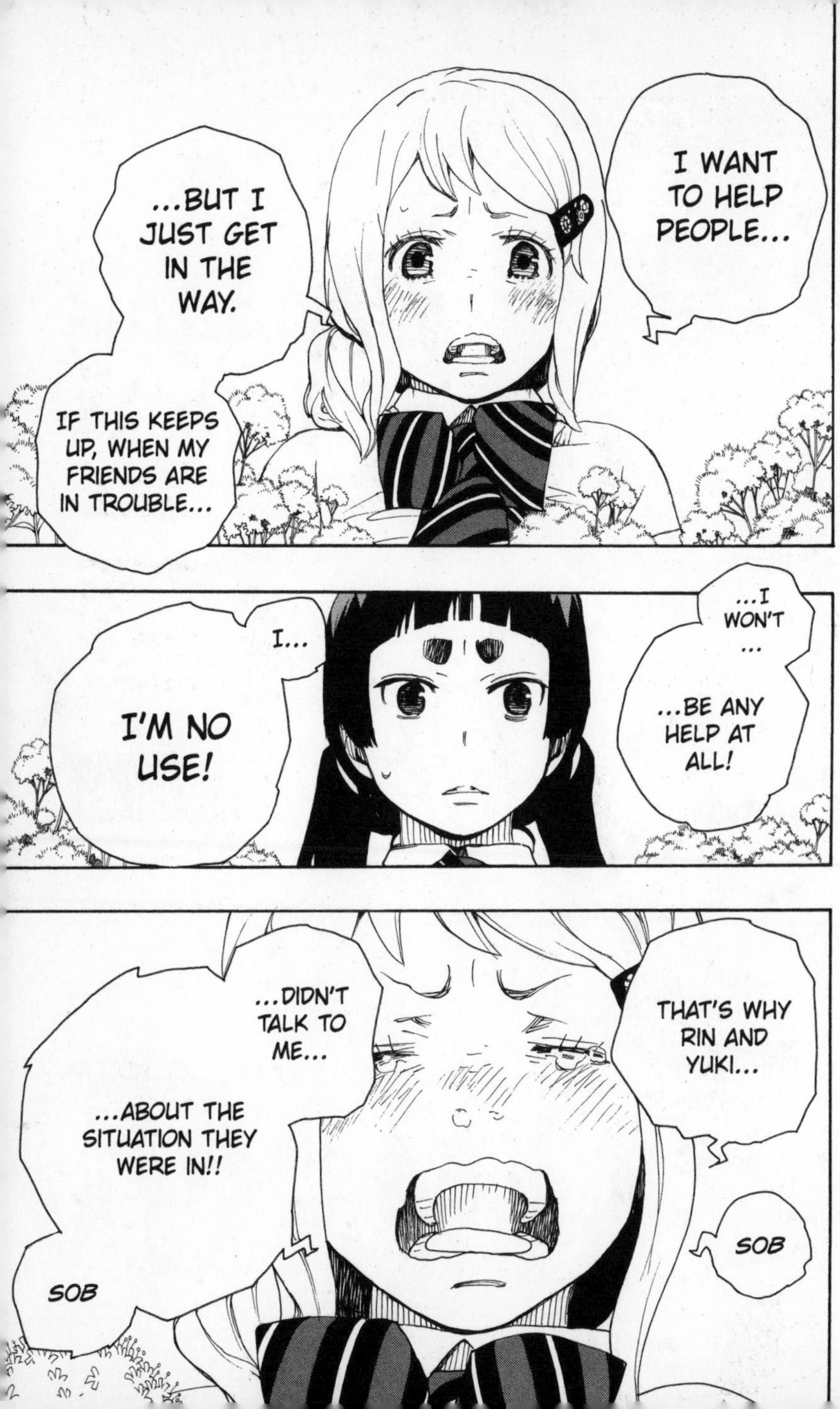
I WANT TO HELP PEOPLE...
...BUT I JUST GET IN THE WAY.
IF THIS KEEPS UP, WHEN MY FRIENDS ARE IN TROUBLE...
...I WON'T ...
...BE ANY HELP AT ALL!
I...
I'M NO USE!
THAT'S WHY RIN AND YUKI...
...DIDN'T TALK TO ME...
...ABOUT THE SITUATION THEY WERE IN!!
SOB
SOB

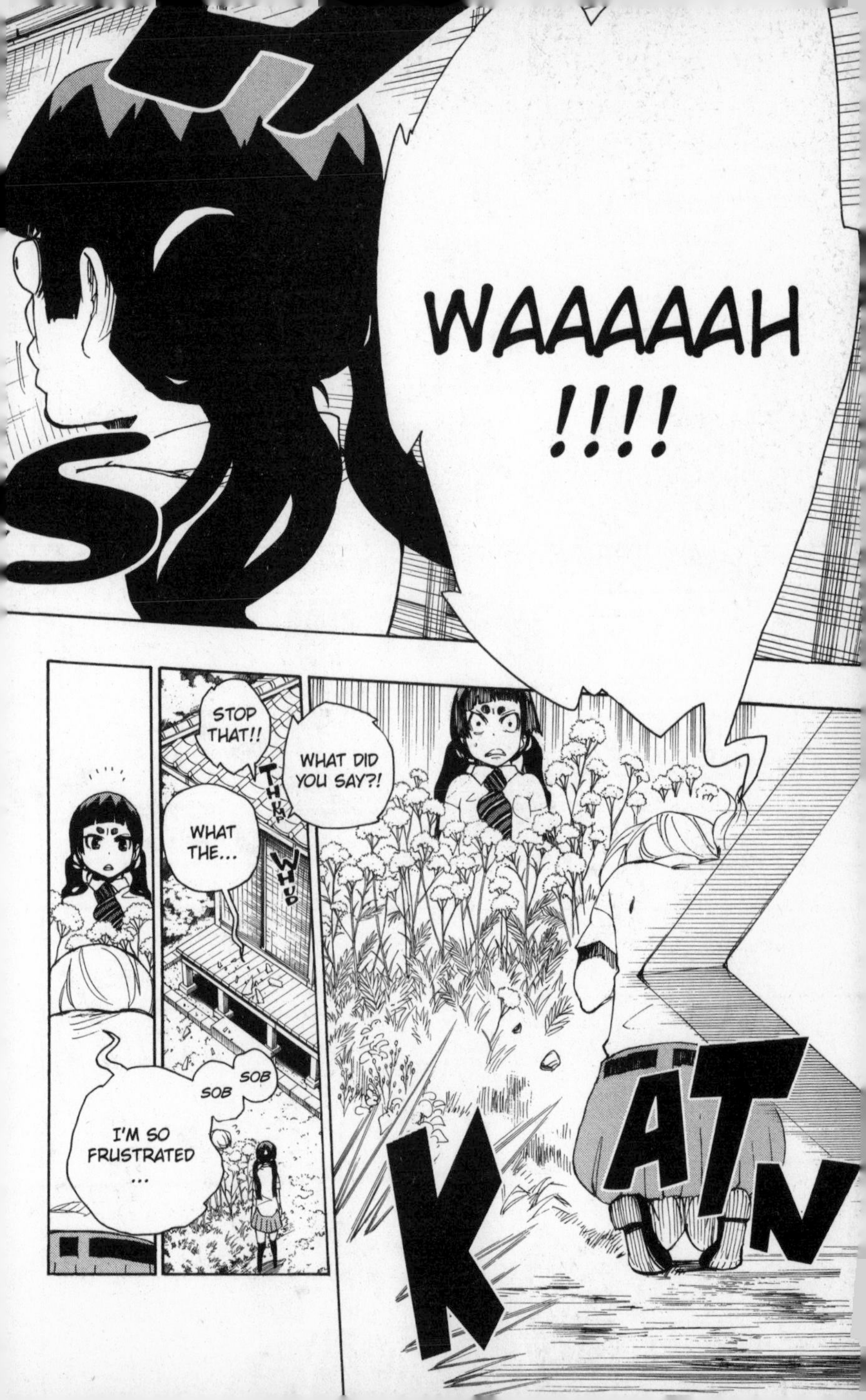
WAAAAAH !!!!
KATN
WHAT DID YOU SAY?!
STOP THAT!!
THUMP
WHAT THE...
WHUD
SOB SOB
I'M SO FRUSTRATED ...

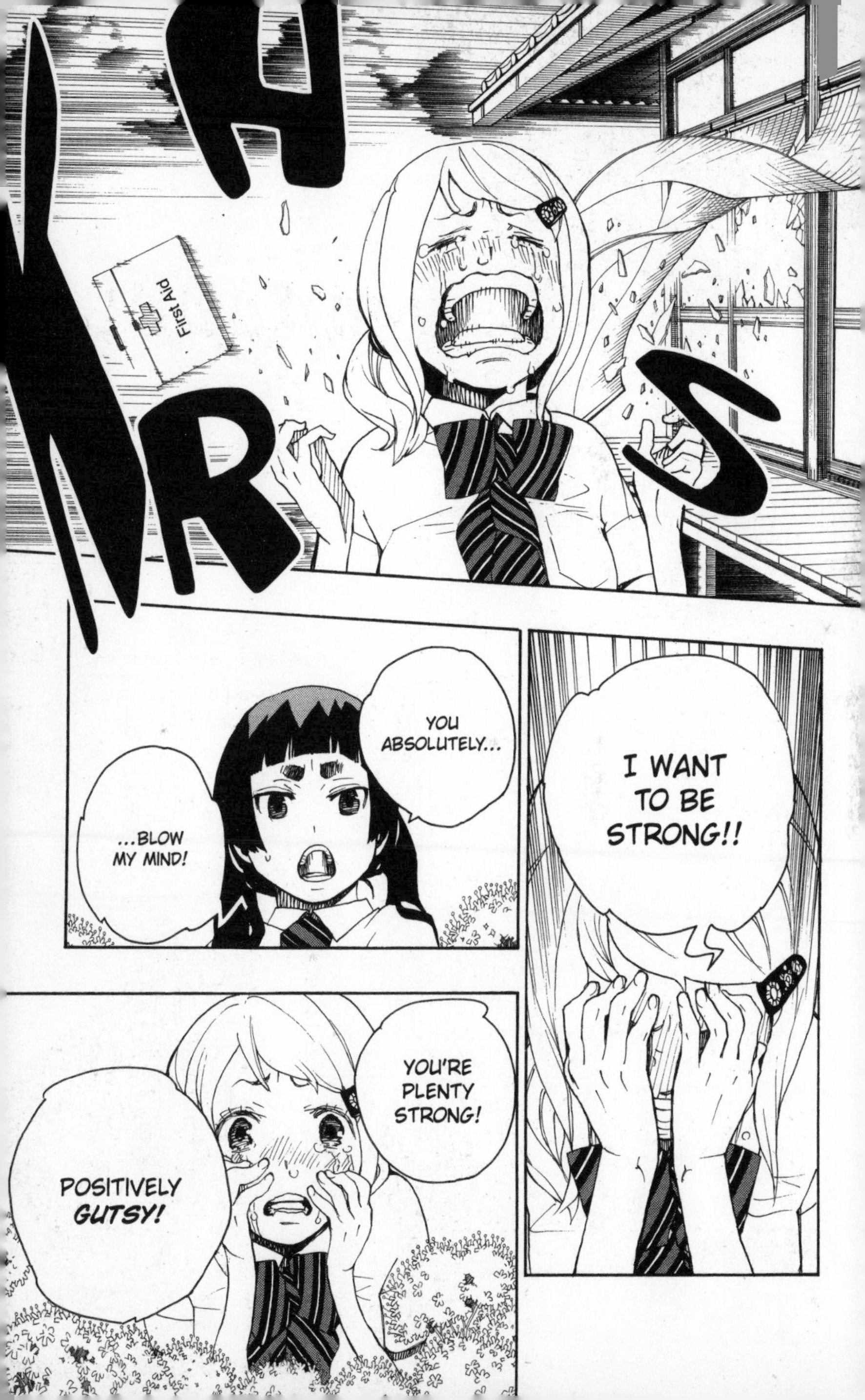
First Aid
I WANT TO BE STRONG!!
YOU ABSOLUTELY...
...BLOW MY MIND!
YOU'RE PLENTY STRONG!
POSITIVELY *GUTSY!*

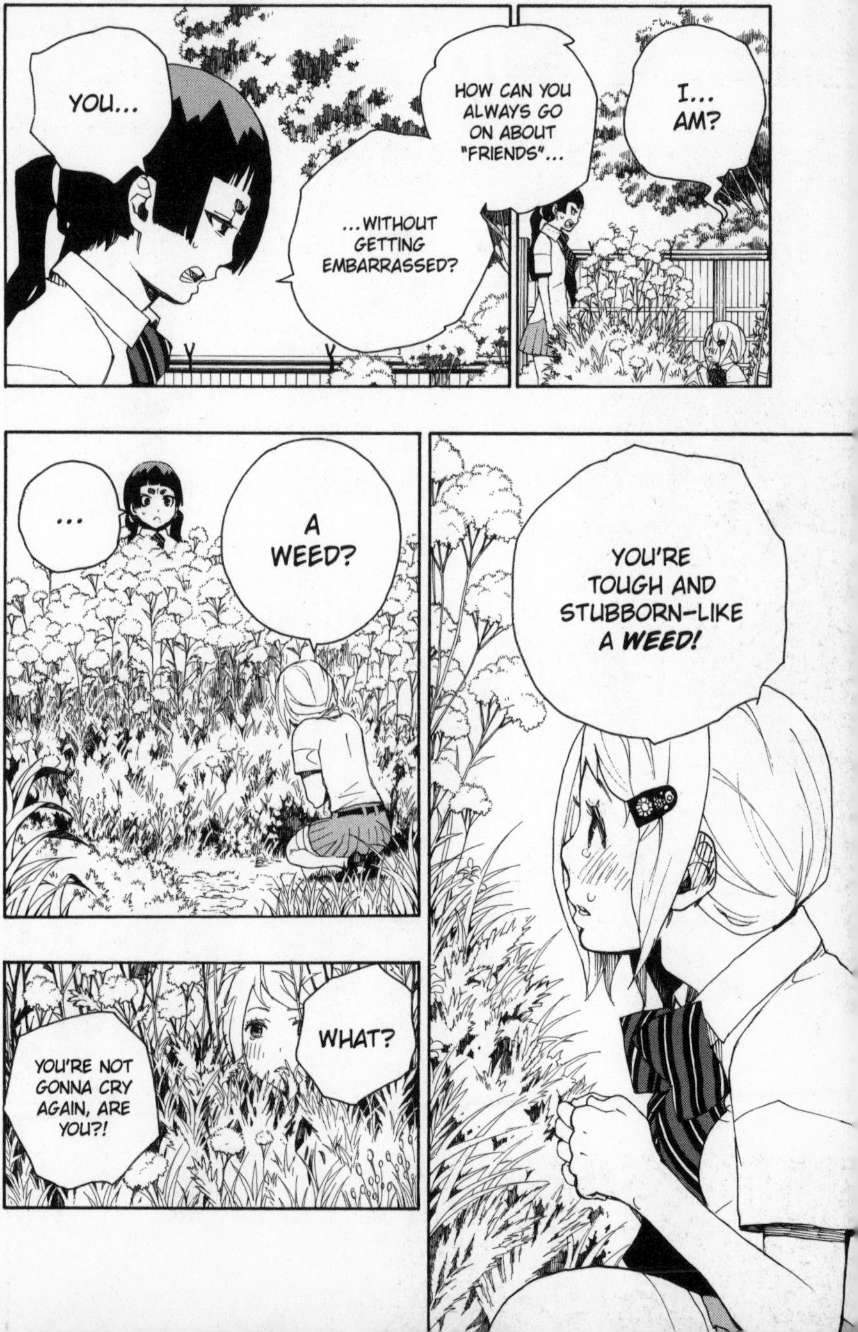
I... AM?
YOU...
HOW CAN YOU ALWAYS GO ON ABOUT "FRIENDS"...
...WITHOUT GETTING EMBARRASSED?
YOU'RE TOUGH AND STUBBORN-LIKE A *WEED!*
A WEED?
...
WHAT?
YOU'RE NOT GONNA CRY AGAIN, ARE YOU?!

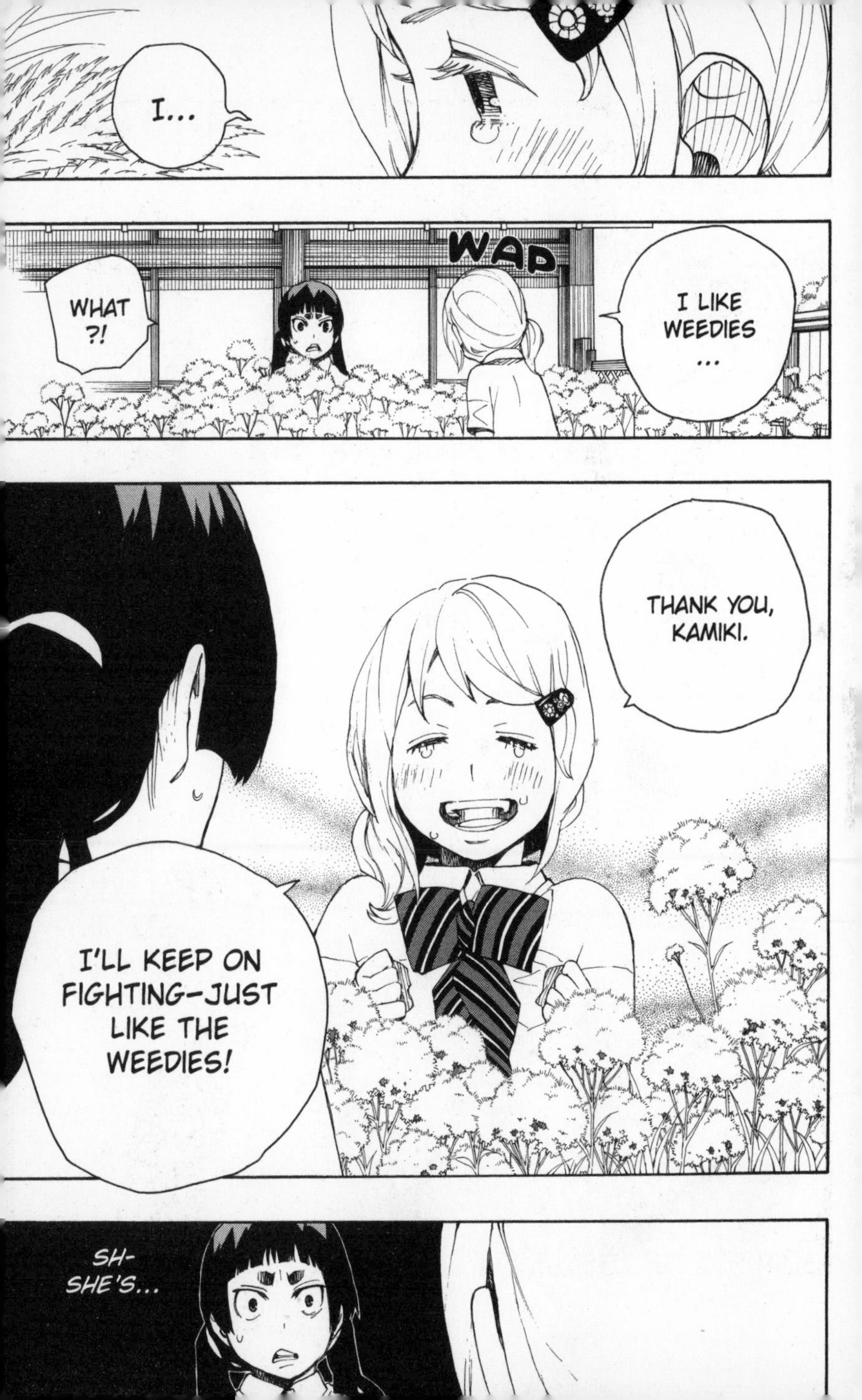
I...
WAP
I LIKE WEEDIES ...
WHAT ?!
THANK YOU, KAMIKI.
I'LL KEEP ON FIGHTING—JUST LIKE THE WEEDIES!
SH- SHE'S...

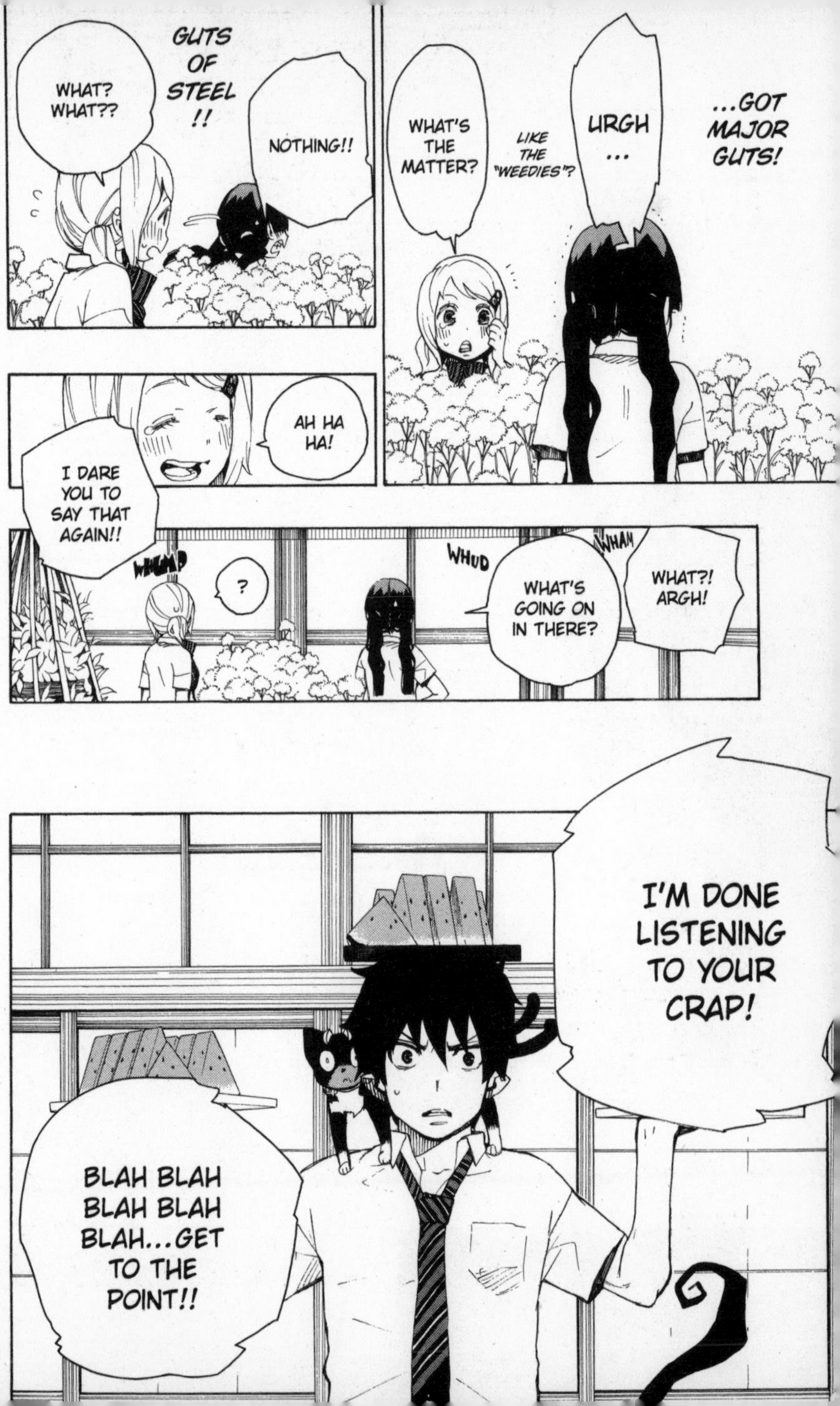
...GOT MAJOR GUTS!
URGH ...
LIKE THE "WEEDIES"?
WHAT'S THE MATTER?
NOTHING!!
GUTS OF STEEL!!
WHAT? WHAT??
AH HA HA!
I DARE YOU TO SAY THAT AGAIN!!
WHAT?! ARGH!
WHAM
WHAT'S GOING ON IN THERE?
WHUD
?
I'M DONE LISTENING TO YOUR CRAP!
BLAH BLAH BLAH BLAH BLAH...GET TO THE POINT!!

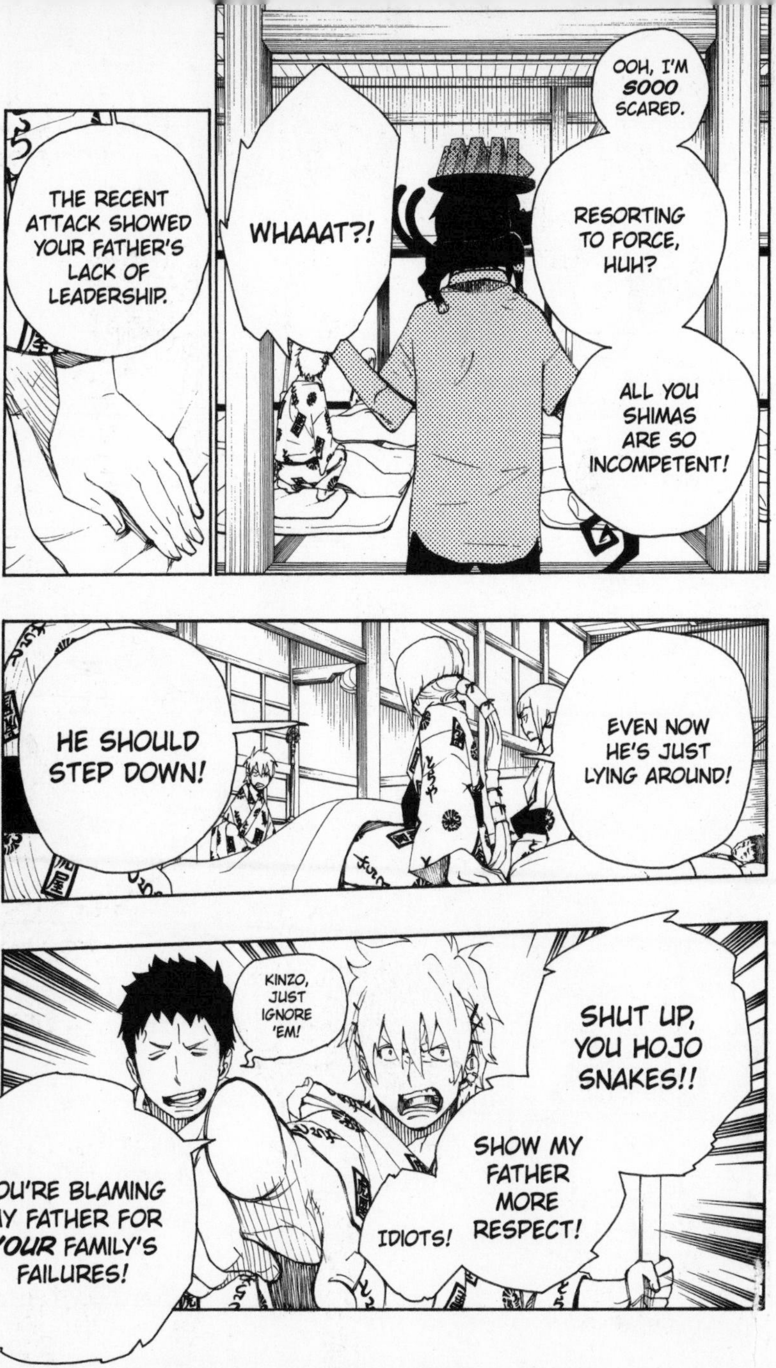
OOH, I'M SOOO SCARED.
RESORTING TO FORCE, HUH?
ALL YOU SHIMAS ARE SO INCOMPETENT!
WHAAAT?!
THE RECENT ATTACK SHOWED YOUR FATHER'S LACK OF LEADERSHIP.
EVEN NOW HE'S JUST LYING AROUND!
HE SHOULD STEP DOWN!
SHUT UP, YOU HOJO SNAKES!!
KINZO, JUST IGNORE 'EM!
SHOW MY FATHER MORE RESPECT!
IDIOTS!
YOU'RE BLAMING MY FATHER FOR YOUR FAMILY'S FAILURES!

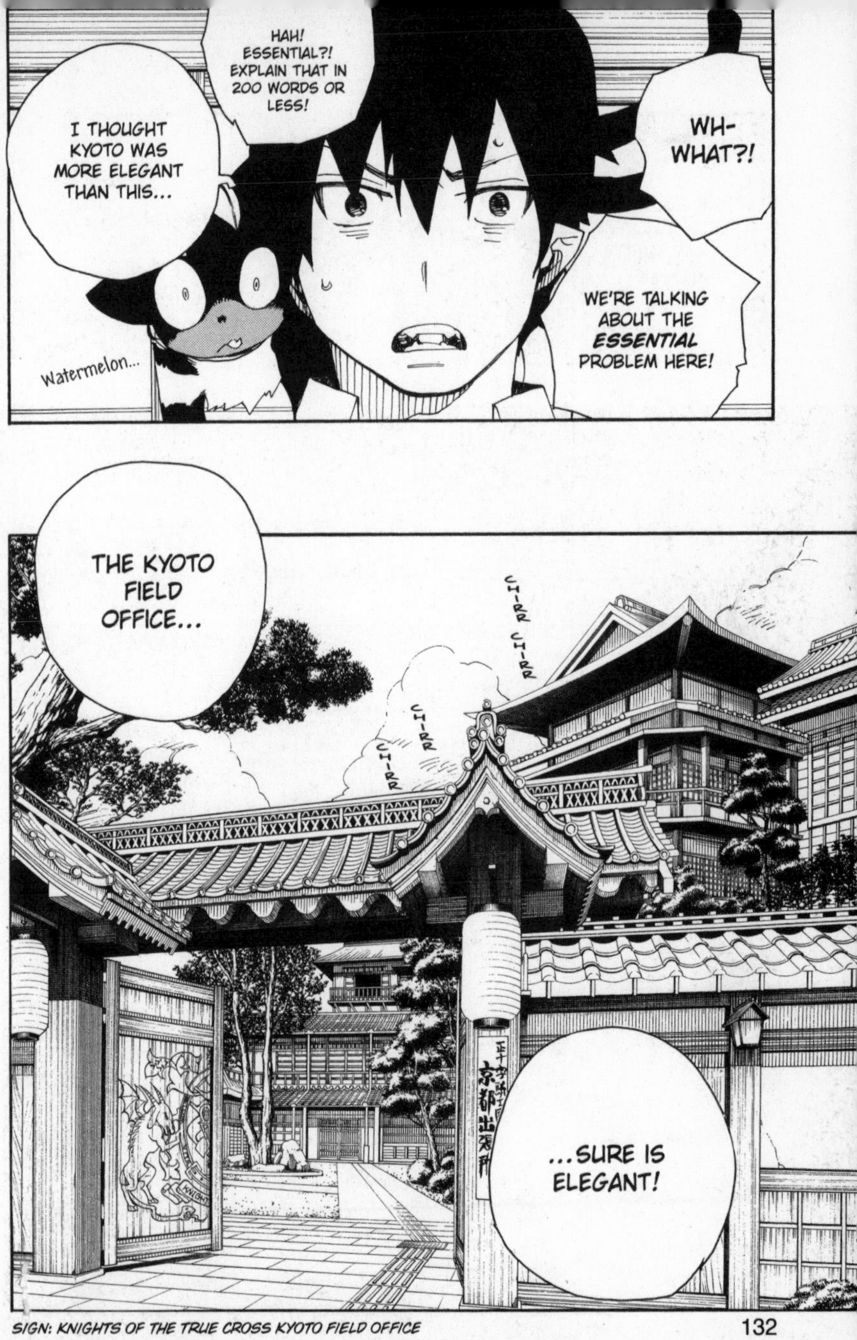
WH- WHAT?!
HAH! ESSENTIAL?! EXPLAIN THAT IN 200 WORDS OR LESS!
WE'RE TALKING ABOUT THE ESSENTIAL PROBLEM HERE!
I THOUGHT KYOTO WAS MORE ELEGANT THAN THIS...
Watermelon...
THE KYOTO FIELD OFFICE...
CHIRR CHIRR
CHIRR CHIRR
...SURE IS ELEGANT!

SIGN: KNIGHTS OF THE TRUE CROSS KYOTO FIELD OFFICE

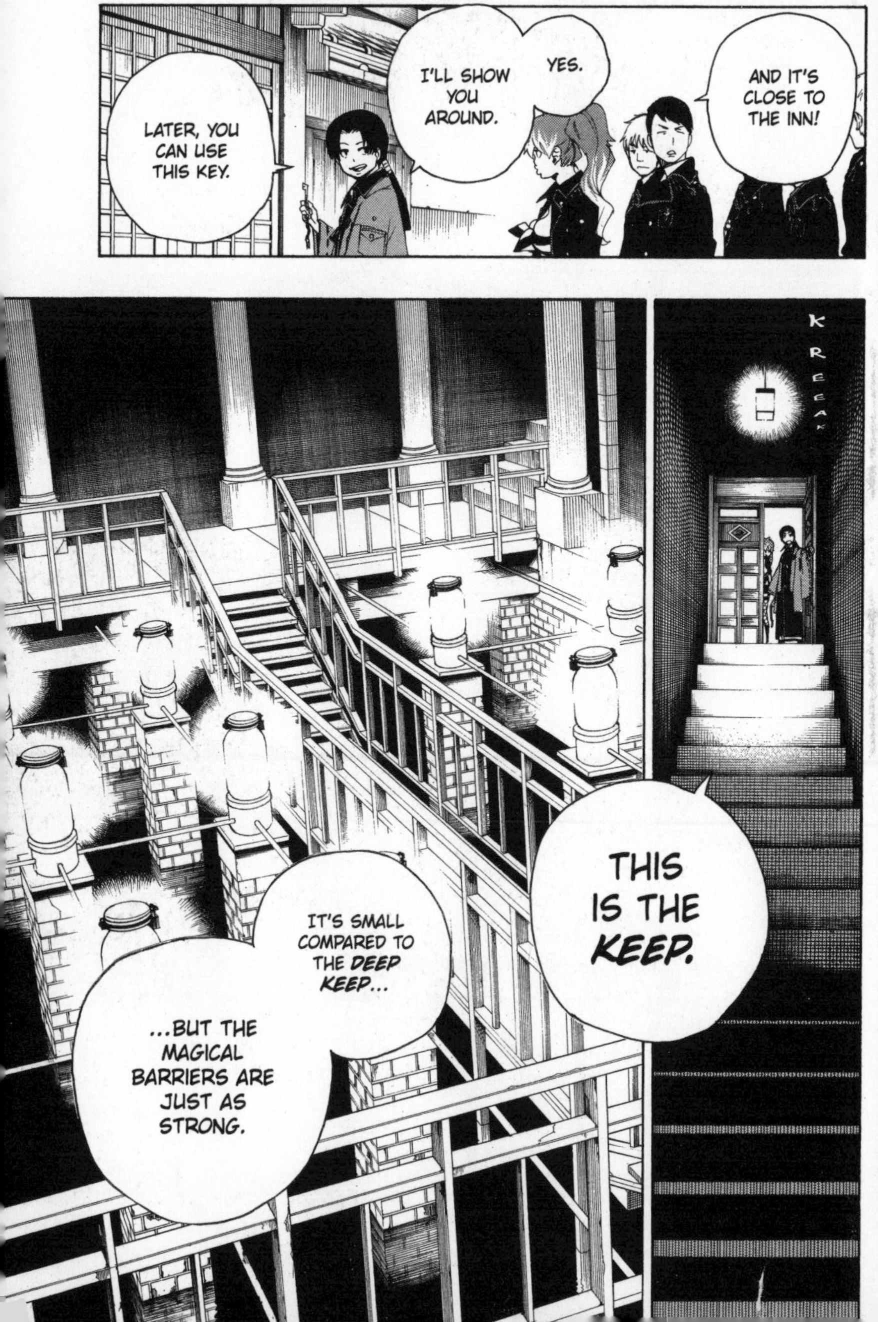
AND IT'S CLOSE TO THE INN!
YES.
I'LL SHOW YOU AROUND.
LATER, YOU CAN USE THIS KEY.
KREEAK
THIS IS THE *KEEP.*
IT'S SMALL COMPARED TO THE *DEEP KEEP*...
...BUT THE MAGICAL BARRIERS ARE JUST AS STRONG.

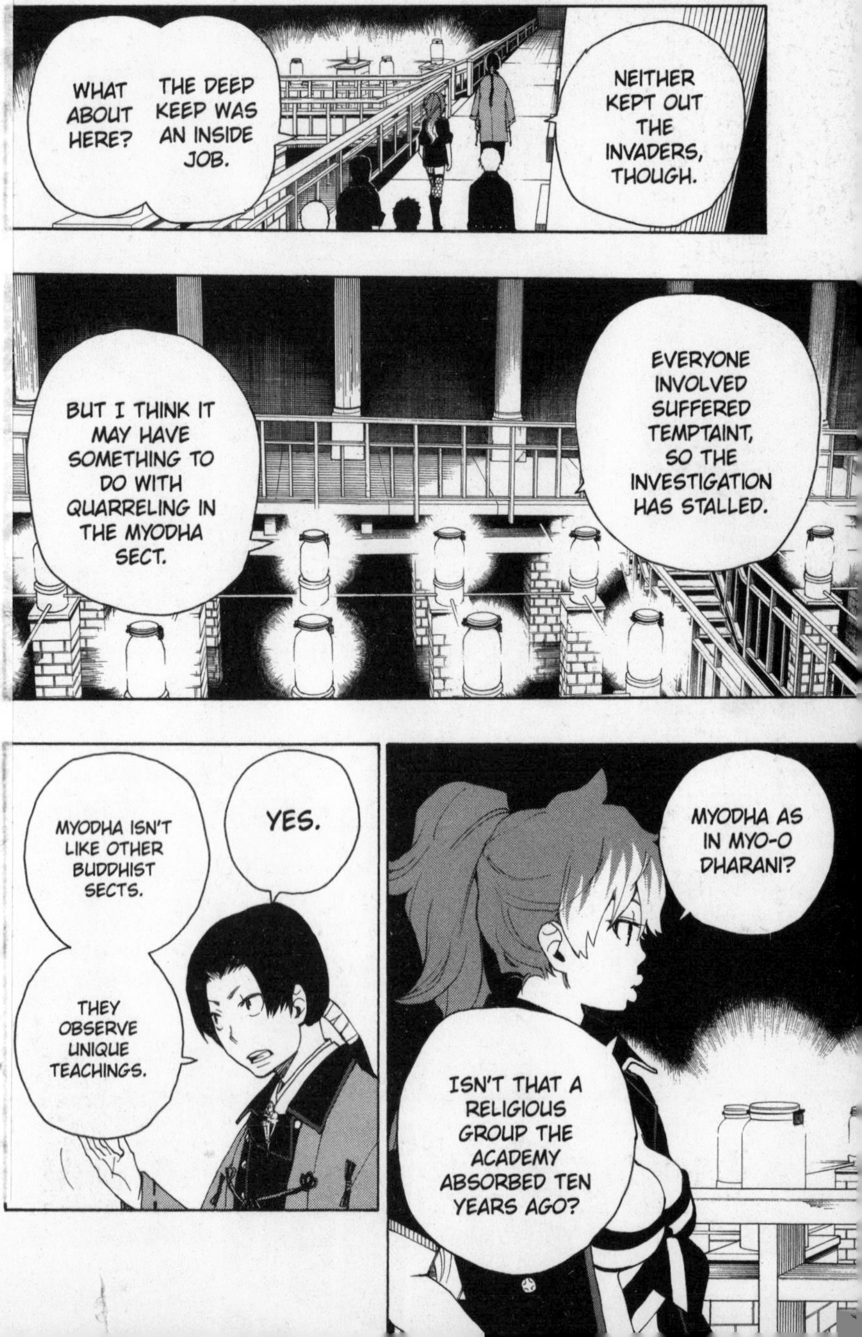
NEITHER KEPT OUT THE INVADERS, THOUGH.
THE DEEP KEEP WAS AN INSIDE JOB.
WHAT ABOUT HERE?
EVERYONE INVOLVED SUFFERED TEMPTAINT, SO THE INVESTIGATION HAS STALLED.
BUT I THINK IT MAY HAVE SOMETHING TO DO WITH QUARRELING IN THE MYODHA SECT.
MYODHA AS IN MYO-O DHARANI?
ISN'T THAT A RELIGIOUS GROUP THE ACADEMY ABSORBED TEN YEARS AGO?
YES.
MYODHA ISN'T LIKE OTHER BUDDHIST SECTS.
THEY OBSERVE UNIQUE TEACHINGS.

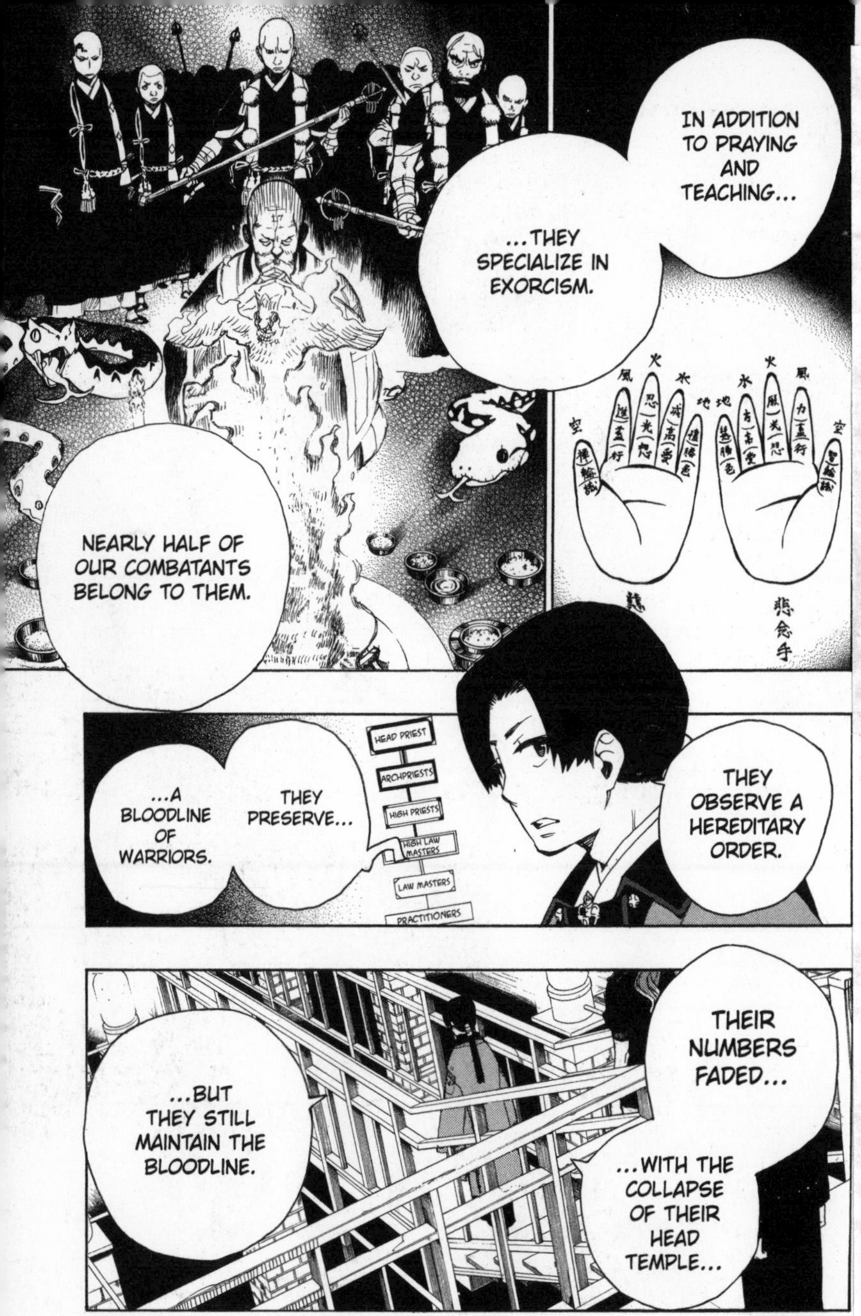
IN ADDITION TO PRAYING AND TEACHING...
...THEY SPECIALIZE IN EXORCISM.
NEARLY HALF OF OUR COMBATANTS BELONG TO THEM.
THEY OBSERVE A HEREDITARY ORDER.
THEY PRESERVE...
...A BLOODLINE OF WARRIORS.
HEAD PRIEST
ARCHPRIESTS
HIGH PRIESTS
HIGH LAW MASTERS
LAW MASTERS
PRACTITIONERS
THEIR NUMBERS FADED...
...WITH THE COLLAPSE OF THEIR HEAD TEMPLE...
...BUT THEY STILL MAINTAIN THE BLOODLINE.

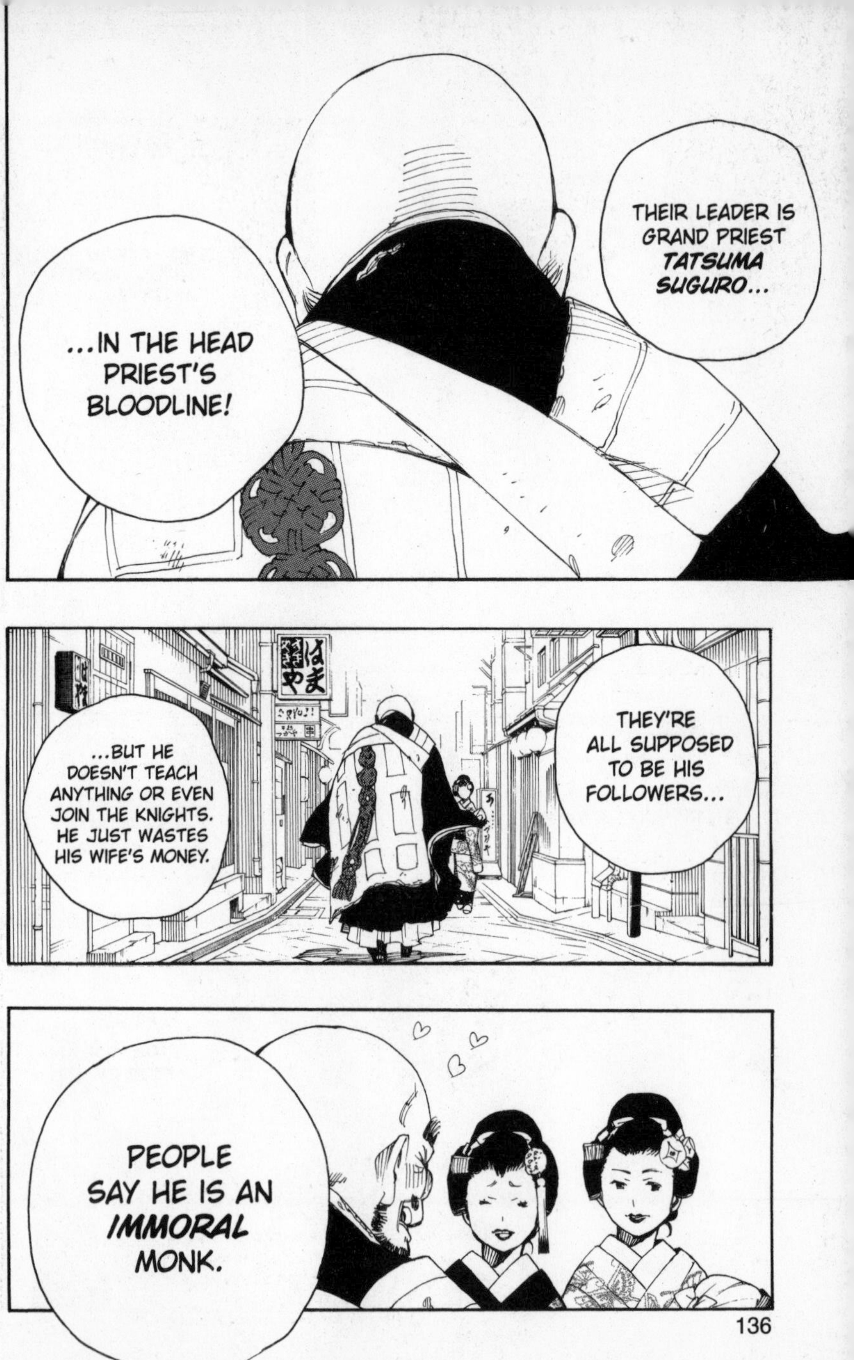
THEIR LEADER IS GRAND PRIEST *TATSUMA SUGURO*...
...IN THE HEAD PRIEST'S BLOODLINE!
THEY'RE ALL SUPPOSED TO BE HIS FOLLOWERS...
...BUT HE DOESN'T TEACH ANYTHING OR EVEN JOIN THE KNIGHTS. HE JUST WASTES HIS WIFE'S MONEY.
PEOPLE SAY HE IS AN *IMMORAL* MONK.

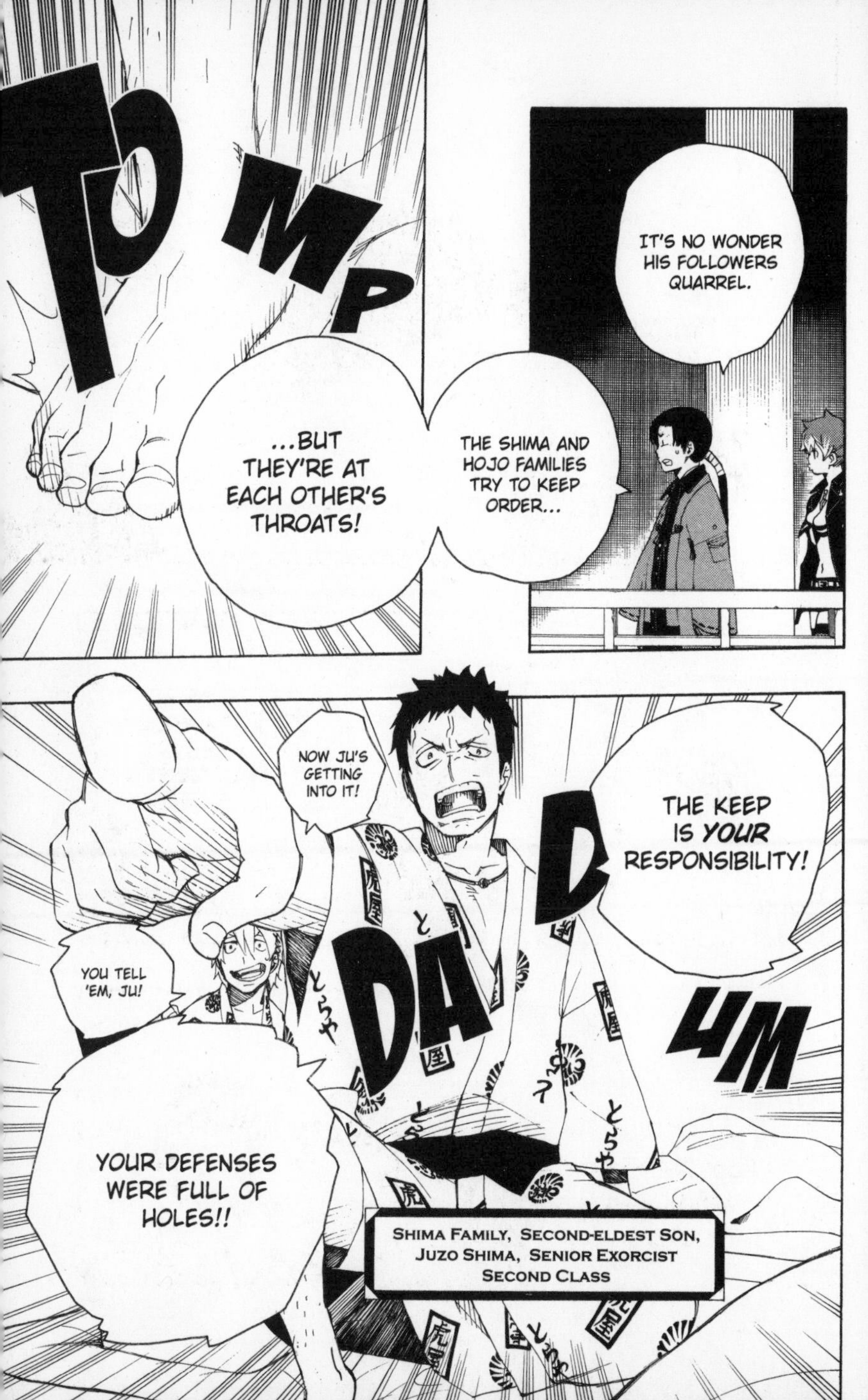
IT'S NO WONDER HIS FOLLOWERS QUARREL.
THE SHIMA AND HOJO FAMILIES TRY TO KEEP ORDER...
...BUT THEY'RE AT EACH OTHER'S THROATS!
TOMP
THE KEEP IS *YOUR* RESPONSIBILITY!
DADUM
NOW JU'S GETTING INTO IT!
SHIMA FAMILY, SECOND-ELDEST SON, JUZO SHIMA, SENIOR EXORCIST SECOND CLASS
YOU TELL 'EM, JU!
YOUR DEFENSES WERE FULL OF HOLES!!

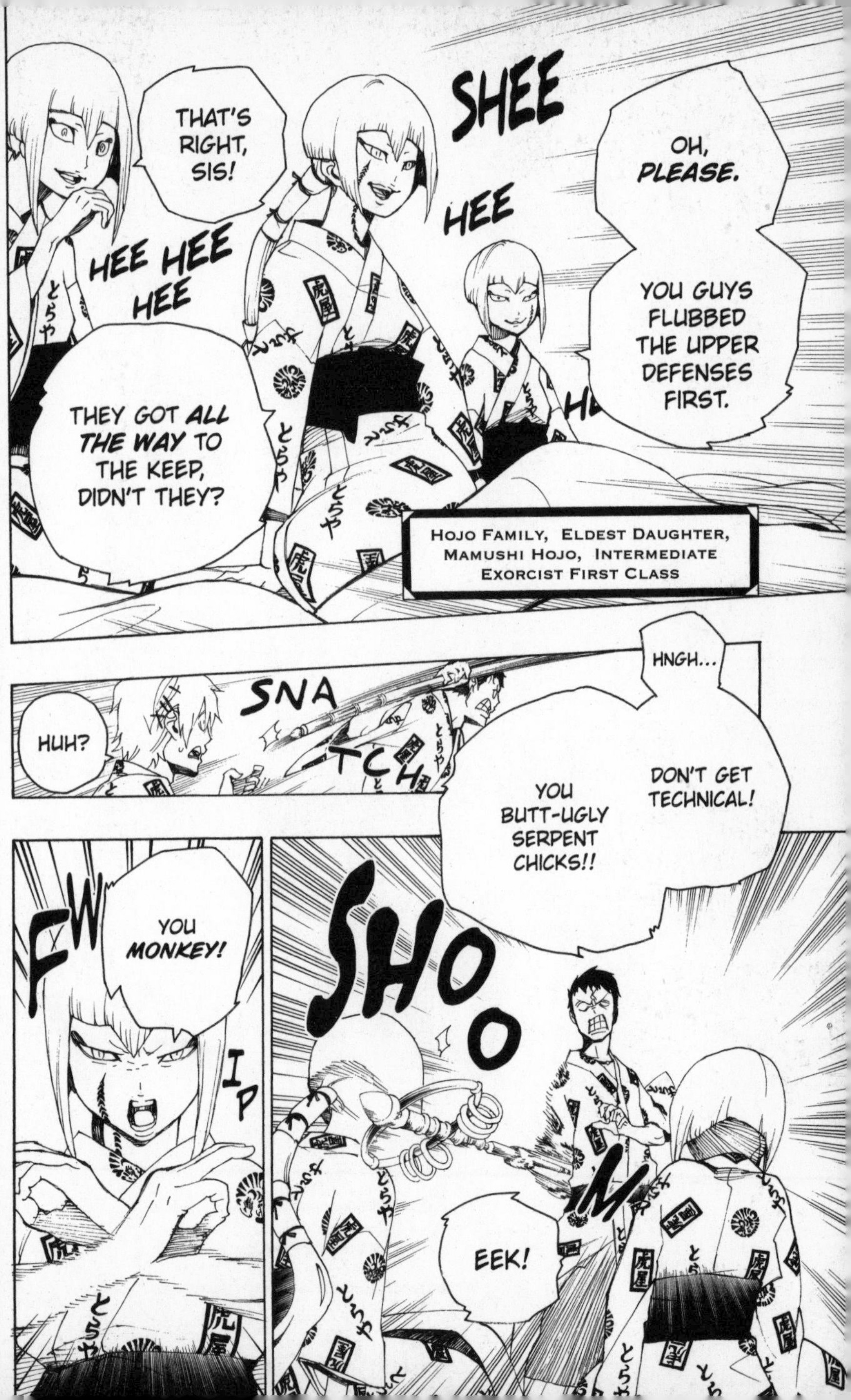

SHEE
OH, PLEASE.
YOU GUYS FLUBBED THE UPPER DEFENSES FIRST.
HEE
THAT'S RIGHT, SIS!
HEE HEE HEE
THEY GOT ALL THE WAY TO THE KEEP, DIDN'T THEY?
HOJO FAMILY, ELDEST DAUGHTER, MAMUSHI HOJO, INTERMEDIATE EXORCIST FIRST CLASS
HNGH...
SNATCH
HUH?
DON'T GET TECHNICAL!
YOU BUTT-UGLY SERPENT CHICKS!!
SHOOM
EEK!
FWIP
YOU MONKEY!

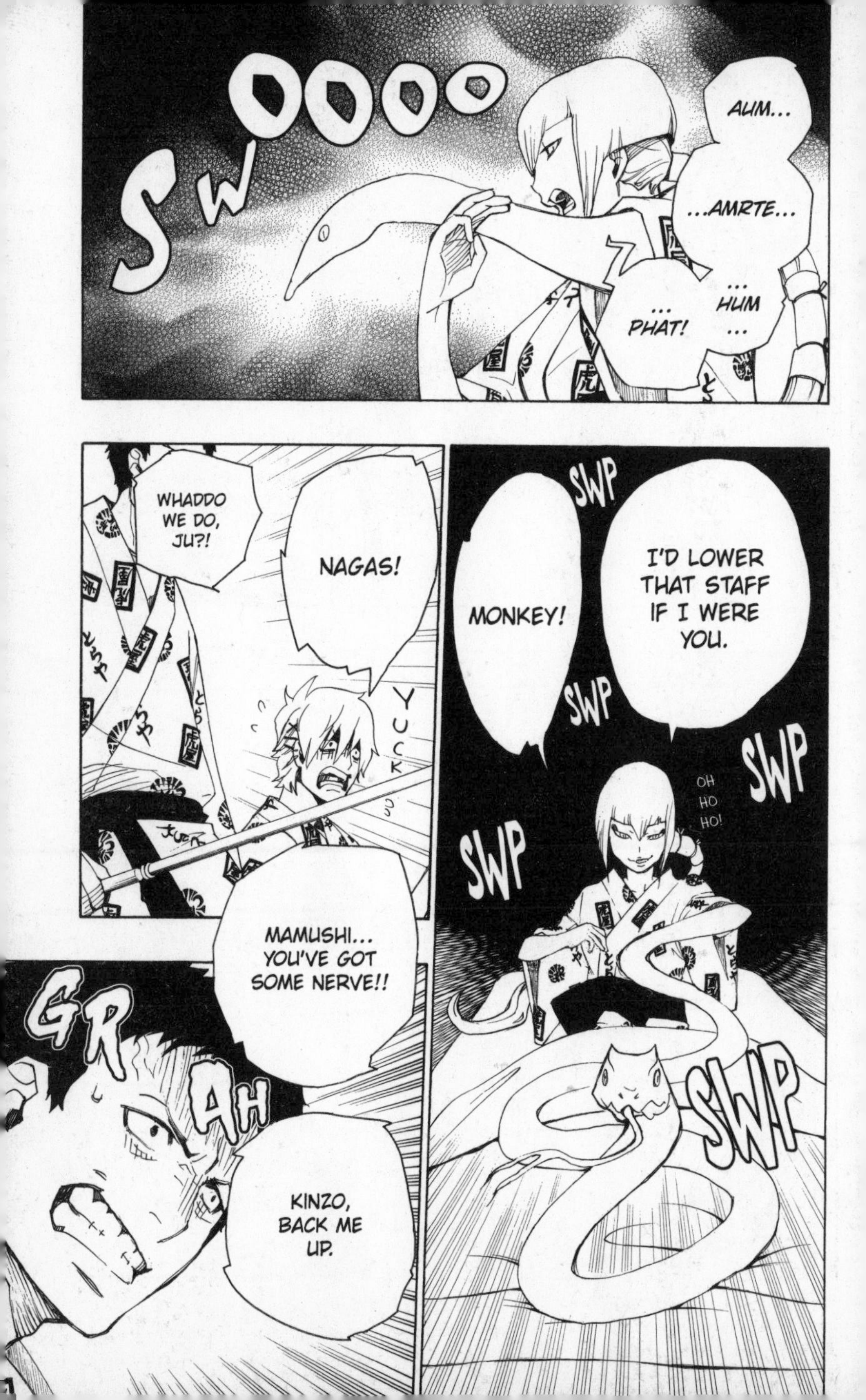
AUM...
...AMRTE...
...HUM...
PHÄT!
SWOOOO
I'D LOWER THAT STAFF IF I WERE YOU.
MONKEY!
SWP
SWP
SWP
SWP
OH HO HO!
SWP
NAGAS!
WHADDO WE DO, JU?!
YUCK
MAMUSHI... YOU'VE GOT SOME NERVE!!
GRAH
KINZO, BACK ME UP.

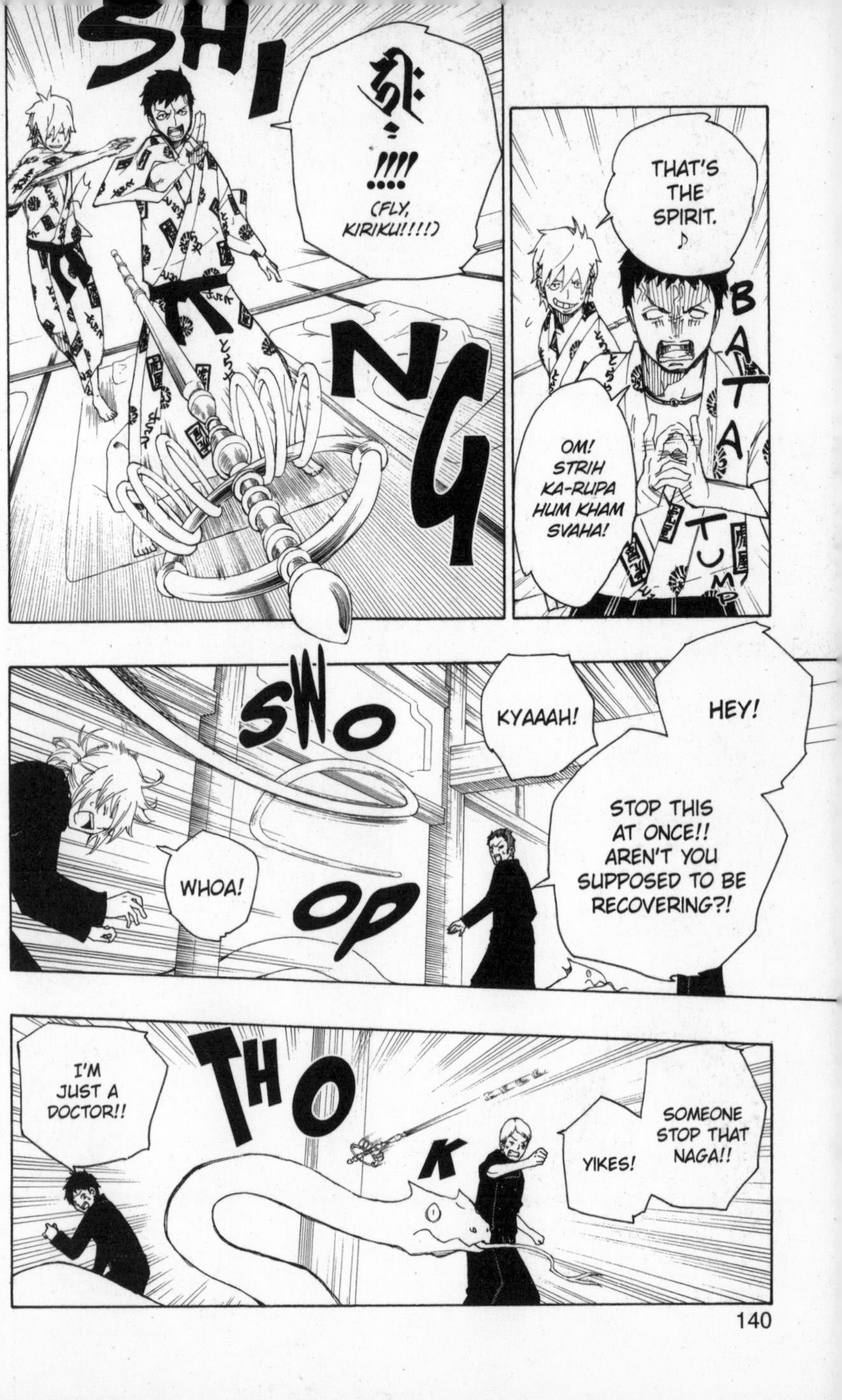
THAT'S THE SPIRIT. ♪
BATA
OM! STRIH KA-RUPA HUM KHAM SVAHA!
TUMP
SHI
!!!!
(FLY, KIRIKU!!!!)
NNG
HEY!
STOP THIS AT ONCE!! AREN'T YOU SUPPOSED TO BE RECOVERING?!
KYAAAH!
SWOOP
WHOA!
SOMEONE STOP THAT NAGA!!
YIKES!
THOK
I'M JUST A DOCTOR!!

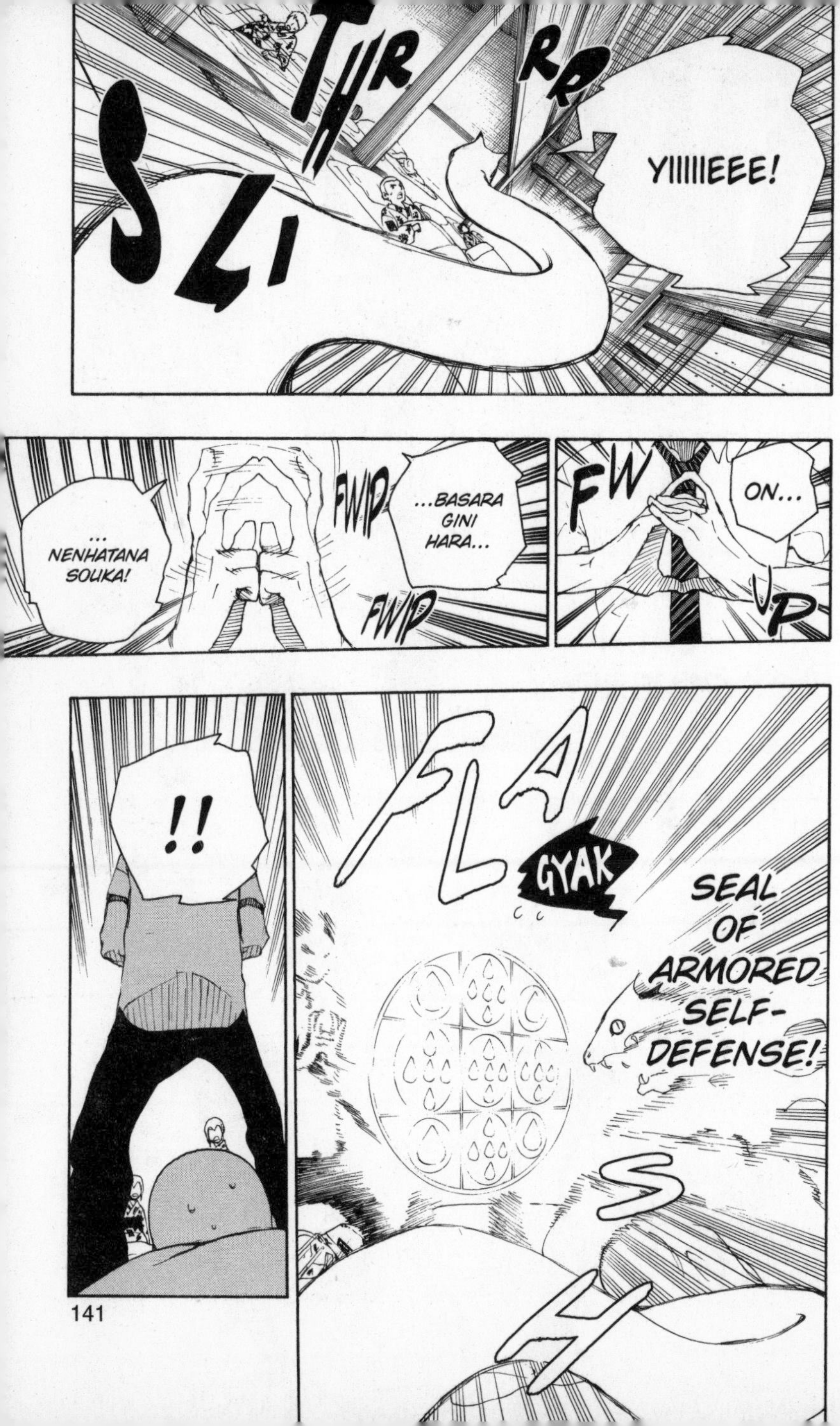
SLITHRR
YIIIIIEEE!
FW
ON...
UP
FWIP
...BASARA GINI HARA...
FWIP
... NENHATANA SOUKA!
FLA
GYAK
SEAL OF ARMORED SELF-DEFENSE!
S
H
!!

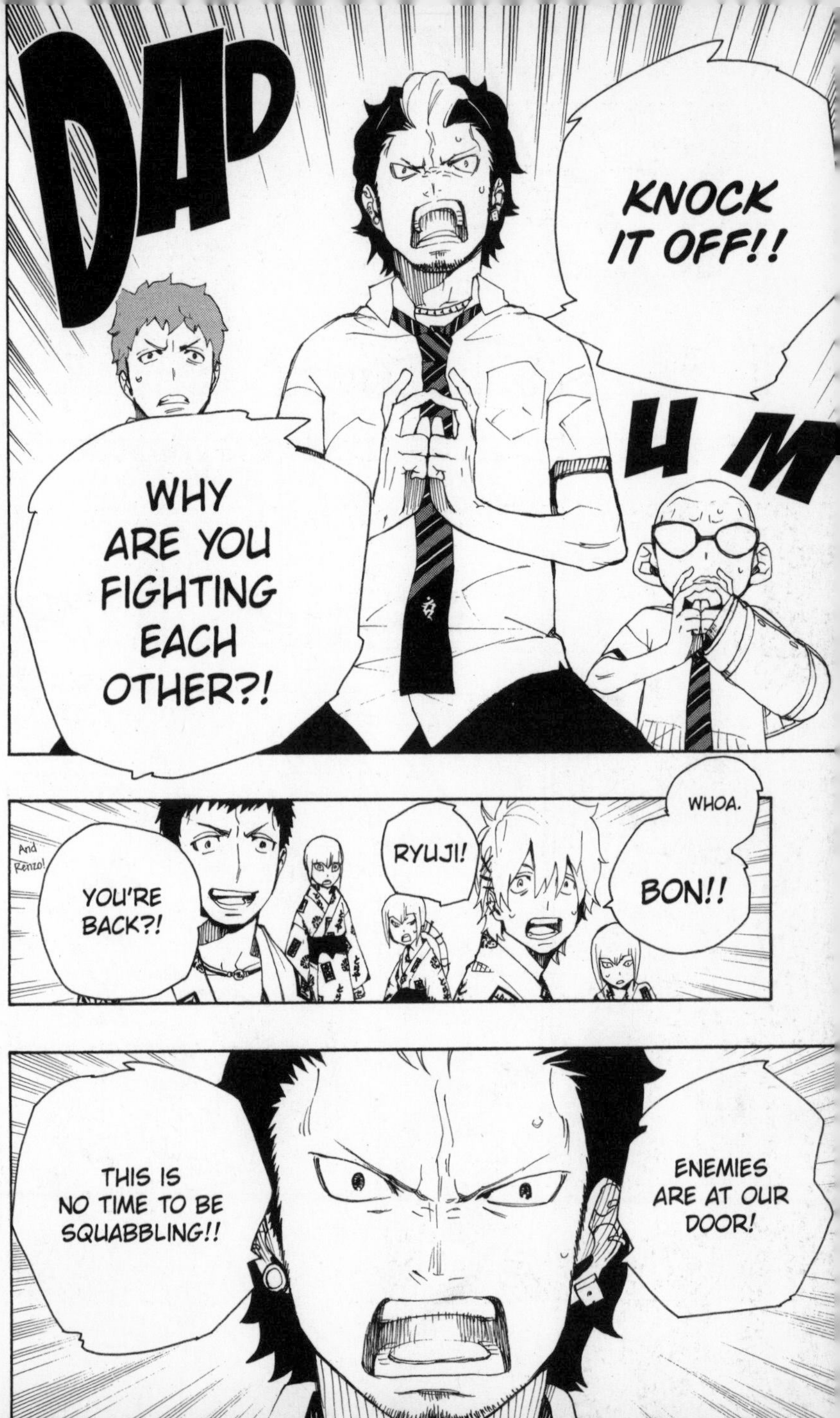
KNOCK IT OFF!!
DAD
UM
WHY ARE YOU FIGHTING EACH OTHER?!
WHOA.
BON!!
RYUJI!
YOU'RE BACK?!
And Renzo!
ENEMIES ARE AT OUR DOOR!
THIS IS NO TIME TO BE SQUABBLING!!

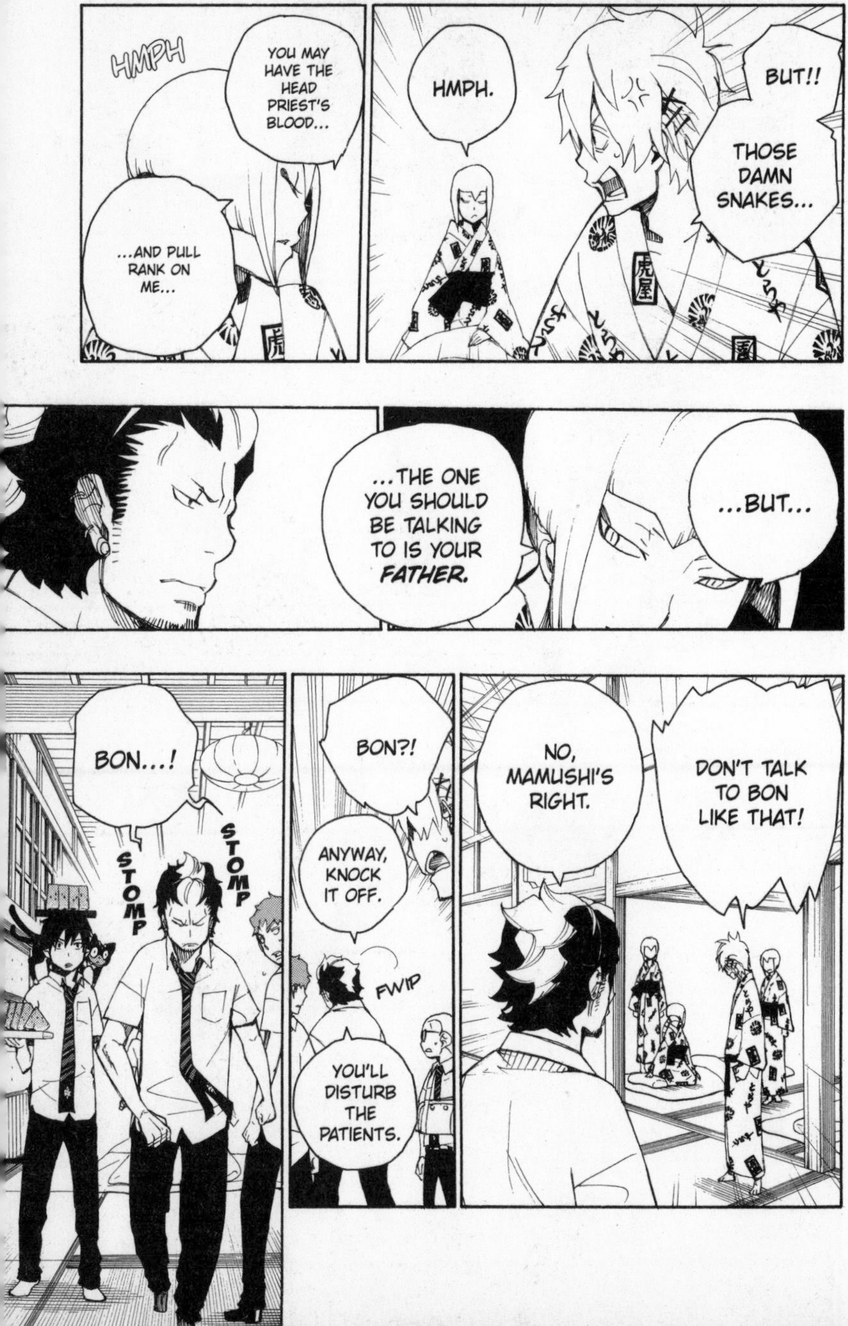
BUT!!
THOSE DAMN SNAKES...
HMPH.
HMPH
YOU MAY HAVE THE HEAD PRIEST'S BLOOD...
...AND PULL RANK ON ME...
...BUT...
...THE ONE YOU SHOULD BE TALKING TO IS YOUR *FATHER.*
DON'T TALK TO BON LIKE THAT!
NO, MAMUSHI'S RIGHT.
BON?!
ANYWAY, KNOCK IT OFF.
FWIP
YOU'LL DISTURB THE PATIENTS.
BON...!
STOMP
STOMP

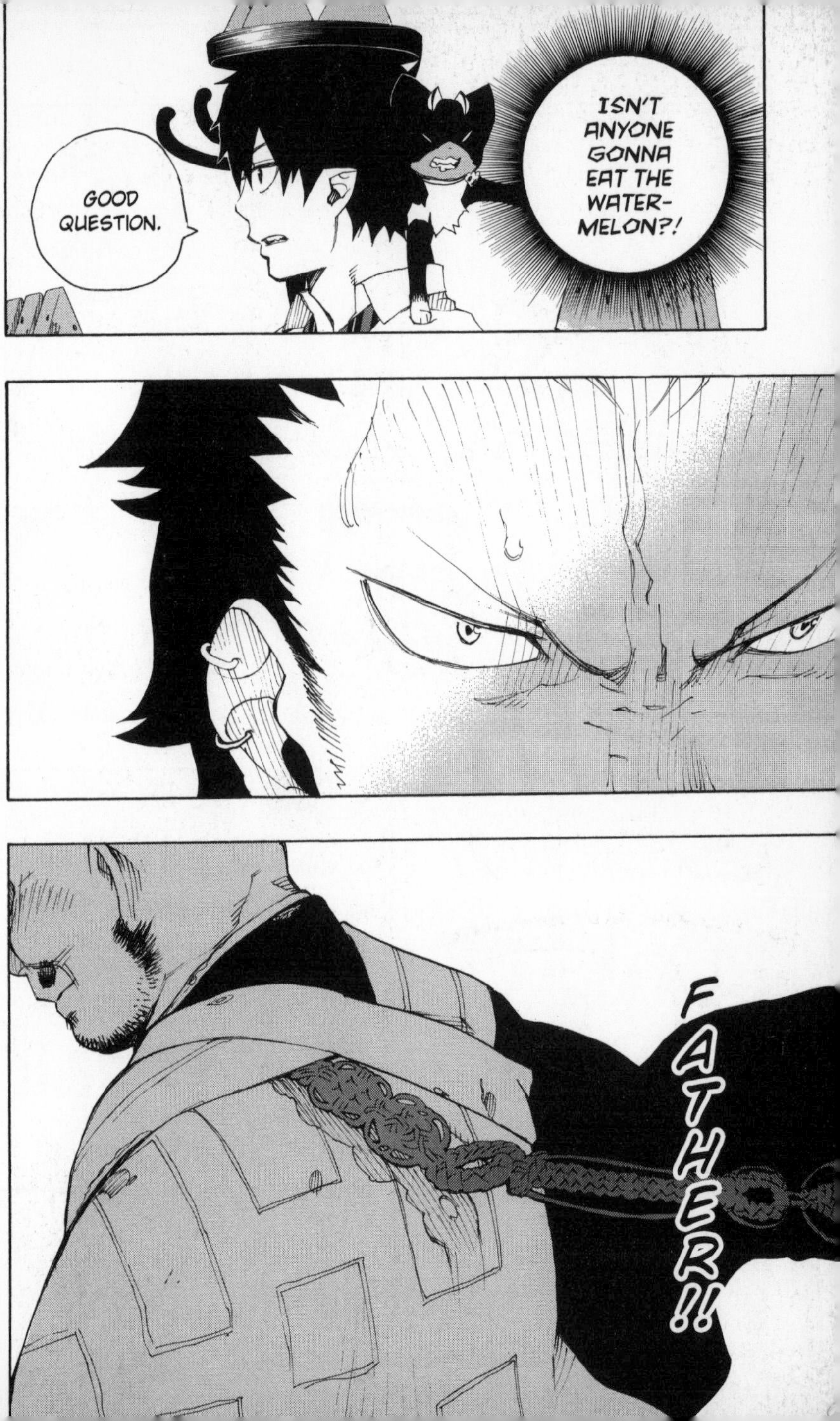
ISN'T ANYONE GONNA EAT THE WATER-MELON?!
GOOD QUESTION.
FATHER!!

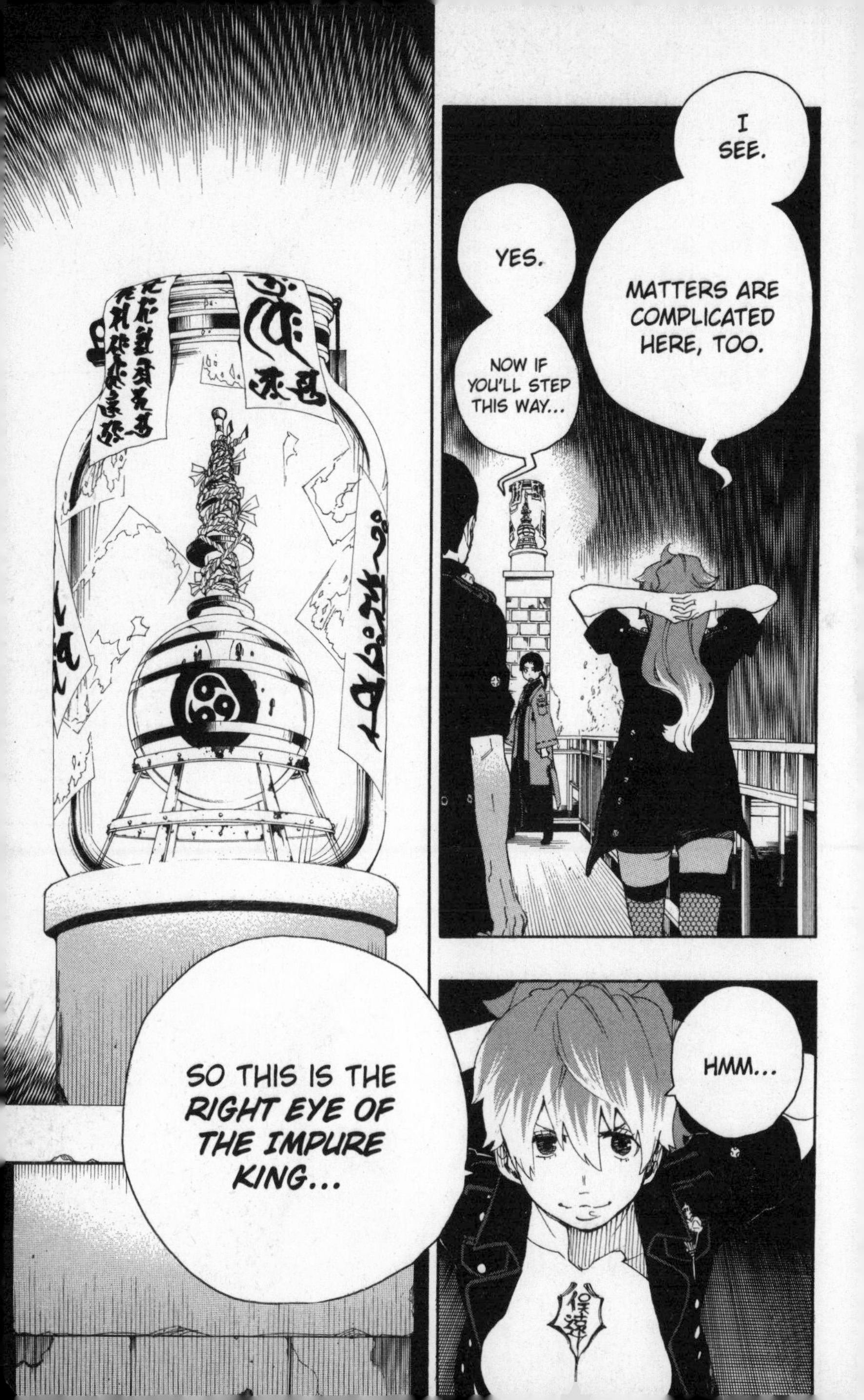
I SEE.
MATTERS ARE COMPLICATED HERE, TOO.
YES.
NOW IF YOU'LL STEP THIS WAY...
HMM...
SO THIS IS THE *RIGHT EYE OF THE IMPURE KING*...

Blue Exorcist Chapter 18 Discord

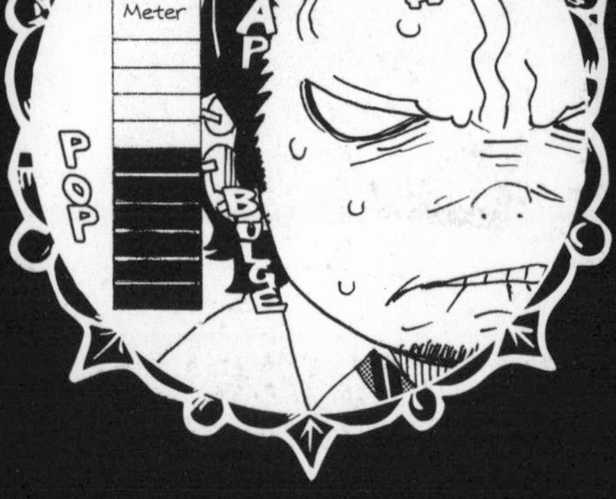
TWITCH
SNAP
BULGE
Suguro Stress Meter
POP

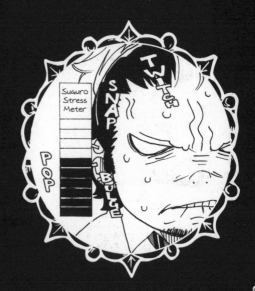

Chapter 19 Drunken Son

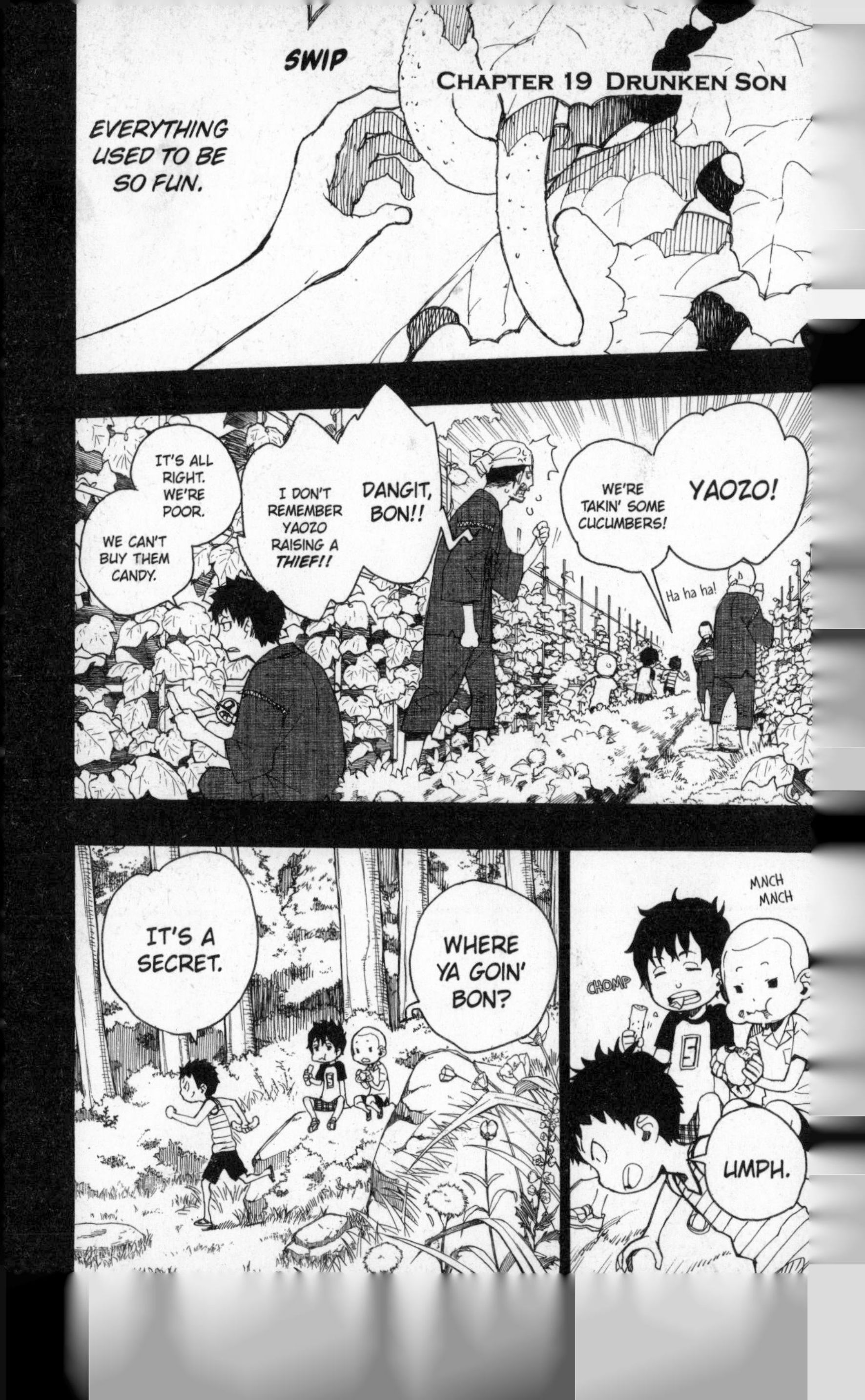
SWIP
EVERYTHING USED TO BE SO FUN.
YAOZO!
WE'RE TAKIN' SOME CUCUMBERS!
Ha ha ha!
DANGIT, BON!!
I DON'T REMEMBER YAOZO RAISING A *THIEF!!*
IT'S ALL RIGHT. WE'RE POOR.
WE CAN'T BUY THEM CANDY.
MNCH MNCH
CHOMP
UMPH.
WHERE YA GOIN' BON?
IT'S A SECRET.

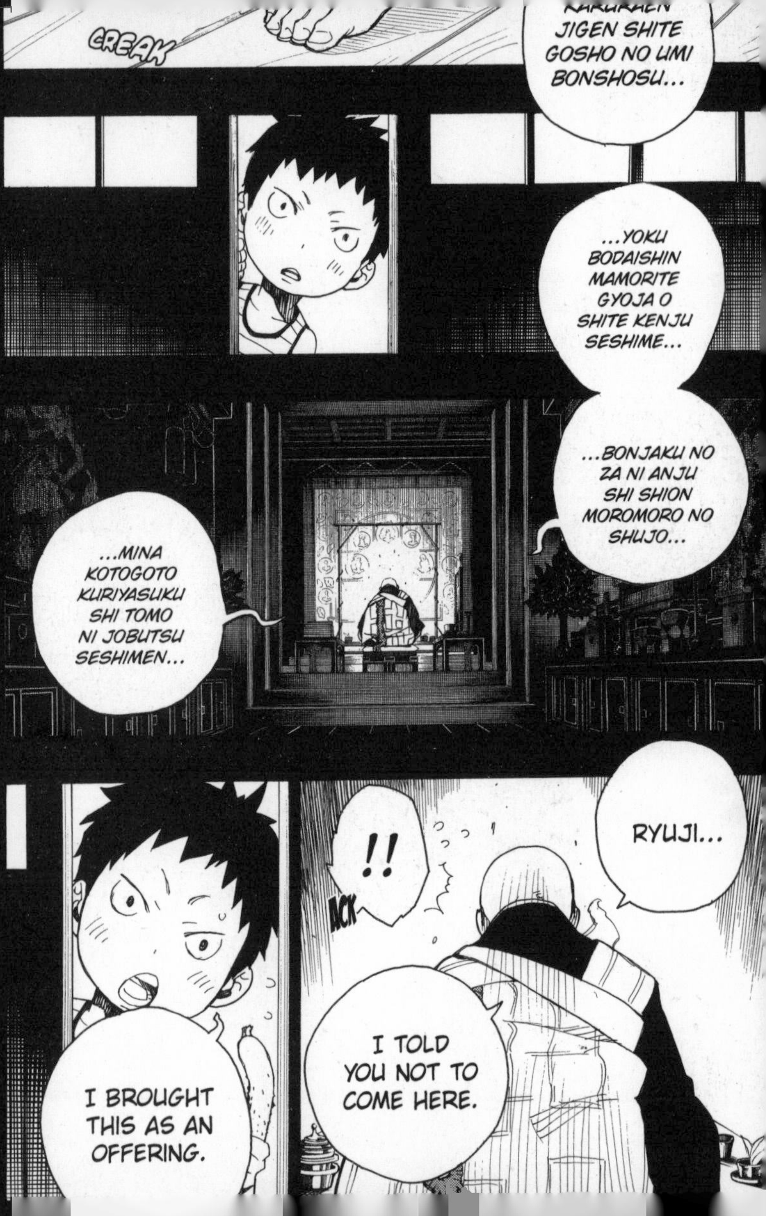
JIGEN SHITE GOSHO NO UMI BONSHOSU...
CREAK
...YOKU BODAISHIN MAMORITE GYOJA O SHITE KENJU SESHIME...
...BONJAKU NO ZA NI ANJU SHI SHION MOROMORO NO SHUJO...
...MINA KOTOGOTO KURIYASUKU SHI TOMO NI JOBUTSU SESHIMEN...
RYUJI...
!!
ACK
I TOLD YOU NOT TO COME HERE.
I BROUGHT THIS AS AN OFFERING.

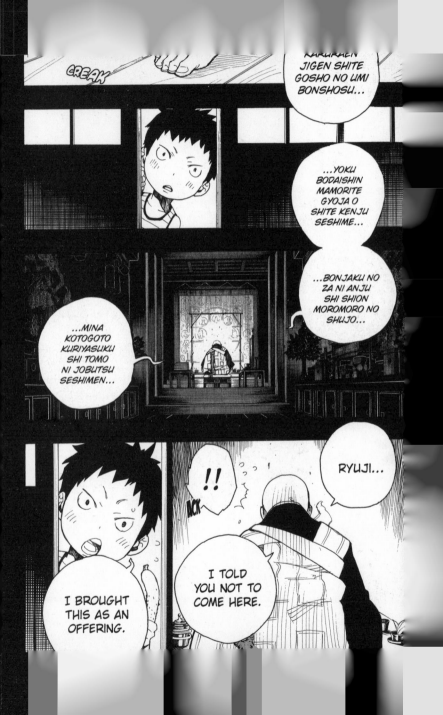

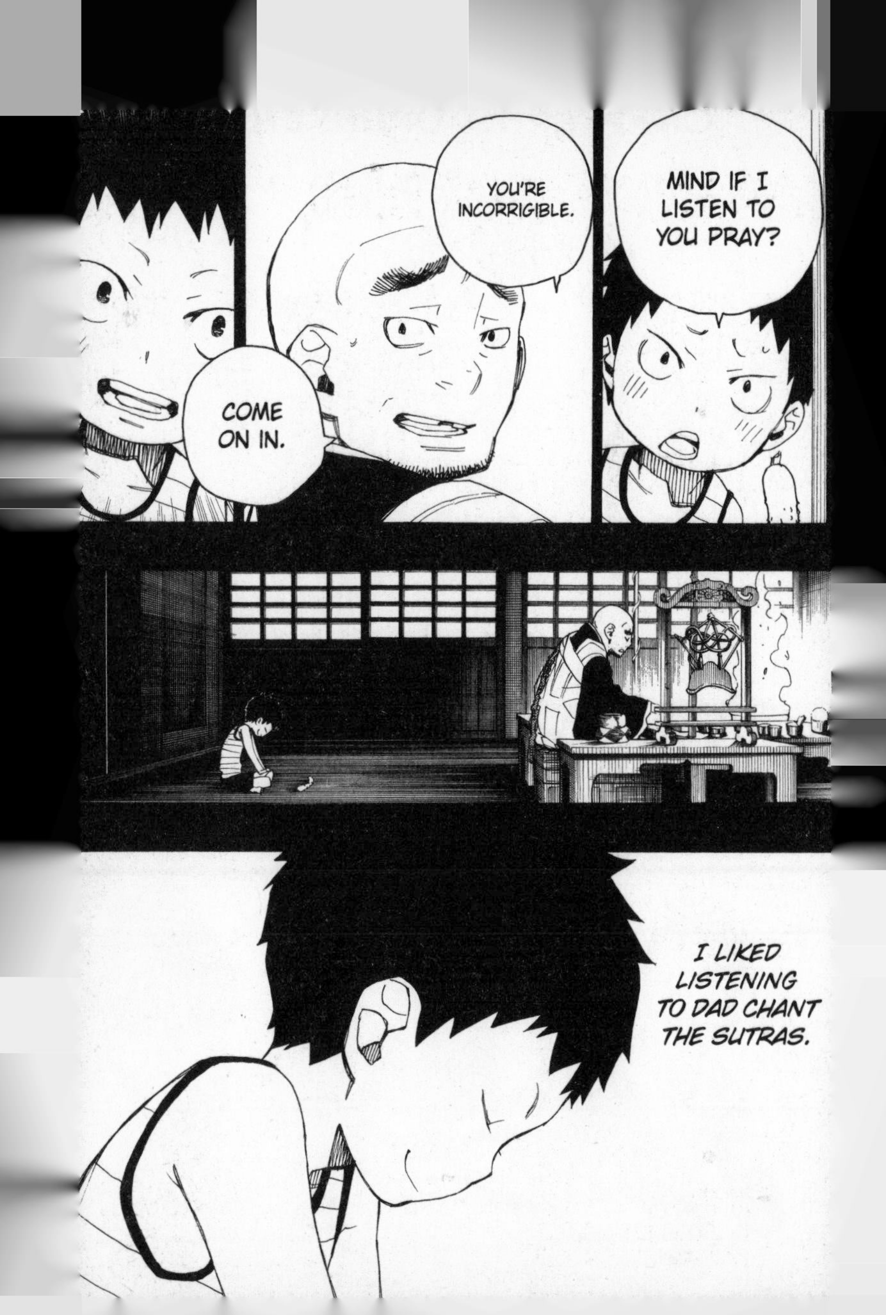
MIND IF I LISTEN TO YOU PRAY?
YOU'RE INCORRIGIBLE.
COME ON IN.
I LIKED LISTENING TO DAD CHANT THE SUTRAS.

CHAPTER 19 DRUNKEN SON

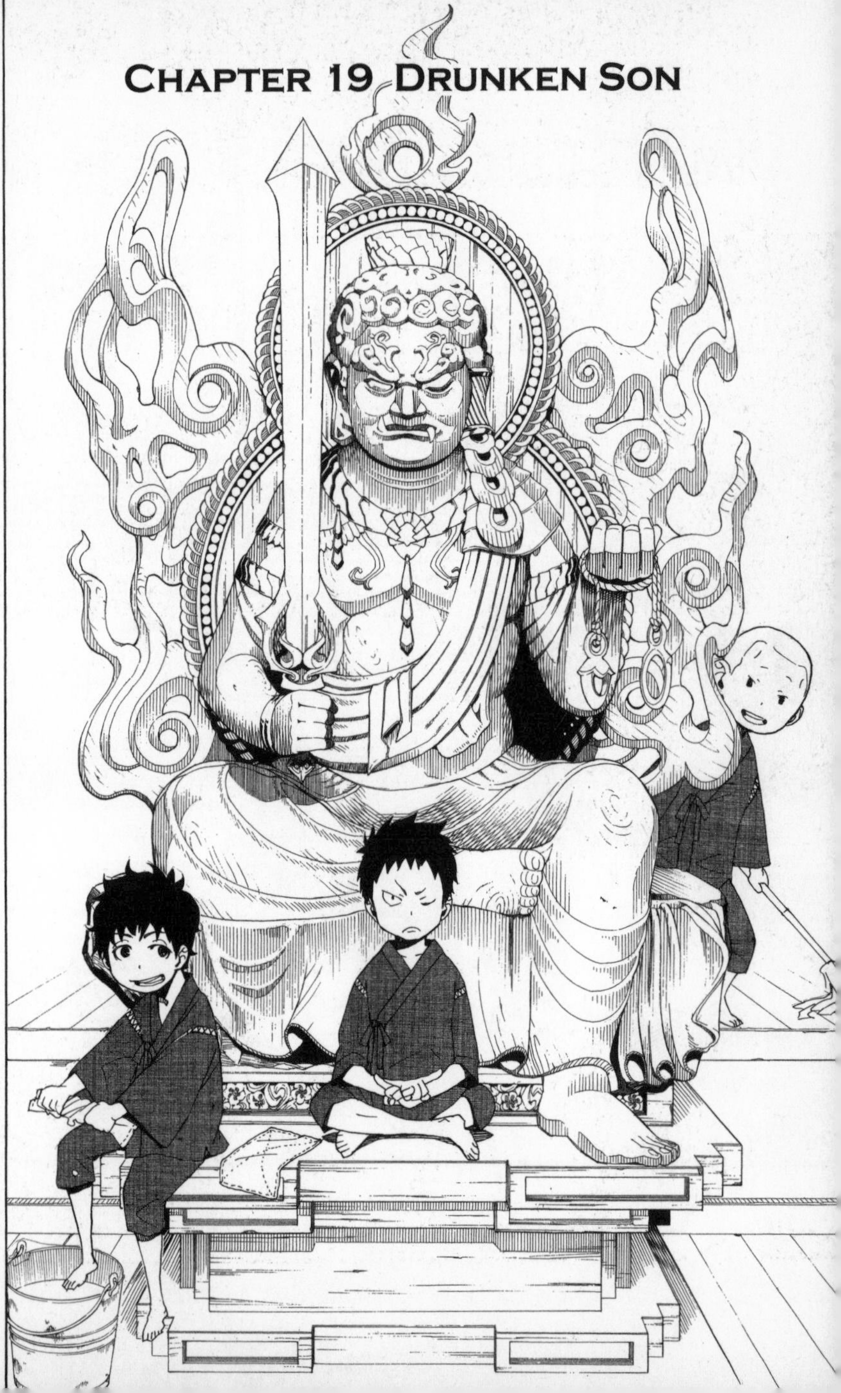

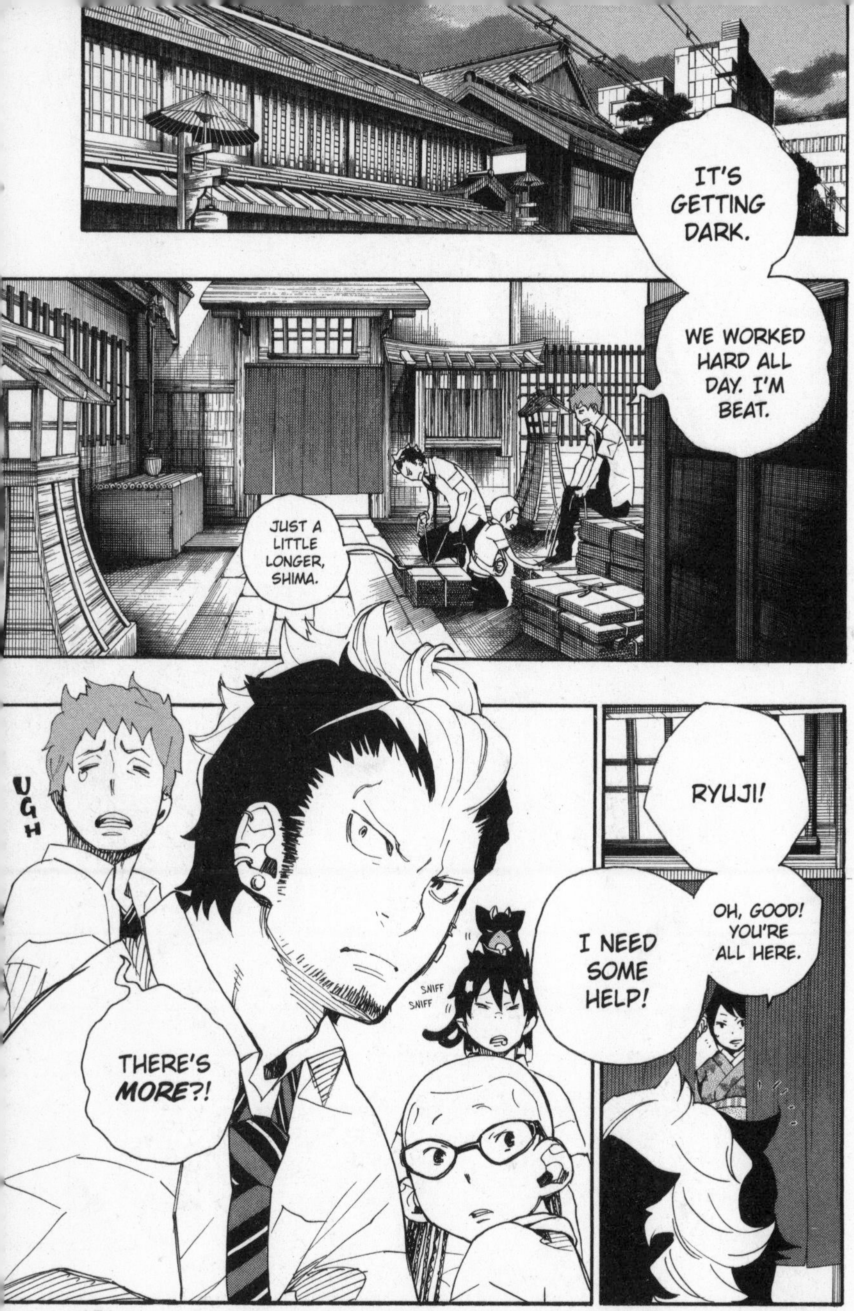
IT'S GETTING DARK.
WE WORKED HARD ALL DAY. I'M BEAT.
JUST A LITTLE LONGER, SHIMA.
RYUJI!
OH, GOOD! YOU'RE ALL HERE.
I NEED SOME HELP!
SNIFF SNIFF
UGH
THERE'S *MORE*?!

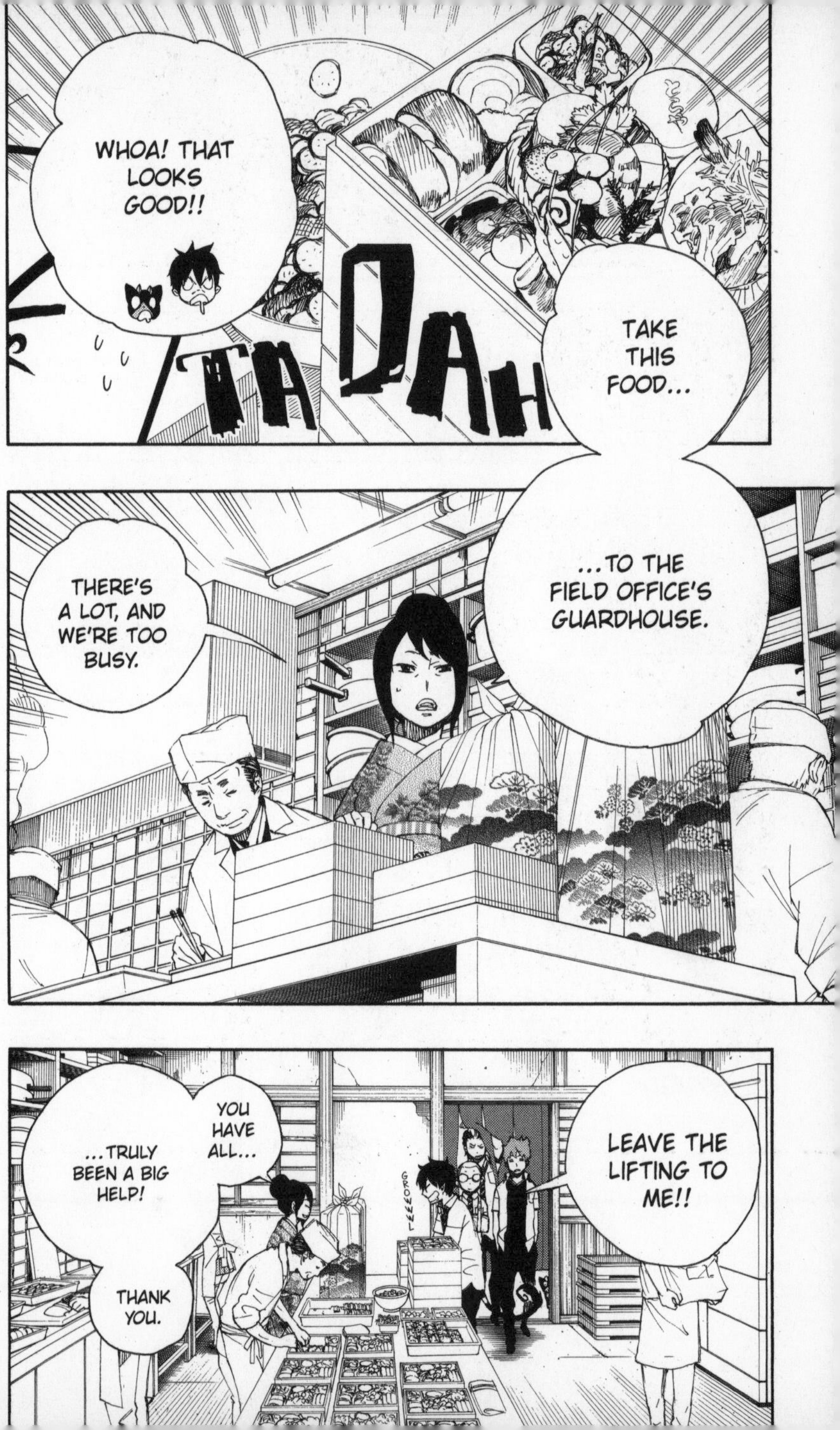
WHOA! THAT LOOKS GOOD!!
TA DAH
TAKE THIS FOOD...
...TO THE FIELD OFFICE'S GUARDHOUSE.
THERE'S A LOT, AND WE'RE TOO BUSY.
LEAVE THE LIFTING TO ME!!
GROWWWL
YOU HAVE ALL...
...TRULY BEEN A BIG HELP!
THANK YOU.

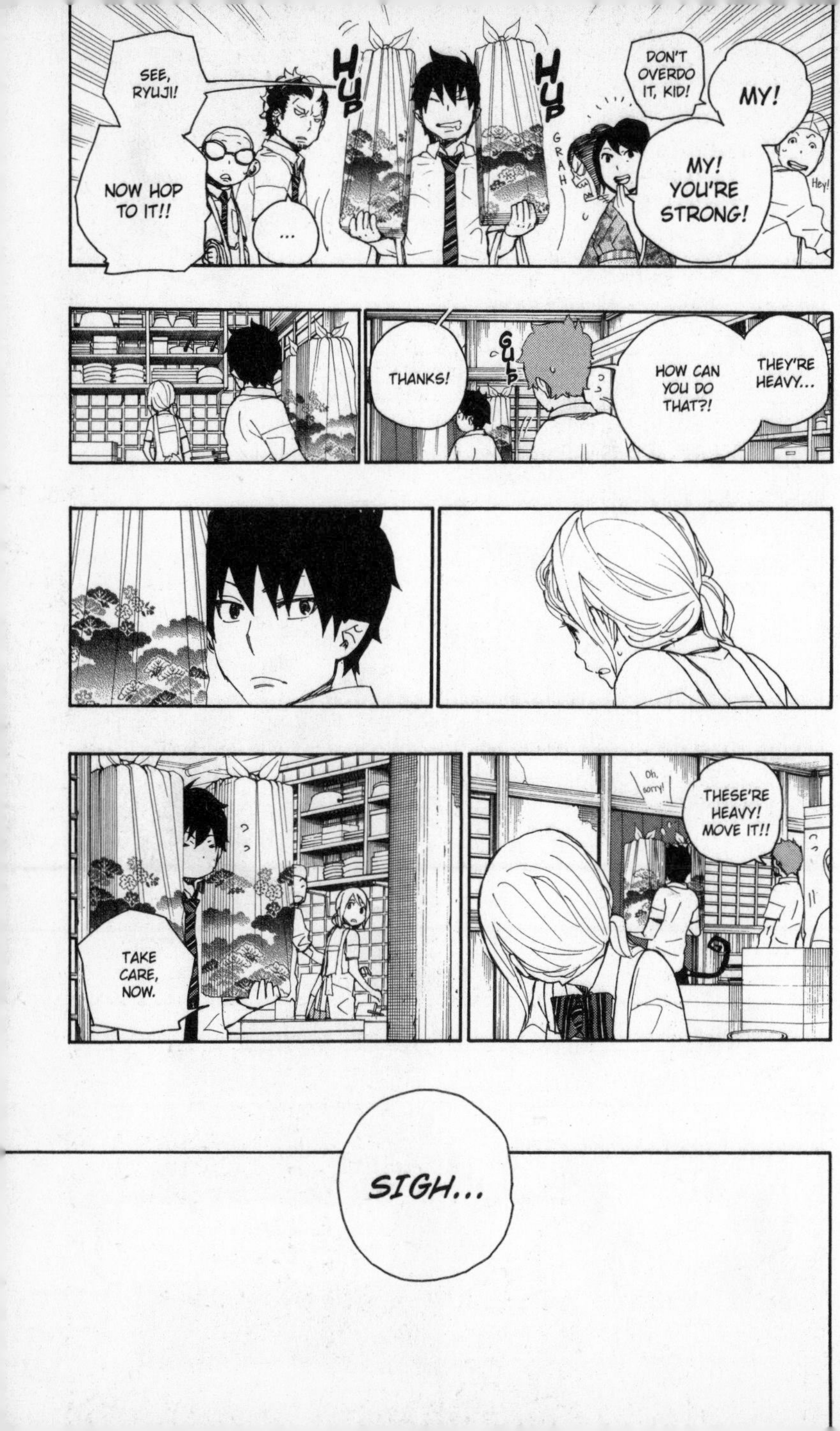
MY!
DON'T OVERDO IT, KID!
Hey!
MY! YOU'RE STRONG!
GRAH
HUP
HUP
SEE, RYUJI!
...
NOW HOP TO IT!!
THEY'RE HEAVY...
HOW CAN YOU DO THAT?!
GULP
THANKS!
THESE'RE HEAVY! MOVE IT!!
Oh, sorry!
TAKE CARE, NOW.
SIGH...

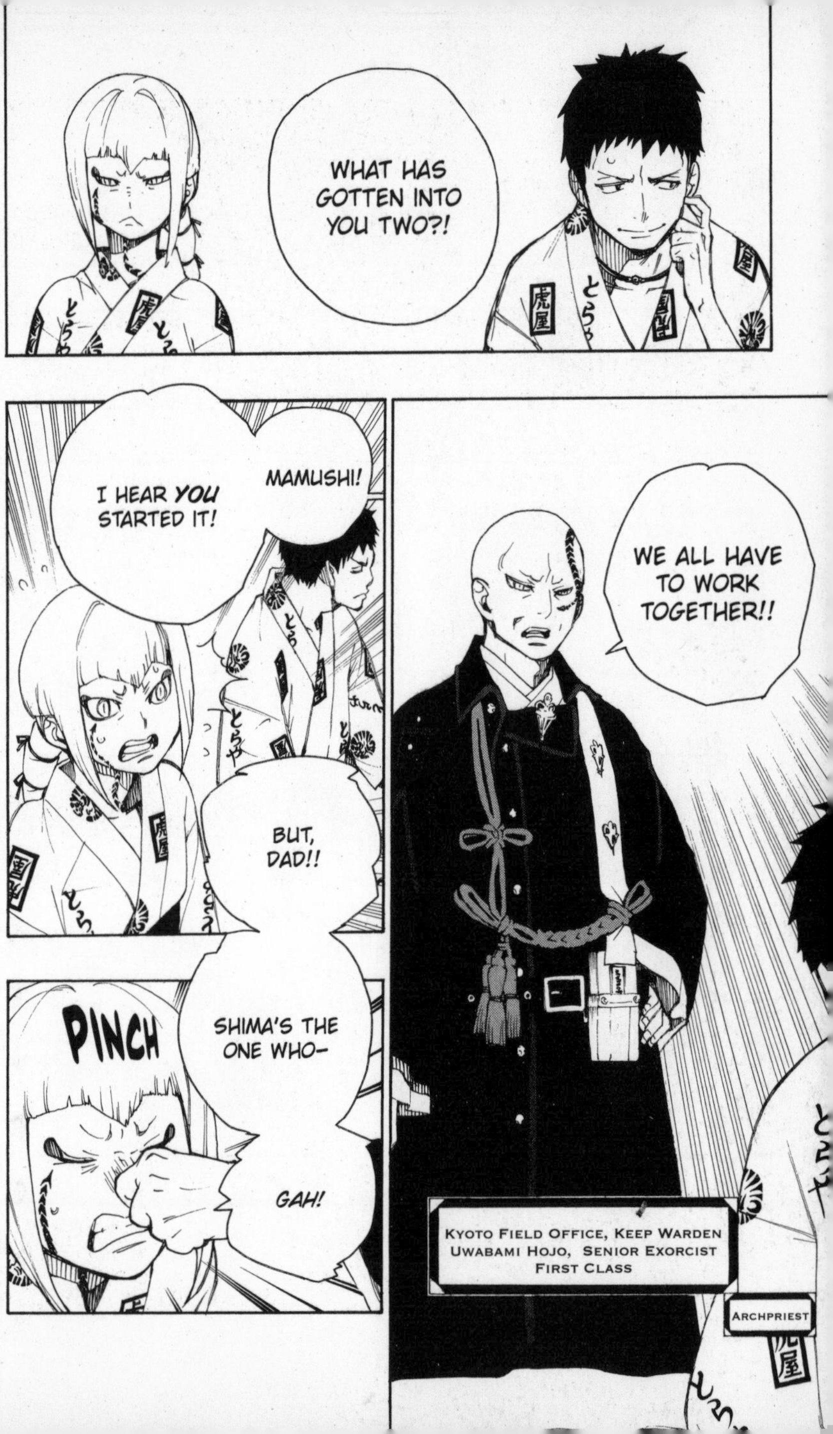
WHAT HAS GOTTEN INTO YOU TWO?!
WE ALL HAVE TO WORK TOGETHER!!
Kyoto Field Office, Keep Warden Uwabami Hojo, Senior Exorcist First Class
Archpriest
MAMUSHI!
I HEAR YOU STARTED IT!
BUT, DAD!!
SHIMA'S THE ONE WHO-
PINCH
GAH!

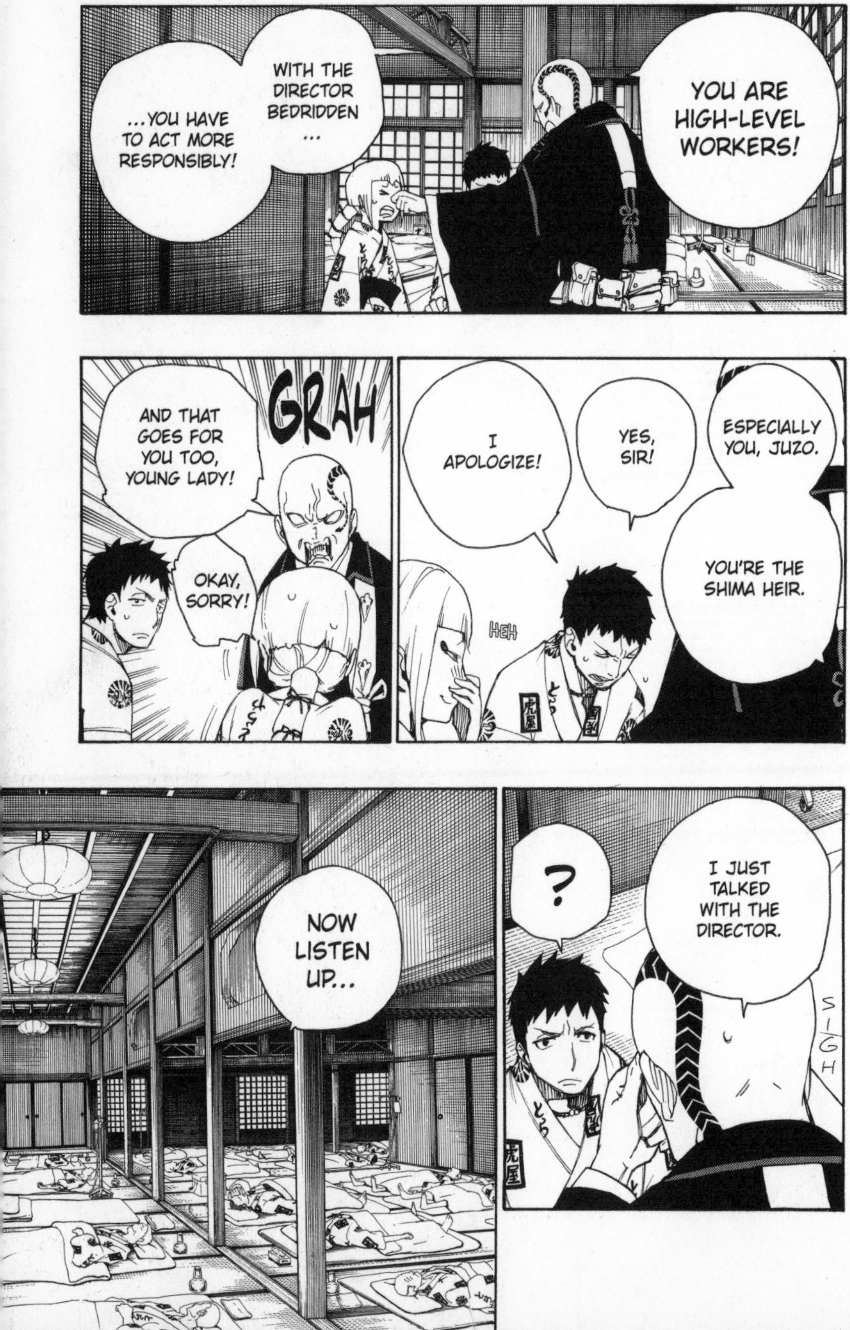
YOU ARE HIGH-LEVEL WORKERS!
WITH THE DIRECTOR BEDRIDDEN ...
...YOU HAVE TO ACT MORE RESPONSIBLY!
ESPECIALLY YOU, JUZO.
YOU'RE THE SHIMA HEIR.
YES, SIR!
I APOLOGIZE!
HEH
GRAH
AND THAT GOES FOR YOU TOO, YOUNG LADY!
OKAY, SORRY!
I JUST TALKED WITH THE DIRECTOR.
?
SIGH
NOW LISTEN UP...

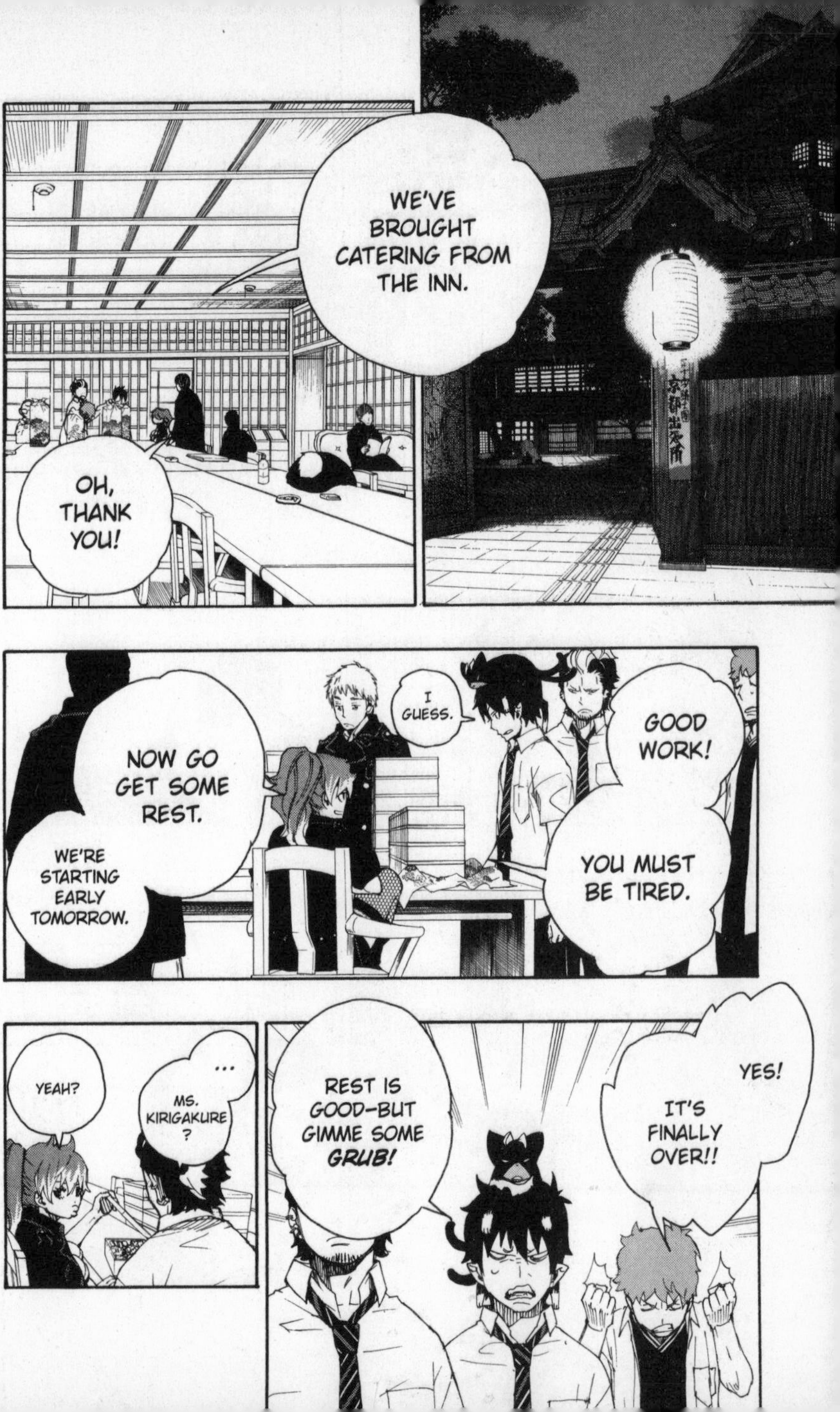
WE'VE BROUGHT CATERING FROM THE INN.
OH, THANK YOU!
GOOD WORK!
YOU MUST BE TIRED.
I GUESS.
NOW GO GET SOME REST.
WE'RE STARTING EARLY TOMORROW.
YES!
IT'S FINALLY OVER!!
REST IS GOOD—BUT GIMME SOME GRUB!
...
MS. KIRIGAKURE?
YEAH?

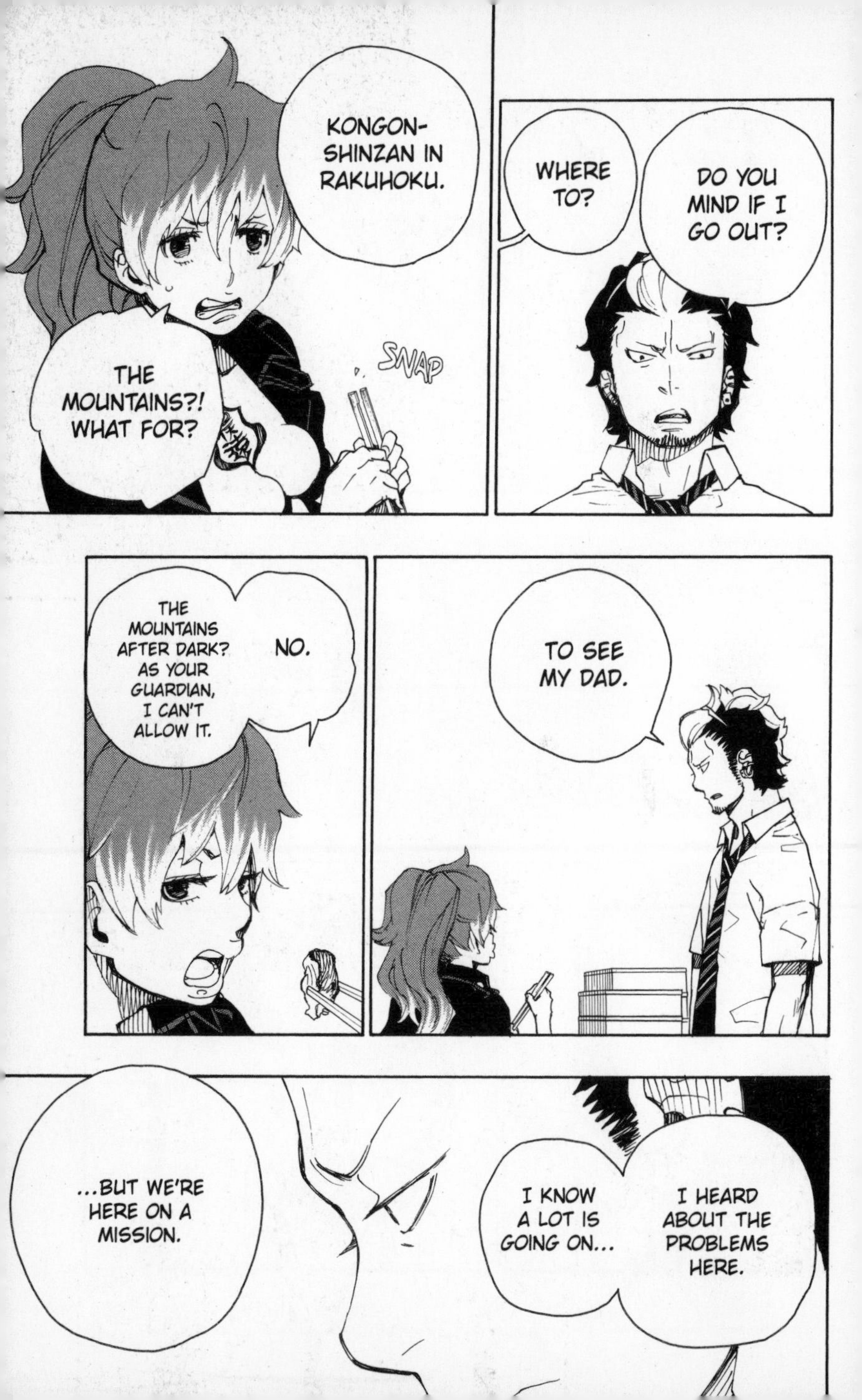
DO YOU MIND IF I GO OUT?
WHERE TO?
KONGON-SHINZAN IN RAKUHOKU.
SNAP
THE MOUNTAINS?! WHAT FOR?
TO SEE MY DAD.
NO.
THE MOUNTAINS AFTER DARK? AS YOUR GUARDIAN, I CAN'T ALLOW IT.
I HEARD ABOUT THE PROBLEMS HERE.
I KNOW A LOT IS GOING ON...
...BUT WE'RE HERE ON A MISSION.

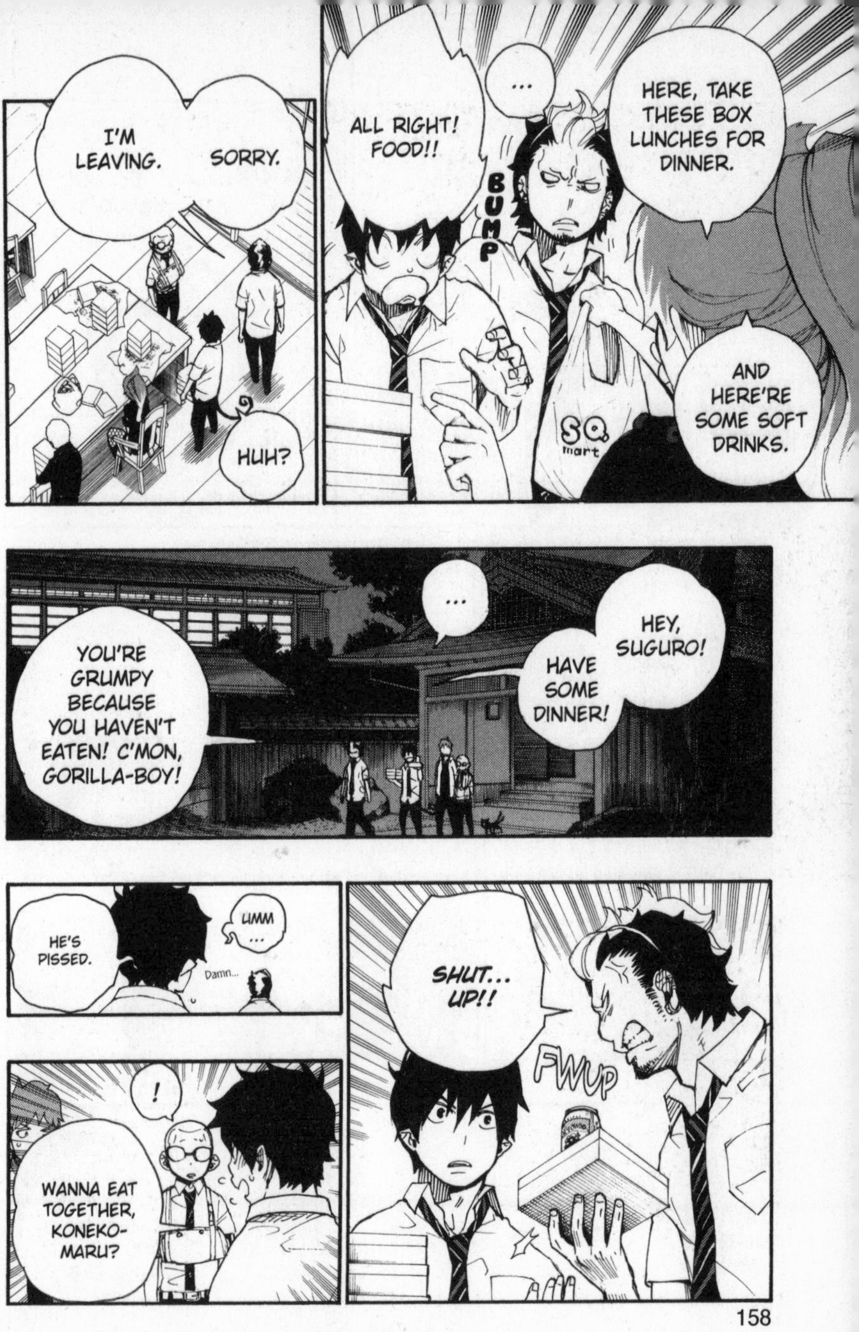
...
HERE, TAKE THESE BOX LUNCHES FOR DINNER.
ALL RIGHT! FOOD!!
BUMP
AND HERE'RE SOME SOFT DRINKS.
SQ mart
SORRY.
I'M LEAVING.
HUH?
HEY, SUGURO!
HAVE SOME DINNER!
...
YOU'RE GRUMPY BECAUSE YOU HAVEN'T EATEN! C'MON, GORILLA-BOY!
SHUT... UP!!
FWUP
UMM ...
HE'S PISSED.
Damn...
!
WANNA EAT TOGETHER, KONEKO-MARU?

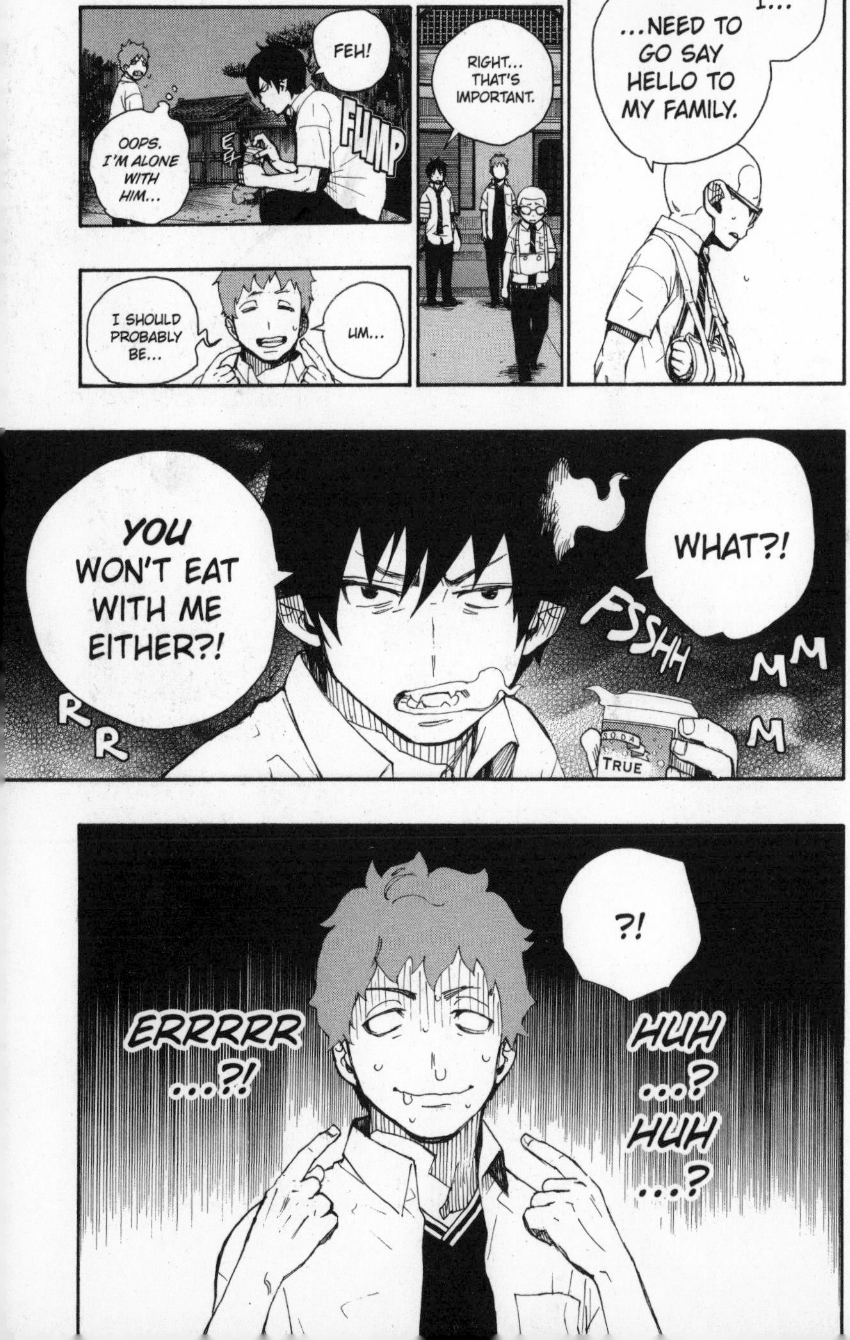
I...
...NEED TO GO SAY HELLO TO MY FAMILY.
RIGHT... THAT'S IMPORTANT.
FEH!
FUMP
OOPS. I'M ALONE WITH HIM...
UM...
I SHOULD PROBABLY BE...
WHAT?!
FSSHH
MMM
YOU WON'T EAT WITH ME EITHER?!
RR
SODA
TRUE
?!
HUH ...? HUH ...?
ERRRRR ...?!

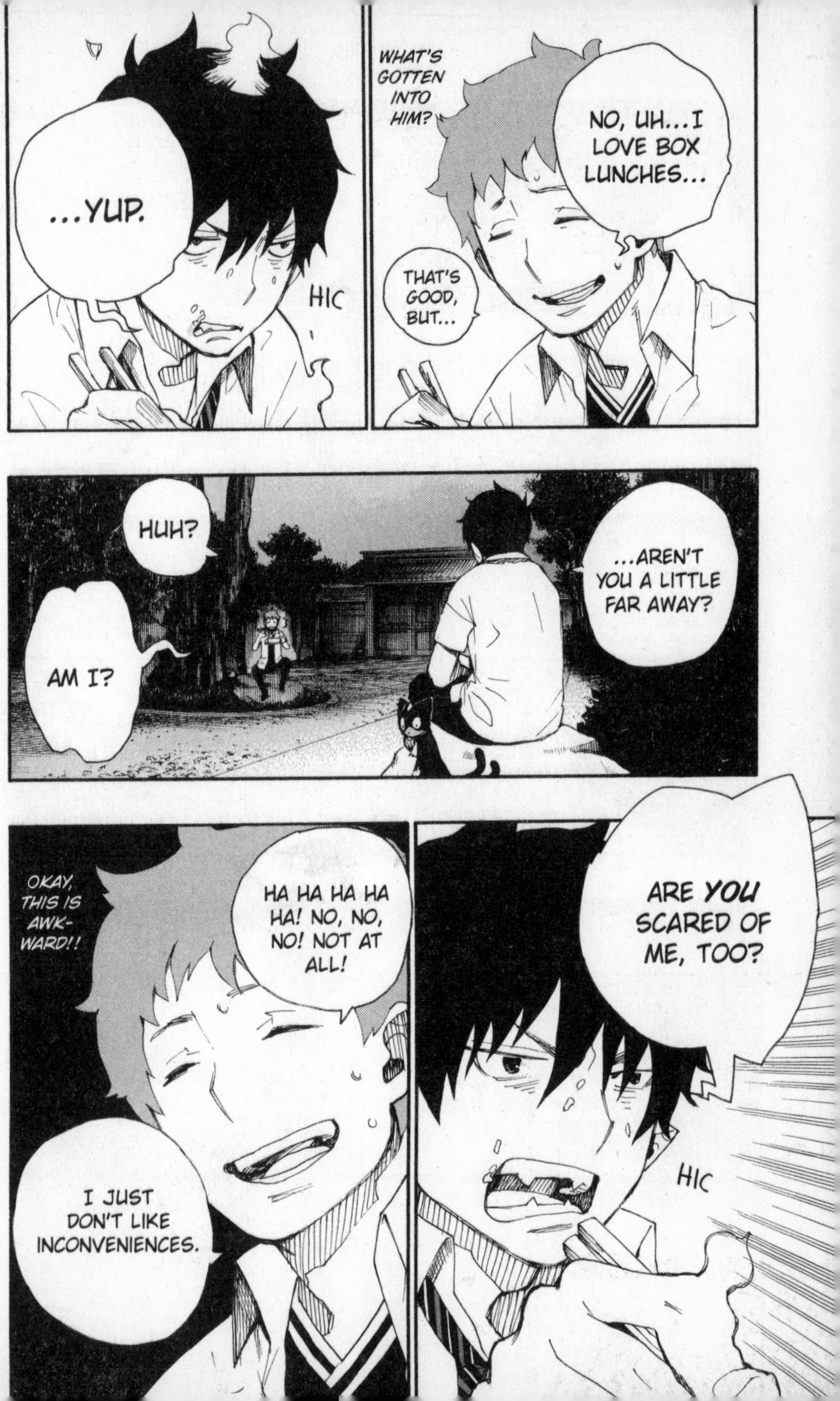
NO, UH...I LOVE BOX LUNCHES...
WHAT'S GOTTEN INTO HIM?
THAT'S GOOD, BUT...
...YUP.
HIC
...AREN'T YOU A LITTLE FAR AWAY?
HUH?
AM I?
ARE *YOU* SCARED OF ME, TOO?
HIC
HA HA HA HA HA! NO, NO, NO! NOT AT ALL!
OKAY, THIS IS AWK-WARD!!
I JUST DON'T LIKE INCONVENIENCES.

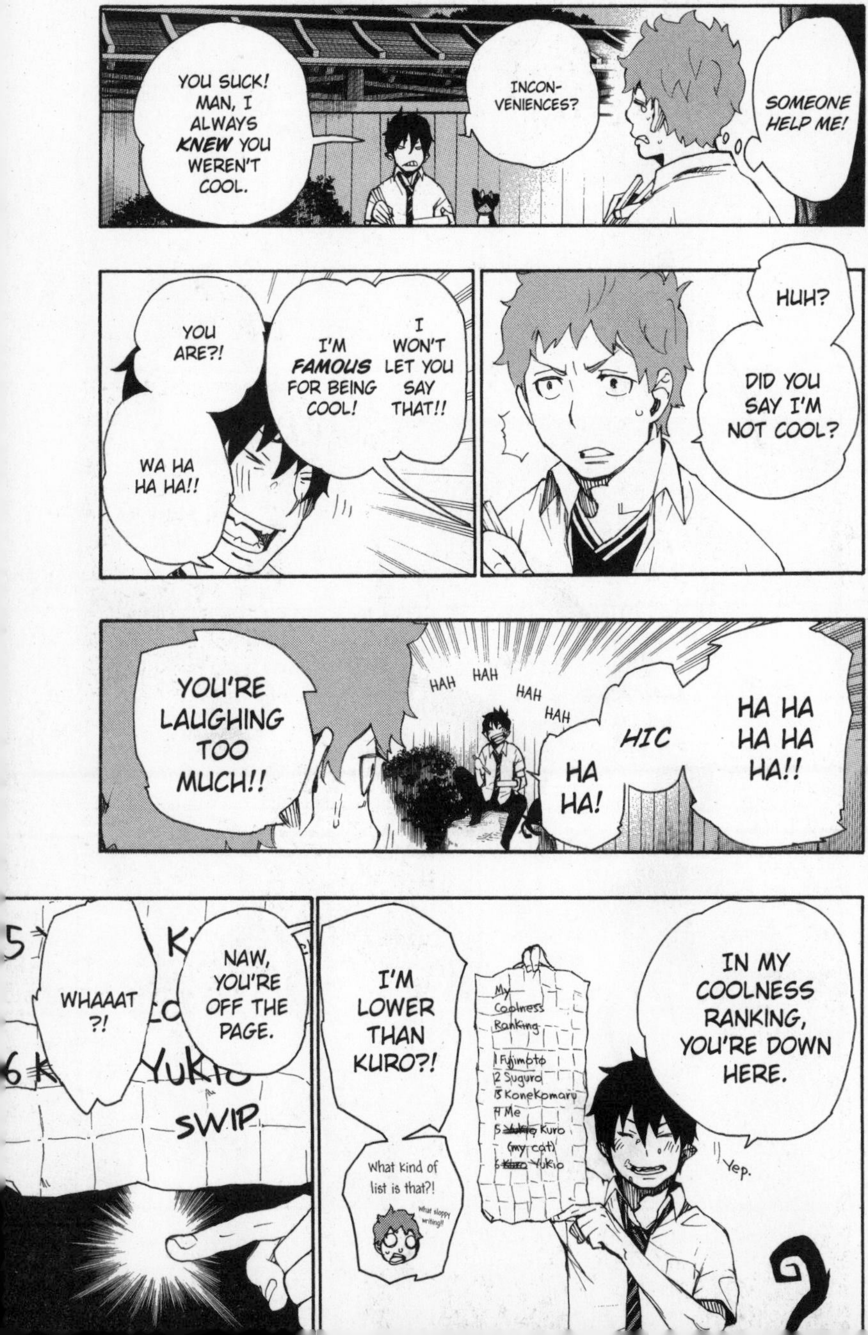
SOMEONE HELP ME!
INCON-VENIENCES?
YOU SUCK! MAN, I ALWAYS **KNEW** YOU WEREN'T COOL.
HUH?
DID YOU SAY I'M NOT COOL?
I WON'T LET YOU SAY THAT!!
I'M **FAMOUS** FOR BEING COOL!
YOU ARE?!
WA HA HA HA!!
HA HA HA HA HA!!
HIC
HA HA!
HAH HAH HAH HAH
YOU'RE LAUGHING TOO MUCH!!
IN MY COOLNESS RANKING, YOU'RE DOWN HERE.
Yep.
My Coolness Ranking
1 Fujimoto
2 Suguro
3 KoneKomaru
4 Me
5 ~~Yukio~~ Kuro (my cat)
6 ~~Kuro~~ Yukio
I'M LOWER THAN KURO?!
What kind of list is that?!
What sloppy writing!!
NAW, YOU'RE OFF THE PAGE.
WHAAAT?!
SWIP

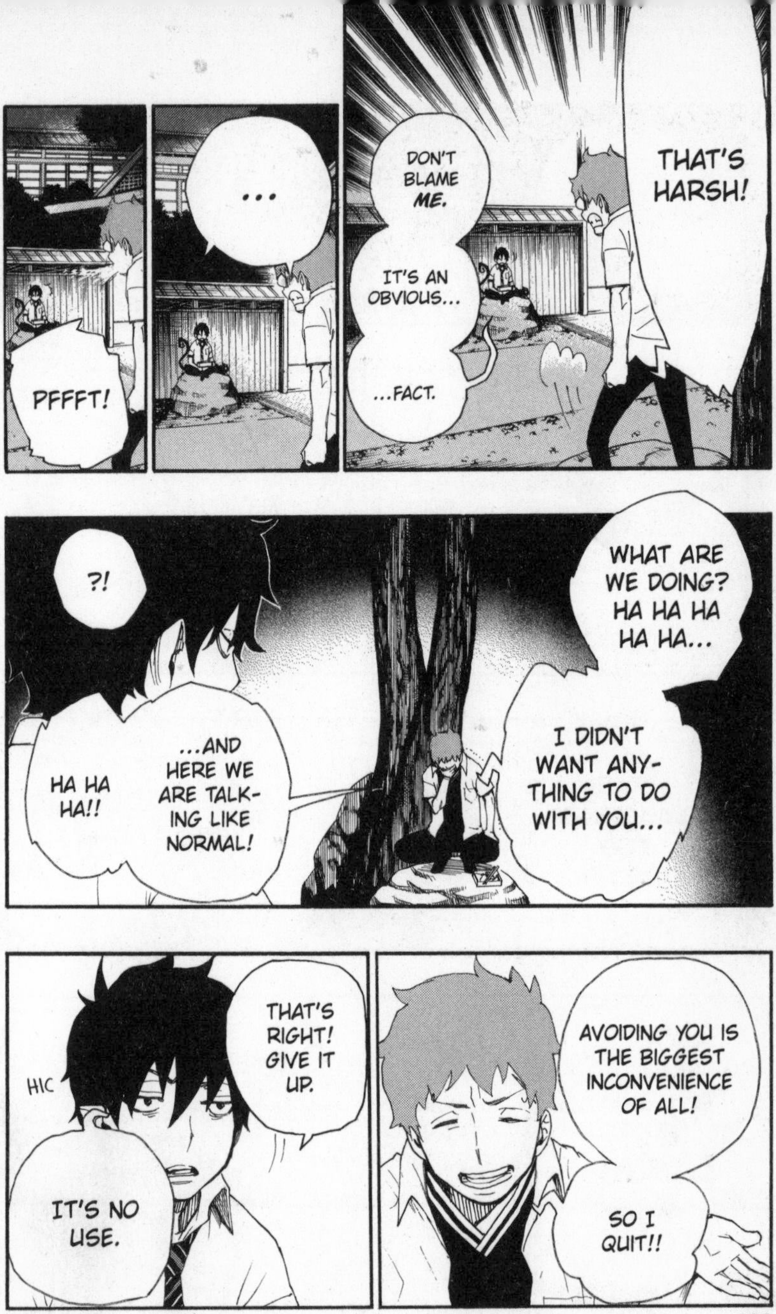
THAT'S HARSH!
DON'T BLAME ME.
IT'S AN OBVIOUS...
...FACT.
...
PFFFT!
WHAT ARE WE DOING? HA HA HA HA HA...
?!
I DIDN'T WANT ANY-THING TO DO WITH YOU...
...AND HERE WE ARE TALK-ING LIKE NORMAL!
HA HA HA!!
AVOIDING YOU IS THE BIGGEST INCONVENIENCE OF ALL!
SO I QUIT!!
THAT'S RIGHT! GIVE IT UP.
HIC
IT'S NO USE.

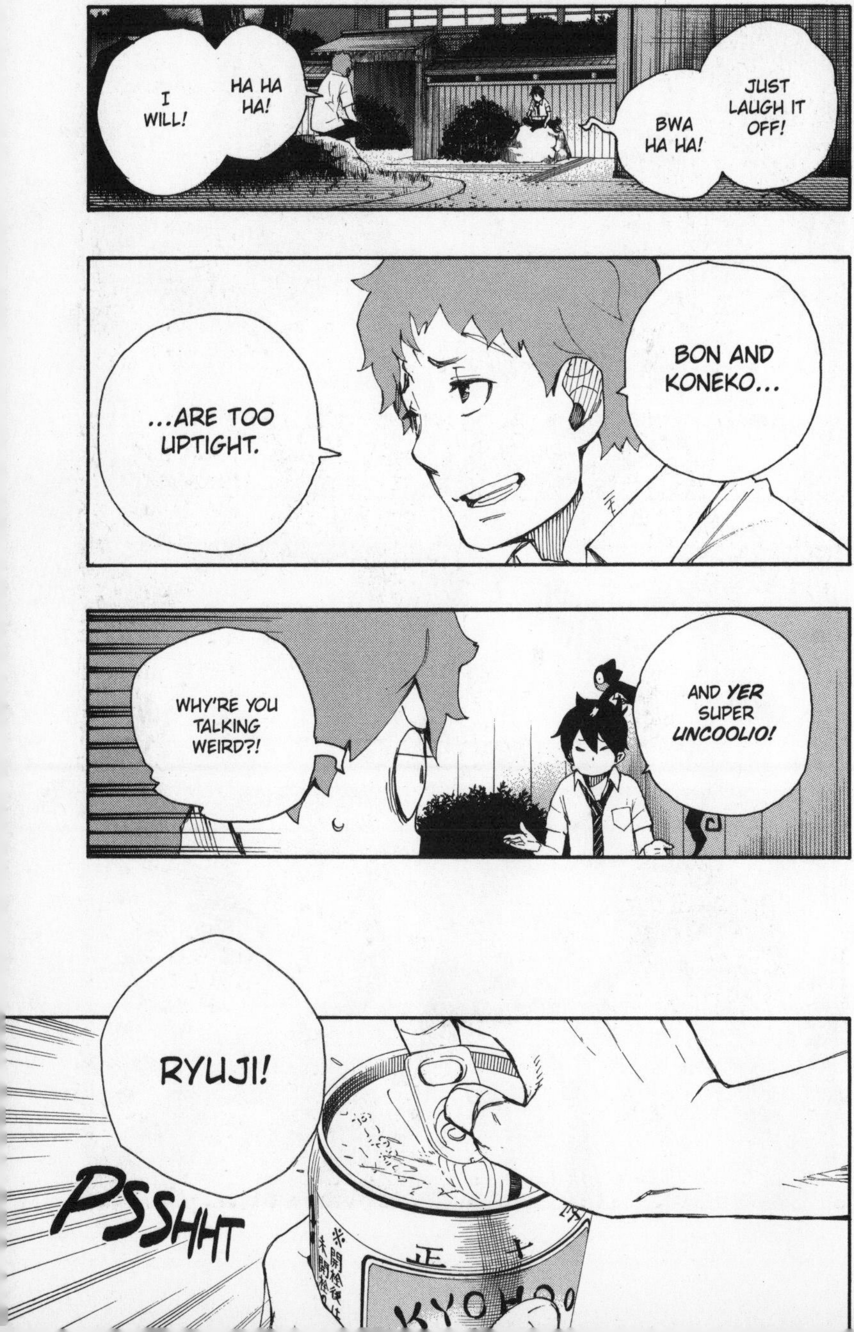
JUST LAUGH IT OFF!
BWA HA HA!
HA HA HA!
I WILL!
BON AND KONEKO...
...ARE TOO UPTIGHT.
AND YER SUPER UNCOOLIO!
WHY'RE YOU TALKING WEIRD?!
RYUJI!
PSSHHT

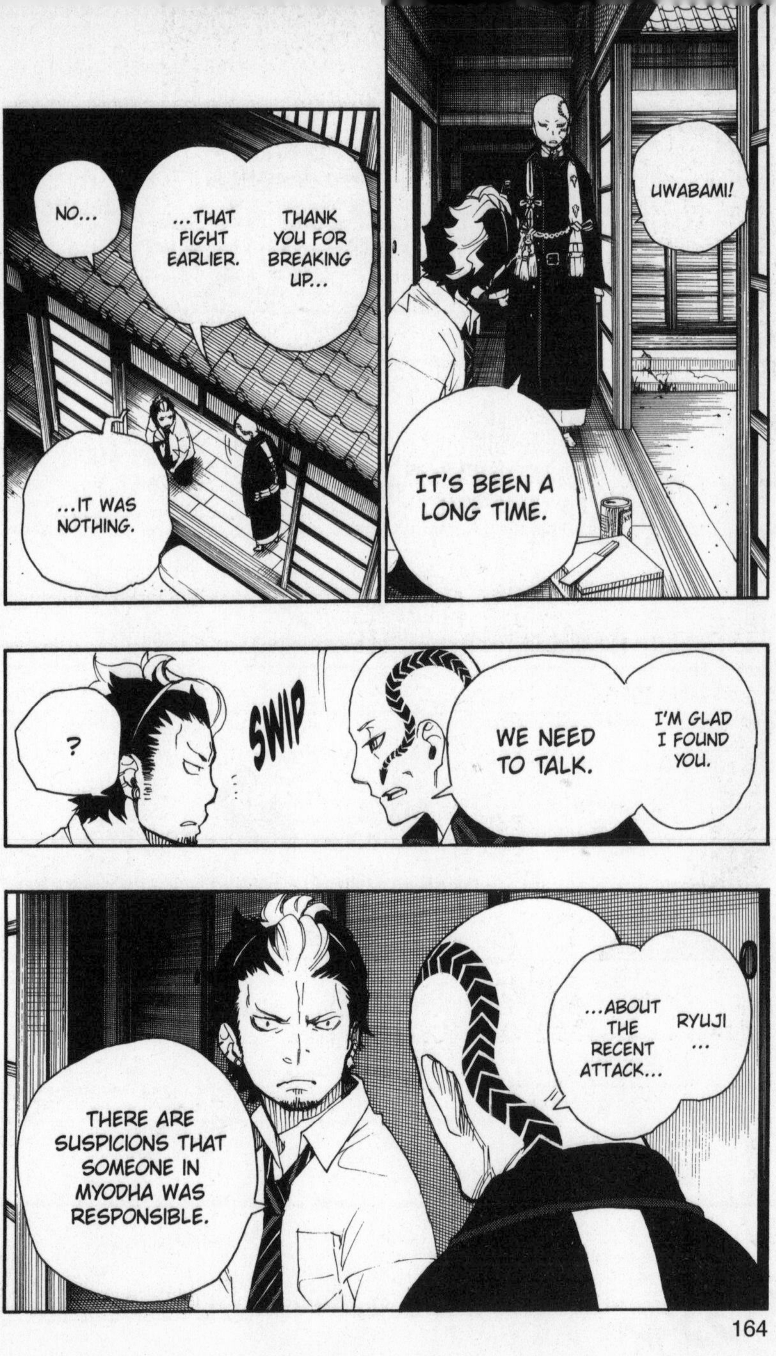
UWABAMI!
IT'S BEEN A LONG TIME.
THANK YOU FOR BREAKING UP...
...THAT FIGHT EARLIER.
NO...
...IT WAS NOTHING.
I'M GLAD I FOUND YOU.
WE NEED TO TALK.
SWIP
?
RYUJI...
...ABOUT THE RECENT ATTACK...
THERE ARE SUSPICIONS THAT SOMEONE IN MYODHA WAS RESPONSIBLE.

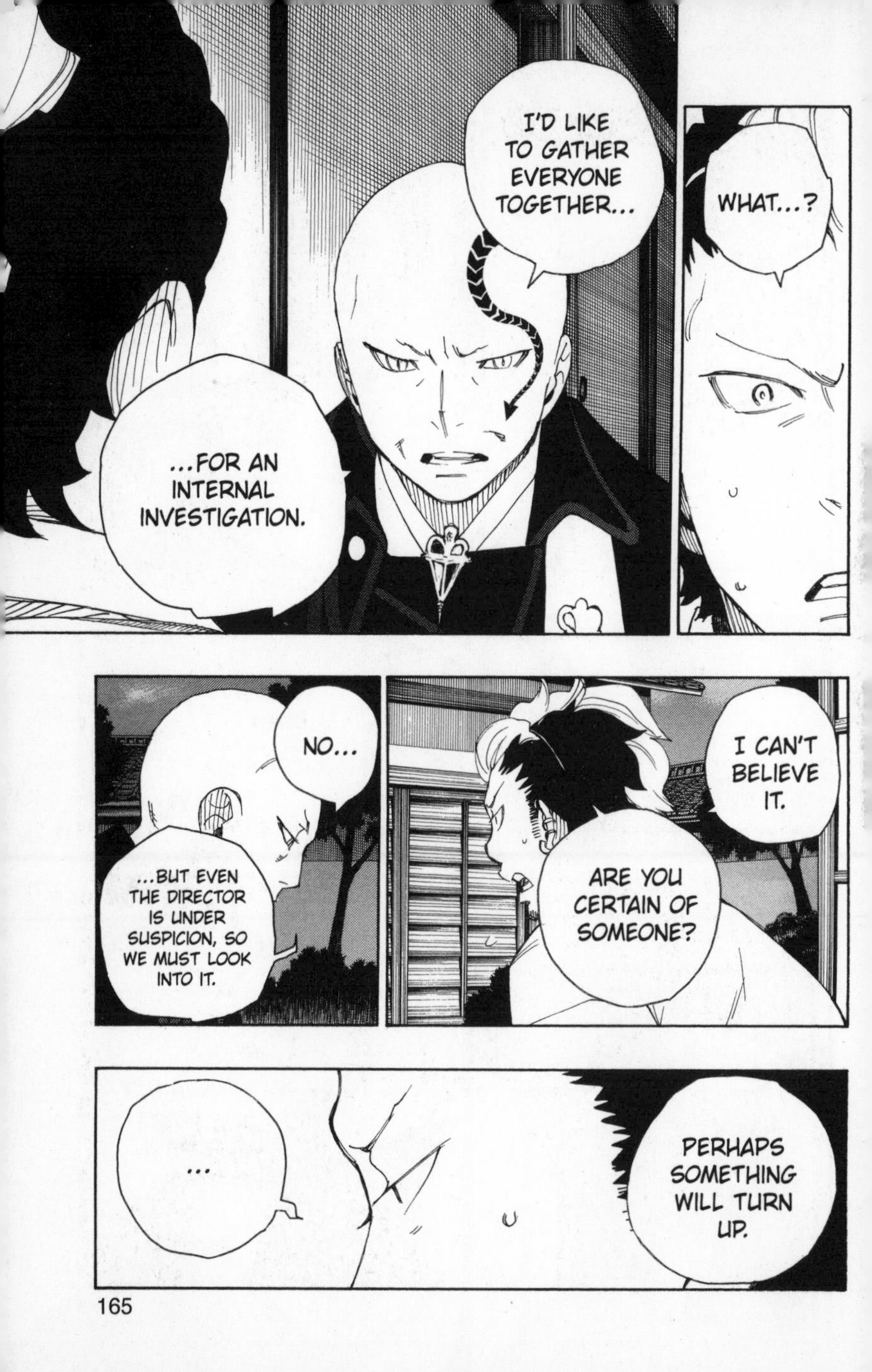
WHAT...?
I'D LIKE TO GATHER EVERYONE TOGETHER...
...FOR AN INTERNAL INVESTIGATION.
I CAN'T BELIEVE IT.
ARE YOU CERTAIN OF SOMEONE?
NO...
...BUT EVEN THE DIRECTOR IS UNDER SUSPICION, SO WE MUST LOOK INTO IT.
PERHAPS SOMETHING WILL TURN UP.
...

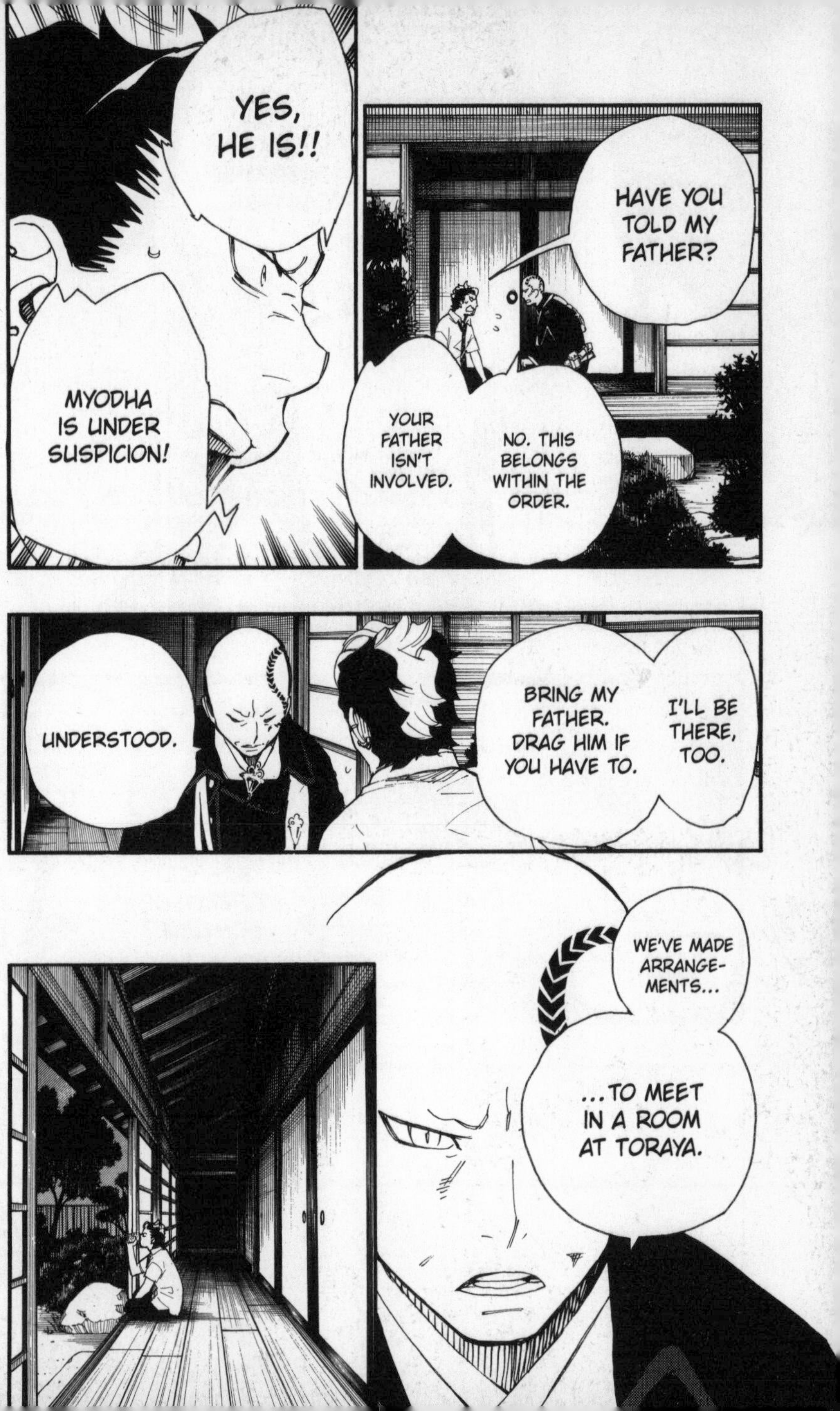
HAVE YOU TOLD MY FATHER?
NO. THIS BELONGS WITHIN THE ORDER.
YOUR FATHER ISN'T INVOLVED.
YES, HE IS!!
MYODHA IS UNDER SUSPICION!
I'LL BE THERE, TOO.
BRING MY FATHER. DRAG HIM IF YOU HAVE TO.
UNDERSTOOD.
WE'VE MADE ARRANGE-MENTS...
...TO MEET IN A ROOM AT TORAYA.

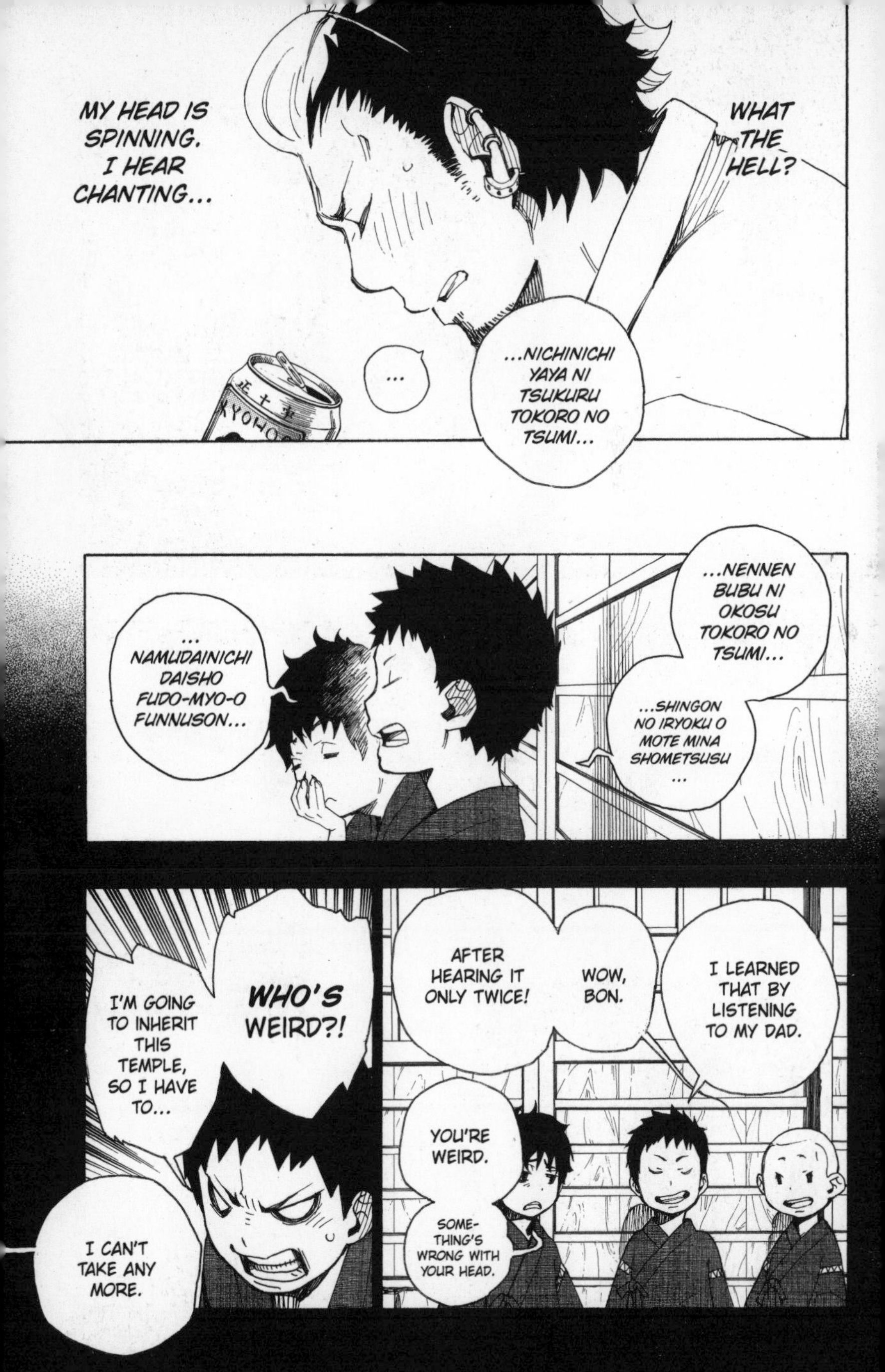
WHAT THE HELL?
MY HEAD IS SPINNING. I HEAR CHANTING...
...NICHINICHI YAYA NI TSUKURU TOKORO NO TSUMI...
...
...NENNEN BUBU NI OKOSU TOKORO NO TSUMI...
...SHINGON NO IRYOKU O MOTE MINA SHOMETSUSU ...
... NAMUDAINICHI DAISHO FUDO-MYO-O FUNNUSON...
I LEARNED THAT BY LISTENING TO MY DAD.
WOW, BON.
AFTER HEARING IT ONLY TWICE!
YOU'RE WEIRD.
SOME-THING'S WRONG WITH YOUR HEAD.
WHO'S WEIRD?!
I'M GOING TO INHERIT THIS TEMPLE, SO I HAVE TO...
I CAN'T TAKE ANY MORE.

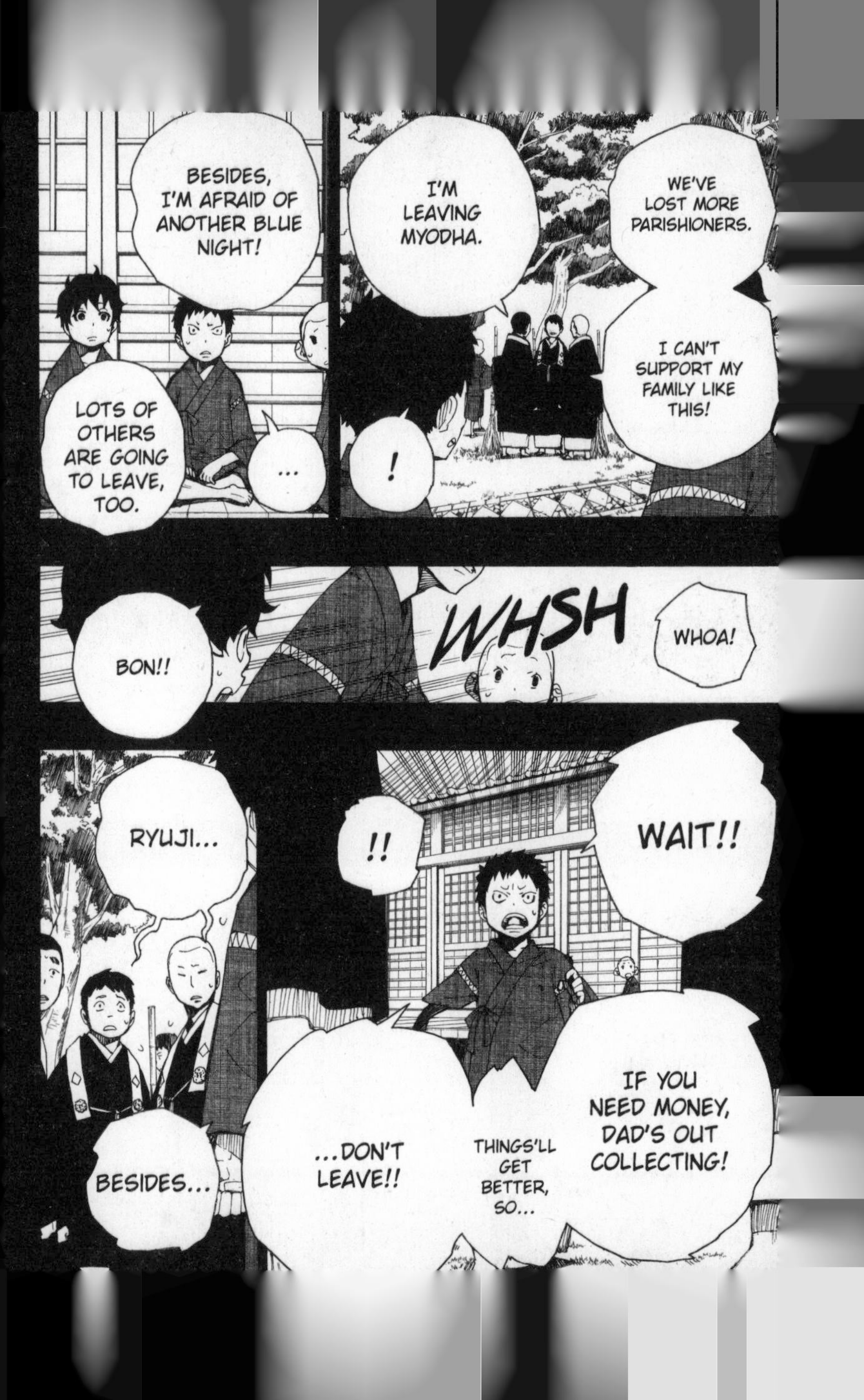
WE'VE LOST MORE PARISHIONERS.
I CAN'T SUPPORT MY FAMILY LIKE THIS!
I'M LEAVING MYODHA.
!
BESIDES, I'M AFRAID OF ANOTHER BLUE NIGHT!
LOTS OF OTHERS ARE GOING TO LEAVE, TOO.
...
WHOA!
WHSH
BON!!
WAIT!!
!!
IF YOU NEED MONEY, DAD'S OUT COLLECTING!
THINGS'LL GET BETTER, SO...
...DON'T LEAVE!!
RYUJI...
BESIDES...

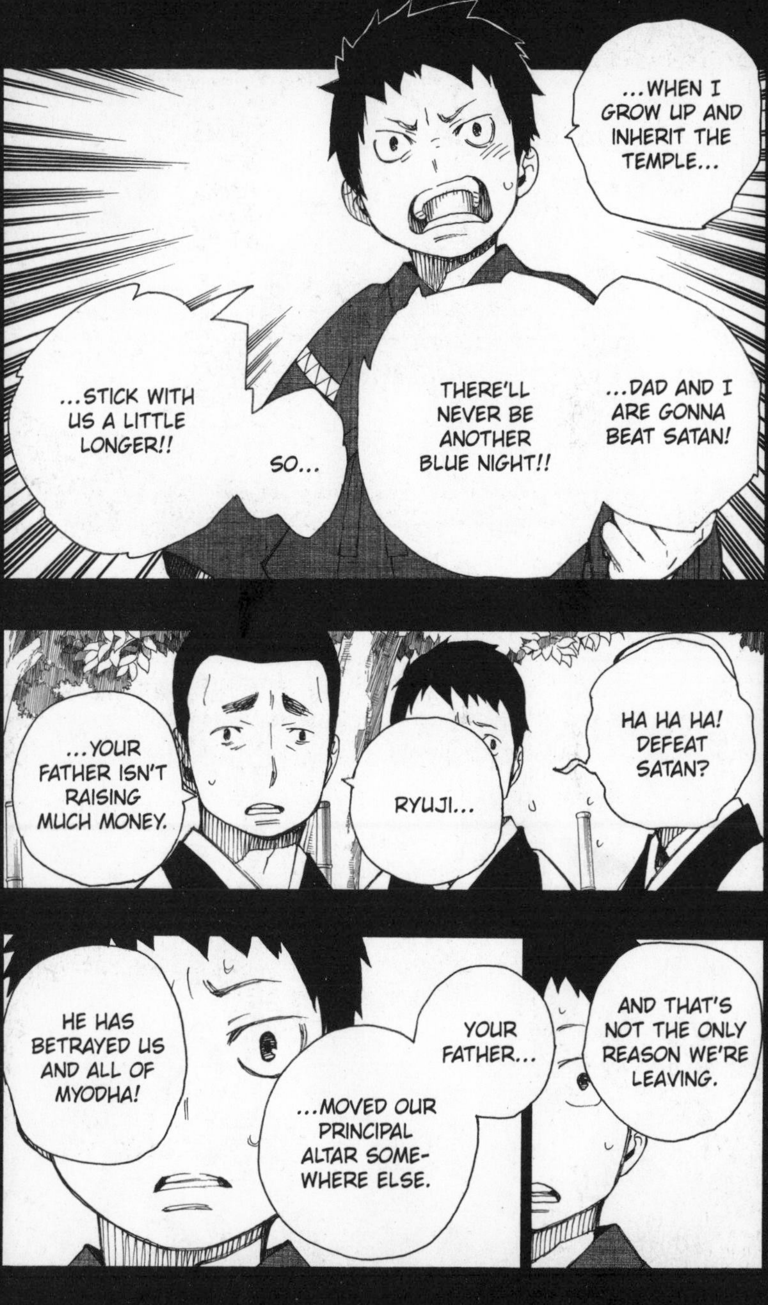
...WHEN I GROW UP AND INHERIT THE TEMPLE...
...DAD AND I ARE GONNA BEAT SATAN!
THERE'LL NEVER BE ANOTHER BLUE NIGHT!!
SO...
...STICK WITH US A LITTLE LONGER!!
HA HA HA! DEFEAT SATAN?
RYUJI...
...YOUR FATHER ISN'T RAISING MUCH MONEY.
AND THAT'S NOT THE ONLY REASON WE'RE LEAVING.
YOUR FATHER...
...MOVED OUR PRINCIPAL ALTAR SOME-WHERE ELSE.
HE HAS BETRAYED US AND ALL OF MYODHA!

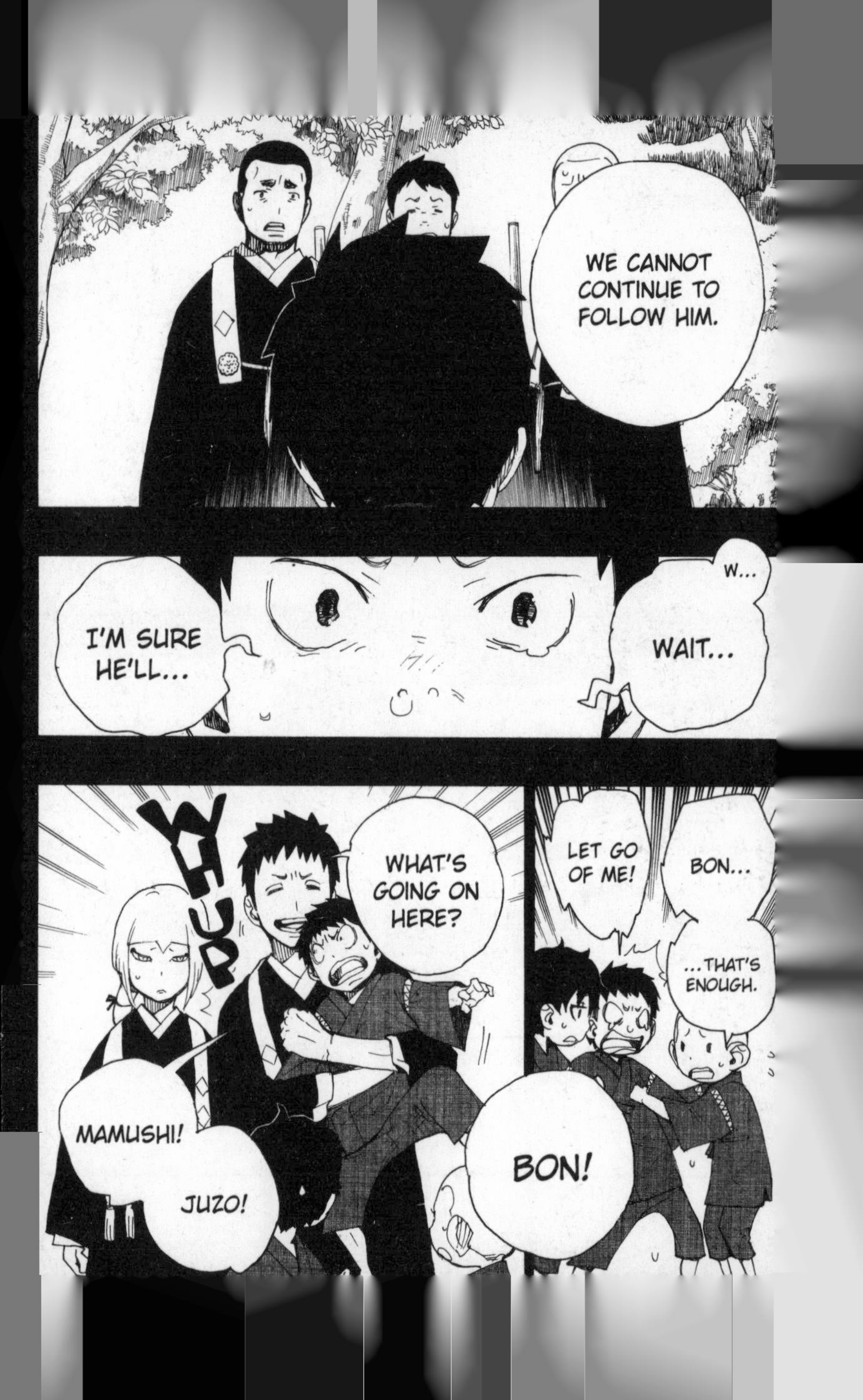

WE CANNOT CONTINUE TO FOLLOW HIM.
W... WAIT...
I'M SURE HE'LL...
BON...
LET GO OF ME!
...THAT'S ENOUGH.
WHAT'S GOING ON HERE?
WHUP
BON!
MAMUSHI!
JUZO!

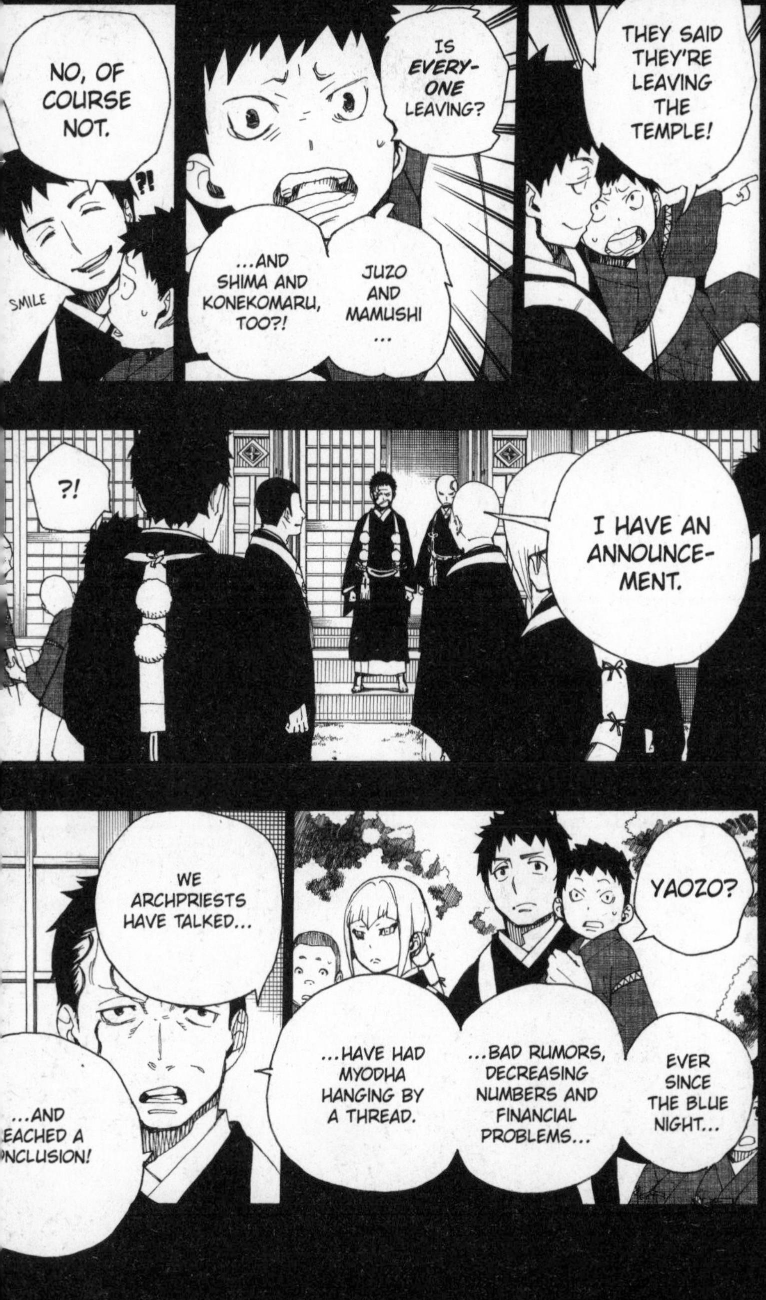
THEY SAID THEY'RE LEAVING THE TEMPLE!
IS EVERY-ONE LEAVING?
JUZO AND MAMUSHI ...
...AND SHIMA AND KONEKOMARU, TOO?!
?!
NO, OF COURSE NOT.
SMILE
I HAVE AN ANNOUNCE-MENT.
?!
YAOZO?
EVER SINCE THE BLUE NIGHT...
...BAD RUMORS, DECREASING NUMBERS AND FINANCIAL PROBLEMS...
...HAVE HAD MYODHA HANGING BY A THREAD.
WE ARCHPRIESTS HAVE TALKED...
...AND EACHED A ONCLUSION!

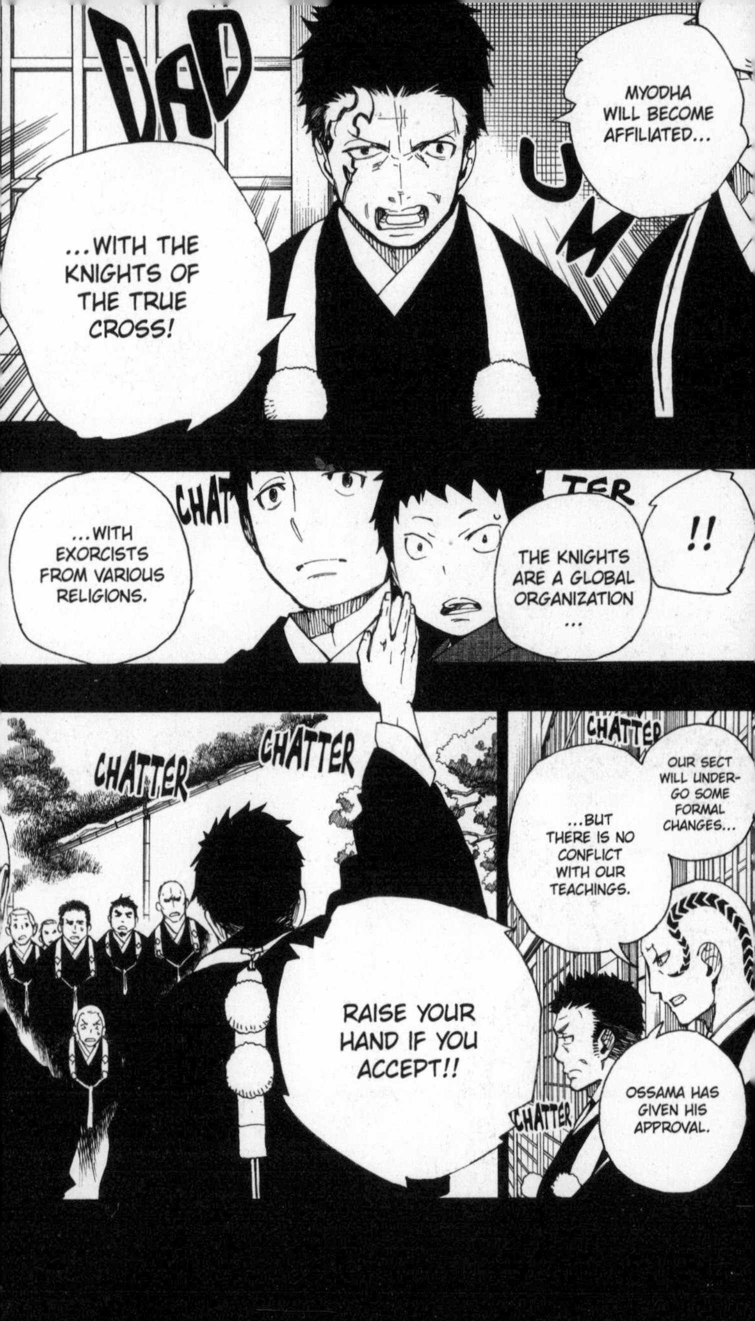
MYODHA WILL BECOME AFFILIATED...
UM
DAD
...WITH THE KNIGHTS OF THE TRUE CROSS!
!!
TER
THE KNIGHTS ARE A GLOBAL ORGANIZATION ...
CHAT
...WITH EXORCISTS FROM VARIOUS RELIGIONS.
CHATTER
OUR SECT WILL UNDER-GO SOME FORMAL CHANGES...
...BUT THERE IS NO CONFLICT WITH OUR TEACHINGS.
OSSAMA HAS GIVEN HIS APPROVAL.
CHATTER
CHATTER
RAISE YOUR HAND IF YOU ACCEPT!!
CHATTER

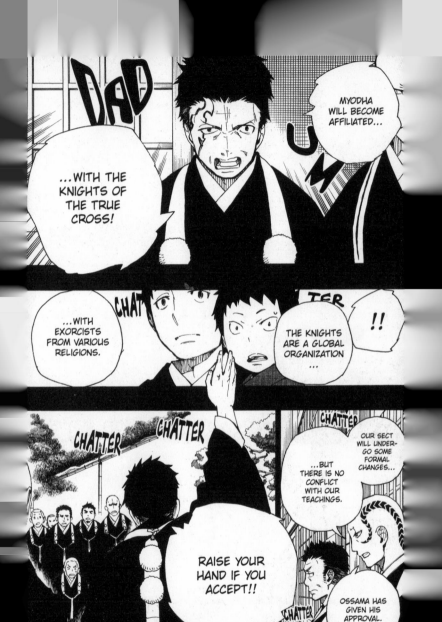

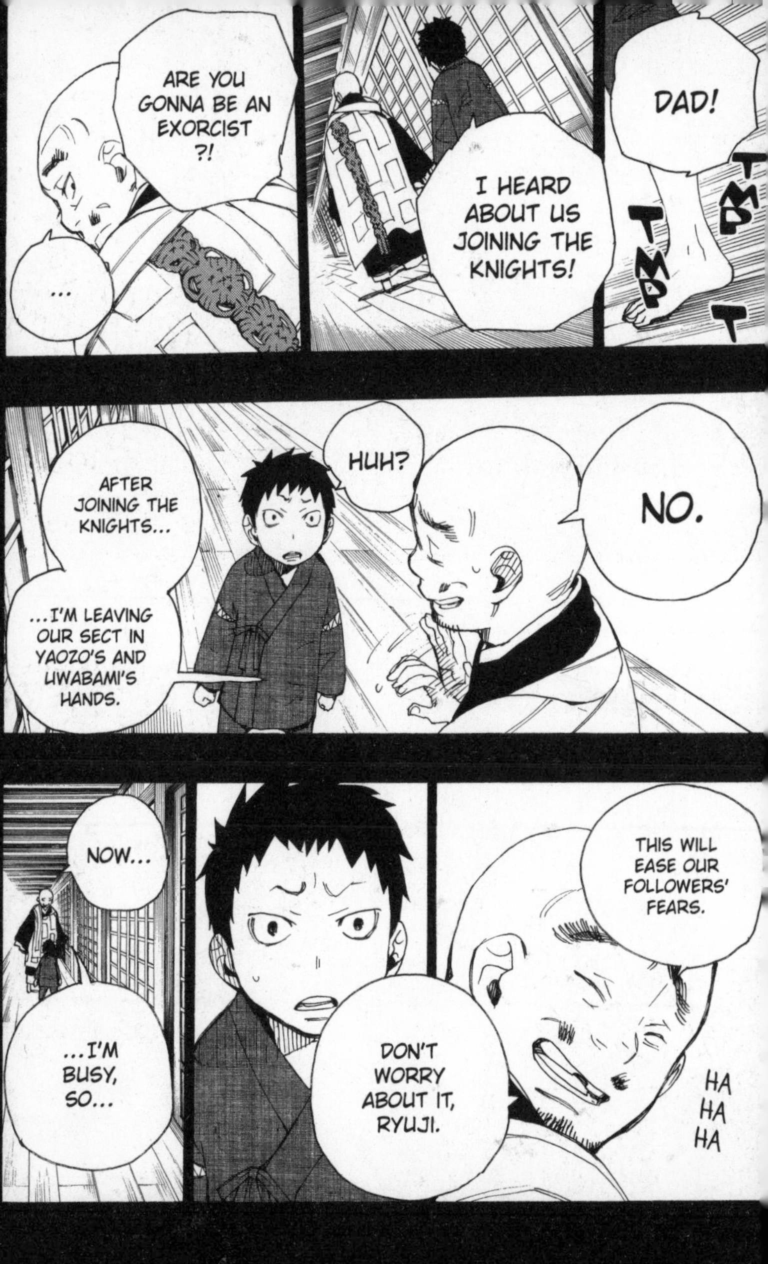
DAD!
TMP
TMP
T
I HEARD ABOUT US JOINING THE KNIGHTS!
ARE YOU GONNA BE AN EXORCIST ?!
...
NO.
HUH?
AFTER JOINING THE KNIGHTS...
...I'M LEAVING OUR SECT IN YAOZO'S AND UWABAMI'S HANDS.
THIS WILL EASE OUR FOLLOWERS' FEARS.
HA HA HA
DON'T WORRY ABOUT IT, RYUJI.
NOW...
...I'M BUSY, SO...

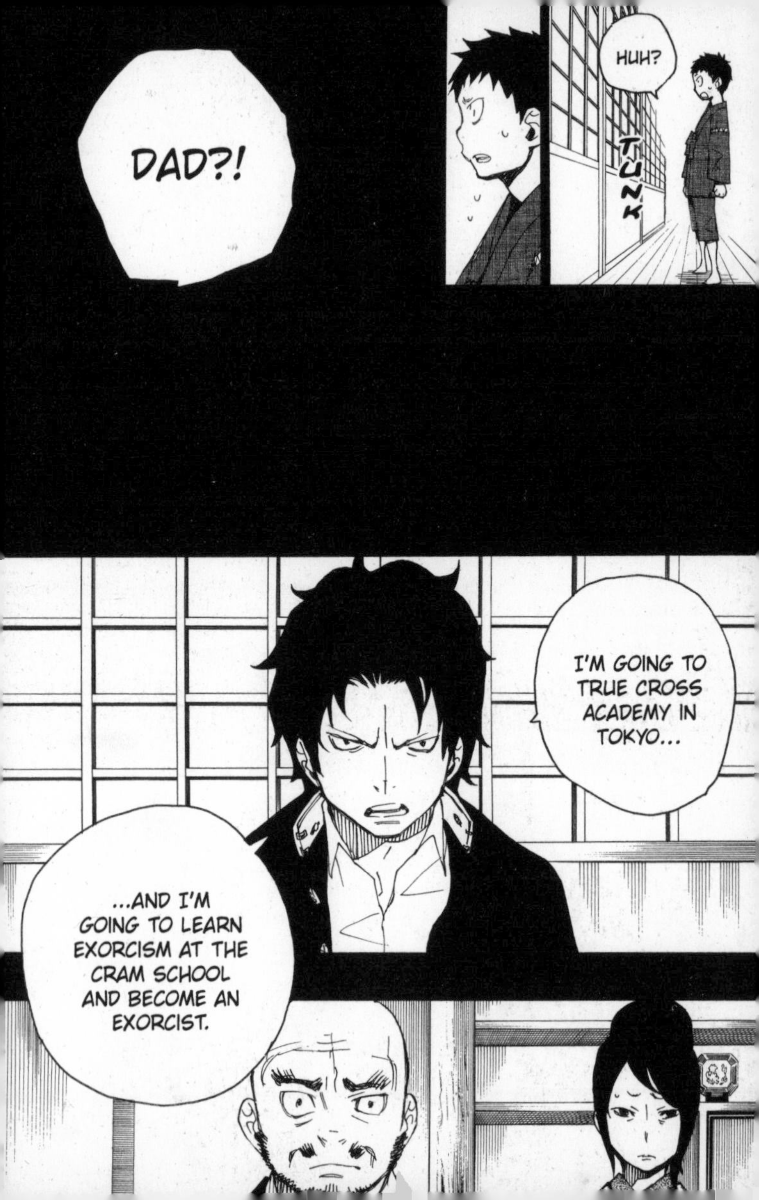
HUH?
TUNK
DAD?!
I'M GOING TO TRUE CROSS ACADEMY IN TOKYO...
...AND I'M GOING TO LEARN EXORCISM AT THE CRAM SCHOOL AND BECOME AN EXORCIST.

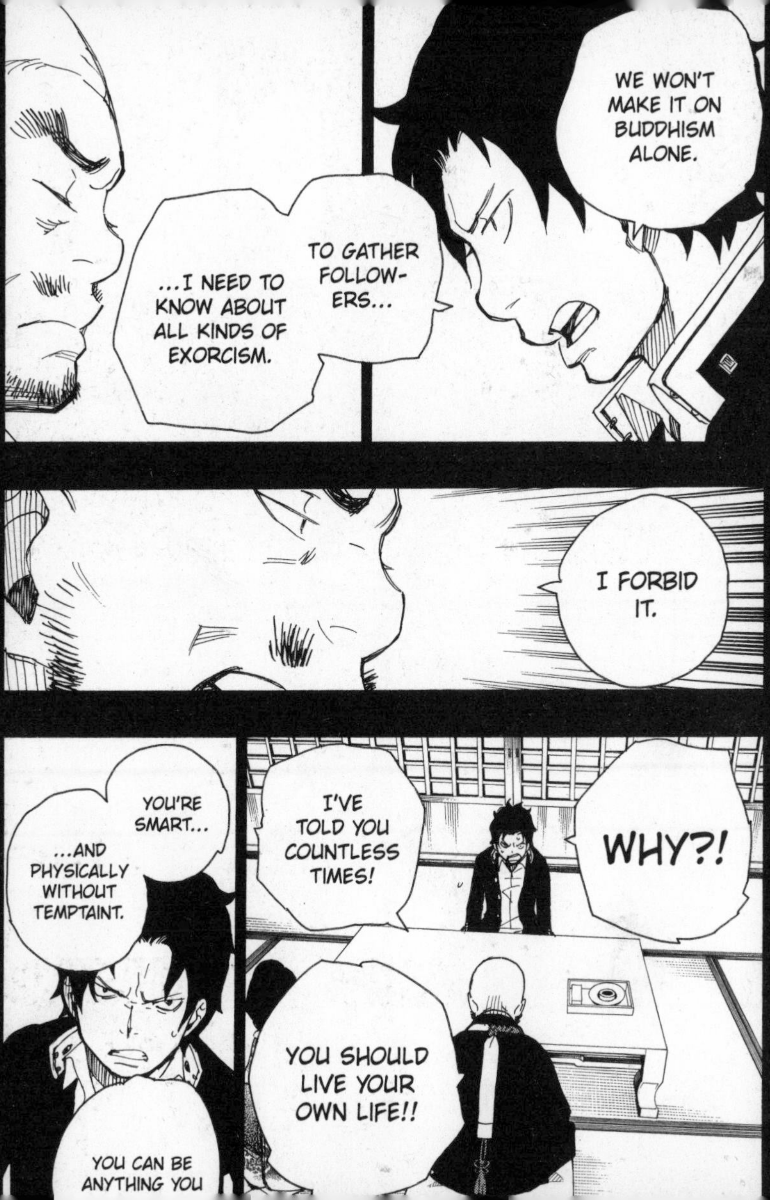
WE WON'T MAKE IT ON BUDDHISM ALONE.
TO GATHER FOLLOW-ERS...
...I NEED TO KNOW ABOUT ALL KINDS OF EXORCISM.
I FORBID IT.
WHY?!
I'VE TOLD YOU COUNTLESS TIMES!
YOU SHOULD LIVE YOUR OWN LIFE!!
YOU'RE SMART...
...AND PHYSICALLY WITHOUT TEMPTAINT.
YOU CAN BE ANYTHING YOU

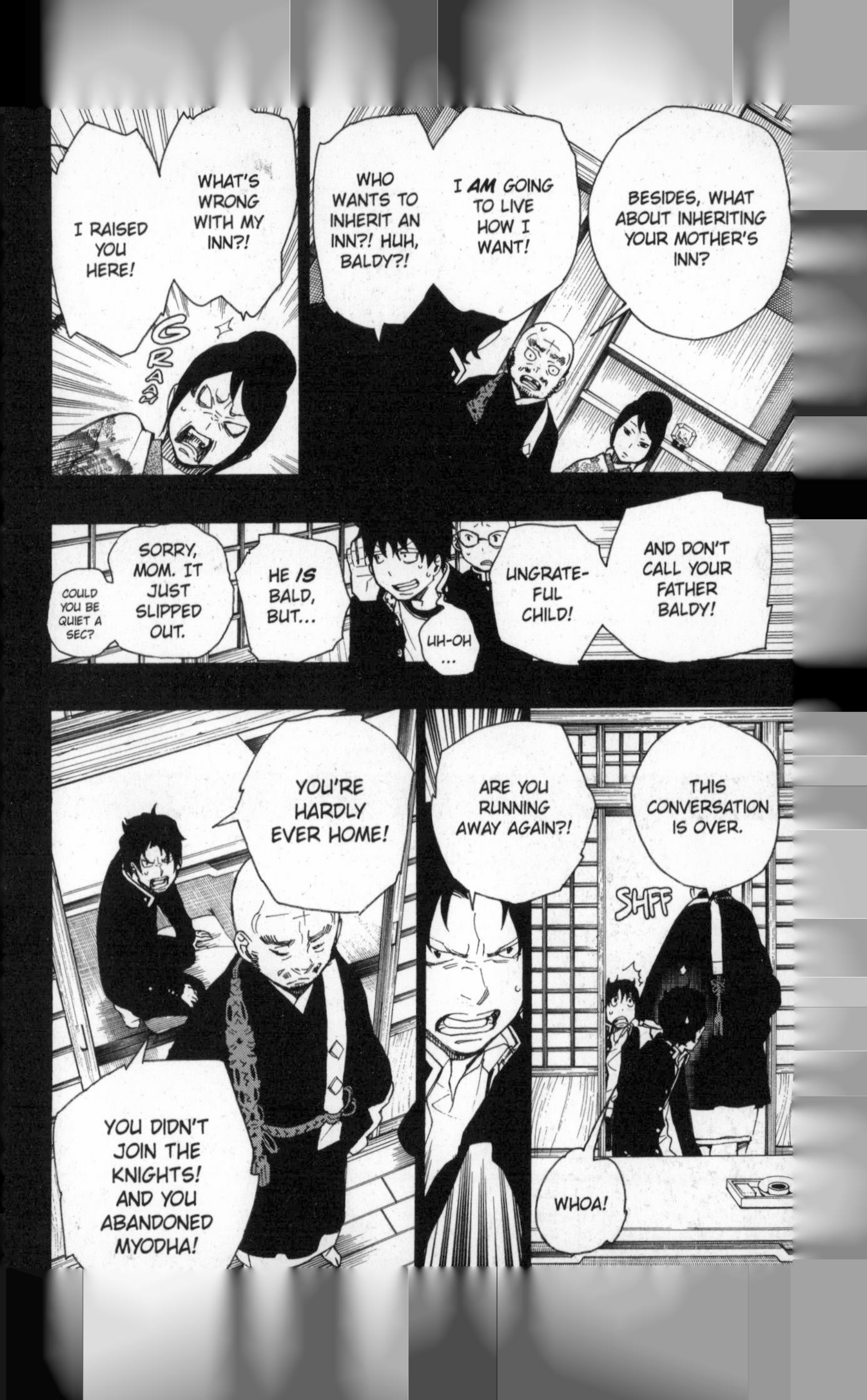
BESIDES, WHAT ABOUT INHERITING YOUR MOTHER'S INN?
I AM GOING TO LIVE HOW I WANT!
WHO WANTS TO INHERIT AN INN?! HUH, BALDY?!
WHAT'S WRONG WITH MY INN?!
I RAISED YOU HERE!
GRAA
AND DON'T CALL YOUR FATHER BALDY!
UNGRATE-FUL CHILD!
UH-OH...
HE IS BALD, BUT...
SORRY, MOM. IT JUST SLIPPED OUT.
COULD YOU BE QUIET A SEC?
THIS CONVERSATION IS OVER.
SHFF
WHOA!
ARE YOU RUNNING AWAY AGAIN?!
YOU'RE HARDLY EVER HOME!
YOU DIDN'T JOIN THE KNIGHTS! AND YOU ABANDONED MYODHA!

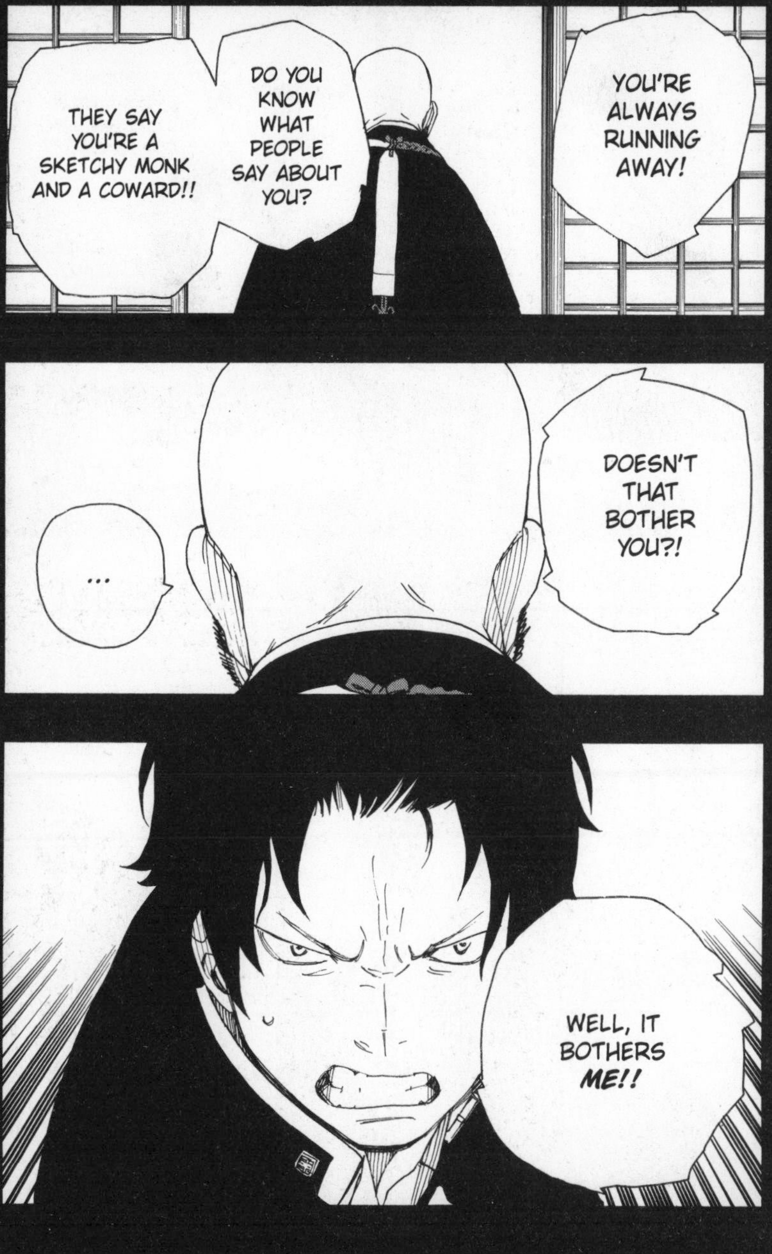
YOU'RE ALWAYS RUNNING AWAY!
DO YOU KNOW WHAT PEOPLE SAY ABOUT YOU?
THEY SAY YOU'RE A SKETCHY MONK AND A COWARD!!
DOESN'T THAT BOTHER YOU?!
...
WELL, IT BOTHERS *ME!!*

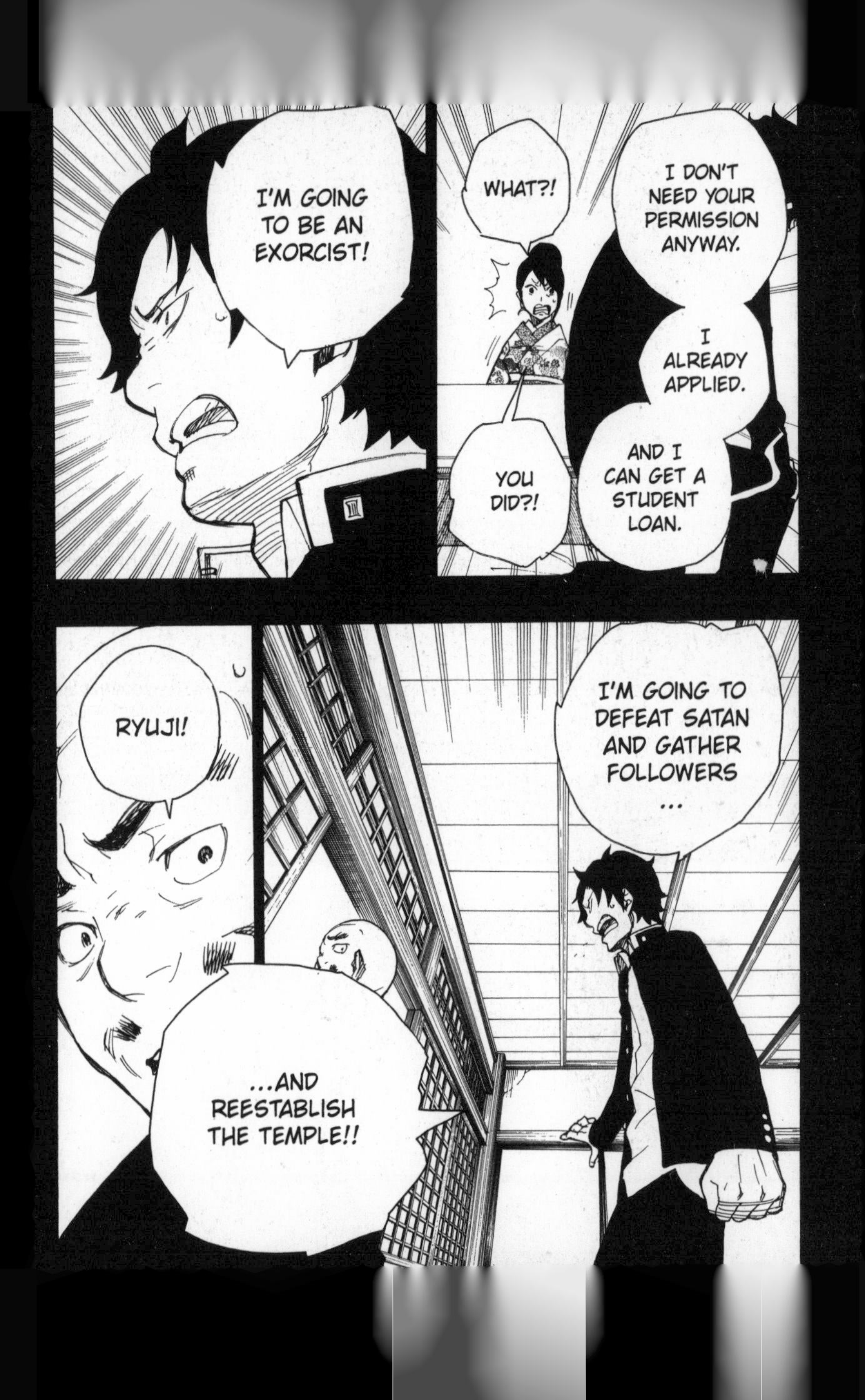
WHAT?!
I DON'T NEED YOUR PERMISSION ANYWAY.
I ALREADY APPLIED.
AND I CAN GET A STUDENT LOAN.
YOU DID?!
I'M GOING TO BE AN EXORCIST!
I'M GOING TO DEFEAT SATAN AND GATHER FOLLOWERS ...
...AND REESTABLISH THE TEMPLE!!
RYUJI!

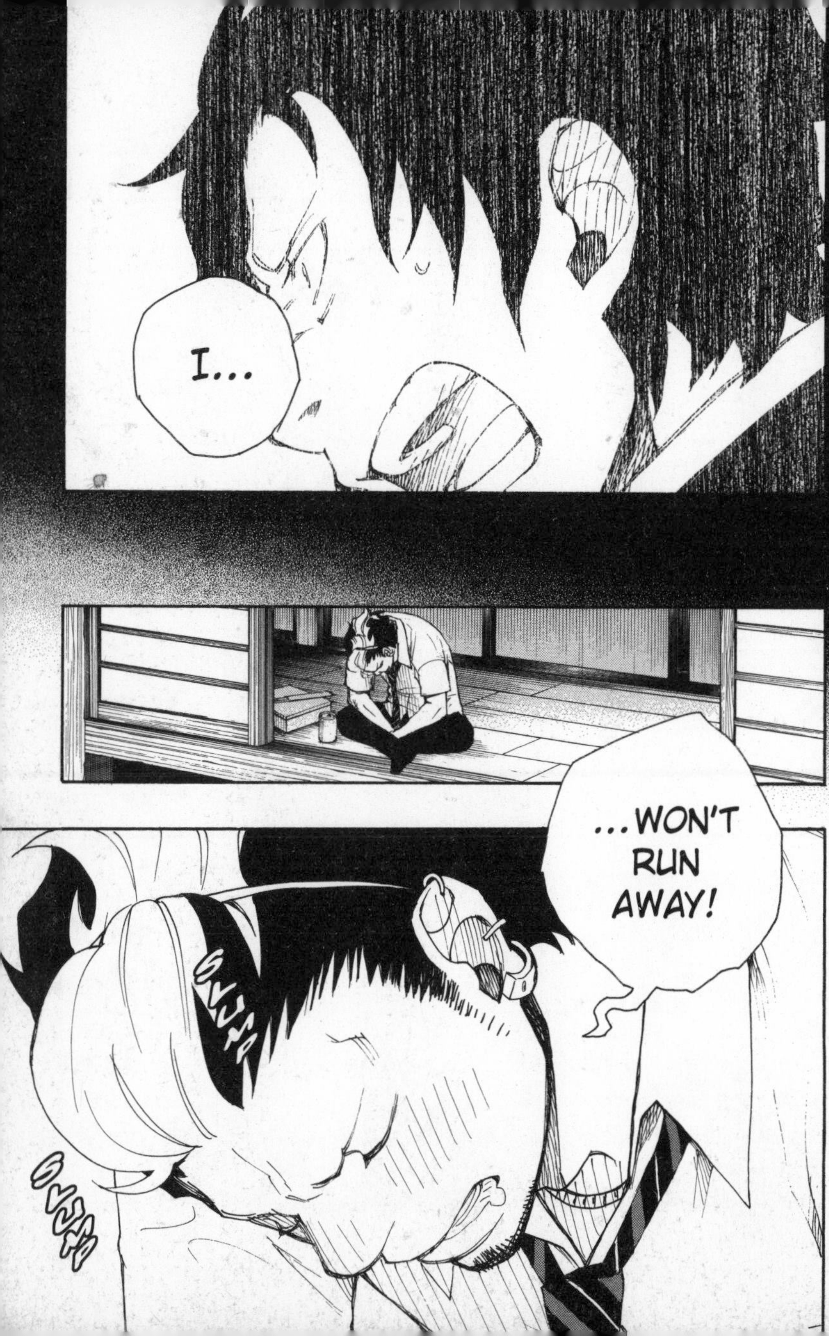
I...
...WON'T RUN AWAY!

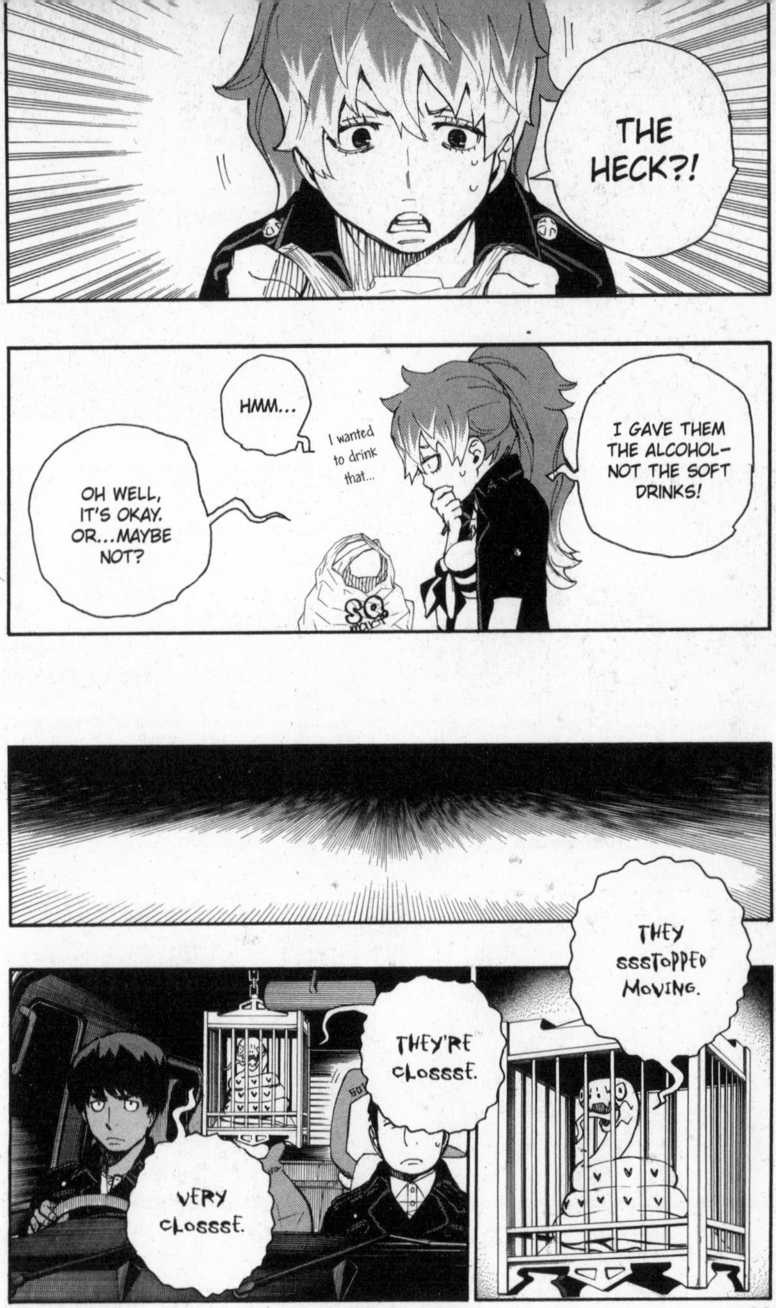
THE HECK?!
I GAVE THEM THE ALCOHOL-NOT THE SOFT DRINKS!
I wanted to drink that...
HMM...
OH WELL, IT'S OKAY. OR...MAYBE NOT?
THEY SSSTOPPED MOVING.
THEY'RE CLOSSSE.
VERY CLOSSSE.

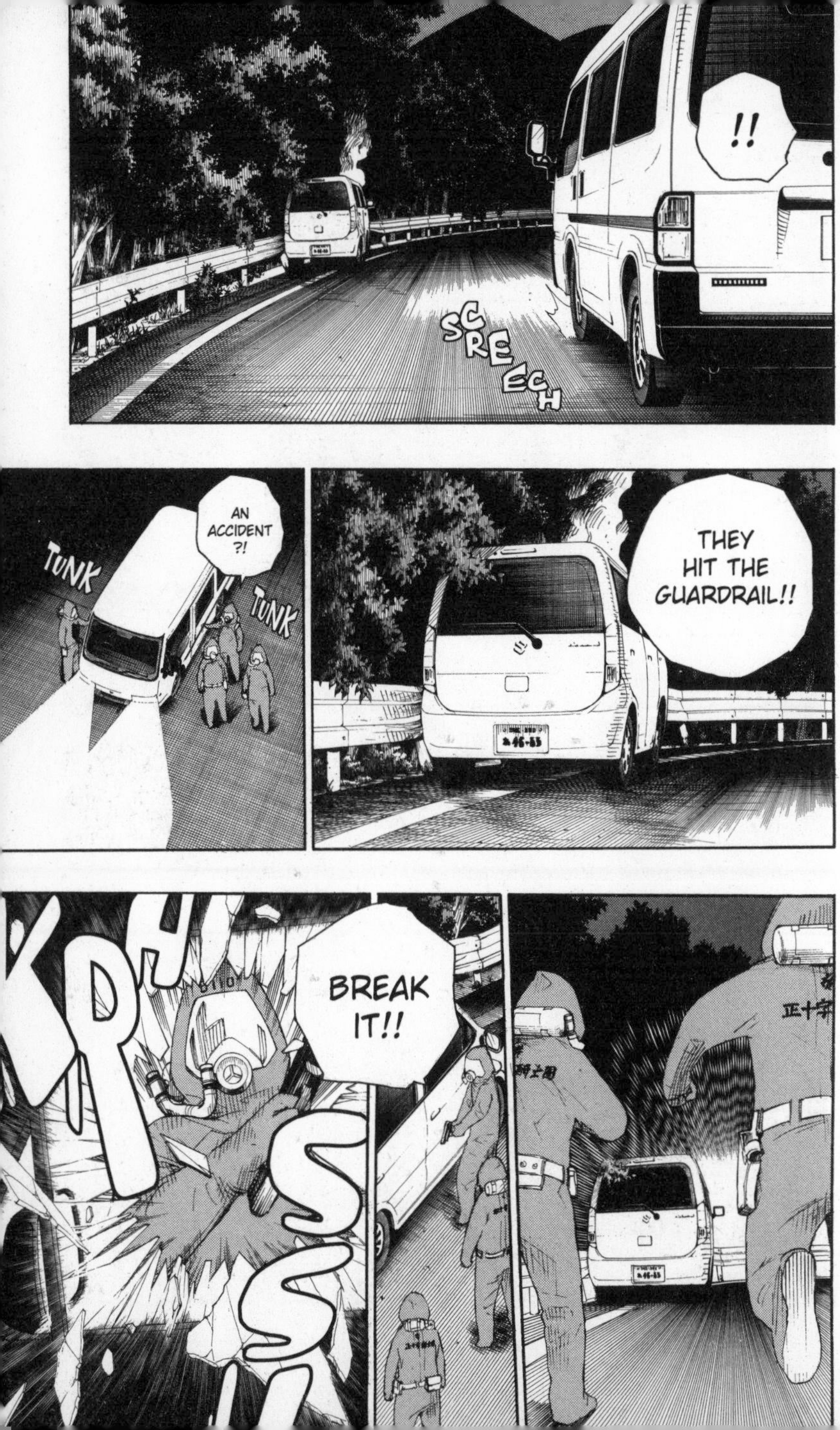
!!
SCREECH
THEY HIT THE GUARDRAIL!!
AN ACCIDENT ?!
TUNK
TUNK
BREAK IT!!

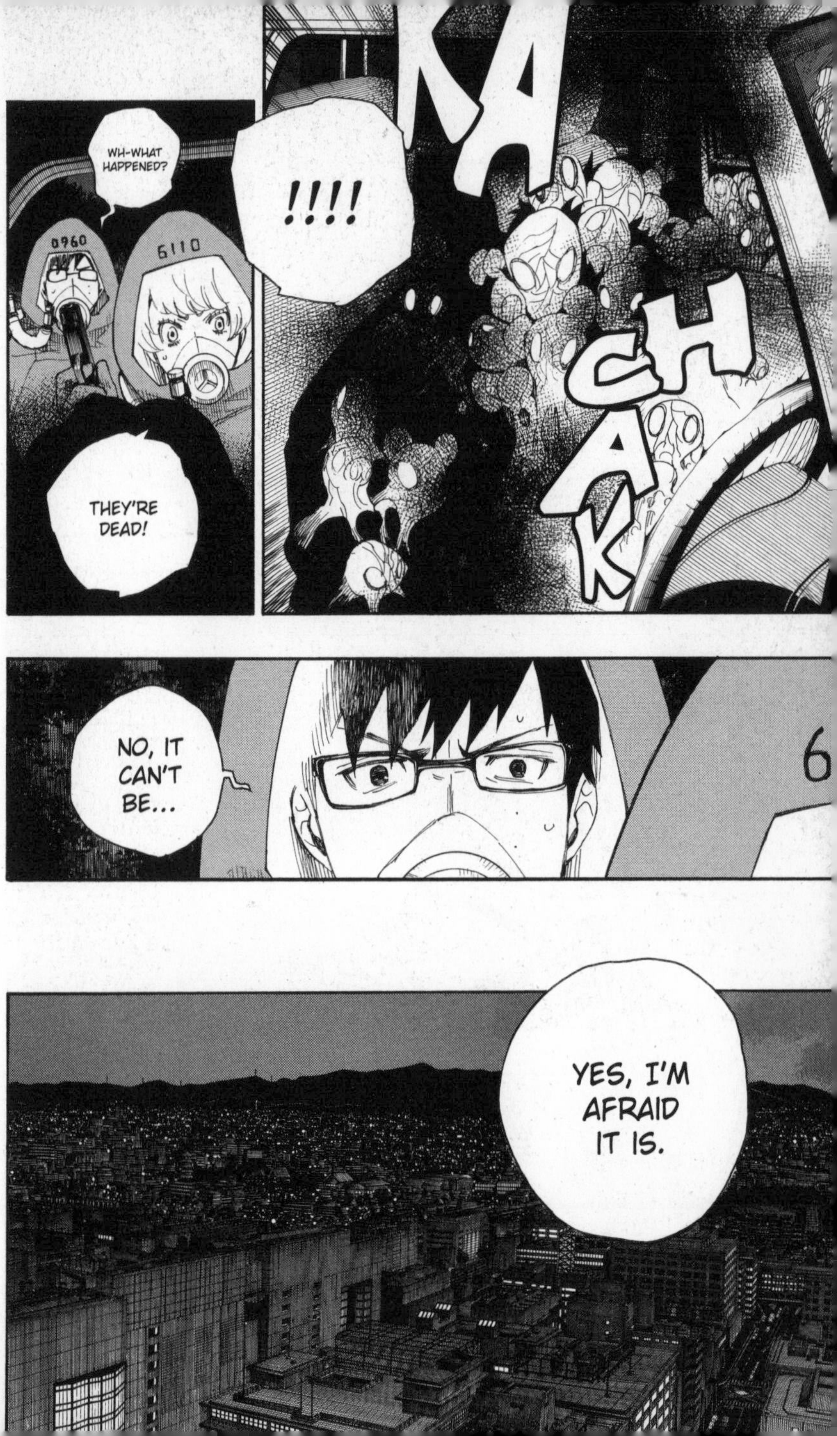
KACHAK
!!!!
WH-WHAT HAPPENED?
THEY'RE DEAD!
NO, IT CAN'T BE...
YES, I'M AFRAID IT IS.

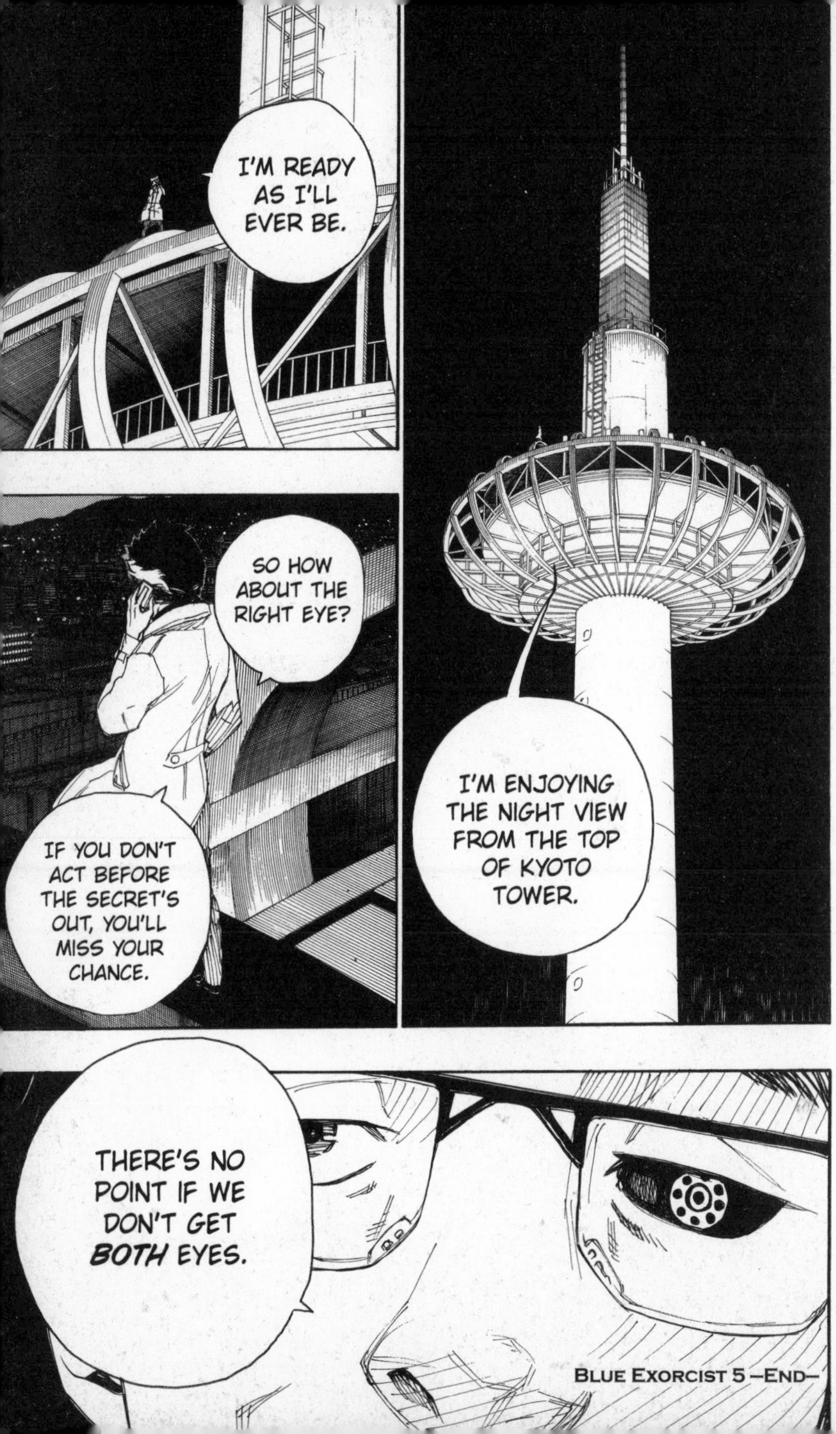
I'M ENJOYING THE NIGHT VIEW FROM THE TOP OF KYOTO TOWER.
I'M READY AS I'LL EVER BE.
SO HOW ABOUT THE RIGHT EYE?
IF YOU DON'T ACT BEFORE THE SECRET'S OUT, YOU'LL MISS YOUR CHANCE.
THERE'S NO POINT IF WE DON'T GET *BOTH* EYES.
BLUE EXORCIST 5 –END–

Blue Exorcist Chapter 19 Drunken Son

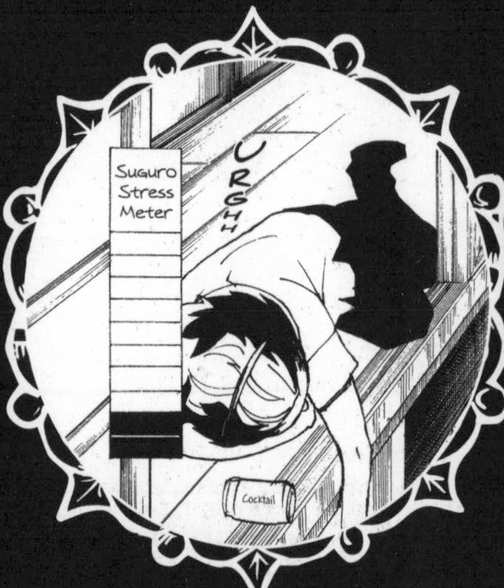
URGHH
Suguro Stress Meter
Cocktail

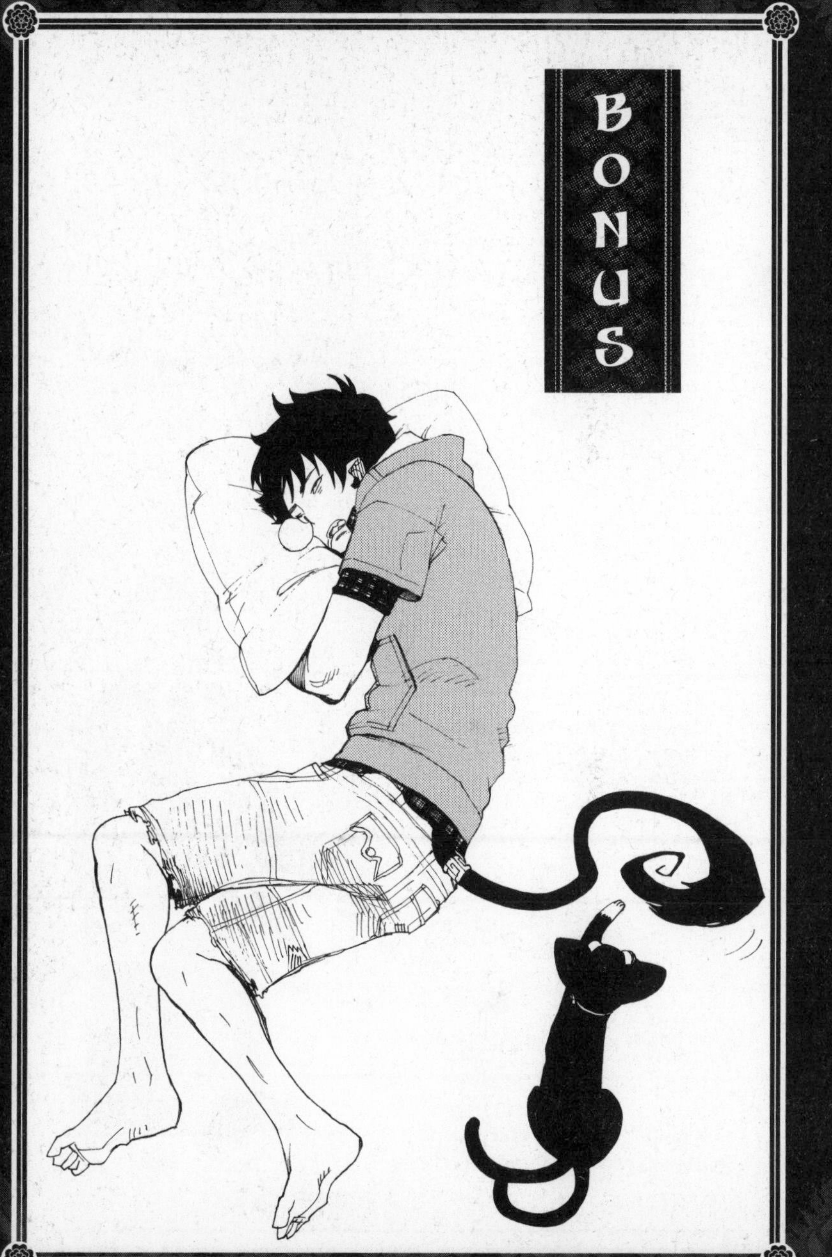
BONUS

True Cross Academy Exorcism Cram School: Exorcists and Students No. 0013

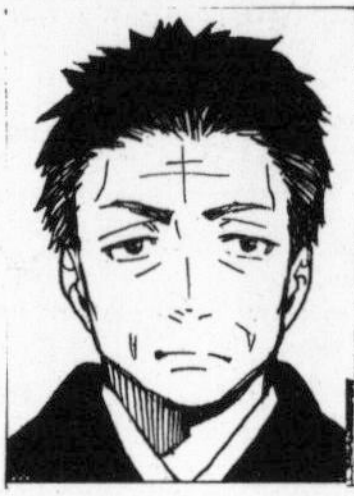

Name	Sex	Age
Yaozo Shima	Male	53

Status:

Senior Exorcist (Buddhist) First Class,
Knights of the True Cross (Titles: Knight, Aria)
Director, Kyoto Field Office

Date of birth

August 10

Blood type

A

Height

177 cm

Weight

62 kg

Pastimes and talents

Japanese chess, home gardening

Average bath time

10 minutes ~~hours~~

Favorite words

Thank you

Favorite music genres (Circle all that apply.)

Rock Pop R&B Hip-hop
American/European Japanese Jazz Anime Soundtracks
Other (Kinzo's band)

How he spends days off

Tending his garden and picking vegetables / casual Japanese chess

Details:

- Father of five boys and two girls
- Serious and straitlaced, so he rarely smiles
- But his wife totally has her way with him

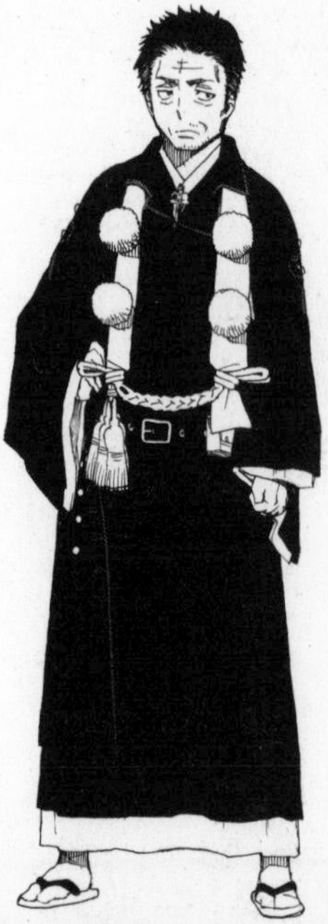

True Cross Academy Exorcism Cram School: Exorcists and Students No. 0014

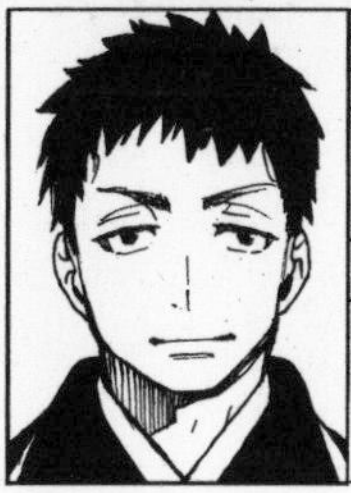

Name	Sex	Age
Juzo Shima	Male	25

Status

Senior Exorcist (Buddhist)
Second Class, Knights of the True Cross (Titles: Knight, Aria)
Unit Commander, Exorcism Unit 1, Kyoto Field Office

Date of birth:	February 5
Blood type	O
Height	178 cm
Weight	70 kg
Pastimes and talents	Mountain hiking, rock climbing
Average bath time	30 minutes ~~hours~~
Favorite words	Even raindrops wear away stone.
Favorite music genres (Circle all that apply.)	Rock Pop R&B Hip-hop American/European Japanese Jazz Anime Soundtracks Other (Kinzo's band)
How he spends days off	Mountain hiking, rock climbing, camping in the mountains

Details:
- The second-eldest Shima son
- Short-tempered and energetic
- Likes children and looks after them
- Popular with girls

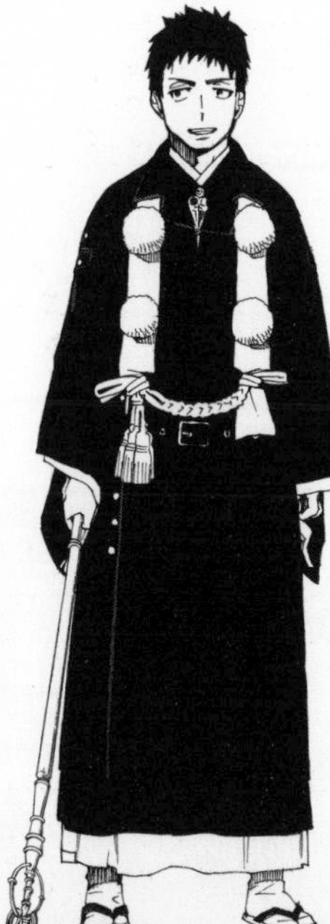

True Cross Academy Exorcism Cram School: Exorcists and Students No. 0015

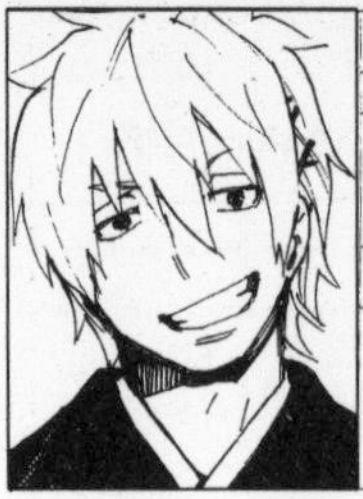

Name	Sex	Age
Kinzo Shima	Male	20

Status:

Intermediate Exorcist (Buddhist)
Second Class, Knights of the True Cross (Titles: Knight, Aria)
Security Unit 2, Kyoto Field Office

Date of birth	November 17
Blood type	O
Height	175 cm
Weight	60 kg
Pastimes and talents	Rock band, Tsugaru-shamisen
Average bath time	15 minutes ~~hours~~
Favorite words	Pace (a mistake—he meant "peace")
Favorite music genres (Circle all that apply.)	Rock Pop R&B Hip-hop American/European Japanese Jazz Anime Soundtracks Other (any kind)
How he spends days off	Practicing or performing with his band

Details:

- Fourth son in the Shima family
- Loves his family, but fights with Renzo a lot
- *Kin* means gold, so he died his hair blond
- Sings in a band

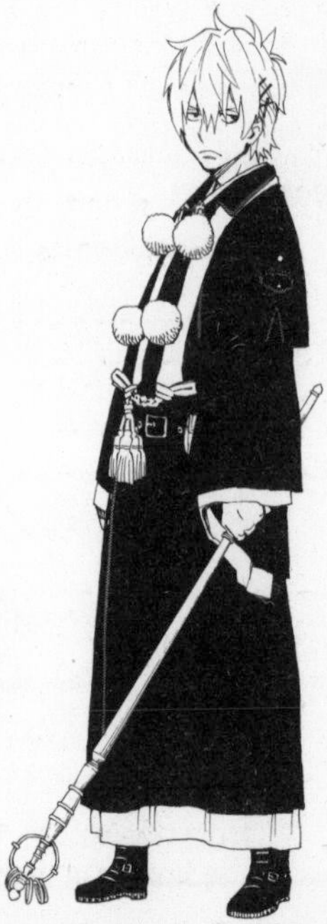

True Cross Academy Exorcism Cram School: Exorcists and Students No. 0016

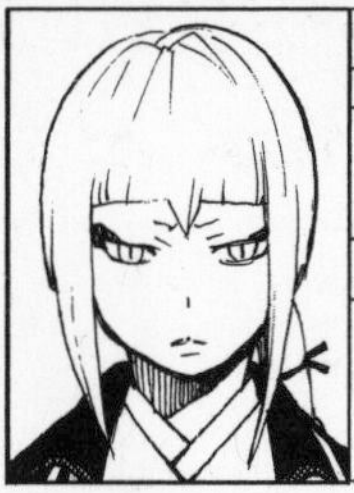

Name	Sex	Age
Mamushi Hojo	Female	24

Status

Intermediate Exorcist (Buddhist) First Class,
Knights of the True Cross (Titles: Tamer, Aria)
Unit Commander, Keep Unit 1, Kyoto Field Office

Date of birth:	June 4
Blood type	A
Height	164 cm
Weight	48 kg
Pastimes and talents	Training, feeding and caring for her Nagas
Average bath time	1 hour
Favorite words	Rain
Favorite music genres (Circle all that apply.)	Rock Pop R&B Hip-hop American/European Japanese Jazz Anime Soundtracks Other (doesn't listen to music)
How she spends days off	If it's raining, she stays inside and watches the rain.

Details:

- The eldest Hojo daughter
- Loves Nagas
- And Nagas love her…so she has trouble making friends

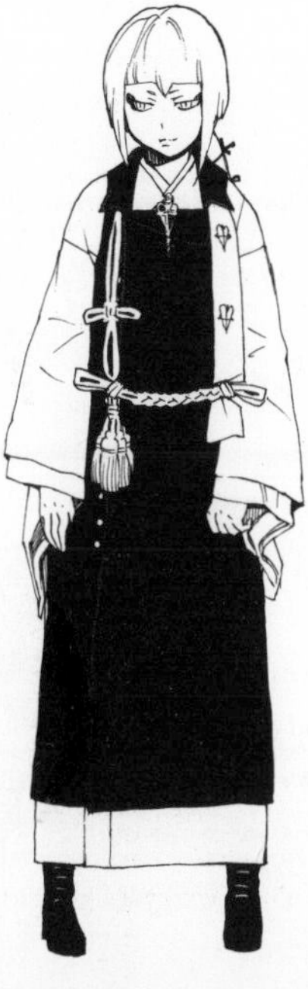

TRUE CROSS ACADEMY EXORCISM CRAM SCHOOL:
EXORCISTS AND STUDENTS

True Cross Academy Exorcism Cram School: Exorcists and Students No. 0017

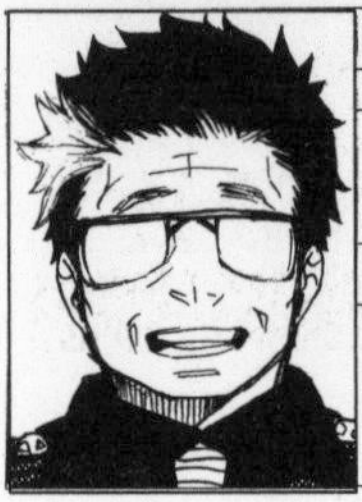

Name	Sex	Age
Saburota Todo	Male	55

Status:

Senior Exorcist Second Class, Knights of the True Cross (Titles: Tamer, Doctor, Aria)
Former first-year Magic Circles and Seals instructor, Exorcism Cram School
Former Warden, Deep Keep

Date of birth	October 10
Blood type	B
Height	170 cm
Weight	71 kg
Pastimes and talents	Tracking down local Japanese sake brews
Average bath time	3 hours
Favorite words	Lonely on a straight road (from a haiku by Santoka Taneda)
Favorite music genres (Circle all that apply.)	Rock Pop R&B Hip-hop American/European Japanese Jazz Anime Soundtracks Other (doesn't listen to music)
How he spends days off	With a bowl of soba noodles and a cup of Japanese sake

Details:

- •Belongs to a famous family of Exorcists
- •His Exorcist's license has been revoked.
- •The Order has issued a warrant for his arrest.

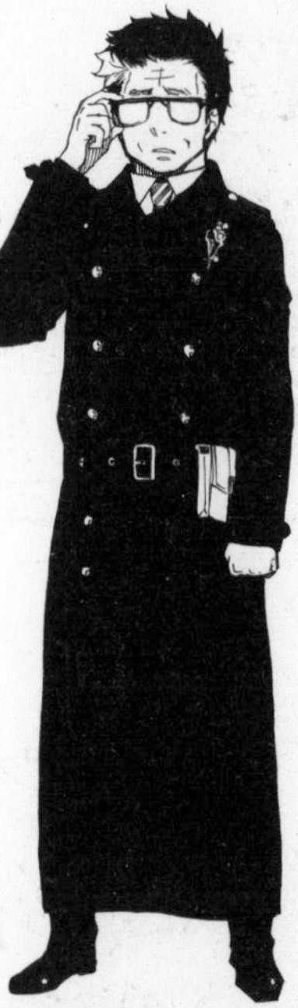

An Illustrated Guide to Demons

CHUCHI
LOW LEVEL

FILE 15

Kin of Beelzebub, King of Insects. Small demons that possess small insects. They swarm around animals, drink their blood, and eat their carcasses.

PEG LANTERN
LOW TO MID LEVEL

FILE 16

Kin of Iblis, King of Fire. Possess manmade lighting equipment. They become active when lit. Various types exist around the world.

NAGA
LOW – MID LEVEL

FILE 17

Kin of Amaimon, King of Earth. Possess serpents. Various species exist around the world. Many are evil, but in Japan, many are revered as gods for the benefit they bring. Their leaders live a long time and are called Nagarajas.

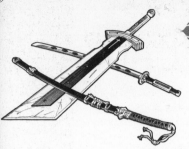

 # MAKEN

FILE 18

A demon sword. If you accidentally become the owner of one, it might kill you. To use one, you have to become the official owner by making a compact with it, much as you would with a familiar.

THE LEFT EYE OF THE IMPURE KING

FILE 19

?

Kin of Astaroth, King of Rot. An object known as the Left Eye of the Impure King. The Impure King was a demon who ravaged Japan in the late Edo Period. The Knights of the True Cross have designated the Left Eye an Extraordinarily Hazardous Demonic Item and kept it sealed away for a long time in the Deep Keep of the Japan Branch.

THE RIGHT EYE OF THE IMPURE KING

FILE 20

?

Kin of Astaroth, King of Rot. An object known as the Right Eye of the Impure King. The Impure King was a demon who ravaged Japan in the late Edo Period. The Knights of the True Cross have designated the Right Eye an Extraordinarily Hazardous Demonic Item and kept it sealed away for about ten years in the Keep of the Kyoto Field Office.

BLUE EXORCIST 5

Art Assistants

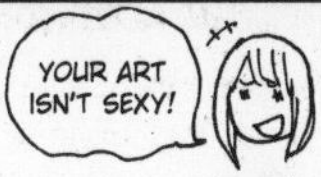
YOUR ART ISN'T SEXY!

Shibu-tama

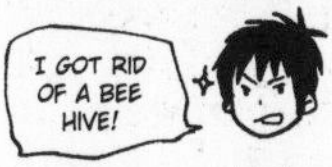
I GOT RID OF A BEE HIVE!

Uemura-san

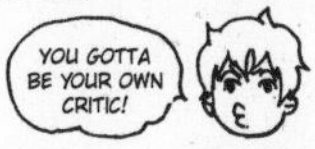
YOU GOTTA BE YOUR OWN CRITIC!

Tae-chin

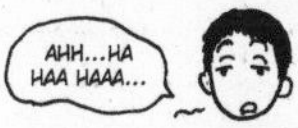
AHH...HA HAA HAAA...

Kimura-kun

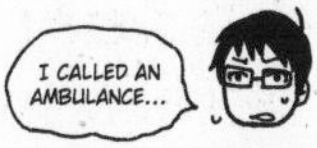
I CALLED AN AMBULANCE...

Hayashi-kun

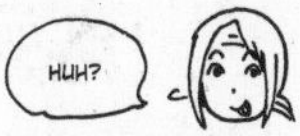
HUH?

Kawamura-san

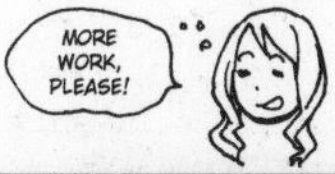
MORE WORK, PLEASE!

Minoru

Editor

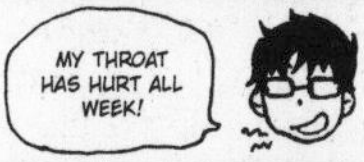
MY THROAT HAS HURT ALL WEEK!

Shihei Rin

Graphic Novel Editor

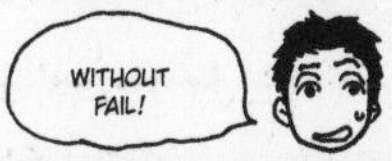
WITHOUT FAIL!

Ryusuke Kuroki

Graphic Novel Design

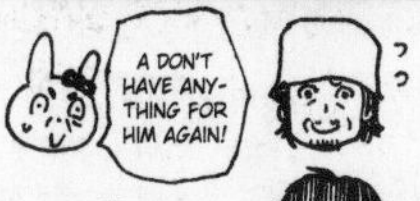
A DON'T HAVE ANY-THING FOR HIM AGAIN!

Shimada Hideaki

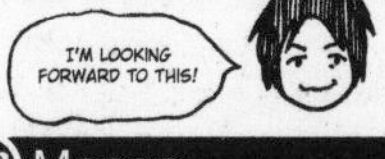
I'M LOOKING FORWARD TO THIS!

Masaaki Tsunoda (L.S.D.)

Manga

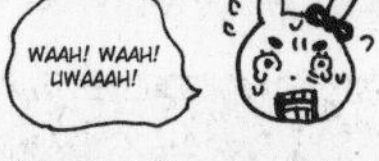
WAAH! WAAH! UWAAAH!

Kazue Kato

(in no particular order)
(Note: The caricatures and statements are from memory!)

Continued in Volume 6! Check it out!

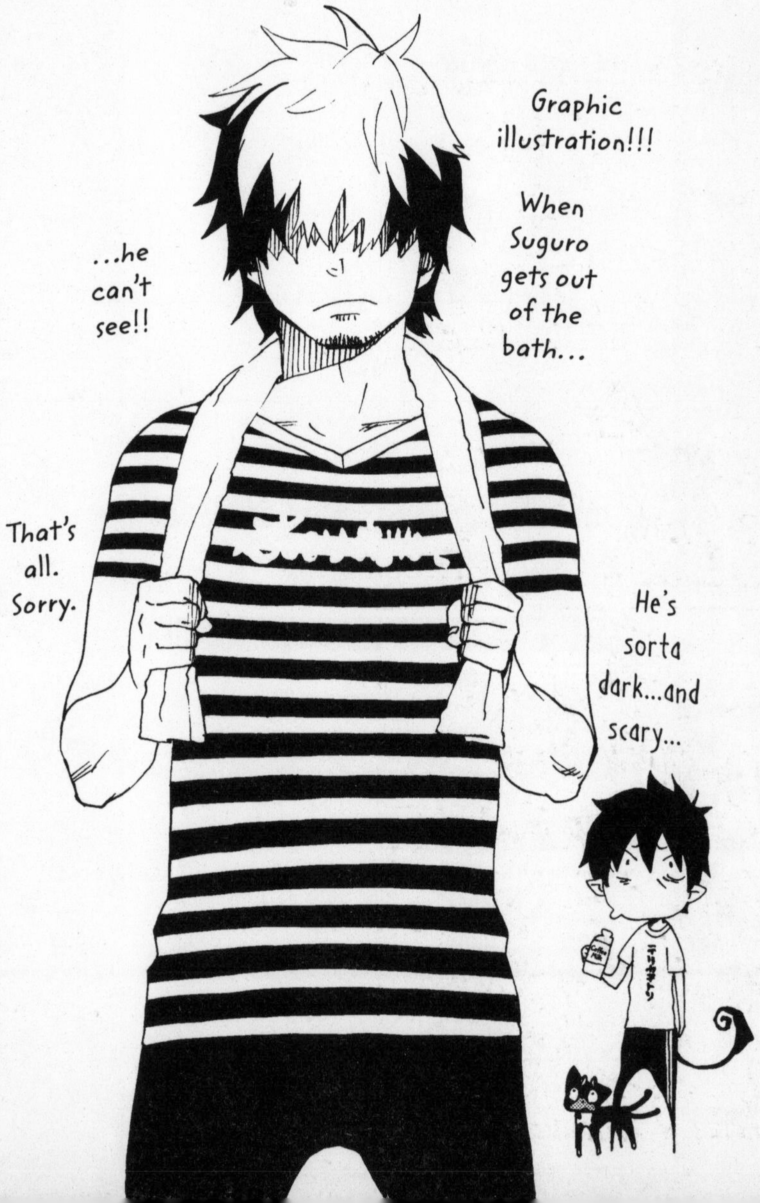
Graphic illustration!!!
When Suguro gets out of the bath...
...he can't see!!
He's sorta dark...and scary...
Coffee Milk
That's all. Sorry.

He Also Studied and Cleaned

...
Dorm
TWEET
TWEET
WAP
AM 5:30
Oh!
You're out early again!
Good morning!!
PANT PANT
TUMP TUMP
AM 6:00
Good morning, Bon...
Mornin'!
AM 7:00
UH-OH
TUMP TUMP
Shima...
Bon already left for school...
Cafeteria
That guy really is perverted!!
AM 8:00

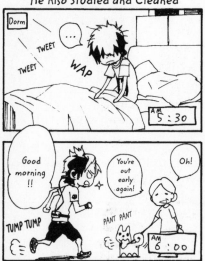

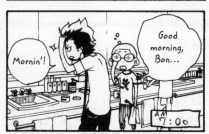

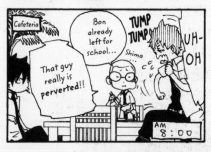

KAZUE KATO

At long last...volume 5! Thank you to everyone who's read along this far!

A fairly long story begins in this volume, so I'm worried about how many people will stick with it...

In any case, go ahead and dive in!

BLUE EXORCIST

BLUE EXORCIST VOL. 5
SHONEN JUMP ADVANCED Manga Edition

STORY & ART BY KAZUE KATO

Translation & English Adaptation/John Werry
Touch-up Art & Lettering/John Hunt, Primary Graphix
Cover & Interior Design/Sam Elzway
Editor/Mike Montesa

AO NO EXORCIST © 2009 by Kazue Kato
All rights reserved.
First published in Japan in 2009 by SHUEISHA Inc., Tokyo.
English translation rights arranged by SHUEISHA Inc.

Printed in the U.S.A.

Published by VIZ Media, LLC
P.O. Box 77010
San Francisco, CA 94107

10 9 8 7 6 5 4 3 2 1
First printing, December 2011

In the next volume...

IF THAT'S TRUE...

...THEN TELL ME THE *TRUTH*...

...IN FRONT OF EVERYONE!!

RIGHT HERE...

The heads of the various Myodha temple families gather to discuss recent events surrounding the Eyes of the Impure King. Revelations at the meeting only deepen suspicion of Suguro's father, Tatsuma, and angry accusations follow. Tatsuma's silence on the matter isn't helping either. Amid all the swirling distrust, Rin tries to make sense of things but struggles to keep his flame in check. Then Rin receives a letter that may shed more light on the current situation, and the secret past!

Includes two bonus stories!

Coming February 2012!

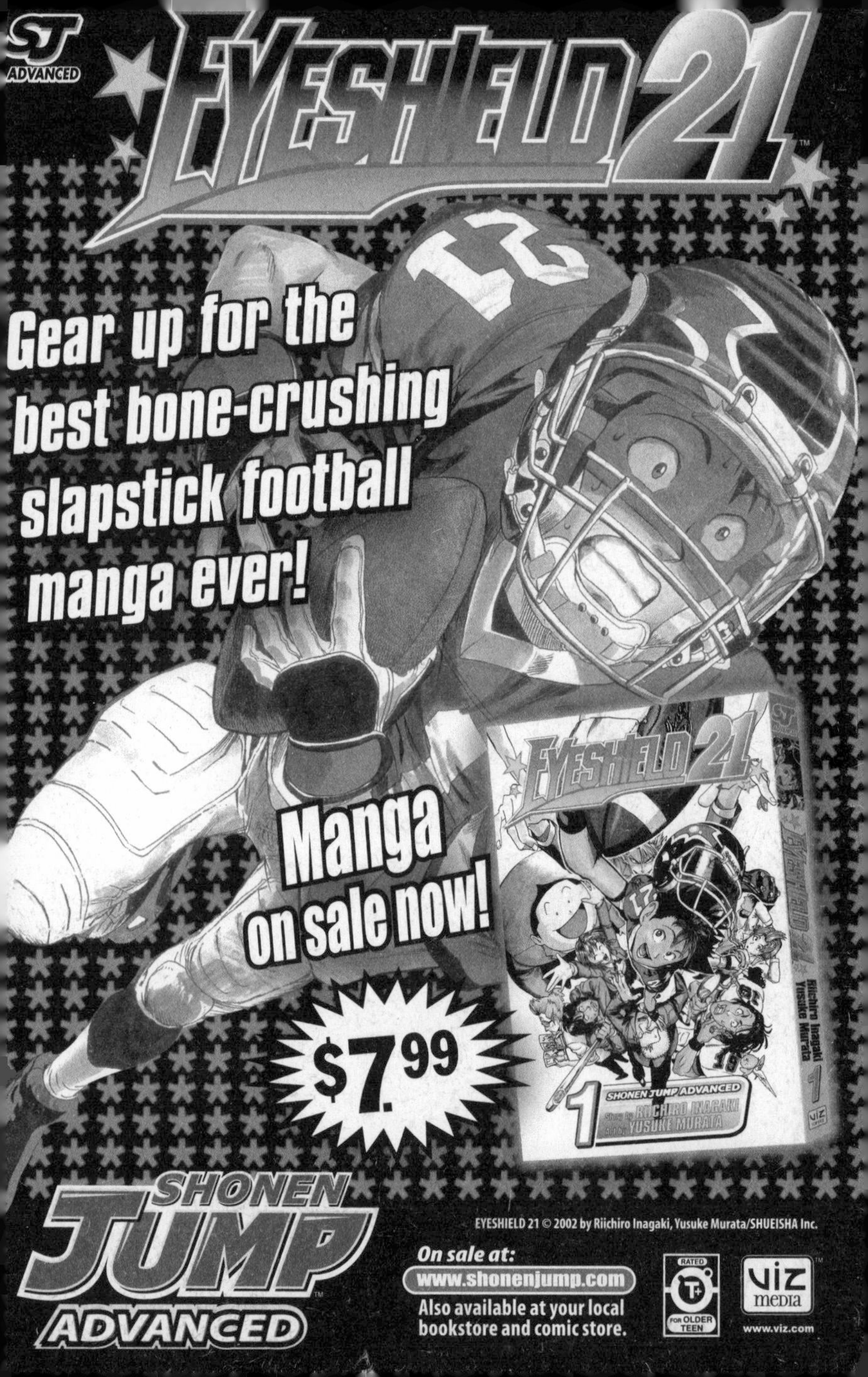
SJ ADVANCED
EYESHIELD 21™
Gear up for the best bone-crushing slapstick football manga ever!
Manga on sale now!
$7.99
EYESHIELD 21
SHONEN JUMP ADVANCED
1
SHONEN JUMP ADVANCED
EYESHIELD 21 © 2002 by Riichiro Inagaki, Yusuke Murata/SHUEISHA Inc.
On sale at:
www.shonenjump.com
Also available at your local bookstore and comic store.
RATED T+ FOR OLDER TEEN
VIZ media
www.viz.com

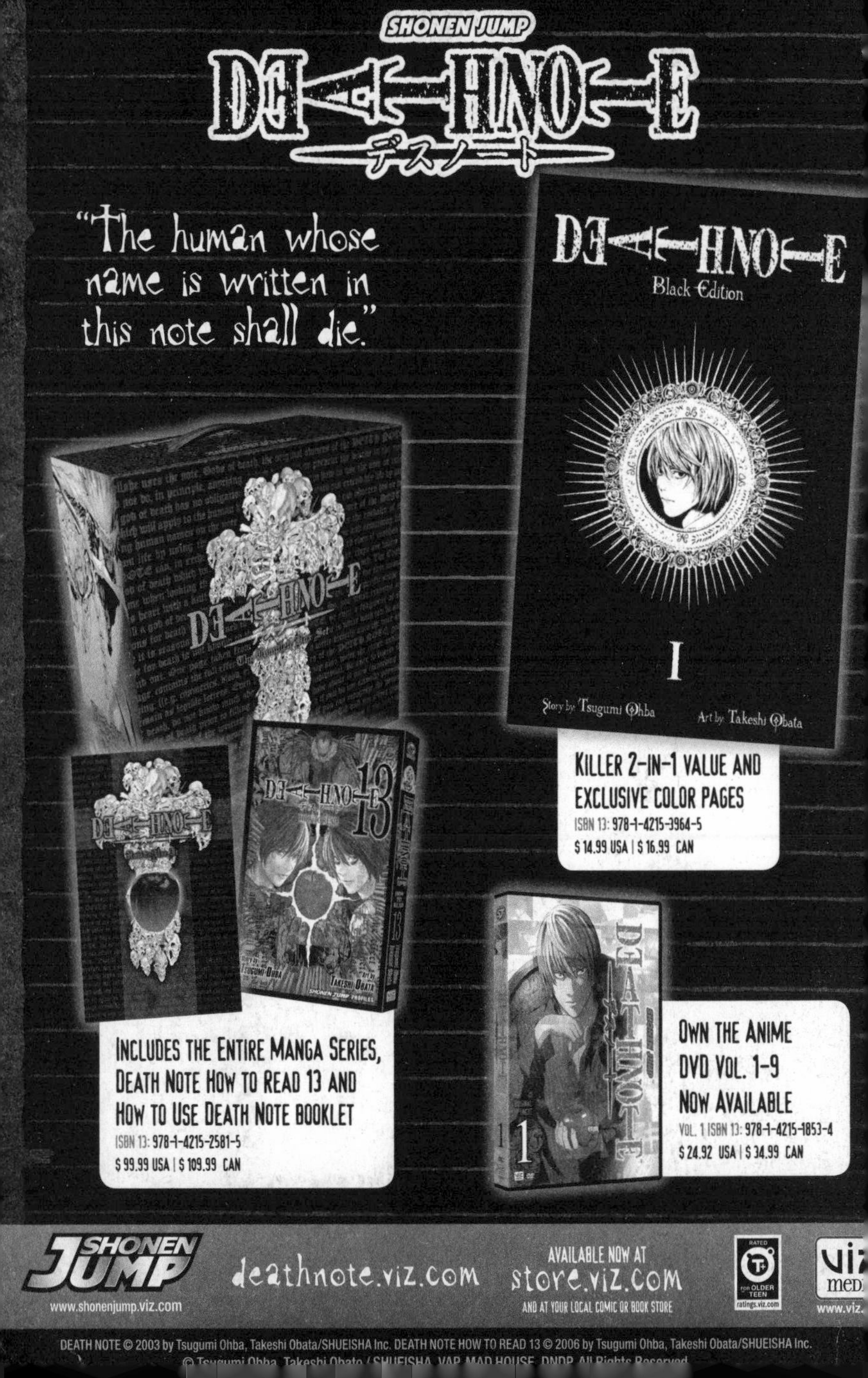
SHONEN JUMP
DEATH NOTE
デスノート
"The human whose name is written in this note shall die."
DEATH NOTE
Black Edition
I
Story by: Tsugumi Ohba
Art by: Takeshi Obata
KILLER 2-IN-1 VALUE AND EXCLUSIVE COLOR PAGES
ISBN 13: 978-1-4215-3964-5
$ 14.99 USA | $ 16.99 CAN
INCLUDES THE ENTIRE MANGA SERIES, DEATH NOTE HOW TO READ 13 AND HOW TO USE DEATH NOTE BOOKLET
ISBN 13: 978-1-4215-2581-5
$ 99.99 USA | $ 109.99 CAN
OWN THE ANIME DVD VOL. 1-9 NOW AVAILABLE
VOL. 1 ISBN 13: 978-1-4215-1853-4
$ 24.92 USA | $ 34.99 CAN
SHONEN JUMP
www.shonenjump.viz.com
deathnote.viz.com
AVAILABLE NOW AT
store.viz.com
AND AT YOUR LOCAL COMIC OR BOOK STORE
RATED T+ FOR OLDER TEEN
ratings.viz.com
www.viz.
DEATH NOTE © 2003 by Tsugumi Ohba, Takeshi Obata/SHUEISHA Inc. DEATH NOTE HOW TO READ 13 © 2006 by Tsugumi Ohba, Takeshi Obata/SHUEISHA Inc.
© Tsugumi Ohba, Takeshi Obata / SHUEISHA, VAP, MAD HOUSE, DNDP. All Rights Reserved.

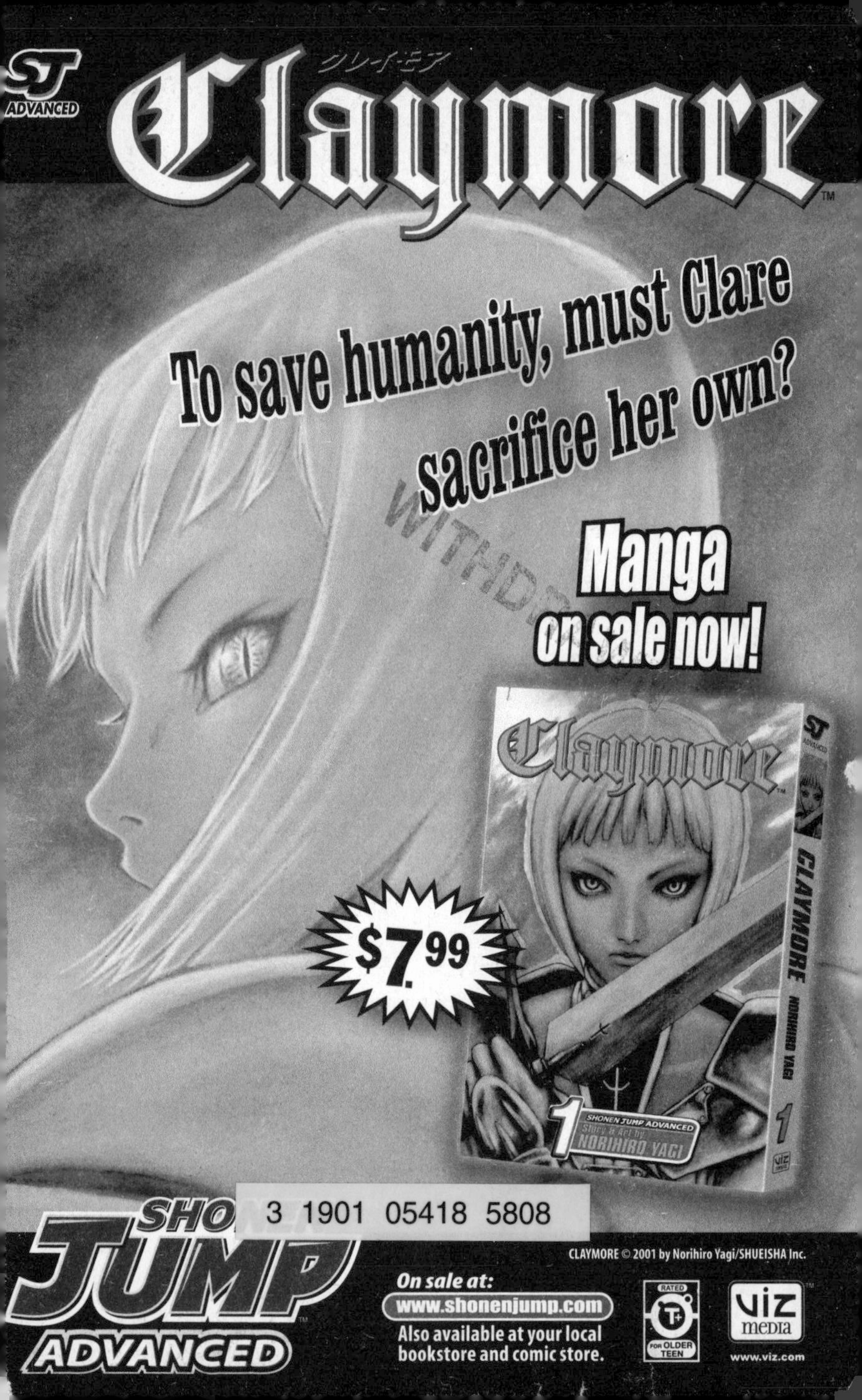
SJ ADVANCED
クレイモア
Claymore™
To save humanity, must Clare sacrifice her own?
Manga on sale now!
$7.99
Claymore™
SJ ADVANCED
CLAYMORE NORIHIRO YAGI 1
1 SHONEN JUMP ADVANCED Story & Art by NORIHIRO YAGI
SHONEN JUMP ADVANCED
CLAYMORE © 2001 by Norihiro Yagi/SHUEISHA Inc.
On sale at:
www.shonenjump.com
Also available at your local bookstore and comic store.
RATED T+ FOR OLDER TEEN
viz media
www.viz.com